ROBIN WOOD
ON THE HORROR FILM

Robin Wood onstage during a postscreening Q&A as part of his American Nightmare program for the Festival of Festivals (now Toronto International Film Festival) in 1979.

ROBIN WOOD
ON THE HORROR FILM
COLLECTED ESSAYS AND REVIEWS

EDITED BY
BARRY KEITH GRANT
WITH A PREFACE BY RICHARD LIPPE

Wayne State University Press
Detroit

© 2018 by Wayne State University Press, Detroit, Michigan 48201. All rights reserved. No part of this book may be reproduced without formal permission.

Library of Congress Control Number: 2018943988

ISBN 978-0-8143-4523-8 (paperback)
ISBN 978-0-8143-4525-2 (hardcover)
ISBN 978-0-8143-4524-5 (ebook)

Wayne State University Press
Leonard N. Simons Building
4809 Woodward Avenue
Detroit, Michigan 48201-1309

Visit us online at wsupress.wayne.edu

Contents

Foreword by Barry Keith Grant   vii

Preface by Richard Lippe: The Journey from *Psycho* to *The American Nightmare*; or, Why Should We Take the Horror Film Seriously?   xi

Psychoanalysis of *Psycho*	3
In Memoriam: Michael Reeves	11
The Shadow Worlds of Jacques Tourneur	25
Disreputable Genre	41
The Creeping Flesh	43
Blood Brides	45
You'll Like My Mother	47
Death Line (*Raw Meat*)	49
The Most Horrible Horror Film Ever?	53
Return of the Repressed	57
Yet Another Terrible Child	63
Race with the Devil	67
An Introduction to the American Horror Film	73
Der Erlkönig: The Ambiguities of Horror	111
The Dark Mirror: Murnau's *Nosferatu*	119
Sisters	133
World of Gods and Monsters: The Films of Larry Cohen	141
Apocalypse Now: Notes on the Living Dead	161
The American Family Comedy: From *Meet Me in St. Louis* to *The Texas Chainsaw Massacre*	171
Neglected Nightmares	181

"Art" and Alligators	201
Burying the Undead: The Use and Obsolescence of Count Dracula	205
Returning the Look: *Eyes of a Stranger*	221
Cronenberg: A Dissenting View	231
King Meets Cronenberg	253
John Carpenter	259
Dead End	261
Cat and Dog: Lewis Teague's Stephen King Movies	265
Notes for a Reading of *I Walked with a Zombie*	281
The Woman's Nightmare: Masculinity in *Day of the Dead*	319
Larry Cohen Interview (Robin Wood and Richard Lippe)	331
Nosferatu	361
The Silence of the Lambs	365
Brian De Palma	369
George Romero	373
Fresh Meat: *Diary of the Dead*	377
Revenge Is Sweet: The Bitterness of *Audition*	385
What Lies Beneath?	399
Notes	407
Acknowledgments	415
Index	421

Foreword

In September 1979 Robin Wood and Richard Lippe programmed a series of sixty horror films for the Festival of Festivals (now known as the Toronto International Film Festival). To accompany the screenings, Wood and Lippe invited several of the filmmakers whose works were included—George Romero, David Cronenberg, Wes Craven, and Stephanie Rothman among them—for introductory discussions and postscreening Q&As. They also assembled a small book of essays on the horror film entitled *The American Nightmare: Essays on the Horror Film*. Sold at the screenings, this slim volume of twelve essays of varying length included two by coeditor Lippe, three by Andrew Britton (all reprinted in *Britton on Film: The Collected Film Criticism of Andrew Britton*, also published by Wayne State University Press), and an important piece on John Carpenter's *Assault on Precinct 13* by Tony Williams. The other half, including the longest and most influential essay, "An Introduction to the American Horror Film," were by Robin Wood.

The American Nightmare was the first serious collection of critical writing on the horror genre (it preceded my own *Planks of Reason: Essays on the Horror Film* by five years), and it has inspired numerous volumes since. This little book (it was fewer than one hundred pages), now a collector's item, went on to become extraordinarily influential, fueling the wave of academic and popular writing on the horror film that followed. Its confluence of Marxist and Freudian theory provided critics with an exceedingly useful and flexible concept that opened the way to explain so much about the horror genre.

Within Hollywood cinema, beginning in the late 1960s during the period known as the New Hollywood, all the popular genres were revisited by a generation of younger filmmakers, many of whom had studied film history. These "movie brats," including Steven Spielberg, Martin Scorsese, George Lucas, and Francis Coppola, among others, brought fresh stylistic approaches and ideological self-awareness to their genre movies, as did Robert Altman. The

Western's ideology was deconstructed, and since then it has never recovered its once-undisputed place as the dominant genre of the studio system (although the genre is not "dead" as some have claimed). And even though horror films have continued to be churned out with consistency, that genre, like the Western, experienced a great but temporary rethinking at the time, with the work of such filmmakers as George Romero, John Carpenter, Wes Craven, Tobe Hooper, and Brian De Palma. Responding to this remarkable resurgence of the horror film was *The American Nightmare*. In "An Introduction to the American Horror Film" Wood offered his ideas of the monster as representing a "return of the repressed" and the tripartite structure of the horror film (normality, monster, and the relation between them). These ideas have since become basic tenets of our critical understanding of horror. Anyone writing about the horror film since then has been obliged to take Wood's model into account, whether to demonstrate it, critique it, or break with it.

In the 1960s and '70s, when film studies was emerging as a legitimate field of scholarship and criticism and coalescing as an academic discipline within universities, genre studies were few and far between in the academic and scholarly literature. The general attitude was that European art cinema and experimental film were appropriate areas for serious discussion, but for the most part, genre films were popular cinema, too lowbrow to take seriously as film art. Genre films might be of some sociological interest but did not constitute "Cinema." In fact, the presence of conventions, a crucial component of genre films, worked *against* them. They were the opposite of art cinema wherein, as David Bordwell and others have pointed out, authorial flourishes and ambiguity were accepted and expected. Popular films clearly provided pleasure, which was regarded with suspicion as a manipulative tool of dominant ideology. It was fine to comment on lowbrow films, as Jean-Luc Godard did in *Breathless* (1959)—the film was dedicated to Monogram Pictures, a "Poverty Row" studio known for its B Westerns and mysteries—but not actually to devote oneself to the *study* of those films. They were, in the words of the magazine *Film Comment*, "guilty pleasures," and that journal dutifully provided a regular forum for filmmakers and critics to confess their sins. (It is no coincidence that Wood would excoriate the very concept of "guilty pleasures," as he does in the essay "What Lies Beneath?") Today, of course, the situation has changed, and the opposite is true. Books on film genres and genre films proliferate, with more devoted to horror and science fiction than any other, and most authors do not feel obliged to justify the seriousness of examining these genres. In the late 1970s a few scholars were taking the study of genre seriously—Stuart Kaminsky, Will Wright, and Steve Neale most notably—but more than any other critic, Robin Wood contributed to this turnaround regarding horror.

Despite the enormous influence of "An Introduction to the American Horror Film" on subsequent critical thinking about the genre, it might seem that Wood's interest in horror was peripheral to his larger work—his more well-known series of early auteur studies in the 1960s on Alfred Hitchcock, Ingmar Bergman, and others, and then his later projects involving ideological critique of Hollywood cinema and Western culture more generally. But, in fact, and as this collection shows, Wood, one of our foremost critics of the cinema, had a sustained critical interest in horror that spanned his entire career and brought together his parallel interests in (to borrow the title of another of his well-known essays) ideology, genre, and auteurism. No matter how one views the consistencies (or contrasts) of interest and emphasis in Wood's early and later writing, he never wavered from taking the horror genre seriously.

Given its scattered publication in widely diverse publications, this important body of work demanded to be collected in one volume. The present collection contains all of Wood's writings from *The American Nightmare* and most everything else he wrote over the years on horror, gathered together for the first time. It begins with the first essay Wood published in a film journal, "Psychoanalysis of *Psycho*," which appeared in *Cahiers du cinéma* (after it was rejected by *Sight and Sound*) in 1960, before that series of remarkable monographs on directors mentioned above. In this early essay one already sees ideas that would be worked through with greater depth in the landmark *Hitchcock's Films* a few years later. And the collection ends, fittingly, with one of Wood's last essays, "What Lies Beneath?," written almost a half century later, in which he reflects on the state of the horror film and horror film criticism since the genre's renaissance in the 1970s. In between are all the remaining essays, reviews, and interviews that Wood wrote on horror over a span of half a century.

Wayne State University Press was working with Wood to revise and reissue his classic early books on important film directors. Before his death in 2009, he managed to revise only the book *Howard Hawks*, as well as an expanded edition of his fascinating collection of essays *Personal Visions* (2006), originally published by a small art gallery in London, England, thirty years earlier. Since his passing, the press has posthumously published an expanded version of *Ingmar Bergman* containing the original monograph from 1969 and four other pieces that Wood had written about the Swedish director, a similarly expanded edition of the 1969 monograph on Arthur Penn in 2014 containing several other pieces and interviews with that director, and a reprint of his detailed analysis of Indian director Satyajit Ray's monumental Apu trilogy in 2016. Because Wood was such an elegant writer, and because his work remains today as fresh and insightful as when it was first published, I am pleased that *Robin Wood on the Horror Film* now takes its place alongside these other distinguished and influential works by him as part of Wayne State University Press's Contemporary Approaches to Film and Media Series.

Wood's prose here—as always, eloquent and lucid—required almost no changes to the text other than the silent correction of typos and a few factual errors, the addition of release dates for film titles in parentheses for the sake of consistency, and the completion of endnotes omitted in the original. Included in this collection is everything Wood published on horror, except for a review of *Next of Kin* (1982) from *Monthly Film Bulletin* because, unlike the other reviews from that magazine included here, this one consisted entirely of a one-paragraph plot summary. Parts of *The American Nightmare* appeared previously in *Film Comment* and subsequently in *Hollywood from Reagan to Vietnam* (1986). "Returning the Look: *Eyes of a Stranger*" was published in *Canadian Forum* magazine in 1982 and in *American Film* the following year as "Beauty Bests the Beast" (in 1987 it was reprinted with the original title in the anthology *American Horrors*, edited by Gregory Waller); the version included here is from *American Film* with the author's preferred title restored. Rather than grouping essays and reviews together into sections, I have chosen to present Wood's writing essentially in chronological order of publication (although I have kept the pieces from *The American Nightmare* previously published in the order in which they appeared in that book) to allow the reader to better appreciate the development and changes in his thinking over the years.

Barry Keith Grant

PREFACE

The Journey from *Psycho* to *The American Nightmare*; or, Why Should We Take the Horror Film Seriously?

ACCORDING TO ROBIN, HIS first encounter with a horror film occurred when his mother took him, as a young child, to a screening of *King Kong*. His mother, whom he described as a genteel woman, didn't fully realize what the film was about until King Kong appeared. He said that she became terribly upset and told him to close his eyes and not to look at the screen. Presumably, they didn't stay to see more of the film. In any case, the experience caused Robin to be wary of horror movies. It was a fear that stayed with him for a long time. In the early 1970s he began to take the genre seriously. John Anderson, who was then living with Robin in Coventry, recalls that the initial horror film to engage his critical interest was Gary Sherman's *Raw Meat* (*Deathline*); soon after that, they saw *Sisters* and *It's Alive!* Yet when it came to *The Texas Chainsaw Massacre*—which was promoted with the tagline "Who will survive and what will be left of them?"—the thought of seeing the film caused Robin to panic to the degree that he was unable to sleep the night before its screening. Perhaps having recently viewed in quick succession several highly intense and disturbing films, the prospect of watching Hooper's film was more than he could consciously handle.

In 1960 Robin's first piece of film criticism, "Psychoanalysis of *Psycho*," was published by *Cahiers du cinéma*. He wrote the article initially in response to Penelope Houston's *Sight and Sound* review of the film in which she dismissed it as a joke on Hitchcock's part. When Houston, as editor of the magazine, rejected his article, Robin was encouraged by his wife and friends to contact the French journal, which argued for the director as an artist, not merely an entertainer. In effect, Robin had *Sight and Sound* to thank for launching his career as a major critic. His sophisticated reading of *Psycho*, with his use of Freudian psychology, introduced a tenet central to his future work. In the film the cause of Marion's feelings of discomfort about her relationship with Sam is the result of social dictates that demand that, as a woman, her sexuality be legitimized by marriage and motherhood. Norman, because of his mother's fanatical rejection of sex, had deeply repressed his sexual desires, which, when aroused, threatened him and needed to be denied consciously. In both cases, their respective guilt is aligned to the nuclear family.

"Psychoanalysis of *Psycho*" illustrates Robin's serious approach to criticism, which he acquired through his literary study with F. R. Leavis at Cambridge. Leavis, addressing content and style, stressed the importance of close textual readings in the process of critical evaluation. As the *Psycho* article illustrates, not only did Robin have an impressive command over the use of language to express himself, he was also sensitive to detail and nuance. In his childhood, he began writing short stories, and later, as a young adult, he hoped to become a recognized novelist. Robin returned to this goal in the late '80s and early '90s by writing several novels and two screenplays. The initial novel, *Trammel up the Consequence*, was published in a limited edition in 2009. It deals with the horrific in a story that involves a brother and sister's extremely violent reaction to an abusive father.

In 1960 Robin was a gay man leading a conventional heterosexual life, recently married and raising a family. At the end of the decade, with its tumultuous social and cultural upheavals, Robin, living with his wife and three children and teaching at Queen's University in Kingston Ontario, openly acknowledged his sexual orientation, leading to the end of the marriage. In hindsight, it is possible to consider his reading of *Psycho* in light of Robin's feelings of being unable to give full expression to his sexuality. I am not claiming that being gay was directly relevant to his analysis of Hitchcock's film; instead, I am suggesting that his criticism became notably more and more personal as his career evolved. As a teacher, he placed emphasis on the personal. When asked by a student what one should look for in watching a film, his reply was in words to the effect that you should begin with a consideration of your own reaction to the work and what produced those thoughts and feelings. Reflecting on his initial writings on Bergman's films, Robin stated that he lacked a sufficient critical distance to comprehend the director's indifference to or suppression of an ideological context in which to place his characters. He attributed this to a preoccupation with his personal life and its conflicts, which led to an overidentification with the director's work. Nevertheless, his close readings of Bergman's films and their thematic preoccupations were insightful and given support through a rigorous analysis of characterization and mise-en-scène.

In 1972 Robin was back in England and living with John. On a professional level, he was fully confronted with the fact that humanist film criticism had become passé. Academic study had taken a scientific approach to the medium with its introduction of semiotics, Lacan, and Althusser. While not shunning film theory and its disciplines, he was troubled by the near outright dismissal of critical practice. He didn't think of criticism as a secondary concern when evaluating a film. Robin's position was that theory became relevant when it was proven to be so through critical practice. Taking Leavis's formulation "This is so, isn't it?" / "Yes, but . . . ," he felt value judgments can be a means to gain an enriched and deepened understanding of works and their meanings. It was during this period of personal, professional, and social upheaval that Robin discovered the contemporary horror film, which was the product of independent American directors working with low budgets. Selective in his response to theory, he adopted the concept of ideology to evaluate their work. Having had a longstanding commitment to mainstream cinema and genre film, which was then denounced as bourgeois indoctrination, Robin detected the political implications of these films. His attention was primarily focused on films dealing with the nuclear family and its underpinnings—patriarchy, capitalism, and bourgeois values.

Film theory embraced the notion of "the death of the author," claiming the author doesn't write but is written by the ideology, being a product of its values. Robin rejected this reductive thinking, adhering to his belief in the individual and the concept of authorship. The films he wrote on were made by imaginative and socially progressive filmmakers. This might not have been evident at the time but, in hindsight, has proven to be the case. With the recent death of a number of these directors—Wes Craven, George Romero, Tobe Hooper—their contributions to the cinema has been widely noted in the mainstream press and online. Their ground-breaking films, as those of John Carpenter, Larry Cohen, and Brian De Palma, remain as powerful and as radical as they were when originally released.

Robin's approach to these films was a humanist one, as it had been when writing on *Psycho* in 1960. Again, he used Freudian psychology to discuss the films' attack on "normality," that is, the maintenance of the ideological status quo and the oppression of blacks, women, and gays. Arguably, the experience of coming out of the closet was instrumental to Robin's response to the intensity and directness of the statements the films made. During the late '70s, and preceding *The American Nightmare*, Robin wrote in quick succession three seminal articles: "Ideology, Genre, Auteur" in 1977 and both "Responsibilities of a Gay Film Critic" and "Return of the Repressed" in 1978. Each of these articles was relevant to his construction of a usable discipline that is inclusive of theory, personal response, and critical practice.

The American Nightmare represents the pinnacle of Robin's commitment to the horror film. His interest in the genre was contingent on the extent to which it was used to challenge conservatism and its reactionary agenda. While not a decisive moment in his rejection of the horror genre as it developed in the '80s, Carpenter's remake of *The Thing* (1983) greatly disappointed him. He considered the film as a grotesque assault on the human body without any justification for its disgusting visuals. Although Robin wrote on few horror films during the '80s and '90s, he moved on to dealing with a range of concerns, including the careers of independent filmmakers such as Jamie Humberto Hermosillo, Gregg Araki, and Richard Linklater, Hollywood teen comedies; gay cinema; and Alice Miller's psychoanalytic writings on childhood and memory repression. Moving into the twenty-first century, he felt the most creative and politically relevant filmmaking was being done in Europe and Asia. In particular, Robin promoted the work of Michael Haneke, Tsai Ming-Liang, and Patrice Chéreau. As for a revival of the genre with such works as *Hostel* and *Saw*, he found those films merely sterile and sadistic.

Robin's last article on an American horror film was "Fresh Meat," his 2008 review of George Romero's *Diary of the Dead*. I think Robin would have appreciated the fact that the piece pays tribute to the director who did so much to legitimize the genre while serving as a fitting farewell to his writings on the horror film.

The American Nightmare: A Retrospective of American Horror Films

In October 1978 Wayne Clarkson, recently appointed the executive director of the Festival of Festivals, invited Robin and I to meet for dinner, saying he had something to discuss. At the dinner, Clarkson, who had met Robin in London during the mid-'70s, was introduced by Gary Sherman, the director of *Raw Meat*. It was Clarkson who proposed the idea that eventually became *The American Nightmare*. He suggested we mount a program of horror films and provide an accompanying book containing essays on the genre. Robin had fairly recently moved to Toronto, in the summer of 1977, and his reputation as an internationally known film critic was already well established.

We were totally taken aback and thrilled to be given this opportunity. Robin wasn't the kind of person who promoted himself. The notion of approaching the Festival's board members with such a proposal never would have occurred to him. Clarkson provided us with an assistant, Martine Becu, as part secretary and part creative advisor in putting the book together. Martine was a big help and a pleasure to work with. Judging from the attendance and audience response, it's safe to say that the event was a big success.

As Barry Keith Grant mentions in his foreword, the result of a year's planning was the screening of sixty films from September 7 through September 15 of 1979. We were given a large venue, the Bloor Cinema, which still exists although it's been renamed and updated, that accommodated at least several hundred people. Screenings began at 9:30 a.m. each day, with the final one beginning at 10:00 p.m. or later. On Saturday, September 8, in addition to the regular format, we held an "All Night Horror Special," beginning at midnight with *Curse of the Demon* and concluding with a 4:30 a.m. screening of the original *King Kong*. A series pass was $25, and individual tickets were $3. The opening screening on Friday, the seventh, was *Nosferatu* (1922), and the closing screening on Saturday, the fifteenth, was *Halloween*. One of the highlights of the event was the North American premiere of Herzog's *Nosferatu the Vampyre* (1979). The first four days dealt essentially with the history of the genre, and the next five were devoted to more contemporary films, with *Psycho* and *The Birds* being a transition of sorts between the classical and postclassical cinemas. As the inclusion of the *Nosferatu* films indicate, the screenings weren't strictly of American films. Wiene's *The Cabinet of Dr. Caligari* was screened, as were the British films *Burn, Witch, Burn!*, *The Sorcerers*, and *Peeping Tom*; as for the Canadian cinema, there were the Cronenberg films, and Bob Clark's *The Night Walker* (*Deathdream* or *Dead of Night*). A number of '50s films were screened that are identified generically as being science-fiction works: *Creature from the Black Lagoon*, *The Incredible Shrinking Man*, *Them!*, *The War of the Worlds*, *The Thing from Another World*, and the original *Invasion of the Body Snatchers*. Given that we chose to begin the program with a historical overview of the horror film, Robin and I spent a considerable amount of time deciding on which films should be included.

We were honored to have a number of notable directors partaking in the event: John Carpenter, David Cronenberg, Wes Craven, Brain De Palma, Tobe Hooper, George Romero, and Stephanie Rothman. A "seminar" was held on a daily basis at 11:00 a.m. at which either Robin or the both of us interviewed a specific director. The mood was relaxed, and the discussions were lively. It was particularly welcome to have Stephanie Rothman's participation, as she offered a feminist perspective on the genre and discussed her working relationship with Roger Corman. The Rothman films shown were *Terminal Island* and *The Velvet Vampire*. Of the other directors, we screened five Romero films (*Night of the Living Dead*, *The Crazies*, *Jack's Wife*, *Martin*, and *Dawn of the Dead*), three by Craven (*The Last House on the Left*, *The Hills Have Eyes*, and *Stranger in Our House* [*Summer of Fear*]), two by Hooper (*The Texas Chainsaw Massacre* and *Eaten Alive* [*Death Trap*]), two by Carpenter (*Assault on Precinct 13* and *Halloween*), Cronenberg's *Shivers* and *The Brood*, and De Palma's *Sisters* and *Carrie*. Larry Cohen was unable to attend but his presence was definitely felt with the inclusion of four films: *Bone*, *It's Alive!*, *Demon*, and *It Lives Again*. Another director who was invited but didn't attend was Gary Sherman, whose film *Raw Meat* was screened. The nine-day program was an extraordinary experience: the ongoing screenings, the seminars, and the energy generated by the audiences attending combined to make the entire event seemingly go by in a flash. The frontispiece photograph in this book of Robin onstage features one of the T-shirts he designed for the event.

The American Nightmare: Essays on the Horror Film had a small printing of a couple hundred copies. Andrew Britton and Tony Williams, who both contributed to the book, had been Robin's students while he was teaching at the University of Warwick and strongly shared his interest in the horror-film genre. I contributed essays on Richard Loncraine's *Full Circle* (*The Haunting of Julia*) and George Romero's *Martin*. These contributions were among my earliest writings, and I was pleased to be included in the book.

With the publication of *Robin Wood on the Horror Film*, Robin's work on the horror film will now reach an even wider audience than it did originally. I am especially pleased that the essay "Der Erlkönig: The Ambiguities of Horror" is included, as he particularly valued the essay because it gave him the opportunity to combine his passionate commitments to classical music, literature, and the cinema.

Richard Lippe

ROBIN WOOD ON THE HORROR FILM

Psychoanalysis of *Psycho*

After the relaxation of *North by Northwest* (1959), *Psycho* (1960) marks the director's return to a more serious tone and to some of *Vertigo*'s themes. In *Vertigo* (1958), the hero's desire to reimpose illusion on reality took the form of a macabre quest; now, once again, the triumph of illusion signifies the psychic death of an individual.

Taking the familiar and the everyday as its starting point, the film plunges deeper and deeper into the abnormal. Immediately after the credits, the camera gives us a commonplace view of a city and its rooftops. Suddenly, in an absolutely arbitrary way, we are given the date and the hour, to within a minute. The camera approaches some buildings, hesitates a moment, then with the same apparent arbitrariness selects a window and leads us there to have a look. It could—or so it seems—be any window, any time. We thus find ourselves plunged into the familiar and detailed world of the normal, better prepared for the banality of the brief love scene which follows, with its conversation about money worries. This world, precisely because it has been situated in time and space with so much particularity, is our world; these characters are like us. Identification with Marion Crane is crucial to Hitchcock's themes: links between the normal and the abnormal; the universal potential for abnormality; and, following on from this, connections between free states of mind and those that aren't free, and the gulf which separates them.

Psycho's technical structure differs significantly from that to which Hitchcock accustomed us in his previous films, notably the three most recent ones to feature James Stewart. In *Rear Window* (1954) and *Vertigo*, for example, we saw everything from the point of view of the central character, who, as clearly defined as he was, remained an everyman with whom we had no trouble identifying. His discoveries were ours. In *Psycho* the investigation is shared among several characters, none presented in much detail: the private investigator, Marion's lover, and Marion's sister. Our consciousness all the more readily identifies with theirs, at crucial moments, because they are mere puppets. The result is that the film is depersonalized: its interest lies in *what is discovered*, not (as in *Vertigo*) in the reactions of the one doing the discovering. Thus, to a superficial observer, *Psycho* may appear less coherent and more fragmented (in the image of Saul Bass's brilliant credit sequence, a premonition of things to come later in the film, as so often in Hitchcock), which is well suited to the subject of the disintegration of a consciousness incapable of managing reality.

The noted absence of personality in the investigators also helps us to focus our attention where Hitchcock wants it: on the two characters on whom the construction and meaning of the film turn, Marion Crane and Norman Bates (and, if you like, Norman's mother).

THE CONCEPTION OF THE film may be summed up in the simultaneous opposition and alignment of Marion's normality and Norman's madness. At the beginning of the film we see Marion in the grip of an irresistible impulse whose intensity destroys her freedom of choice. From the moment she steals the money (and, subtly, Hitchcock never shows her deciding to take it—she never gets to the point of deciding—rather, she is gradually possessed by her decision), Marion, under the sway of fear, becomes unable to think and act rationally. An instant's reflection would be enough to show her that she has no chance of succeeding, as the accusing voices which speak to her in the car tell her clearly: she alone could have stolen the money, her chances of escaping the police and finding a safe hiding place are so slight that no sensible person could take them seriously. She knows that even her lover will refuse the money and the solution it offers (she doesn't manage to finish the imaginary conversation she has with him in her head as she drives). In fact, her behavior is very close to that of Norman, who is himself "possessed," a detail which their later conversation will make explicit.

The sequence with the suspicious policeman and the exchange of cars underlines this well. Since she has been noticed, there is absolutely no point in changing cars: the policeman will find the new one as easily as the old. She wastes $700 in the process, but she is unable to act otherwise. Having abandoned herself to her criminal impulse (we learn a little later that Norman similarly succumbed to an even more terrible impulse several years before), she is no longer in control of her will. In fact, Marion's essential function in the film

Marion's behavior is close to that of Norman in *Psycho* (1960).

is to bridge the gulf between everyday normality and psychosis: without these first twenty minutes, which some critics find pointless, the film would lose its universality and become a simple description of a particular psychological case.

Our impression of being inexorably dragged along, in spite of ourselves, is brilliantly conveyed by simple means. We see Marion's face as she drives, eyes fixed on the road as if in a trance (Hitchcock excels, throughout the film, in the telling and expressive use of eyes), and then we take her place and see the ribbon of road roll out before us, so that we end up identifying with Marion and sharing her distress, her feeling of being taken over by an irresistible force. Obviously, the policeman, his stare inscrutable behind dark glasses, by and large represents, for Marion and for us, our conscience: conveying, in this case, the certainty that she will be unable to escape the consequences of her act.

THE CONFRONTATION BETWEEN MARION and Norman is the key to the film, especially in the conversation they have while eating sandwiches just after

Marion has overheard the quarrel between Norman and his mother. Their conversation clearly touches on the underlying themes of the film: free will and psychological predetermination. And it's thanks to this conversation that Marion succeeds in freeing herself from her obsession, that she decides to return the money through an impulse as natural as her previous impulse to steal it, thus escaping the trap in which she was caught like a bird. In fact she frees herself thanks to her intuitive perception of Norman's condition: he is unable to escape. Seeing him, she discovers that she has regained her freedom of choice.

Birds play a central role in the scene—the birds that Norman has stuffed—and their significance is complex. He thinks of Marion as of a bird, at first, in quite a sinister way, and at this moment a bird of prey hangs ominously above her head, its gaze turned toward Marion. There is a double visual metaphor here: Norman is at the same time the bird of prey and the victim, himself a prisoner of his own distress and absence of willpower. He is, truth be told, a victim precisely *because* he is a bird of prey. His acts have condemned him, like Macbeth, to a perpetual state of loss of will where each instant predetermines the next. Marion, for her part, is a bird because she is free—not a bird of prey, but an unconfined, spontaneous, and natural being. And it's because she is a bird that she is killed, the stabbing, of course, being a violent substitute for rape.

The whole sequence offers an example of the supreme technical and stylistic mastery which Hitchcock has attained. It is a mastery which goes much further than what is ordinarily understood by "technique" and "style," for here technique is inseparable from what it expresses. Hitchcock persuaded Janet Leigh to live her role as no actress had done before, while stripping Perkins of all those mannerisms which were becoming intrusive, eliciting in their place a performance of thoroughgoing interiority. The subtle evolution of the connections between the two characters, the concentrated and psychologically profound dramatic irony, Marion's liberation as a result of gaining insight into Norman, and the freedom which provokes her death—all this is magnificently realized. The characters are situated with extreme precision in their environment: the composition of the image, the framing, playing roles equivalent to those of the actors. Marion, visibly not especially out of her element in a motel setting, nonetheless shows some discomfort here. Her movements, her way of

Norman and his stuffed birds (*Psycho*, 1960).

sitting down, reveal her uneasiness. Norman, in contrast, despite his nervousness, is as comfortable in the room decorated with his stuffed birds as in his office. However, the childish mannerisms in his speech and gestures also link him to a setting in which we never actually see him—his bedroom. When Vera Miles explores the house a little later in the film, we instinctively recognize it precisely as having to be Norman's room from the knowledge that we possess of Norman himself.

At the moment when Norman leaves her, Marion, having made her decision, becomes a different creature from the Marion of the car journey. When Norman watches her undress through a hole in the wall, it is *his* eye which is as if entranced, whereas Marion has rediscovered her equanimity. She moves toward the shower in order to feel the purifying water flow coolly down her face and body, frees herself from her anguish, and washes herself with the naturalness of a bird. What follows is the most horrific murder ever shown on screen: horrific not only in its physical hideousness but in its pointlessness. Marion dies for no reason, victim of the lewd desire of the enslaved to destroy that which is pure and free. The murder is as irrational as the theft of the money. It is essential for the Hitchcockian thematic to show the continuity between the normal and the abnormal. After Marion's death, the investigation develops around the psychotic personality of a being permanently incapable of exercising his will.

Hitchcock is one of those rare artists who can effortlessly work on two levels, the level of popular melodrama and a deeper psychological/metaphysical level. A perfect example of this is the extraordinary camera movement which accompanies the carrying of the mother from her room on the first floor, the camera pausing, turning, gently rising in order to observe her emergence from above. At one level, our curiosity is maintained through our being prevented from moving in too closely as we look. At another level, the emphasis is on the distance that separates us from Norman, and thus on the objectivity with which we watch him act. *Psycho*, as has been well noted, is crammed with symbols borrowed from fantastic tales and Victorian melodrama: haunted house, imprisoned madwoman, dark room and sinister recesses, secrets hidden in attic and cellar, doors that open stealthily, etc. But, after Freud, we no longer take such things at face value: a secret passage, a closed chest or cupboard, a madwoman in the cellar—these symbols were in wide circulation at a time when the subconscious suffered the repercussions of severe sexual repression. Hitchcock knowingly uses our reactions to such symbols so that the horror and his psychological interpretation feel intimately linked. Given that Norman's condition is the result of a long period of sexual repression, the reference to Victorian melodrama is appropriate. Take, for example, the sequence where Vera Miles explores the house. Simply at the level of horror, it's brilliant. We see her move slowly forward toward the staircase with a timid step, the camera preceding her all the way up the stairs as if it exerted a magnetic pull, then we take her place and we're the ones who mount the staircase leading to the darkened room. The technique is familiar: we identify with the heroine in danger, in the act of climbing these stairs where a brutal murder has already been committed. She visits the rooms, makes some significant discoveries in each of them: the room where Norman went to look for his mother, the attic where he sleeps, and finally the cellar. But at the same time we explore a personality subject to a psychosis whose secret workings we follow with terror. It is easy to seize upon the symbolism of the cellar and the attic: they make an impression on our subconscious whether we are familiar with psychology or not. The attic represents the sick man's conscious mental development: strange confusion of the childish and the adult (the toys, the record of the *Eroica* symphony). The cellar is the source of repressed sexuality: it is where we find the mother.

Lila Crane (Vera Miles) explores the Bates house (*Psycho*, 1960).

The psychiatrist's explanation deserves some comment: it too lends itself to a double interpretation. As an explanation it is slight and superficial, though authentic and adequate enough if we see the film as a simple thriller. If the film were no more than that, we would doubtless be licensed to look no further. In fact, in its context, this verbosity risks masking the truth. The final scenes, which immediately follow, constitute an implicit refutation: it's not simply a matter of a "case," and the extreme abnormality is not as distant from us as we imagine it to be.

If we recall *Vertigo*, we will understand why *Psycho* must be Hitchcock's first "horror movie." His art led him to a point where it became inevitable that he would envisage the possibility of final and irremediable horror. Never has a human being been as irretrievably alone as the defenseless creature seated, trembling, in the cell clasping a blanket. The destruction of the freedom of a personality is total here. The moment where Norman spares the fly leads us briefly back to Marion's murder—the two acts being equally arbitrary and pointless—and Marion's death clearly makes no more sense to a deranged mind than the murder of a fly. This gesture of pity toward the fly constitutes a sort of expiation in the face of a cruel and uncomprehending society. So the features of the corpse superimpose themselves on the living face: Norman's identity is finally drowned by illusion.

It is this finally that gives the film, in the last analysis, its curious effect of serenity—a serenity completely free from complacency. We watch a permanently incurable madman through the lucid and objective eyes of a director whose art is above all a triumph of will and of character. The final horror has been surmounted, since no horror can surpass Norman's condition. We can return to life and to optimism. Serenity and optimism are the essence of Hitchcock's art.

And it's thus that the final image of the car emerging from the mud leads us back to Marion, to ourselves, and to the idea of liberty.

(1960)

Translation by Deborah Thomas

With thanks to Susan Spitzer and Ginette Vincendeau

In Memoriam: Michael Reeves

Ideally, perhaps, one should see everything—certainly the early work of all new directors—to search it for signs of promise. In practice, of course, it is virtually impossible. I made no pilgrimage to see *Revenge of the Blood Beast* (*The She Beast*, 1966); it never occurred to me to do so, nor to distinguish it from other Blood Beasts. Nor did I go to see *The Sorcerers* (1967) when it appeared. I wouldn't have gone to see *Witchfinder General* (*The Conqueror Worm*, 1968) either, if it hadn't turned up at the local and if it hadn't been for Tom Milne's short notice in the *Monthly Film Bulletin*.[1] It seems nicely ironic, when one looks back over the history of British film criticism in the last decade, that the director who perhaps came nearest to fulfilling the wishes of *Movie* for a revival in the British cinema—a director working at the heart of the commercial industry, making genre movies without apparent friction or frustration—should have been discovered by *Films and Filming* and the associate editor of *Sight and Sound*. I came out of *Witchfinder* telling myself that the next time a Michael Reeves film appeared I would review it for *Movie* and try to secure an interview with its director. Now there will be no interview, and *Witchfinder General* will have no successor: Michael Reeves is dead, at the age of twenty-five, leaving behind him only three and a half films. So what should have been an enthusiastic recognition of his great promise becomes a sad and (I hope) balanced assessment of his limited but striking achievement.

First, the problematic half. *Castle of the Living Dead* (*Il castello dei morti*, 1964) is credited to Warren Kiefer, coauthor of the scenario. Reeves was associated with it throughout as assistant director; his work on it earned him the opportunity of directing *Revenge of the Blood Beast*. He is said to have taken over altogether the last fortnight's shooting, which in terms of low-budget Italian-British coproduction must account for about half the film (he was scarcely in his twenties at the time). I have been unable to obtain any official confirmation of precisely which scenes he directed or what he contributed to other scenes or to the script; I can only offer my own deductions, on stylistic and thematic grounds. (The film's cameraman, Aldo Tonti, who has worked for Visconti, Rossellini, Fellini, and Fleischer, may also have made a significant contribution; certainly in the best parts of the film the camerawork is highly distinguished, equalled in Reeves's output only by that of Johnny Coquillon on *Witchfinder General*.) The film is startlingly uneven. Most of the first half is at best routine stuff, completely undistinguished in mise-en-scène, the camerawork merely restless. It is difficult to judge dubbed dialogue scenes fairly, but the acting seems mostly nondescript. There is no sense of any strong controlling presence: stock horror-film characters are unimaginatively presented. Then, at the point where the action moves to the castle exteriors, the whole film lifts. One feels, I think, the point where I suppose Reeves to have taken over as certainly as one feels the moment where Shakespeare took over *Pericles* (I hope no one will think a qualitative comparison is intended!). And one feels it primarily not from any stylistic mannerisms but from the film's sudden quickening into life. Not everything that follows need necessarily be Reeves's (just as not everything that precedes it need necessarily *not* be); but from the appearance of the coachman with the scythe, the film ceases to be a standard horror movie and takes on the closely knit organization of poetry. For a start, we are suddenly in the presence of a *director*, someone who knows where to put the camera and where and when to move it. The acting noticeably livens. The remarkable decor of the castle grounds is really *used*, becoming an important presence, and when the film returns to the interiors, the level of invention is sustained. Suddenly we find, after the awkwardness of the first part, a flowing of ideas. Reeves can't convert the central characters from stock figures, but they become dislodged from the center in favor of the hitherto-subsidiary dwarf. The film, from which one might have walked out from sheer boredom during the middle stretches in the castle interior, becomes extremely exciting: it might have been a minor masterpiece. As it is, it offers a salutary reminder of the supremacy of pure mise-en-scène in the art of cinema.

The distinction between great *metteur-en-scène* and auteur inaugurated by certain French critics seems to me fallacious, however. A genuine engagement with one's material inevitably involves expressing one's attitudes and hence defining one's themes, whether consciously or not. The quality and something of the content of Reeves's personal vision is already impressively clear in *Castle of the Living Dead* (if my attribution is accurate). The first part of the film is peopled by the stock characters of the horror genre, the notably gaunt, sinister count and gaunt, sinister coachman (both have their honorable ancestry in *Nosferatu* [1922], but the coinage has been much devalued since then). There is one scene only in which one would like to think Reeves had a determining influence: that in the market-square, with its macabre public-hanging joke and its establishment of hostilities between dwarf and coachman. Then, about halfway through, comes the moment when the intruding vindictive actor, still dressed in his Harlequin suit, lost in the castle's underground passages, emerges into the grounds. Low-angle shots show the coachman, with his gaunt death's head, holding an immense scythe that crosses the whole foreground of the screen. Abruptly, here and in the ensuing murder, the stock character takes on new resonances: he becomes a figure of monstrous cruelty and power; the image relates him to the traditional personification of death. In subsequent scenes the dwarf, with his sturdy energy and pluck, his valiant efforts to protect the heroine, comes to represent for us the positive promptings of life. The two figures, both physically grotesque yet incongruous opponents, alternately pursue and ambush each other among the weird, huge statuary of the castle grounds. The scenes, almost painfully exciting at "thriller" level, take on an allegorical or morality-play resonance.

If I am right in assuming that Reeves was the controlling influence in the latter half of the film, then what he seems to have done is to grasp the implicit subject—for even the most routine material can reveal a subject to the diligent inquirer—and around it organize characters, incidents, and images into a coherent poetic unity. The plot concerns a deranged Count Draco (Christopher Lee) who lures people to his castle (by means of his coachman-servant-assassin) and murders them in order to embalm them by a special instantaneous process that immortalizes them in death by preserving the flesh eternally. His dead wife, subject to an experiment before the fluid was perfected, is slowly decaying on a bed; in another room he is assembling a kind of waxwork museum of corpses held in permanent suspension (among whom one may spot Reeves himself as a dashing mustachioed officer). Clearly, there is a far-from-negligible subject lurking here—the theme of transience and mortality, one of the great subjects of English poetry. To grasp something of the "poetic" organization of the latter half of the film, consider the underlying interconnections between the following:

a) The coachman as death kills Harlequin with the scythe; cut to a shot of him tranquilly scything grass.

b) At the (supposed) burial of another victim, the count recites over the grave the text about the grass that "in the morning is green and groweth up, in the evening it is cut down and withered."

c) The count is obsessed with a desire to perpetuate beauty in death. His wife's unsuccessfully embalmed corpse on the bed is set holding a hand-mirror, to stare with glassy eyes at her own beauty forever; around and over her we see cobwebs, a spider, rats. The heroine Laura exclaims, "That's what he wanted to do to me!"

d) The dwarf is Laura's protector; gradually he emerges as the true hero of the film ("Smallest of the small, bravest of the brave," as his friend the witch says), defender of life against death (the coachman). He is the answer to the count's obsession with a useless, aesthetic beauty: aesthetically ugly and stunted, as a character he becomes increasingly beautiful throughout the latter part of the film.

e) The witch, the dwarf's patroness, once beautiful, victim of an early experiment, is now devoted to destroying the count. Her ugliness and degradation (the fact that the role is visibly played by a man is itself macabrely expressive) add another component to the complex of ideas and images unified by the theme of transience.

f) The struggle between dwarf and coachman is played out against time-worn monuments that decorate the castle grounds; one of these, beneath which the dwarf meets the witch, looks like an allegorical figure of age.

I must confess to a special affection, within Reeves's work, for these later scenes of *Castle of the Living Dead*: the obsession with evil and violence that characterizes the subsequent films is here more muted and balanced, reminding us that there can be advantages, for an immature genius, in working from other people's material. If they were in fact directed by Warren Kiefer, would Mr. Kiefer please step forward?

If the initial stimulus and justification for wanting to talk about Reeves lie in certain stunning set pieces of mise-en-scène (of which the precredit sequence of *Witchfinder General* can stand as an example), one's sense of his great promise is determined by the way in which, in only three and a half films, he had already established himself as an auteur, with a coherent (if still somewhat raw) view of life. *Revenge of the Blood Beast*, *The Sorcerers*, and *Witchfinder General* were written as well as directed by him, from subjects of his own choosing (within the bounds of that elastic term, the "horror film"), and he had virtually complete control of the shooting and editing. One notices various incidental similarities over the four films that suggest the more superficial aspects of a "signature." In both *Blood Beast* and *Witchfinder* a body falls away from a wall to reveal a blood smear left behind it. The witches in *Castle* and *Blood Beast* are both played by men; though the former is a force of good and the latter a force of evil, the overwhelming way they assault people (the former, Christopher Lee; the latter, everyone in sight) is strikingly similar. Played off against them in both films are ineffectual comic policemen. The following progression, and the degree of development it shows, suggest something central to Reeves's work. In *Castle*, the Harlequin-clad actor climbs the castle wall, inadvertently looks in through the window where the heroine is preparing for bed, and stays to watch; later, he is murdered with a scythe. In *Blood Beast* an innkeeper deliberately peers in at the room where the young honeymooning couple are making love in bed, and subsequently tries to rape another young girl; later, he is hacked to bits with a sickle. In *Witchfinder*, the central character, sexually depraved, seduces the heroine by agreeing to spare her uncle; at the end of the film, he is savagely and hideously mangled with an axe. His henchman spies on the witchfinder's love-making through a window; at the end, he gets one of his eyes kicked out. The odd film out—*The Sorcerers*—is so only in so far as there is no sharp instrument involved in the leading characters' destruction and in so far as the issue is much more complicated. Of the three leading characters, one (under hypnosis) performs the actions of a homicidal sex maniac and the other two experience them through a kind of glorified empathic voyeurism; all three are burnt to death. What is striking in this progression is the way in which the sexually depraved character moves increasingly toward the center of the film and the corresponding increase in the violence and intensity of the punishment he receives. Beneath these surface resemblances, the films Reeves scripted reveal a deeper unity.

Revenge of the Blood Beast (the Italian title, *La sorella di satana*—"Satan's sister"—is rather more meaningful) is an untidy and often clumsy film, made very cheaply (about £13,000) and swiftly, and sometimes looking it. The scenario was more or less made up as they went along, and adjusted to such factors as the vagaries of weather and the fact that Barbara Steele (nominally the star) was only available for four days' shooting. It contains unfortunate incongruities of tone, notably in a comic car chase with a would-be surrealist joke about a recurring motorcyclist that was shot (to save time) by an ad hoc second unit (the only time Reeves used such a thing); the result displeased Reeves, but neither time nor money permitted retakes. Nevertheless, when one looks back on it from the two later films, one is struck by the completeness with which *Blood Beast* sets forth Reeves's outlook and the essential themes of his work; it also contains one of his finest passages—the flashback that shows the witch Vardella.

The sequence starts with the intercutting of a funeral service in a chapel (the bell being rung by a dwarf) and shots of a boy running across a darkening hillside, across a landscape at once ominous and beautiful. The boy bursts in on the service with the news that his brother has been killed by the witch; enraged priest and congregation immediately set out to destroy her. The ragged procession sweeps out of the dark chapel under trees silhouetted against the night sky, carrying feebly flaring torches: the visual-dramatic sense of *Witchfinder General* is already striking and sure. Then the witch's cave, a yawning black hole from which an apparently decomposing hand gropes. Vardella is summoned out, and the nightmarish quality of the scene becomes manifest. She is an obscenely disgusting figure, her face hideously wrinkled and decomposed, yet her onrush suggests great power. The horror is intensified by the sense that she is nearly but not quite human, an obscene freak of nature, a suppressed and perverted force from the darkness. In the semidarkness she and her assailants become a struggling mass as she claws at men's faces before being overpowered. The rapid cutting and closeup details increase the sense of messy confusion. Vardella is dragged to the lake and placed in an elaborate ducking chair (it was in fact a siege catapult left over from an epic: a nice example of Reeves's flair for rapid improvisation!). A red-hot metal spike is driven through her, and she is repeatedly ducked, while the priest intones prayers of exorcism. Reeves cuts to a medium-long shot from the lake, the hideous figure impaled in the chair struggling and screaming, thick bare legs convulsively outstretching, as the chair rises and falls, the holy, white-clad ministers and the congregation forming a semicircle behind, the faces of the women impassive. The vileness of the witch is matched by the horror of what is being done to her: victim and destroyers are reduced to a common bestiality. Or, if you like, Vardella's viciousness is felt as being reflected in the righteous who surround her, an ineffaceable universal principle. The scene evokes comparison with the nightmare visions of Hieronymus Bosch; it belongs in a better film than *Revenge of the Blood Beast*. Its sense of horror and cruelty is so intense as to suggest a painful hypersensitivity in its creator: not a balanced view, certainly.

Nothing else in the film quite equals this, but several other sequences have something of the same force: the intercutting between the resurrected (and indestructible) Vardella and the brutish innkeeper, just before his attempted rape of the young girl who comes to him for protection, again suggesting that the witch is being used as an image for a universal evil inherent in human nature; the sequence of the cockfight, where a young boy is attacked by Vardella as through a high window he watches with pleasure the brutal sports of his fellow humans. The whole concept of the film is centrally Reevesian. "Transylvania Today," the opening title tells us, and we see a vintage car jogging through some very traditional woods. "Transylvania Today" proves to be a Communist state peopled mainly by idiotic policemen and a voyeuristic rapist innkeeper. This could appear a cheap and childish sneer at Communism, or even at foreigners; in retrospect from the other two films, the idea reveals itself as more serious. On the one hand there is the state, which thinks it has solved all human problems by politico-social means; on the other is Vardella the witch, symbol of eternal and indestructible evil. (From this viewpoint the film becomes a sort of pop *Switchboard Operator* [1967].) The visual joke, which is the thing most people seem to remember from the film, is in fact organic and fundamentally serious: after hacking the innkeeper with a sickle, Vardella contemptuously casts it aside so that it falls neatly over a hammer. In Reeves's films policemen are *necessarily* ridiculous and ineffectual, because evil is ineradicable and ultimately all-powerful, all-overwhelming. *Castle of the Living Dead* is his only optimistic film (in so far as it is his); one wonders if

Reeves was responsible for adding the opening commentary—"The war is over but the killing goes on . . ." The excessive violence with which Ian Ogilvy beats up *Blood Beast*'s innkeeper looks gratuitous at first sight but can be seen as making, rather clumsily, the basic point of *Witchfinder General*, whose ending it strikingly anticipates: that evil infects everyone, "villain" and "hero" alike, that we all carry within us a terrific latent violence that awaits a chance or pretext for erupting. The apparently "happy" ending of *Revenge of the Blood Beast* is completely undermined by Barbara Steele's last words ("I will return"), with their implication that Vardella, officially laid to rest forever, lives on in her and is only awaiting an opportunity to surge to the surface again. (Reeves wanted to end the film with the young couple safely back in their London flat. They make love. Later, the man wakes up in the moonlight and turns to gaze tenderly into the face of . . . Vardella. Time, budget, and Barbara Steele's unavailability for further shooting forced him to substitute the present more innocuous but quite unambiguous ending.)

The Sorcerers occupies a curious position in Reeves's little oeuvre because it is at once the finest of his films in conception and the worst in execution. It is as if the creative impulse had expended its energies at the script stage: the realization of ideas that could have been the basis of a masterpiece is generally unenterprising and ordinary. One feels, especially in scenes centered on subsidiary characters, that Reeves has been too easily content with B-feature solutions.

The film concerns an old practitioner of medical hypnosis (Boris Karloff), disgraced and reduced to poverty by journalistic exposure, who has perfected a method of hypnosis that not only gives him and his wife complete telepathic control (at whatever distance) over their victim but also enables them to experience, with complete physical empathy, whatever sensations the victim is experiencing. Gradually, two decisive facts emerge: that his wife (Catherine Lacey), apparently a sweet old lady whose chief interest in life is to support and encourage her husband, carries within her a great reservoir of perverted and sadistic desires, which, once the floodgates are opened, proves absolutely uncontrollable; and that her will is very much stronger than that of her humane and appalled husband, so that it is she who effectively determines what the young man does. The film is centered on the three-minds-in-one-body conflict: the young man, will-less whenever the couple chooses to exert their control over him, becomes a battleground for their opposed wills.

The Sorcerers really has two subjects, both very rich and suggestive. From the point of view of the young man, it can be seen as an allegory about psychosis, with Catherine Lacey as unmanageable id and Karloff as ineffectual superego: the young man is completely at the mercy of what seem (since he remembers nothing of his meeting with the old couple) uncontrollable inner compulsions, and he is not aware afterward of what he has done. What he has done includes the gratuitous murder of two girls, one with scissors, one by strangulation. He is as helpless as Norman Bates, and his mental relationship with Catherine Lacey strongly recalls the mother-son interaction in *Psycho* (1960). From the point of view of the old couple, on the other hand, the film becomes, fascinatingly, an allegory about the cinema and the vicarious experience of the spectator. Catherine Lacey discovers the delights of experiencing anything she wishes to experience, with no consequences: especially, the delights of danger and violence, which even her nice old husband can't deny that he rather enjoyed. From the point in the film where we are alerted to such implications, our own response becomes uncomfortable and self-questioning: To what extent do we, like Catherine Lacey, want the young man to commit horrible murders while we sit back in our seats sharing the sensations in second-hand security? And are we so sure that that "security" isn't a delusion? Are we, like the old woman, contaminated? Does the release of our baser instincts threaten to overwhelm and obliterate all our finer feelings? What do we go to horror films for, anyway?

At the core of *The Sorcerers*—and by no means unrelated to such questions as the popularity of the horror film—is Reeves's recurrent preoccupation with the universality and the irresistible power of evil. The most frightening (and best realized) thing in the film is the tracing of Catherine Lacey's rapid and unprotesting surrender to her worst destructive impulses, from that first ominous moment when she delightedly orders her victim to crush an egg in his bare hand. The theme is given a further extension through the interaction of the minds and desires of the old woman and the young man, and the ambiguities arising from it. When responding to telepathic orders, he appears merely zombie-like, the medium through which her perverse desires can be realized; yet it is established at the outset of the film that the experiment will only work if the guinea pig is "willing." The young man's character is not explained or developed in detail, but we are given a few tantalizing hints suggestive of inner disturbances and conflicts. He is associated with two strongly contrasted decors—his modern flat, decorated with contemporary abstract paintings, and his dowdy and cluttered antique shop where he spends most of his days. At the start of the film he expresses his boredom and dissatisfaction with life, his desire to have things happen: his behavior, abruptly and arbitrarily leaving his sweetheart with a (male) friend and going off for a solitary hamburger in a Wimpy bar, suggests a neurotic restlessness. Both the murders he is driven to commit carry (like the shower scene in *Psycho*) violent sexual overtones: the repeated upward lunge with the scissors with which he stabs the first girl, the position of the bodies as he strangles the second. We are left to ask exactly whose perverted desires are being fulfilled, his or the old woman's?

As the film progresses the young man becomes increasingly its focal point. This is doubtless partly explainable in that what happens to him is more "cinematic" than the experiences of the old couple, who are for most of the film confined to a single room. But in relation to the Reeves's oeuvre the character assumes a particular significance. He is completely at the mercy of the evil forces that have been released, be they within him or without, forces he can neither control nor understand, forces that make him both destroyer and destroyed. The role is played by Ian Ogilvy, a personal friend of Reeves, who appears in all three films and with whom one can assume a certain degree of identification on Reeves's part. Can it be coincidence that this character, who seems to embody so much that is central to the personal vision of Michael Reeves, is called Michael Roscoe?

If *The Sorcerers* is perhaps the most theoretically interesting of Reeves's films, *Witchfinder General* is certainly his most successfully achieved work. It is easy to make *The Sorcerers* sound a much better film than in fact it is: its virtues are primarily on the level of ideas. In *Witchfinder* what one is immediately struck by is the assurance and intensity of what is on the screen. The precredits sequence—again concerned with the execution of a "witch," though she is not here a force of evil, merely a wretched victim—instantly reveals a regaining of the creative intensity of the best scenes of *Revenge of the Blood Beast*, and although this level of inspiration is not consistently maintained, there are no serious lapses. The film has, unfortunately, a central flaw. Vincent Price does not really belong in it. It is not just that his accent repeatedly jars in an otherwise all-British cast: one can persuade oneself to overlook such incidental defects. He gives a very accomplished performance, but he remains always Vincent Price in costume. *Witchfinder General*, while certainly horrific, is not really a genre horror film, and it is the genre that Price's presence continually evokes. One guesses that Reeves found difficulty in "directing" an actor whose screen persona is so fully formed and familiar. The scenes introducing Price promise, in fact, a richer and more complex character than ever actually materializes. Michael Walker pointed out to me that Matthew Hopkins and his sadistic, brutish henchman Stearne are like a parody of the knight and squire in *The Seventh Seal* (1957), and once one has seen it the likeness is striking. But the hint of genuine religious zeal felt as intermixed with Hopkins's corruption on his first appearance is never developed: he becomes an altogether more melodramatic villain, a mere hypocrite, differing from Stearne in his greater refinement rather than in any greater complexity of motivation. Reeves wrote the part with Donald Pleasence in mind, and, though one is not altogether happy about this idea either, it certainly throws light on the director's original conception of the role.

It is easy to demonstrate *Witchfinder*'s consistence with Reeves's other work. The theme of the morally outraged seeking a revenge that ultimately

Vincent Price as Matthew Hopkins in *Witchfinder General* (1968).

degrades them to the level of their quarry—a theme so fundamental to human experience that it has inspired outstanding work in most ages, in Greek tragedy, Elizabethan drama, the Western—is one to which Reeves would be expected to respond strongly. Primary interest in the film is divided between two figures: the debased witchfinder Hopkins, and the young Cromwellian officer Richard Marshall (Ian Ogilvy again). Marshall's fiancée allows herself to be seduced by Hopkins in the belief that he will then spare her uncle-guardian; later she is raped in the fields by Hopkins's assistant Stearne (Robert Russell); the guardian is publicly executed for witchcraft. The first half of the film shows an England where the disorders of civil war allow evil, cruelty, and violence (thinly disguised as religious righteousness) to run riot. There is the sense that Hopkins is everywhere; not only that, his excesses are condoned and applauded by educated and ignorant alike. The second half centers upon Marshall's quest for vengeance and culminates in the overwhelmingly horrible scene where it is executed, and we see that he, too, has become more beast than human.

But *Witchfinder* offers more than thematic repetition: there is marked development. *Revenge of the Blood Beast* and *The Sorcerers* are dominated almost entirely by destructive evil; the weakest aspects of both films are those involving positive or constructive feelings—the Ian Ogilvy / Barbara Steele relationship in the former, the Victor Henry / Elizabeth Ercy characters in the latter, all conceived perfunctorily in very conventional terms, with little sense of interest or involvement on Reeves's part. In *Witchfinder*—although there is again the disturbing sense throughout that sanity and goodness are powerless against the all-pervading corruption and violence—there is also a strong feeling for positive potentialities, with emotions like love and tenderness becoming real presences in the tone of the film, so that through their destruction it moves closer to true tragic feeling than either of its predecessors. The love relationship is handled with poignance; so is the girl Sara's feeling for her uncle, and the sacrifice it prompts her to make in a scene which Hilary Dwyer plays very touchingly. The film pivots on the church scene: Marshall returns to find the guardian dead and Sara cowering in the chapel, terrified and feeling herself defiled. Kneeling with her by the altar he declares them married and swears vengeance, a scene that could easily have lapsed into melodramatic absurdity but which Reeves and his actors bring off magnificently. After it, Marshall rides off again, and as he kisses Sara goodbye we understand that for him, too, the girl is degraded—that he has difficulty in bringing himself to caress her and that the tenderness he felt for her has now become converted into the single-minded lust for revenge. His reaction interestingly echoes that of Hopkins when he learns that Sara has been raped by Stearne: he wants no more to do with her and promptly breaks his pact, sentencing the guardian to death.

The use of landscape in the film is felt as an extension of this awareness of human positives. Reeves's grasp of the importance of decor is one of his best qualities: one thinks of the garden in *Castle of the Living Dead*; the innkeeper's littered primitive room, with its incongruous fridge, in *Revenge of the Blood Beast*; the Karloff-Lacey flat in *The Sorcerers*. In *Witchfinder General*, from the first shot of a "natural" cross formed by sunlight streaming through trees, the English countryside is felt as a real presence: it is difficult to think of other films in which it has been used so sensitively and meaningfully. With it is associated Paul Ferris's theme music, which suggests a traditional air without being actual quotation. Against the peace and fertility of nature is set the depravity of men. The last seconds of the film are very striking. After Marshall has hacked Hopkins to death, the camera returns us to Sara's face (she is bound on a torture table, face down). In the sudden stillness she begins to scream,

Richard Marshall (Ian Ogilvy) takes his revenge on Hopkins (*Witchfinder General*, 1968).

and we realize that her mind has given way, perhaps permanently, under the strain of so much horror. Reeves cuts in shots of the castle's deserted staircases and corridors, along which the screams echo, then returns us to the face and freezes the image. As the final credits come up over it, they are accompanied by the "nature" music, over which the screams continue: the juxtaposition chillingly expresses our sense of all that has been lost.

Reeves's death is a tragic loss for the British cinema, the more so in that none of his films is completely satisfactory, that one is aware of far more promise than achievement. In discussing his work I have not attempted to minimize its unpleasant aspects, its neurotic quality. It is certainly true that his direction springs to life most startlingly in scenes involving excessive cruelty and horror, and, although his treatment of violence is never in the least titillating, neither does it strike one as balanced or mature. But, in the very lack of balance that the films reveal, he shows the kind of intensity of vision out of which great art often develops, and his work, in its consistency and in the development shown over so short a period, is more impressive in its sum than in its components. There is little to be gained, now, in talking of his promise: if it were solely a matter of promise, this article would scarcely be worth writing. And of course there can be no promise without some degree of achievement. The achievement represented by these three and a half films is sufficient, I think, to repay the attention of anyone interested in movies and in what could be done within that most discouraging of areas—the British commercial cinema.

I WISH TO THANK Ian Ogilvy and David Austen for their generous cooperation in the preparation of this article.   R.W.

(1969–1970)

The Shadow Worlds of Jacques Tourneur

The series of horror films (for want of a better term) produced by Val Lewton in the '40s can stand as at once a demonstration of the limitations of the auteur theory and its vindication. They are usually regarded, and with some justice, as essentially Lewton's films. Much of their taste, intelligence, and discretion is attributable to his planning and supervision, and it becomes peculiarly difficult—in the last resort impossible—to sort out the precise contributions of producer, writer, and director. Yet important discriminations remain to be made. None of the series, not even *Bedlam* (1946), is without interest; and to be the producer of an interesting film directed by Mark Robson is in itself evidence of distinction.

Perhaps *The Body Snatcher* (1945)—which I thought on first viewing (mistakenly, as I now believe) the finest of the whole series—testifies best to Lewton's quality. It is a marvelously constructed film, a moral fable on the subject of dehumanization carefully structured in terms of its characters—brutalized body snatcher, experienced doctor tormented by his complicity yet too involved to extricate himself, young doctor in continual danger of getting drawn into the same trap—yet given considerable complexity by the varying play of sympathy elicited for each (Karloff's body snatcher remains disturbingly human). Yet, if one places it beside *Cat People* (1942) and *I Walked with a Zombie* (1943), one cannot but be aware of a comparative crudeness of sensibility apparent in the realization. Insofar as it is a Lewton film, *The Body Snatcher* is a potential masterpiece (a *producer*'s film cannot be more than potential); insofar as it is a Robert Wise film, it is inferior to certain of its companions.

Cat People and *Zombie* were both directed by Jacques Tourneur. Interestingly, they exhibit not only stylistic but thematic features that at once connect them with each other and distinguish them from other films in the series.

And similar features are discernible in *The Leopard Man* (1943), the other film Tourneur directed for Lewton. Though it contains several excellent—and recognizably Tourneuresque—sequences, *The Leopard Man* is notably inferior to its predecessors, striking one as at once overexplicit and underdeveloped, as if its makers had become too conscious of the thematic level of their work. I shall not discuss it here, as it does little that is not done better in the two earlier films, but it is useful in offering confirmatory evidence for the decisive influence on the films of Tourneur's personality—decisive on their precise character and to some extent on their quality. And memories of *Curse of the Demon* (*Night of the Demon*, 1957) made later without Lewton, and exhibiting very much the same character and quality, tended further to support my growing sense of Tourneur as essential auteur.

But before going the whole auteurist hog and regarding *Cat People* and *Zombie* as Tourneur movies *tout court*, it is salutary to glace at some of his other work. My own experience here has been disconcerting. In the excitement of discovering Tourneur's Lewton films I managed to unearth six of his nonhorror movies. With *Canyon Passage* (1946) and *Out of the Past* (1947) I began to wonder what Tourneur was doing outside Mr. Sarris's pantheon, and felt confident I had discovered one of the great unacknowledged masters of the American cinema; *Days of Glory* (1944), *Experiment Perilous* (1944), *Berlin Express* (1948), and *Easy Living* (1949) constituted four successive blows to that confidence.

Not that they offer any incontestable refutation: everyone makes bad movies sometimes (even directors with total control over their material and free choice of subject matter, like Mr. Dennis Hopper), and a Hollywood contract director has the right to claim forgiveness for any number of unredeemable fiascoes. One could not possibly ask an artist of any intelligence and sensibility to interest himself passionately in the scenario of, for example, *Berlin Express*, which is of a stupidity one would find unbelievable were one not hardened by so many precedents.

What raises some doubt is the nature of the failure of these films. Tourneur's visual style—characterized by a penchant for long shot and camera movement—is intermittently recognizable in all of them (except perhaps *Easy Living*, overall the most competent but least Tourneuresque of the four).

But it is simply applied to the subject matter externally, without in any way transforming it. One begins to question, tentatively, the strength and force of Tourneur's creativity; to ask oneself on which side of the shadowy borderline between creator and interpreter he belongs. An inability to enter deeply into not entirely congenial subject matter, to penetrate its surface and transform it from within, is not inconsistent with the excellence of the Lewton films or of *Canyon Passage* or *Out of the Past*.

Related to this is one's general sense that Tourneur is not a particularly distinguished director of actors. In a Nicholas Ray movie, for example, no one ever gives a bad performance, not even Curt Jurgens or Robert Taylor or even, heaven help us, Mr. Quinn. But in both *Cat People* and *Zombie* Tom Conway remains, unshakably, Tom Conway. If there are few really bad performances in Tourneur's films there are no great ones (with the possible exception of Mitchum in *Out of the Past*; and Mitchum, to adapt Michel Mourlet's famous remark about Charlton Heston, is an axiom).[2] His best scenes are typically either atmospheric (certain sequences in the Lewton films discussed below) or ensemble scenes (the wedding in *Canyon Passage*, where the connecting camera movement leads one to compare the status of the various couples present) in which individual performances are subordinated to a sense of relatedness between the parts.

It is obvious that all directors are dependent on their scripts; Tourneur appears unusually so. His chief qualities—words like "reticence" and "delicacy" come first to mind, rather than Mr. Sarris's somewhat belittling "gentility" (see his maddening, indispensable *The American Cinema*, the most-thumbed reference work in my book collection)—are not necessarily negative ones but can easily become so. His bad films have nothing actively offensive about them; they are simply colorless and boring. Perhaps he could be fairly described as a born collaborator in search of someone with whom to collaborate. On the other hand, the humility that led him to accept whatever chores were thrown his way, however unpromising, is a quality that, in his best work, assumes great positive significance: *I Walked with a Zombie* is, in its humble and masterly way, a lesson in humility.

Though I think it is Tourneur's contribution that distinguishes them from their companions in the series, I feel, then, that *Cat People* and *Zombie* should be regarded as group achievements, with due credit to Lewton and the scriptwriters—DeWitt Bodeen and Curt Siodmak, respectively. Both films are beautifully planned and mostly (minus a few lapses into triteness) well written; under Tourneur their implicit poetry reaches sensitive visual expression.

I HAVE SUGGESTED THAT the two films are linked thematically as well as stylistically. Both are about honest, upright, uncomplicated Americans (in *Zombie*, in fact, a Canadian nurse primly commended by her employer and potential lover for her "clean, decent thinking") who are impinged upon by outside "foreign" forces at once sinister, mysterious, and fascinating. The sociologically inclined will doubtless like to interpret the films in terms of American isolationism (as Mr. George A. Huaco in *The Sociology of Film Art* explains *Nosferatu* [1922] for us as reflecting "the growing economic crisis in 1922").[3] The treatment is in fact extremely complex and ambivalent.

Tourneur's father, Maurice, was not, as ignorant people like myself tend to assume, a director in France who emigrated to America to complete his career in Hollywood. It was precisely the other way round: from 1914 to 1926 he made films in America then went to Europe where he continued making films, mostly in France, until 1948. Jacques, born in 1904, spent parts of his childhood in Europe and in fact began his career in France in 1931, where he made three films before settling in America in the late '30s. One would scarcely wish to claim him as a cinematic Henry James, but one can perhaps assume that the intermixture of American and European culture in his background gave him a particular sensitivity to the ambivalences inherent in the subject matter of his Lewton films. (The presence, or at least the potential, of a similar ambivalence in the subject matter of *Experiment Perilous* makes the failure of that film—Tourneur's inability, for whatever reason, to transcend the melodramatic banalities of the script—all the more disappointing.)

If the American protagonists embody a norm of straightforward decency, all the poetry emanates from the foreign elements, and in both films the decency is revealed as decidedly limited. One small, specific clue to Tourneur's sympathies can surely be found in the fact that the little song he gave Irena in *Cat People* is a French lullaby he remembered from his childhood. One is led to forget about geography and interpret the films in terms of an opposition between day consciousness and night consciousness, between a surface world of conventional and unimaginative "normality"—for want of a better word—and a far richer underworld of dangerous and fascinating dreams.

Some such opposition is, of course, a common and universal theme in the arts; it manifests itself in the American cinema with both frequency and intensity. It is there in *Sunrise* (1927), in the comparison (implicit in the imagery) of the Woman from the City to a cat. (The fact that in that film sympathies are reversed, and the "underworld" is presented as almost exclusively evil and destructive, is more characteristic of German Expressionism than of Hollywood.) One need only mention—to suggest the variety of tone and manner, the range of genres in which it can clothe itself—*Bringing Up Baby* (1938) and *Marnie* (1964), both of which use cats (leopard and jaguarundi, respectively) prominently in their imagery of the dangerous instinctual world on whose suppression bourgeois stability depends. Thematically, *Marnie* in particular offers fascinating and detailed parallels to *Cat People*, rendering explicit that film's psychological implications.

Cat People (1942) employs the common association of women with cats.

Confronted, however, with such delicate and reticent works, one wants to preserve a corresponding reticence in the interpretation. *Cat People* and *I Walked with a Zombie* both suggest, and in a more conscious and sophisticated way than is the case in the majority of horror films, that the myths they draw on are capable of psychological interpretation; neither is reducible to clear-cut psychological allegory. They work by means of poetic suggestiveness rather than of clearly definable "meaning," and any attempt to "explain" them beyond a certain point can only do them harm. The sexual overtones of *Cat People* are clear enough: Irena is afraid that her "cat" nature will be released if she is sexually aroused, and it eventually is released by sexual jealousy. Similarly, *I Walked with a Zombie* hints at an equation between the zombie state ("the living dead") and emotional death. But the filmmakers have in both cases respected the poetic power of the myth. Psychological meaning remains a matter of suggestion; it is never insisted upon or spelled out. Rather than attempt an allegorical interpretation (which would, inevitably, become an interpretation of the script), I want to examine some of the films' poetic detail, or poetic movement, to show something of their richness of suggestion.

THE PRIEST IN GREENE'S *The Power and the Glory* regards ironically the tendency of the good, and incorrigibly "innocent," Americans he meets to place cleanliness next to godliness—but only just. *Cat People* opens (after an impressive-sounding quotation about sin lingering on in the unconscious like fog in low places, from *The Anatomy of Atavism* by "Dr. Louis Judd," who turns out later to be the glib and skeptical psychiatrist played by Tom Conway) with a similarly ironic association of surface cleanliness with ignorance of deeper evils. Irena (Simone Simon) is making her obsessive sketches, before the panther's cage in the zoo, of a panther transfixed by a sword. When a discarded drawing fails to reach the litter basket, a young man (Kent Smith) retrieves it and draws Irena's attention to the sign nearby: "Be it not said, and said unto your shame / That all was beauty here until you came." The same idea is referred to unobtrusively in one of the film's climactic scenes: the buildup to the famous sequence where Irena pursues Alice (Jane Randolph) along a shadowy sidewalk at night is twice punctuated by brief scenes in which a cleaning woman meticulously flicks cigarette ash off her uniform.

Such details point to the film's central opposition. Oliver, the young man at the zoo, is a draftsman in a ship designer's offices. As with Professor Cary Grant in *Bringing Up Baby*, the impersonal scientific activity represents a surface consciousness whose order depends on ignorance or rejection of the potentially chaotic world of unconscious forces and instincts; and, like Professor Grant, Oliver is involved with two girls, one who shares his work (it's nice that in both films she is called Alice) and one who embodies exactly those drives that threaten the surface order. But whereas Katharine Hepburn was content to own a leopard, Irena actually turns into a panther. Imagery derived from this basic opposition pervades the film. Even the apparently banal and incongruous movement when Oliver dismisses Irena-as-panther by brandishing a cross and exclaiming "in the name of God!" is partly redeemed by the fact that they are in the draftsmen's office and the cross is a set square.

The film's delicate life is in the wealth of poetic invention. Oliver and Irena are in her dimly lit apartment. In the background an armchair casts its shadow on the wall. Oliver, lying on the sofa, declares his love for Irena. She draws back, disturbed, and her head becomes superimposed upon the shadow so that the uprights of the chair become cat's ears—the shape is very like that of the Egyptian cat-goddess beside which Irena pauses, later, in the museum. Characteristically, Tourneur does nothing to force the point—he neither cuts nor tracks in; the effect is conveyed solely through the actress's movement. Nor are such points underlined with music; credit for the discreet and sparing way in which music is used in these films (even truer of *Zombie* than of *Cat People*) doubtless belongs to Lewton as much as Tourneur, the score being one of the last things over which a Hollywood contract director is likely to have control. Later in the film, when Irena is spying on Oliver and Alice before her first attempt to kill her rival, Alice says, shuddering, as she and Oliver emerge from the building, "A cat walked over my grave." Tourneur cuts to Irena standing before the window of a flower shop, with a wreath behind her. Most unobtrusive touch of all: the chain that bars Irena from the panther's cage during her nocturnal wanderings has, at the end of the film, when her animal nature has been released, mysteriously vanished.

But it would be false to give the impression of a series of isolated touches. To suggest how this delicate poetry pervades the movement of the whole film it is necessary to examine some extended sequences. Consider the sequence of the wedding night and the scenes that follow. During the celebration in the Serbian restaurant Irena is confronted by the catlike woman who addresses her as "my sister." Afterward, on the sidewalk outside Irena's apartment (where the couple are to live), she tells Oliver she can't sleep with him yet, and asks him to be patient with her. Irena goes to the bedroom. We see Oliver standing helpless outside the closed door; cut to the other side of the door, where Irena is crouching, still hesitant. The mood is intensified by the snow falling outside the window in the background of the image. Irena's hand rises to the doorknob; the panther's cry comes through the night from the zoo; her hand draws back. Again, Tourneur's reticent style is crucial to the effect of the scene: a single, static shot, the camera at some distance from Irena at right of the screen, so that the darkness of the room behind her, the falling snow beyond the window in the left background, the distant, disturbing wail all make, unforced, their contributions.

The next scene shows another of Irena's obsessive visits to the panther's cage and her dialogue with the keeper who, in response to her remarks about the panther's beauty, insists upon its ugliness and refers her to the book of Revelations and the worst "beast" of them all, which was "like unto a leopard." The image of the snarling animal suggests both its beauty and its cruelty. The door that separated Irena from Oliver is paralleled by the cage that separates her from the panther: divided between two worlds, she is barred from access to either. The idea is taken up in the closing quotation—genuine, this time—from Donne's "Holy Sonnet V": "But black sin hath condemn'd to endless night / My world, both parts, and both parts must die."

From this we are moved back to Irena's apartment. The sequence opens with an image that beautifully links what has gone before with what is to come: the painting of a black panther on a screen, over which falls the shadow of the cage of the bird Oliver has given Irena. The image provides a visual link with the previous scene, taking up the "caged panther" motif, and connects the panther with the bird. From this the camera moves back to take in Irena at her drawing board, connecting her with the panther/bird image where cutting would have separated. She is working at a slick, commonplace fashion design, the image again suggesting the opposition between surface consciousness and unconscious forces. Irena stands back and gives a little stretch, slightly drawing up her shoulders and curling her fingers, like a cat. Then she moves to the birdcage, opens it, tries to take the bird in her hand. The bird flutters in wild hysteria, and an ambiguous smile comes on Irena's face: tender or sadistic? The bird dies of shock. The sequence ends with a long shot of Irena standing desolate with the bird in her hand. In the foreground is the model of a ship, reminding us of Oliver and his work, balancing the expression of Irena's mysterious, suppressed nature with the idea of conscious control.

There follows the scene where Irena takes the dead bird to the zoo and throws it to the caged panther, an action that crystallizes for us the ambiguity of her relationship to the beast. Most obviously (since Irena herself, at moments of crisis, assumes its form), it represents her alter ego. Yet it was emphasized earlier that it is a male panther; we may see it as an alternative potential mate to whom she is taking food, and the point is strengthened by the fact that the bird was originally a gift from Oliver. The action also suggests an act of propitiation, with the panther as some kind of dark god that Irena must appease with an offering.

Almost wherever one looks in the film one finds a similar accumulation of suggestive detail. The sequence of Irena's pursuit of Alice at night, and its aftermath, are particularly rich. Alice is alone in the draftsmen's office; Irena phones to ascertain that she is there, without herself speaking. The images of the two women, each with the receiver in hand, are very exactly balanced. Alice is lit from below by an illuminated table used for design work, Irena by a table lamp. Beside Irena is the statue of King John of Serbia holding a speared panther aloft on his lance; beside Alice is a gentle domestic cat (called John Paul Jones). The sequence of the pursuit is a locus classicus of unnerving effects achieved with the utmost reticence and simplicity of means: movement, rhythmic editing, lighting, culminating in the film's one shock effect—the more startling for being unique—as the bus slides into the frame with a loud hissing noise just at the moment we expect the unseen panther to spring. This is followed by the shot of the dead, savaged sheep on which Irena has vented her animal fury (when we next see the panther, there is a leg of lamb in its cage!), with paw marks deep in the mud; then by the simple, magical tracking shot along the sidewalk as the paw marks change, step by step, into the marks of high-heeled shoes and we see Irena walking slowly away, dazed—the juxtaposition recalling that of the panther painting and the fashion sketch in her apartment. Later, when Irena has returned home, we see the base of her bathtub, resting on a foot shaped like an animal's claw, and the camera moves up to show Irena above, sitting in the bath, weeping, the unbroken camera movement connecting her to the claw foot, subtly underlining our sense of her divided self and of her poignant helplessness.

There follows the brief sequence of Irena's dream, one of the finest dream sequences in the cinema because it is so packed, complex, and suggestive. Black panther shapes move outward gracefully and ominously toward the camera. From behind them emerges what at first appears to be an erect panther figure but then reveals itself as Dr. Judd, the psychiatrist, dressed in chain mail as King John, the avenger. It was Judd who, earlier, at the zoo, brought to consciousness Irena's desire to steal the key of the panther's cage. In the dream his sword becomes the key, and she wakes up knowing she must steal it. The dream is rich in ambiguities that relate to the role Judd plays but are characteristic of the manner of the whole film, at once concrete and mysterious, always eluding clear-cut definition.

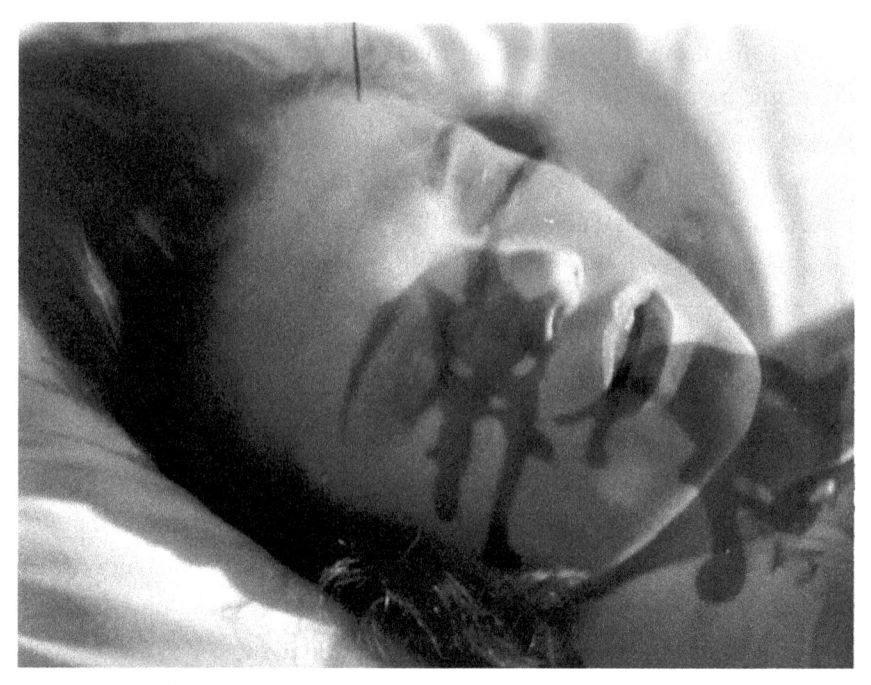

Irena's dream (*Cat People*, 1942).

Judd is ostensibly the doctor whose job it is to banish Irena's irrational fears, but he is also another potential mate. Therefore, in the dream he is both panther and avenging knight; he carries the sword that should destroy the panther, but it becomes the key that will release it. The sword is also of course associated with the blade inside his cane, which later transfixes Irena. Yet his identification with King John is always at least half-ironic: if he eventually kills the panther, he is also destroyed by it. The dream, in drawing together so many threads, concisely embodies the film's sense of life itself as a shadow world in which nothing is certain, no issue is clear-cut, nothing is what it seems. The film's attitude to psychology is also very interesting. Coming somewhat in the vanguard of Hollywood's belated discovery of Freud as a subject for more than party jokes in the '40s (it antedates Hitchcock's *Spellbound* [1945] and Lang's *Secret Beyond the Door* [1947] by several years), it suggests the possibility of psychological interpretation while regarding such interpretation with a healthy skepticism.

I AM GLAD TO find that Tourneur considers *I Walked with a Zombie* the finer film of the two and, with *Stars in My Crown* (1950) and *Out of the Past*, one of his three best movies.[4] He also claims it as (again with *Stars in My Crown*, which I have not been able to see) one of the only two of his films which he has been in on right from the original conception. Though Tourneur's claim that he had the idea of doing "Jane Eyre in the West Indies" is contradicted by DeWitt Bodeen, who says the idea was Lewton's,[5] it doesn't finally matter. It is clear from the way Tourneur talks about *Zombie* that he regards it as one of his most personal works, and this is certainly confirmed by the film itself.

Tourneur's style, and the natural way it associates with Lewton's taste and intelligence, can be fittingly illustrated by *Zombie*'s most celebrated atmospheric set piece: the scene in which Betsy, the Canadian nurse (Frances Dee), takes her patient to a nocturnal voodoo meeting in a desperate attempt to cure her. The sequence is introduced by a medium-long shot from a medium-low angle of an unnaturally tall, gaunt Negro standing in the shadowy moonlight at a crossroads in the middle of the cane fields. We don't know at this point who he is or what he is doing there; the image has a dreamlike quality—inexplicable, haunting, beautiful, and sinister. It creates unease without any suggestion of a shock effect. It also perhaps gives us a sense that the journey to the voodoo meeting is a journey into dream.

The women's departure is shown in a camera movement that spatially connects the central characters. We see the front of the house from a medium-shot position, the foreground of the screen in darkness, with the foliage of the garden suggesting the night world beyond the safety of the lighted house; the half brothers, Paul (Tom Conway) and Wesley (James Ellison), are disclosed in turn, the former working, the latter drinking, in separate parts of the building. As the camera turns, the two women, in distant long shot, emerge from the door leading to the tower where Paul's invalid wife is kept, and the camera follows them, still keeping its distance, as they move away from the possibility of male protection and toward the darkness and (we presume) that strange, enigmatic, dominating figure. The shot combines all the functions of long-shot / camera-movement style: it connects different lives being lived separately but simultaneously. By placing the characters in an environment (where a close-up

The nocturnal walk through the cane fields (*I Walked with a Zombie*, 1943).

would detach them from it), it enhances the atmospheric qualities of the scene. By keeping different characters in our minds simultaneously and by preserving physical distance, it also encourages a certain emotional distance. We never become identified with Betsy or her actions, hence we are free to consider their implications judicially.

The ensuing progress through the cane fields evokes memories of the sidewalk pursuit in *Cat People*; there is a similar delicacy and simplicity. The women's movement is filmed mostly in medium-long shot, often with foliage intervening between characters and camera; and the various sinister details en route, signposting the way, are introduced without overemphasis, the entire sequence being notable for a total absence of music (until the voodoo drums become audible through the night). Especially characteristic is the introduction of the giant Negro at the crossroads: the camera follows the light from Betsy's torch as it moves forward along the ground, until it suddenly encounters a dark foot. There is no shock cut, no crashing chord; the frisson arises from the simple process of discovery, without underlining. The sequence, recalling others like it in this and other Tourneur movies, is unlike the work of any other American director I can think of. The director it evokes, for me, irresistibly, is Mizoguchi—the Mizoguchi of *Ugetsu monogatari* (1953).

The theme of "clean, decent-thinking" North Americans impinged upon by disturbing outside forces—or of the relationship between the day world and the night world—is handled more subtly and complexly in *Zombie* than in *Cat People*. Leaving aside for a moment the film's supernatural elements, consider the use Tourneur makes of the calypso singer, Sir Lancelot. Though black/white oppositions play a characteristically ambiguous part in the poetic texture of the film, the racial issue never becomes a dominant theme. It is, however, touched upon and has its relevance in the pattern of associations the film sets up: voodoo–darkness–the subconscious; zombie-ism–emotional paralysis–spiritual death; psychological repression–slavery–the continuing resentment of the black people toward the whites.

Tourneur expresses satisfaction in the fact that he has always treated Negroes with respect in his films, taking a stand against the pervasive tendency to restrict them to undignified roles,[6] and his satisfaction is certainly justified. There can't be many Hollywood movies of the early '40s in which a colored character is permitted to make sly, malicious fun of whites who are neither comic nor villainous—with the film's at least partial endorsement—and get away with it. One could, I think, find Tourneur's use of Sir Lancelot more acceptable, in its unobtrusive way, than the pious (hence insidiously condescending) treatment of blacks in the later '40s movies that began to handle racial issues explicitly.

The end of the sequence in which Sir Lancelot appears draws together several threads of the film. As the singer approaches Betsy and the unconscious Wesley (he has drunk himself to sleep at the table) out of the darkness in a slow, threatening advance, singing his insultingly personal calypso, he becomes associated with the mysterious, disturbing forces by which Betsy feels herself menaced. Yet the fact that, previously, his dignity, intelligence, and irony have engaged our sympathy serves to detach us further from Betsy; we cannot simply share her awareness of him as a threat. Although, obviously, she is the heroine of the film, our consciousness of the overall action is never limited to her point of view.

The superiority of *I Walked with a Zombie* over *Cat People* is primarily one of structure: of—in so far as the distinction is possible—poetic structure rather than narrative structure. The linear progression of the earlier film, the development of its story, leaves nothing to be desired; but in *Zombie* the poetic resonances, the suggestive ambiguities and uncertainties, are more meaningfully organized. It is by no means a matter of explaining, resolving, or simplifying them—if anything, the contrary. In *Cat People* the opposition between the day characters and the night world remains clear-cut. Only Oliver's attraction to Irena implicates him in the mysterious urges she embodies; he never reveals anything corresponding to them within himself. But in *Zombie* such barriers are dissolved. The night world pervades everything and implicates everyone, even Betsy. To analyze the film is but to define its ambiguities.

At its center are two related figures: T-Misery and Carrefour. T-Misery is the name the blacks give to the figurehead (now a statue in the garden, streaming with water like tears) from the boat that brought the first slaves. He is himself an ambiguous figure, fusing the film's oppositions. All stuck with arrows, he is St. Sebastian, the Christian martyr; yet he is also unmistakably negroid and to the blacks the embodiment of slavery. Carrefour, the guardian of the crossroads, bears a striking facial resemblance to him. He is a zombie, and, as his name suggests, the intermediary between the two worlds, the messenger the night world sends to claim its dues.

The clue to reading the film is given us in Paul's speech on the boat that brings Betsy to the island (itself called St. Sebastian). He tells her that the beauty she is admiring is illusory, the phosphorescence that makes the ocean seem alive is produced by a myriad of dead and decomposing creatures; she is coming to a world where nothing is what it seems. By the end of the film everything has proved to be other than what it seemed—even the motives of clean, decent-thinking Betsy herself.

The quiet, intense poetry of the film is evident in the scene of Betsy's first encounter with her patient, Jessica. It opens with a shot of T-Misery and with the sound of weeping (seeming at first, disturbingly, to emanate from the statue), which awakens Betsy. She crosses the courtyard to the tower door, from which the crying is issuing. When she has climbed the stairs, she is pursued by Jessica, unnaturally tall and gaunt, moving like a sleepwalker. The heroine threatened by a sinister figure—yet Betsy is in black, Jessica in white.

This poetic ambiguity is developed in the cane fields sequence, where each woman is given a lace badge that will allow her to be "passed" by Carrefour and will gain her admittance to the voodoo meeting; Betsy, in black, has a white badge (which catches, unnoticed, on the foliage as they push their way through), Jessica, a black, in white. The weeping is subsequently explained. It was the maid mourning the birth of her sister's child; for the tradition has been handed down through generations of slaves that one mourns birth, rejoices at death.

Uncertainty, ambiguity, the reversal of expectations pervade every aspect of the film. Who is responsible for Jessica's state? Betsy's lover, Wesley, with whom she was about to run away? Her husband, Paul, who (according to Wesley—and Paul's treatment of Betsy offers some confirmation) destroys all sense of beauty, all feeling for life? Their mother, Mrs. Rand, who believes herself responsible for Jessica's being a zombie, deadening spontaneous instinct to preserve family unity? What is Betsy's real motive for persuading Paul to give permission for Jessica to have insulin shock treatment (which the doctor warns may kill her) or, later, for taking her to the voodoo meeting? Does she (already in love with Paul) want to cure Jessica (as she clearly believes she does) or to kill her? She is, in Paul's words, the "nurse who's afraid of the dark," which means, in the terms suggested by the film, afraid of her own subconscious.

I remember, during my first viewing of the film, at the end of the "insulin" sequence, thinking, "But don't Tourneur and Lewton realize that Betsy probably wanted Jessica to die?" as she and Paul are expressing their disappointment that the treatment has had no effect. At which precise moment Wesley stepped out of the shadows and accused them of just that. Which shows how one can still underestimate the possible subtleties of an unassuming little Hollywood thriller. The ambiguities come nearest to explicitness in the revelation of Mrs. Rand's involvement with voodoo. Is she Christianizing voodoo or voodooizing Christianity ("I should have known there's no easy way to do good, Betsy")?

The shadows and half lights of the film's haunting atmospheric quality are in fact but the expression of its moral and spiritual world, in which nothing is fixed or certain, nothing is as it seems: a world subtly dominated by the subconscious, a world of shadows in which we can do no more than cautiously and hesitantly grope. The last, magical, sequence of the film beautifully and movingly unifies many of its poetic motifs. The emotional paralysis that deadens the lives of the characters is dissipated not by the exercise of conscious reason but by a cathartic gesture activated by the subconscious: Wesley at last kills Jessica, and then himself. He kills her by driving through her heart an arrow plucked from T-Misery; his actions are subconsciously induced by voodoo. He carries her body out into the sea, which in Paul's speech on the boat became an embodiment of simultaneous beauty and horror, and drowns himself. As he carries her down the shore, he is followed by Carrefour, arms outstretched; and it is Carrefour who bears Jessica's body back to the house when it is retrieved by fishermen, at night, their spears and torches adding a visual poetry to the poetry inherent in the ideas. The film ends with a track-in on T-Misery. *I Walked with a Zombie* is a small masterpiece—perhaps the most delicate poetic fantasy in the American cinema.

(1972)

Disreputable Genre

The horror film is the most disreputable of the genres, the disrepute partly deserved, partly not. No genre is richer in potential, its thematic material rooted in archetypal myth and the darker labyrinths of human psychology and having analogies with dream and nightmare. Yet no genre lends itself more readily to debasement, whether through commercial opportunism or rhetorical pretentiousness. The proliferation in England at present, however, may well be building the kind of tradition out of which work of real distinction can develop. Already Peter Sasdy's *Hands of the Ripper* (1971) has revealed a sensibility of some subtlety, and Piers Haggard's curiously constructed *The Blood on Satan's Claw* (1971), a genuine original talent striving for expression. Now, even more convincingly, there is the remarkable *Raw Meat* (*Death Line*, 1972), directed by Gary Sherman and based on his own idea.

Predictably, the critical reaction (Nigel Andrews honorably excepted)[7] has been quite uncomprehending, "absurd" and "disgusting" being the favored epithets. The latter is understandable: *Raw Meat* is the most horrible horror film I have ever seen, and the only surprise here is that the outcry against it has not been more heated. Mr. Sherman clearly anticipated difficulties: a billboard figuring prominently in one scene announces, "Censor in Trouble" (one critic, incredibly, regarded this touch as "accidental"!). But the features of the film that arouse disgust are not gratuitous. It is central to Mr. Sherman's purpose to create an underworld (located in disused tunnels of the London Underground) that represents the most horrible conditions in which human life, and human feeling, can survive—one of the traditional functions of the horror story (Hitchcock's *Psycho* [1960] is the supreme example) being to force us to confront the worst of which humanity is capable.

The charge of absurdity is curious: do critics really expect neorealist verisimilitude in a horror fantasy? It is not the artist's function to reproduce reality but to comment on it by constructing a coherent world that relates to it. It is the inner coherence of *Raw Meat* that is so impressive. Sherman sets in relation to each other three sets of characters: the LSE (London School of Economics) students, male and female, likeable but variously complacent people of the contemporary surface world; Donald Pleasence's police inspector (a splendid comic creation), sturdily independent and resilient, his strength depending on and necessitating a complete lack of human involvement; the underground "family," man and dying pregnant woman, living in unthinkable degradation amid rotting half-eaten corpses, yet still recognizably human, still capable of tenderness and deep attachment.

The film, which is characterized by the kind of creative intensity that manifests itself in a startlingly expressive sureness of technique (the extraordinary claustrophobic circular camera movement that introduces the cannibals and creates their world; the sustained static long shot wherein the man, after the woman's death, expresses his misery and frustration in useless violence on an abandoned platform), moves toward the moment where Pleasence is at last confronted with the buried underworld.

If the film, for all its horror, strikes one finally as affirmative, it is partly through the Pleasence character, but more through the irrepressible urge for life of the plague-ridden, unimaginably deprived, brutalized but human creature he comes up against, one of the cinema's most pitiable and terrible monsters since Karloff's Frankenstein creation. It is he, fittingly, who is allowed the film's last words.

(1972)

The Creeping Flesh

London, the late Victorian era. In an attempt to convince a new assistant of his discovery of the principle of evil and its imminent victory, Professor Emmanuel Hildern (Peter Cushing) relates the following incident from his past. Returning from New Guinea with a giant skeleton (the remains of a prehistoric man, earlier than Neanderthal but more advanced), he reads a legend that suggests that ancient evil will be resurrected by rain, and he accidentally discovers that the application of water to one of the skeleton's finger bones recomposes the flesh tissues. Emmanuel has kept from his daughter Penelope the fact that her mother was at the time of her death an inmate in the asylum run by his brother James (Christopher Lee); and fearing, when Penelope learns the truth, that the shock has induced the beginnings of insanity, Emmanuel tries to inoculate her against evil by injecting her with a serum taken from the recomposed and amputated finger. Under the serum's influence, Penelope becomes sensual and violent, killing Lenny, a patient escaped from James' asylum, before being herself imprisoned by her uncle. From a sample of Penelope's blood, James—who has also been conducting experiments on his patients to discover the source of evil—guesses something of Emmanuel's discovery. He steals the skeleton with the help of one of his inmates, but the carriage in which they are transporting it is overturned during a storm, and the skeleton, exposed to rain, is resurrected. It returns to Emmanuel and removes one of his fingers before disappearing into the night. Emmanuel, it transpires, is imprisoned with Penelope in James's asylum; no one will believe his story.

After the crudities of *Tales from the Crypt* (1972), *The Creeping Flesh* (1973) comes as a welcome surprise. The film is hampered by an obtrusively contrived narrative and by the fact that the parallels between the brothers and their experiments are somewhat schematic; but the theme of the different attempts to locate and hence control evil (with the ultimate irony of evil being released as a result of their convergence) is interestingly and sensitively worked out. The preponderance of long shots ensures that, despite the presence of Britain's two most prominent horror stars, *The Creeping Flesh* is above all an ensemble film, concerned with the interconnection of actions and drives. It also distances the spectator, encouraging him to see each action in the context of the total pattern rather than isolating effects for the sake of impact. This comparative restraint accords well with the film's overall melancholy and pessimism. The effect on Penelope of discovering the truth about her mother is quietly expressed in the toppling over of the paper marionette in the miniature theater with which she has been playing; and the climactic sequences, right up to the final attack on Emmanuel, gain particularly from the reticent treatment of the resurrected embodiment of evil—a black-hooded, monk-like figure moving in long shot slowly, silently, and relentlessly through the darkness. Paul Ferris's score, less striking than his *Witchfinder General* (1968) music, is also used with restraint to establish the pervasive tone of melancholy and desolation rather than of simple horror.

The film suffers from the somewhat squalid bourgeois morality which afflicts so much British popular art (the equation with evil of all displays of energy or overt sexuality, the consequent implication that all expressions of spontaneous vitality must be ruthlessly punished); but in this case, the intelligence and vivacity of Lorne Heilbron's performance arouse so much sympathy for Penelope's release from Victorian repression that the total effect is more ambiguous.

(1973)

Blood Brides

Fashion designer John Harrington (Stephen Forsythe) is aware that he is a psychopath and multimurderer, unable to control his compulsion to kill brides, since each murder brings to consciousness a further detail in a traumatic childhood experience involving his mother's death. Although embittered by his failure to consummate their marriage, his rich Catholic wife Mildred (Laura Betti) refuses to divorce him; while John, genuinely attracted to Helen (Dagmar Lassander), a new model in his bridal salon, resists her advances for fear of harming her. John murders Mildred but realizes that people still see her beside him and that she is haunting him; he has also aroused the suspicions of Inspector Russell, who questions him repeatedly. John knows that if he kills one more woman, the last details of his childhood experience will be revealed to him; and having failed to murder another model on her wedding night, he dresses Helen in a bridal gown and is about to strike her when he remembers: it was he who murdered his mother and her second husband on their wedding night. Helen escapes, and as John is taken away in the police van, he finds Mildred beside him: they will be together for all eternity.

Mario Bava's claim to attention arises principally from the fact that, since he usually photographs as well as directs his films, they are very consciously conceived in terms of the potentialities of the camera and as a result are, in a somewhat crude sense, "cinematic." *Blood Brides* (*Un Hacha para la Luna de Miel* / Hatchet for the Honeymoon) offers several examples: the water running from a tap turning a subjective red at the onset of one of John's attacks; Mildred's face reflected in the gleaming hatchet that is about to kill her; her hand, dripping blood, reflected in the glass-topped table as John is questioned by the police. The creation of elaborate effects through camera movement, stylized color, focus distortion, and the use of varied lenses is, however, no guarantee of quality; and the effects in *Blood Brides* appear merely self-conscious and self-indulgent. There is no sense of exploration or dynamic progress, only a complacent acceptance of decadence, heightened by the protagonist's voice-over commentary, placing him in a confiding relationship with the audience and drawing us into his sickness, from which nothing else in the film attempts to detach us.

(1973)

You'll Like My Mother

Pregnant young widow Francesca Kinsolving (Patty Duke) visits her dead husband Matthew's mother, whom she has never met. In the lonely house, now cut off by a snowstorm, also lives Kathleen (Sian Barbara Allen), a retarded teenager introduced as Matthew's sister. Francesca sees a portrait of Matthew's sadistic young cousin Kenny (Richard Thomas), and Kathleen later shows her a newspaper clipping which reveals that Kenny is wanted for rape and murder. Francesca also learns that Matthew's mother is in fact dead, and that his aunt (Rosemary Murphy) has secretly usurped her place. When Francesca, cut off from all outside help, gives birth to a baby girl, the aunt tells her that the child is dead and orders Kathleen to bury it; but when Francesca is able to get up, Kathleen takes her to the attic, where she has hidden the baby, alive and healthy. Francesca discovers that Kenny is in the house, hidden from the police by his mother. The snow is now sufficiently clear for Francesca to attempt to escape from the house with her baby. Kenny traps her in the garage and is about to murder the child, when Kathleen stabs him.

    Films about helpless, persecuted heroines often fall into the trap of harrowing the spectator quite unprofitably, there being no easier way of manipulating the audience through a painful emotional experience that proves neither cathartic nor particularly meaningful (*Fright* [*Night Legs*, 1971] and *Blind Terror* [*See No Evil*, 1971] are two recent instances). Lamont Johnson's film is better than either, largely free of the blatant sadism of the former and the pointlessness of the latter, with the presence of the baby and the release of generous human impulse in Kathleen providing the struggle between healthy and perverted forces with a strong positive center. Nevertheless, the narrative's many implausibilities make it impossible not to feel that one is being manipulated at many points for the sake of nothing beyond an empty suspense. The casting is of great interest: Sian Barbara Allen is made to look remarkably like

Patty Duke in *The Miracle Worker* (1962), and Patty Duke—inadvertently, at least, her savior—has come slightly to resemble Anne Bancroft. The scene where Kathleen reveals the baby's presence to Francesca—one of the film's most affecting moments—clearly evokes the scene with the chick hatching from the egg in Penn's film, with something of the same overtones of the birth of new consciousness and hope in the girl.

(1973)

Death Line (Raw Meat)

After the last train has gone, two students, Alex (David Ladd) and Patricia (Sharon Gurney), find a well-dressed man unconscious in a tube station and learn his name, Manfred (James Cossins), from a card in his wallet. When they return with a policeman, the man has disappeared. Next day, Inspector Calhoun (Donald Pleasence) interrogates the students. The vanished man is a high-ranking Ministry of Defence employee, and he has not turned up for work. Calhoun remembers that a series of people have disappeared from the tube stations at night, and learns of a cave-in during the construction of a proposed tube station under the British museum in 1892, when men and women were buried alive. Meanwhile, in the disused tunnels, a man (the Man), last of the descendants of those who were buried, tries but fails to save the life of the last woman by feeding her Manfred's blood. Despite an attempt by Stratton-Villiers of MI5 to prevent further inquiries, Calhoun pursues his investigations when three night workers are murdered on the underground. Patricia, accidentally stranded on the station platform, is carried off by the Man as a replacement for his mate. Alex explores the tunnels, saves her from rape, and mortally injures the Man. Calhoun arrives to confront the horrors of the underground world.

A rat is nibbling at a bloody arm, along which the camera slowly pans left, revealing it as severed and half-eaten; the camera continues, passing over decomposing bodies with flesh torn from them, then pausing on a living man—unkempt, filthy, and covered with running sores—bending in tender concern over a dying, pregnant woman. The movement resumes, revealing a tunnel-like opening, more bodies, eventually completing the full 360 degrees and coming to rest on the original arm; whereupon the camera begins to track slowly into the tunnel, leading us backward through darkness, then along dimly lit vaulted tunnels, part of the abandoned underground structure, to the point of access to the world above—the world of tube trains and modern civilization.

The core of the film is contained in that shot; the meaning is essentially created by the technique. The circular movement of the camera in a constricted space—our sense that everything revealed in the 360-degree pan is in virtual close-up—creates the claustrophobia of this appalling world, both prison cell and womb. The scene communicates—from the hideous conditions, the permanent entrapment, the subterranean location—the idea of hell; but it is a hell in which humanity still survives, not merely with life but human feeling. The backward track out (despite a concealed cut, the *effect* is of continuity) suggests an umbilical cord connecting this terrible underworld with the world above. Perhaps the title not only refers to railways but is an ironic play on "lifeline." Certainly the film is a powerful and terribly distressing embodiment of the descent myth, built on the relationship between our complacent surface world of technology, social progress, and moral emancipation and an underworld that represents the very worst conditions in which life and "humanity," however degraded, can survive.

Against this underworld are set the LSE (London School of Economics) students, Alex and Pat, he armed with his insulated New York callousness, she with her limited compassion: sufficiently sympathetic and close to us for the moment when Alex kicks in the Man's head to save Pat from rape (and plague) to be intensely disturbing. More impressively, there is Donald Pleasence's inspector, set against both "couples," his absolute separateness (he has no close

The Man (Hugh Armstrong) is horrible and repellent yet irrefutably human (*Death Line* [*Raw Meat*], 1972).

human ties, no deep attachments) the condition for his independence and splendid resilience. But the Man is the film's real hero, unutterably horrible and repellent yet irrefutably human; ourselves, as we might survive in the most terrible conditions imaginable.

Sadly, critical reaction to the film has been insensitive in the extreme. But its director, Gary Sherman (besides imagination and the audacity to push ideas to their logical conclusion, however appalling), clearly has a sense of humor, so perhaps he is still laughing at the critic who complained that the Man's reiterated, half-articulate cry of "Mind the doors!" became unintentionally funny. In fact, the macabre humor is the indispensable and perfectly judged release that prevents the horror from becoming unendurable. The film, a coherent whole in which the parts interrelate suggestively rather than schematically, and rich in mythological overtones, represents one of the most remarkable debuts of recent years.

(1973)

The Most Horrible Horror Film Ever?

It has been argued by English critic David Pirie (who develops the thesis in a forthcoming book) that the horror movie is the essential British genre—as mythically central to Britain as the Western to America. I find it easy to accept the notion theoretically without accepting what is for Pirie its corollary—that a great many British horror movies are of high quality; in particular, his estimate of the stolidly unimaginative Terence Fisher is quite incomprehensible to me.

However, it remains true that much of the most interesting work in the British cinema during the past decade has been in the horror field (hence seldom noticed, except with repugnance, by the British critical establishment), though it has been achieved either outside, or against the general trend of, Hammer Films, who still dominate the scene. There were the films—variously flawed, but variously promising—of the late, young Michael Reeves (*The Sorcerers* [1967], *Witchfinder General* [1968]) and, since Reeves's death, several films of character and distinction by different directors: Piers Haggard's *The Blood on Satan's Claw* (1971), which, with *Witchfinder General*, is one of the few films to make really expressive use of the English countryside; Peter Sasdy's subtle and delicate *Hands of the Ripper* (1971), a variant on the *Marnie* (1964) theme with murders instead of thefts and the "flashback" shifted to the precredits; and Gary Sherman's *Death Line* (1972). I would sit through any of these again in preference to the painstaking, and fundamentally uncreative, literary fidelity of *The Go-Between* (1971) or the pretentious and derivative obsoleteness of *O Lucky Man!* (1973).

Death Line, perhaps the most remarkable of these films, has, for the benefit of American audiences, been equipped by American International with a new and greatly inferior title (*Raw Meat*) and a publicity campaign of the kind of unimaginative ugliness and irrelevance (voluptuous female ghouls in off-the-shoulder shrouds) specially reserved for horror movies. It is also rumored to have been cut and substantially re-edited. I must ask the reader to attribute any discrepancies between my account and the film actually on view to the fact that I am familiar only with the British prints (which almost, though not quite, correspond to the director's wishes). The original idea for the film was Sherman's; he and Ceri Jones collaborated on the script from an early stage, and as Sherman, an American, has only recently settled in London, it seems reasonable to credit Jones with idiomatic dialogue ("The Queen, God bless her, flogging her pretty little guts out . . .").

The basic premise of *Death Line* is that, in the Victorian period, there was a cave-in during the construction of the London Underground beneath the British Museum which trapped a number of men, women, and children whom it was expedient to leave for dead; that they and their descendants survived, eventually resorting to cannibalism and the kidnapping of travelers at Russell Square station. British critics were quick to pounce on minor "naturalistic" implausibilities but largely ignored the premise's rich potentialities. All the best horror movies are rooted in universal psychology or universal myth; at the basis of *Death Line* is one of the most potent myths of all, that of the underworld and the descent (one may think of Persephone and Orpheus, or of *Nosferatu* [1922] and *Psycho* [1960]). The film's structure (in a sense in which "structure" is inseparable from, but not identical with, plot) is strong without being schematic; one can't talk of allegory in the strict sense, but the action consistently carries resonances beyond its literal meaning.

The relationship between underworld and overworld is strengthened by parallels between the different groups of characters the film sets in opposition. The desperate, totally committed need of the underground cannibal for his dying wife is set against the casualness of the young American student, who can manage little beyond a shrug when his girl, Pat, walks out on him. According to Gary Sherman, the American distributors were to remove this scene: it's not very interesting in itself, but it's essential to the pattern, its significance pointed to by the cut from Pat's return and the lovers' equally casual reconciliation to the underground woman dead, the man distraught with grief. No one would argue that David Ladd's ineffectual performance is an asset to the film, but it doesn't unduly damage it; as in *Nosferatu*, the point lies partly in the superficiality of the "surface" characters against the intense desires and needs of their underworld counterparts. The monstrous, pitiable cannibal (he is in the tradition of the screen's great sympathetic monsters) subsequently becomes an alternative "husband" for the girl; Sherman's crosscutting between the two men searching for her (one with a torch, one with a lantern) in the underground labyrinth evokes memories of the intercut journeys of *Nosferatu*.

The structure is given greater complexity by the introduction of a third term of comparison, Inspector Calhoun (one of Donald Pleasence's most brilliant creations). Against the coolness of the student and the desperation of the cannibal is set his tough resilience, the sarcasm, invective, and cynicism that are his protection against loss and aloneness (he is a widower—or so I deduce from his isolation and his reference to "the night poor Maggie died"). The theme of isolation is extended in the film's emphasis on time: the amplified heartbeat that accompanies the long take introducing the cannibals; the still-ticking watch of the victim that becomes (in the timeless world of the underground) a memorial ornament on the dead woman's breast, part of the tribal ritual of the underworld, taken up and parodied in the trivial clicking of the student's "perpetual motion" desk toy; Calhoun's incessant imbibing of tea and beer to fill the emptiness of his existence (the unemphasized detail of the teapot and cup beside his bed is eloquent about his loneliness).

Death Line vies with *Night of the Living Dead* (1968) for the most horrible horror film ever. It is, I think, decidedly the better film: more powerfully structured, more complex, and more humanly involved. Its horrors are not gratuitous: it is an essential part of its achievement to create, in the underground world, the most terrible conditions in which human life can continue to exist and remain recognizably human. Sherman's first feature, it also reveals a filmmaker groping toward a personal style, an artist who can think and feel—at least intermittently—in terms of his medium. One can instance the extraordinary shot that introduces the cannibals. The camera moves slowly right to left, along a severed arm gnawed by rats and maggots; over dead bodies hanging as in a butcher's shop; over the latest victim, still alive (the sound of dripping water giving place to the sound of slow heartbeats); past an aperture; hanging meat; offal. The circle completed, the camera tracks back, apparently through the aperture, into another room. We see stores of candles and lamps, and first hear, then see, the man, unkempt and hideously covered with running sores, bent over the dying woman. The camera tracks further backward through arches; we hear sounds of work and tunnel collapse, a ghostly echo from the past, before the camera comes to rest on the rubble beyond which we can hear the noise of trains, the world of modern technology. All this in one shot; then cut to Pat on Russell Square station platform. In that one shot the whole underground world is created for us—its decay, its claustrophobic constriction, its life surviving amid, and on, the most obscene horrors. The continuous camera movement (worked out, Gary Sherman told me, after he'd discovered the location, an abandoned tunnel near Shoreditch) connects that world to our own (the title of the film is perhaps an ironic play on "lifeline") as with an umbilical cord: the essential meaning of the film is there.

(1973)

Return of the Repressed

Two elementary Freudian theses: in a civilization founded on monogamy and the family, there will be an immense, hence very dangerous, surplus of sexual energy that will have to be repressed; what is repressed must always struggle to return, in however disguised and distorted a form.

Where should one look, in our culture, for this inevitable return to manifest itself? Certain conditions must be met. The repressed must not be immediately recognizable as such (though, in Juliet Mitchell's phrase, the unconscious is "knowable"[8]); hence the need for disguise; hence also its tendency to erupt within contexts we don't take seriously, despise, laugh at, where it can evade our scrutiny. Dreams, nightmares, and the "Freudian slip" are the areas that psychoanalysis has found most deserving of exploration. It is also rewarding to look at popular culture, especially those areas of it we feign most to despise ("It's just entertainment"): above all, the horror film. Commercial cinema has analogies with mass dreaming; in examining the evolution of a genre one finds oneself studying the evolution of civilization's unconscious; horror films are our collective nightmares.

Five recurrent motifs (frequently interlinked) dominate the American (or American-influenced) horror film from the early '60s to the present: the schizophrenic personality (initiated by *Psycho* [1960], subsequent examples include *Homicidal* [1961], *Sisters* [1972], *Schizo* [1976]); cannibalism (*Night of the Living Dead* [1968], *Raw Meat* [*Death Line*, 1972], *Frightmare* [1974], *The Texas Chainsaw Massacre* [1974]); Satanism (initiated by *Rosemary's Baby* [1968], also *The Exorcist* [1973], *The Antichrist* [1974], *The Omen* [1976]); the monstrous child (*Rosemary's Baby*, *The Exorcist*, *Night of the Living Dead*, *It's Alive* [1974], *The Omen*, and, one should add, though it is not strictly a horror film, *The Sailor Who Fell from Grace with the Sea* [1976]); and the revenge of nature (initiated by *The Birds* [1963], also *Night of the Lepus* [1972], *Frogs* [1972]; *Squirm* [1976]).

All of these have antecedents, but only since the '60s has their confluence become clear and significant. One master motif—the "figure in the carpet" that makes sense of its intricate patternings—unites them all: the family. Its centrality is immediately obvious in the overlapping Satanist and monstrous-child cycles. The cannibalism is generally shown as the family's means of sustaining itself; more rarely, it takes the form of its members devouring each other. The various psychopaths of the schizophrenia cycle disown their violence by projecting it onto mother (*Psycho*) or sister (*Homicidal, Sisters*). In the nature films the eruption of "natural" forces is linked to sexual and familial tensions, most expressively in *The Birds* and *Squirm*.

A complete account of how this "return of the repressed" has come about would involve a lengthy and systematic analysis of both the horror tradition and the treatment of the family in the American cinema generally. Before the '60s, the association of the two is sporadic or peripheral. Many horror films play on the plot device of the monogamous couple threatened by the monster; the notion seems fundamental to vampire mythology, though perhaps only Murnau in *Nosferatu* (1922) really explored its implications. On the other hand, those much-loved comedies of the 1930s, '40s, and early '50s whose passing is so often lamented, which apparently celebrated American family life, now tend to look somewhat different. Space necessitates the strictest economy, so I limit myself to two '40s films.

I Walked with a Zombie (1943), directed by Jacques Tourneur and produced by Val Lewton, stands out by virtue of its explicit identification of horror with sexual repression and its location at the heart of the family (the mother being the repressive force); in its gentle and reticent way, this most poetic of all American fantasy films now seems a remarkable anticipation of developments to come. Almost contemporary with it is Minnelli's musical *Meet Me in St. Louis* (1944), received in its day as a touching celebration of family solidarity, now revealed as a film built almost single-mindedly on family strains and tensions. Two scenes stand out, in both of which the younger daughter Tootie (Margaret O'Brien) symbolically "kills" parent figures: the famous Halloween sequence, which draws elaborately on the iconography of the horror movie (creepy music; isolated, vulnerable figures; darkness; wind; rustling leaves) and a later scene in which she hysterically hacks her "snow people" (who are dressed in adult clothes) to bits with a spade in the night as her father looks on from a window.

It is a commonplace that the (ostensibly) celebratory family film disappeared from the American cinema in the '50s. What happened was that its implicit content became displaced into the horror film. What is enacted symbolically in *Meet Me in St. Louis* is realized in George Romero's *Night of the Living Dead*. The premise here is that unburied dead come back to life as ghouls to kill and devour the living. The film opens with a quarrel between brother and sister in a graveyard, where they have come, resentfully, to tend the father's grave; the brother teases, frightens ("They're coming to get you . . .") and angers the sister; the first ghoul lurches forward, as if the direct product of their tensions, and strangles him. Later, a group of people, including a couple with a young daughter, are besieged by the ghouls in an isolated house. The little girl, sick, is kept in the cellar; her father goes down and doesn't return. When the mother follows, she finds her daughter (who has meanwhile "died") eating the father's hand; whereupon the little girl hacks her mother to death with a builder's trowel. Tootie is no longer satisfied with symbolism.

The devil has traditionally been civilization's image for repressed (but ultimately irrepressible—like Dracula he is never really destroyed) energies, regarded as "evil" so that they can be disowned; of all Freud's theories, that of infantile sexuality has always been the one society has been most reluctant to accept (or even grasp). The recent fusion of the image of the devil with that of the child—the devil revealed as the product of the family—becomes enormously suggestive in the light of such ideas. The films characteristically emphasize the sweetness and light of the home: the happy couple of *Rosemary's Baby*, the ideal family of *It's Alive*, the apparent intimacy and affection of the mother/daughter relationship of *The Exorcist*. Beneath this ostensibly happy, somewhat complacent surface, the terrible forces prepare themselves. Rosemary gives birth to the Antichrist, the mother of *It's Alive* produces a devouring monster that slaughters all the nurses and doctors in the delivery room on its release from the womb, Regan in *The Exorcist* actually becomes the devil—a devil characterized very explicitly by violently assertive sexuality.

Another striking general development: the pretense that the released forces can be effectively overpowered or destroyed, and the traditional order restored, has been largely dropped. One registers this with one's disappointment at the end of *Squirm*, where the survival of the young couple and the heroine's sister is felt to run counter to the film's logic: the world totally overwhelmed by eruptions of devouring worms that develop, initially, out of familial constraints and sexual possessiveness. *Rosemary's Baby* ends with the acceptance of the Antichrist by its mother. *It's Alive* ends with the destruction of the child-monster—followed immediately by the announcement over the car radio that another has been born.

Two recent horror films—interestingly, from opposite ends of the production spectrum—appear to carry this movement to its logical culmination; the question of where the horror film goes next is of far more than academic interest or curiosity value. *The Texas Chainsaw Massacre* is crude, brutish, cheaply and roughly made with an unknown and largely untalented cast; its aesthetic deprivation and ugliness become positively expressive, as the eruption of a spirit of total negation and destructiveness. *The Omen*, if it wasn't particularly expensive, certainly wants to appear so: glossy, superprofessional, with respectable stars and plenty of what are called "production values," it seems the bourgeois entertainment par excellence. The former has become a disreputable cult movie in America (deservedly, I think) and looks like it is achieving the same status in London (greatly aided by the censor's ban); the latter has been breaking box-office records at respectable big-chain cinemas. Between them, they represent our collective nightmare made manifest on screens for the entire range of audiences.

The Texas Chainsaw Massacre opens with a hideous parody of domesticity: two decomposed corpses, dug up from a graveyard, one male, one female, the woman perched on the man's lap. An ensuing sequence tells us that the age of Aquarius (as celebrated in *Hair*) has given place to the age of Saturn, that everything is beyond control and ultimate disaster imminent. The film is about the slaughter and dismemberment of a group of "healthy," quasi-liberated young Americans by a family of variously degenerate psychotics. The young people are largely uncharacterized and unmemorable with the significant exception of the crippled brother, who represents an extension of the psychotic world into the apparently healthy world, underlining the sense that we are seeing two sides of the same coin. All the film's considerable energy is channeled into the terrible family, which has three significant aspects: its older generation were slaughterhouse workers (the family represents an exploited and debased proletariat revenging itself on capitalist society—they run a café on the highway where they sell hamburgers and hot dogs as to whose meat content we are left in no doubt); it also represents an obscene parody of traditional family unity and devotion (the apparently dead grandfather lovingly revived with drinks of human blood); its most striking member (whose pig mask, it is hinted, conceals something much worse underneath) is an embodiment of repressed sexuality returned and uncontrollable—his appalling vitality and the phallic nature of the constantly whirring chainsaw he brandishes makes such a reading irresistible. The ending of the film recuperates little or nothing. One girl is rescued, but she is by now reduced to gibbering idiocy; the chainsaw maniac remains free, his tool still active, raging in psychotic frustration.

I find *The Omen* astonishing, while not valuing it highly as a work of art. *The Exorcist* is by far the more "serious" film, with a disturbing intensity that bears witness to personal engagement; the cost of this is its final, somewhat unconvincing, restoration of order and its influx of compensatory religious uplift. *The Omen* is an extremely skillful and shrewd fabrication, a cunning entertainment that audiences can enjoy with relative equanimity; for this reason, paradoxically, it is able to follow through its implications with uncompromising ruthlessness, becoming the joint culmination of the twin, simultaneously developing cycles of Satanist and disaster movies.

The Omen is explicitly about the end of the world (conceived, like the "age of Saturn," as inevitable, guaranteed by prophecy). Yet the film defines "the world" very precisely: the bourgeois-capitalist couple, who inadvertently adopt and raise the devil; the state establishment they eminently represent (the father—Gregory Peck, perfectly cast—is the American ambassador to England, his best friend is president of the United States); the church, as servant of the state (though its services are unappreciated and its warnings ignored until too late); the rational consciousness, represented by the photographer (David Warner) who, with splendid appropriateness, gets his head cut off. The powers of "evil" also get quite precise definition: the devil-child (ironically named Damien, after the priest in *The Exorcist*), protected and guided by the independent woman (Billie Whitelaw). (It is not, I think, irrelevant to point out that in the United States there is an active and developing children's-liberation movement, closely linked to women's liberation.) The two are supported by untamed and unfettered animal life in the form of demonic dogs that generally erupt out of darkness (one is finally suppressed by Peck under a trapdoor in the cellar), contrasted with animals offered as safe bourgeois spectacle in the sunlit Windsor Safari Park. Inevitably, a reading of the film tends to become a reading *against* it: one longs to reverse all its terms. Yet the rigor with which the implications are seen through to their logical conclusion is exemplary: the systematic annihilation of *all* the "establishment" characters as the devil prepares to take over the world; a last ten seconds that it would be cruel to give away to those who have not seen the film, but which most satisfyingly clinches its inexorable progress and, one might argue, the progress of the whole Hollywood cinema.

The implication of these films—of the whole movement of popular cinema—is that the norms by which we have lived must be destroyed and a radically new form of organization (political, social, ideological, sexual) be constructed; the alternative is "the end of the world." It is an implication the films are unable consciously to confront; the conscious discourse does not even serve the unconscious discourse even as the unconscious discourse asserts itself. What our civilization needs is a cinematic William Blake, capable of daring to imagine the devil as hero.

(1976)

Yet Another Terrible Child

Carrie (1976) simultaneously confirms the significance of two fascinating cinematic phenomena: the recent development of the American horror film, and the career of Brian De Palma.

With *Sisters* (1972), *Obsession* (1976), and *Carrie*, a trilogy of variations on Hitchcock relating to *Psycho* (1960), *Vertigo* (1958), and *Marnie* (1964), respectively, De Palma has established himself as one of the most distinctive and remarkable artistic personalities in the contemporary American cinema. In that context, he is unique among his distinguished confreres: unlike Penn, Altman, Peckinpah, Schatzberg, Pakula, Ritchie, he has shown no overt interest (at least since his two experimental early movies *Greetings* [1968] and *Hi, Mom!* [1970]) with the state of America; instead, he has immersed himself in the conventions of a genre and the technique of a particular director. Many films have imitated Hitchcock and remained mere imitations, without creative force. The first thing that strikes one about De Palma's films is their intensity. Hitchcock's stylistic and structural devices are here not decorative flourishes applied from outside; they have been completely assimilated, becoming the medium for another man's personal vision, related yet distinct.

It is useless to look in De Palma's films for qualities traditionally valued by British critics such as reticence, understatement, "good taste": the intensity is partly a readiness to pull out all the stops, to carry actions through to the most excessive (though logical) conclusions. This effect is qualified everywhere by an equally extreme and insistent artifice—tracking shots so elaborate that they draw attention to themselves, "special effects," slow motion, and (in *Sisters* and *Carrie*) an inventive use of split screen. The peculiar tone of the films derives from the tension generated by the violent fusion of apparent opposites: irresistible élan and obtrusive artifice; unrestrained energy and sophistication; romanticism and a bitter, despairing skepticism.

One can illustrate this from two characteristically flamboyant, moving, and disturbing climactic sequences in *Obsession* and *Carrie*, both employing similar technical devices. (Both derive, in fact, from the celebrated 360-degree tracking shot around James Stewart and Kim Novak in *Vertigo* that is not a 360-degree tracking shot at all: it uses a revolving stage and back projection.) At the end of *Obsession* the man (Cliff Robertson) and the woman he loves but thinks has betrayed him (Geneviève Bujold) rush toward each other, their movements interminably suspended by slow motion, across the vast space of an airport corridor; he is going to shoot her, she is going to throw herself into his arms.

As they at last meet, the slow-motion spell is broken, and she cries out one word. Reunited in each other's arms, they turn and turn as the camera circles them in an excess of lyrical ecstasy. The most celebratory of all happy endings? But on the man's face is a look of increasing bewilderment and disturbance as he reviews the whole past and his total immersion in a suddenly shattered romantic illusion: the word she spoke was "Daddy."

At the climax of *Carrie* the ugly duckling grows into a swan and (to mix one's fairy tales) dances at the ball with Prince Charming. De Palma employs every means—notably, again, the ecstatically circling camera—to draw the audience into Carrie's surrender to a dream come true, the realization of a happiness that had seemed unthinkable. But we already know, and never forget, that the cruelest imaginable trick is being prepared for Carrie backstage, and we know enough about her to guess how appalling the consequences may be.

Carrie takes up certain central motifs of the '70s horror film and develops them with a rigor and intelligence that gives the film a force quite lacking in a formulaic construct like *The Omen* (1976)—the force of personal commitment. Again we have the terrible child (here a generally underdeveloped teenager), the repression of sexuality within the home, and the association of the child's powers with the devil.

The release (at the start of the film) of Carrie's long-denied sexuality coincides with the first expression of her powers of telekinesis. But, at last, the identification of repressed sexuality with diabolism is "placed." The association is insisted upon, not by the film, but by the heroine's fanatical and perverted mother; the film blames not the devil, but repression enforced in the name of religion—one aspect of a society whose general sickness encompasses Carrie's brutal pseudoliberated classmates and the well intentioned liberal PE teacher, all of whom contribute to and suffer in the culminating catastrophe. De Palma's idiosyncratic fusion of passionate romanticism with a savagely bitter irony gives *Carrie* a flavor achieved by no other recent horror film.

(1977)

Race with the Devil

In a much-quoted and justly influential article, the editors of *Cahiers du cinéma* attempted to categorize films according to their relationship to the dominant ideology; within the mainstream American cinema, the crucial distinction (descriptive and, by implication at least, evaluative) was between films that simply embody the ideology unquestioningly and films in which (generally, it transpires, through the intervention of an auteur, though this is not made explicit) the ideological project is undermined and subverted: the films of John Ford and, in a subsequent "exemplary" analysis, specifically *Young Mr. Lincoln* (1939), are offered as instances.[9] The weakness of the article (and it seems to me a fundamental one, producing an argument that, while valuably stimulating and provocative, is riddled with its own "gaps" and "dislocations") is that it treats "the dominant ideology" as if this were in itself monolithic and coherent, or at least as if the great majority of American films succeeded in making it appear so: no doubt they did, but then so did, for over thirty years, *Young Mr. Lincoln*. In fact, one can't get far in attempting to define the ideology expressed, overall, by the Hollywood cinema without becoming aware of the most violent contradictions and extreme incompatibilities inherent in its very basis. To take an obvious example, it is not just the films of Ford, but Westerns in general, not to mention innumerable comedies, thrillers, musicals, and domestic dramas, that are based on the tension between ideals of settling and wandering, home and freedom, the virile adventurer as ideal male and the wife and mother as ideal female.

One explanation of the development and coexistence of the genres is that they are produced out of such ideological splits: in their pure forms, they represent efforts to iron out the contradictions by removing one of the terms. I am troubled by some doubt as to whether these "pure forms" exist in practice. One would be forced, searching for them, to represent the Western by Roy Rogers and the family comedy by Andy Hardy, and even there it is uncertain whether the ideology is as clear-cut as one retrospectively assumes: are adventure and domesticity convincingly reconciled in that interesting family Roy Rogers / Dale Evans / Trigger? It is also doubtful whether the presence of ideological tensions and contradictions carries any evaluative weight whatever: they exist at all levels of achievement and are no guarantee of distinction or even more than cursory interest.

However, such an approach does, by implication, attribute particular interest (not necessarily distinction) to films that strikingly combine otherwise discrete, seemingly mutually exclusive genres. I am confident that the disturbing power of *Shadow of a Doubt* (1943) must be attributed primarily to the presence of Hitchcock; yet it also seems clear that it arises partly out of that film's fusion of small-town domestic comedy and film noir. *Race with the Devil* (1975) is scarcely a work of comparable distinction, precisely because it lacks the presence of any defined individual sensibility; nevertheless, its fusion of genres gives it a particular force and importance for anyone interested in the progress of the American cinema. (It is also, be it said, an efficient and exciting movie: I no more wish to "write off" Jack Starrett than to enroll him prematurely in the auteur register.)

The two subgenres here (neatly announced in the first two shots of the credits, road and dead tree) are what I have defined elsewhere as the "male-duo" road movie (here linked to its cousin, the bike movie: the lineage *Wild Angels* [1966]–*Easy Rider* [1969]–*Race with the Devil* is clear enough, Peter Fonda being common to all three), and the "Satanist" movie. One should have deduced that there must be a connection between them, because they both established themselves around the same time (*Rosemary's Baby* [1968] and *Easy Rider* were crucial in defining their respective natures and themes) and developed side by side (up to, and beyond, *The Exorcist* [1973] and *Thunderbolt and Lightfoot* [1974]). Neither should be seen in isolation from neighbor genres: the male-duo movie (and the bike movie) have their roots in, and continuing affinities with, the Western; the Satanist movie is only one aspect of the development of the horror movie. The link is the widespread disillusionment with, or questioning of the ideal of domesticity, the American home. The male-duo move represents an overt rejection of the home-and-family syndrome in favor of a "freedom" (often ultimately equated with emptiness, as in *California Split* [1974] or the excellent, still-unreleased *Loose Ends* [1975]) from which woman is largely barred, the dominant ideological image of woman still being the figure of wife and mother: the homosexual undercurrents critics have found in these films are, I think, there, but as a by-product, the absence of woman leaving a gap to be filled. The horror movie, I argued previously, has gravitated with startling insistence toward the family, horror now being located at the heart of domesticity: the mother gives birth to the Antichrist (*Rosemary's Baby*) or a powerful, destructive monster (*It's Alive* [1974]), or her child becomes the devil (*The Exorcist*). The potential implications of "crossing" these subgenres are convincingly realized in *Race with the Devil*.

The premise of the film: Roger (Peter Fonda) and Frank (Warren Oates) take off with their wives for a vacation in a glorified caravan that is high-class capitalist domesticity on wheels, their motorcycles strapped onto the back luggage rack. Much is made of the luxury: color TV, four-channel stereo, fully-stocked bar, microwave oven. The wives seem curiously superfluous: for all the intimacy we are shown, they might as well be casually encountered "chicks." Both men are swiftly characterized in terms of complementary contradictions relating to the central ideological opposition of domesticity/freedom. Roger has absented himself from the men's motorcycle business and made himself late for departure by practicing on the local track, yet he is by far the more acquiescent in domestic entrapment, expecting to sleep in a motel, ready to return home in answer to his wife's plea; the couple own the archetypally cute dog Ginger, ultimate emblem of the domestic. Frank is the one who is proud of (and dependent on) the luxuries as the fruit of their achievement ("We've put it all together," he remarks complacently, just before the apparition of the Satanists) yet also the one who continually resents domestic constraints (a motif introduced when he discovers Ginger's presence in the caravan).

One can distinguish (for the sake of clarity) three main levels of ideological tension in the film, though they are not really separable and continually interact. I have already indicated the most obvious and pervasive (and the most traditional, rooted as it is in the archetypal garden/wilderness, settling/wandering oppositions of the Western), beautifully epitomized in the contradictions of the camper itself, the vehicle in which the men can express their independence ("We don't need anything from anybody"), find their "private road to seclusion" (a road that leads directly, with a striking sense of narrative inevitability, to the Satanists' tree) and assert their freedom by escaping to the wilderness (the bikes strapped on behind) yet which is a precise embodiment of the material rewards of technological capitalism.

Linked to this is the level of suppressed sexual resentment. In ideological terms, woman is both the reason for and validation of domesticity; the men of *Race with the Devil* appear to need their wives solely as sexual objects, their chief desire being to break away on their bikes together. One might adduce here Stephen Heath's perception that *Jaws* (1975) is structured on the elimination of women.[10] Interestingly, the wives are the only ones who attempt (on the simple narrative level, that is) to find an explanation for what is happening to them (by stealing reference books on witchcraft from a public library); but rational/intellectual explanation proves to be as useless as appeals to the establishment authorities (who are either inaccessible or revealed as Satanists themselves). Otherwise, the wives do little in the film but have hysterics and get in the way; they are quite useless in every emergency.

Thirdly, there is the level of capitalistic envy. One must be wary in watching American films from the perspective of the much more stratified British class system, but it seems valid, for instance, to read the monstrous family of *The Texas Chainsaw Massacre* (1974) (ex-slaughterhouse workers) as representing an exploited and degraded proletariat. Similarly, contrast is made throughout *Race with the Devil* between the luxuriously appointed caravan and the nondescript or decrepit service trucks and gas stations that appear to be operated exclusively by Satanists. Envy and resentment of wealth are expressed most overtly through the Hendersons, the macabre couple who "befriend" the reluctant principals and bully them into going out for the evening.

Almost every detail in the film becomes interesting in relation to one or all of these levels. I shall restrict myself (in the interests of economy) to a brief examination of the key episodes: the introduction of the Satanists, the incident of the rattlesnakes, and the ending. The Satanists' appearance is prepared for in the scenes immediately preceding it. The "private road to seclusion" up which Frank turns to park for the first night leads to a location whose precise layout is established in the high angle shot showing the caravan pulling to a halt, and insisted upon by the zoom-out that follows two shots later: to the left, the parked caravan; to the right, the dead tree (anticipated in the credits) under which the Satanists will appear; separating the two, the shallow river, a boundary dividing the "normal" from the horrific rather as the cinema audience are divided from the screen—a screen, in this case, on which fantasies will be manifested as realized nightmares, and a boundary that proves all too easy to cross. The next scene intercuts the men's bike race with the wives out walking (one says to the other, "It seems to me you could get away from your bike for five minutes on a vacation"). Ginger is suddenly nervous; Kelly (Roger's wife, ambiguously sensitive/paranoid) looks across at the dead tree, feels cold, and wants to go back.

The scene introducing the Satanists is in two parts, one inside the caravan, one outside in the darkness. Inside, all is apparent domestic bliss, conviviality, and capitalistic self-satisfaction. Frank toasts "the wife I know I'll love forever" and the "friends I know I don't deserve." Outside, it is full moon, and just across the river (though we don't see it yet) is the land where suppressed desires are made manifest. The wives, inside, talk of the hangovers their men will have in the morning. Outside, Frank calls Roger, lovingly, "the straightest guy I've ever known in my life." No play on words is intended by the character or seems intended, at conscious level, by the script; but if one agrees that the male-duo movie carries implicit homosexual connotations (if only by default, as it were), the insistence on "straightness" at this crucial moment of the film may not appear merely accidental. On Roger's response ("I'm with you"), we cut to a view of the tree across the river. A bonfire flares up; the Satanists' orgy begins, watched by our heroes through binoculars. It is centered on a masked, demonic male figure and the murder by him of a naked girl (it is Frank, the one with the greater resentment of domesticity, who actually sees / conjures up the murder). The development of the action hinges on mutual recognition across the river, and from that moment the whole world changes: everyone is sinister, "normality" no longer exists. The attack on the caravan (stuck in the "boundary" river) that immediately ensues vividly recalls Indian attacks in the classical Western, with hordes of Satanists swarming out of woods and darkness: there is a direct line of ideological descent from, say, the burning of the home in *Drums along the Mohawk* (1939) to the repeated attacks on the "home" of *Race with the Devil*.

The rattlesnake scene is preceded by Kelly's paranoid terror in the campsite swimming pool (everyone is watching her, every smile is suddenly sinister) and the evening out with the Hendersons. They represent a grotesque parody of bourgeois domesticity and its repressions—the wife extolled for her cooking and her polishing, the couple hideously delighting in the violence of the brawl in the diner. When the principals return to the caravan, they find Ginger (dead) hanging from the door. Frank drives off wildly, Ginger's body is stowed in a low cupboard, Frank's wife (to quiet Kelly's hysterics) decides to make coffee and opens the door of a high food cupboard; two rattlesnakes (one for each man?) leap out, one actually springing on top of Kelly. The close juxtaposition of emblems of domesticity (Ginger) and the wilderness (the snakes) is underlined and its significance extended by the sexual symbolism and by the snakes' violent eruption from imprisonment.

The end of the film is somewhat perfunctory (the two audiences with whom I have watched it have been audibly disappointed), yet appropriately apocalyptic in conception. The quartet, adversaries apparently defeated, a town near, feeling themselves safe, but with their headlights smashed, draw off the road again as darkness descends. As they prepare to get drunk to celebrate ("It's all over"), Satanists appear all around them and the caravan is enclosed in a rectangle of flame. Freeze: the end. What is most interesting is that Kelly's vision, which earlier appeared paranoid, is vindicated as the true one: it seems that the entire population of America (outside the caravan, which is both fort and trap) really are devil worshippers. (One assumes, then, in retrospect, that the Hendersons deliberately led the couples away while Ginger was killed and the rattlesnakes installed.) Complaints about the film's implausibility are patently ridiculous: its whole force lies in its refusal to explain or limit its Satanists. They are the nightmare surrounding—and annihilating—the American dream.

(1976–1977)

Wilderness invades domesticity in *Race with the Devil* (1975).

An Introduction to the American Horror Film

I. Repression, The Other, The Monster

THE MOST SIGNIFICANT DEVELOPMENT—IN film criticism, and in progressive ideas generally—of the last few decades has clearly been the increasing confluence of Marx and Freud, or more precisely of the traditions of thought arising from them: the recognition that social revolution and sexual revolution are inseparably linked and necessary to each other. From Marx we derive our awareness of the dominant ideology—the ideology of bourgeois capitalism—as an insidious all-pervasive force capable of concealment behind the most protean disguises, and the necessity of exposing its operation whenever and wherever possible. It is psychoanalytic theory that has provided (without Freud's awareness of the full revolutionary potential of what he was unleashing) the most effective means of examining the ways in which that ideology is transmitted and perpetuated, centrally through the institutionalization of the patriarchal nuclear family. The battle for liberation, the battle against oppression (whether economic, legal, or ideological), gains enormous extra significance through the addition of that term "patriarchal," since patriarchy long precedes and far exceeds what we call capitalism. It is here, through the medium of psychoanalytic theory, that feminism and gay liberation join forces with Marxism in their progress toward a common aim, the overthrow of patriarchal-capitalist ideology and the structures and institutions that sustain it and are sustained by it.

Psychoanalytic theory, like Marxism, now provides various models, inflecting basic premises in significantly different ways. It is not certain that the Lacanian model prompted by (among others) *Screen* magazine is the most satisfactory.[11] On the evidence so far it seems certainly not the most potentially *effective*, leading either to paralysis or to a new academicism perhaps more sterile than the old, and driving its students into monastic cells rather than the streets. I want to indicate briefly a possible alternative model, developed out of Freud by Marcuse and given definitive formulation in a recent book by Gad Horowitz, *Repression*:[12] a model that enables us to connect theory closely with the ways we actually think and feel and conduct our lives—those daily practicalities from which the theorizing of *Screen* seems often so remote. The book's subtitle is *Basic and Surplus Repression in Psychoanalytic Theory: Freud, Reich, Marcuse*. It is the crucial distinction between basic and surplus repression that is so useful in relation to direct political militancy and so suggestive in relation to the reading of our cultural artifacts (among them our horror films) and, through them, our culture itself. Horowitz has developed a dense, often difficult, and closely argued book on the subject; in the space at my disposal I can offer only a bald and simplified account.

Basic repression is universal, necessary, and inescapable. It is what makes possible our development from an uncoordinated animal capable of little beyond screaming and convulsions into a human being; it is bound up with the ability to accept the postponement of gratification, with the development of our thought and memory processes, of our capacity for self-control, and of our recognition of and consideration for other people. Surplus repression, on the other hand, is specific to a particular culture and is the process whereby people are conditioned from earliest infancy to take on predetermined roles within that culture. In terms of our own culture, then, basic repression makes us distinctively human, capable of directing our own lives and coexisting with others; surplus repression makes us into monogamous heterosexual bourgeois patriarchal capitalists ("bourgeois" even if we are born into the proletariat, for we are talking here of ideological norms rather than material status). *If* it works; if it doesn't, the result is either a neurotic or a revolutionary (or both), and if revolutionaries account for a very small proportion of the population, neurotics account for a very large one. Hardly surprising. All known existing societies are to some degree surplus repressive, but the degree varies enormously, from the trivial to the overwhelming. Freud saw long ago that our own civilization had reached a point where the burden of repression was becoming all but insupportable, an insight Horowitz (following Marcuse) brilliantly relates to

Marx's theory of alienated labor. The most immediately obvious characteristics of life in our culture are frustration, dissatisfaction, anxiety, greed, possessiveness, jealousy, neuroticism: no more than what psychoanalytic theory shows to be the logical product of patriarchal capitalism. What needs to be stressed is that the challenges now being made to the system—and the perceptions and recognitions that structure those challenges and give them impetus—become possible (become, in the literal sense, thinkable) only in the circumstances of the system's imminent disintegration. While the system retained sufficient conviction, credibility, and show of coherence to suppress them, it did so. The struggle for liberation is not utopian, but a practical necessity.

Given that our culture offers an extreme example of surplus repressiveness, one can ask what, exactly, in the interests of alienated labor and the patriarchal family, is repressed. One needs here both to distinguish between the concepts of repression and oppression and to suggest the continuity between them. In psychoanalytic terms, what is repressed is not accessible to the conscious mind (except through analysis or, if one can penetrate their disguises, in dreams). We may also not be conscious of ways in which we are oppressed, but it is much easier to become so: we are oppressed by something "out there." One might perhaps define repression as fully internalized oppression (while reminding ourselves that all the groundwork of repression is laid in infancy), thereby suggesting both the difference and the connection. A specific example may make this clearer: our social structure demands the repression of the bisexuality that psychoanalysis shows to be the natural heritage of every human individual and the oppression of homosexuals; obviously the two phenomena are not identical, but equally obviously they are closely connected. What escapes repression has to be dealt with by oppression.

What, then, is repressed in our culture? First, sexual energy itself, together with its possible successful sublimation into nonsexual creativity—sexuality being the source of creative energy in general. The "ideal" inhabitant of our culture is the individual whose sexuality is sufficiently fulfilled by the monogamous heterosexual union necessary for the reproduction of future ideal inhabitants, and whose sublimated sexuality (creativity) is sufficiently fulfilled in the totally noncreative and nonfulfilling labor (whether in factory or office) to which our society dooms the overwhelming majority of its members. The ideal, in other words, is as close as possible to an automaton in whom both sexual and intellectual energy has been reduced to a minimum. Otherwise, the ideal is a contradiction in terms and a logical impossibility—hence the necessary frustration, anxiety, and neuroticism of our culture.

Second, bisexuality—which should be understood both literally (in terms of possible sexual orientation and practice) and in a more general sense. Bisexuality represents the most obvious and direct affront to the principle of monogamy and its supportive romantic myth of "the one right person"; the homosexual impulse in both men and women represents the most obvious threat to the norm of sexuality as reproductive and restricted by the ideal of family. But more generally we confront here the whole edifice of clear-cut sexual differentiation that bourgeois-capitalist ideology erects on the flimsy and dubious foundations of biological difference: the social norms of masculinity and femininity, the social definitions of manliness and womanliness, the whole vast apparatus of oppressive male/female myths, and the systematic repression from infancy ("blue for a boy") of the man's femininity and the woman's masculinity in the interests of forming human beings for specific predetermined social roles.

Third, the particularly severe repression of female sexuality/creativity, the attribution to the female of passivity, and her preparation for her subordinate, dependent role in our culture. Clearly, a crucial aspect of the repression of bisexuality is the denial to women of drives culturally associated with masculinity: activeness, aggression, self-assertion, organizational power, creativity itself.

Fourth, and fundamentally, the repression of the sexuality of children, taking different forms from infancy, through "latency" and puberty, and into adolescence—the process moving, indeed, from repression to oppression, from the denial of the infant's nature as sexual being to the veto on the expression of sexuality before marriage.

None of these forms of repression is necessary for the existence of civilization in some form (i.e., none is "basic")—for the development of our humanness. Indeed, they impose limitations and restrictions on that development, stunting human potential. All are the outcome of the requirements of the particular surplus-repressive civilization in which we live.

Closely linked to the concept of repression—indeed, truly inseparable from it—is another concept necessary to an understanding of ideology on which psychoanalysis throws much light, the concept of the "other." Otherness represents that which bourgeois ideology cannot recognize or accept but must deal with (as Roland Barthes suggests in *Mythologies*)[13] in one of two ways: either by rejecting and if possible annihilating it, or by rendering it safe and assimilating it, converting it as far as possible into a replica of itself. The concept of otherness can be theorized in many ways and on many levels. Its psychoanalytic significance resides in the fact that it functions not simply as something external to the culture or to the self, but also as what is repressed (though never destroyed) in the self and projected outward in order to be hated and disowned. A particularly vivid example—and one that throws light on a great many classical Westerns—is the relationship of the Puritan settlers to the Indians in the early days of America. The Puritans rejected any perception that the Indians had a culture, a civilization, of their own; they perceived them not merely as savage but, literally, as devils or the spawn of the devil; and, since the devil and sexuality were inextricably linked in the Puritan consciousness, they perceived them as sexually promiscuous, creatures of unbridled libido. The connection between this view of the Indian and Puritan repression is obvious: a classic and extreme case of the projection onto the other of what is repressed within the self in order that it can be discredited, disowned, and if possible annihilated. It is repression, in other words, that makes impossible the healthy alternative—the full recognition and acceptance of the other's autonomy and right to exist.

Some versions, then, of the figure of the other as it operates within our culture, of its relation to repression and oppression, and of how it is characteristically dealt with:

1. *Quite simply, other people.* It is logical and probable that under capitalism all human relations will be characterized by power, dominance, possessiveness, manipulation: the extension into relationships of the property principle. Given the subordinate and dependent position of women, this is especially true of the culture's central relationship, the male/female, and explains why marriage as we have it is characteristically a kind of mutual imperialism/colonization, an exchange of different forms of possession and dependence, both economic and

emotional. In theory, relations between people of the same sex stand more chance of evading this contamination, but in practice most gay and lesbian relationships tend to rely on heterosexual models. The otherness and the autonomy of the partner as well as her/his right to freedom and independence of being are perceived as a threat to the possession-dependence principle and are denied.

2. *Woman.* In a male-dominated culture, where power, money, law, and social institutions are controlled by past, present, and future patriarchs, woman as the other assumes particular significance. The dominant images of women in our culture are entirely male created and male controlled. Woman's autonomy and independence are denied; onto women men project their own innate, repressed femininity in order to disown it as inferior (to be called "unmanly"—i.e., like a woman—is the supreme insult).

3. *The proletariat*—insofar as it still has any autonomous existence and has escaped its colonization by bourgeois ideology. It remains, at least, a conveniently available object for projection: the bourgeois obsession with cleanliness, which psychoanalysis shows to be an outward symptom closely associated with sexual repression, and bourgeois sexual repression itself find their inverse reflections in the myths of working-class squalor and sexuality.

4. *Other cultures.* If they are sufficiently remote, no problem arises: they can be simultaneously deprived of their true character and exoticized (e.g., Polynesian cultures as embodied by Dorothy Lamour). If they are inconveniently close, another approach predominates, of which what happened to the American Indian is a prime example. The procedure is very precisely represented in Ford's *Drums along the Mohawk* (1939), with its double vision of the Indians as "sons of Belial" fit only for extermination and as the Christianized, domesticated, servile, and (hopefully) comic Blueback.

5. *Ethnic groups within the culture.* Again, they function as easily available projection objects (myths of black sexuality, animality, etc.). Or they become acceptable in two ways: either they keep to their ghettos and don't trouble us with their otherness, or they behave as we do and become replicas of the good bourgeois, their otherness reduced to the one unfortunate difference of color. We are more likely to invite a Pakistani to dinner if he dresses in a business suit.

6. *Alternative ideologies or political systems.* The exemplary case is of course Marxism, the strategy that of parody. Still almost totally repressed

within our preuniversity education system (despite the key importance of Marx—whatever way you look at it—in the development of twentieth-century thought), Marxism exists generally in our culture only in the form of bourgeois myth that renders it indistinguishable from Stalinism.

7. *Deviations from ideological sexual norms*—notably bisexuality and homosexuality. One of the clearest instances of the operation of the repression/projection mechanism, homophobia (the irrational hatred and fear of homosexuals) is only explicable as the product of the unsuccessful repression of bisexual tendencies: what is hated in others is what is rejected (but nonetheless continues to exist) within the self.

8. *Children.* When we have worked our way through all the other liberation movements, we may discover that children are the most oppressed section of the population (unfortunately, we cannot expect to liberate our children until we have successfully liberated ourselves). Most clearly of all, the otherness of children (see Freudian theories of infantile sexuality) is that which is repressed within ourselves, its expression therefore hated in others. What the previous generation repressed in us, we, in turn, repress in our children, seeking to mold them into replicas of ourselves, perpetuators of a discredited tradition.

All this may seem to have taken us rather far from our immediate subject. In fact, I have been laying the foundations, stone by stone, for a theory of the American horror film which (without being exhaustive) should provide us with a means of approaching the films seriously and responsibly. One could, I think, approach any of the genres from the same starting point; it is the horror film that responds in the most clear-cut and direct way, because central to it is the actual dramatization of the dual concept of the repressed / the other, in the figure of the monster. One might say that the true subject of the horror genre is the struggle for recognition of all that our civilization represses or oppresses, its reemergence dramatized, as in our nightmares, as an object of horror, a matter for terror, and the happy ending (when it exists) typically signifying the restoration of repression. I think my analysis of what is repressed, combined with my account of the other as it functions within our culture, will be found to offer a comprehensive survey of horror-film monsters from German Expressionism on. It is possible to produce "monstrous" embodiments of virtually every item in the above list. Let me preface this by saying that the general sexual content of the horror film has long been recognized, and the list of monsters representing a generalized concept of otherness offered by the first item on my list cannot be represented by specific films.

1. *Female sexuality.* Earlier examples are the panther woman of *Island of Lost Souls* (1932) and the heroine of *Cat People* (1942) (the association of women with cats runs right through and beyond the Hollywood cinema, cutting across periods and genres from *Bringing Up Baby* [1938] to *Alien* [1979]); but the definitive feminist horror film is clearly De Palma's *Sisters* (1972) (coscripted by the director and Louisa Rose), among the most complete and rigorous analyses of the oppression of women under patriarchal culture in the whole of patriarchal cinema.

2. *The proletariat.* I would claim here Whale's *Frankenstein* (1931), partly on the strength of its pervasive class references but more on the strength of Karloff's costume: Frankenstein could have dressed his creature in top hat, white tie, and tails but in fact chose laborer's clothes. Less disputable, in recent years we have *The Texas Chainsaw Massacre* (1974), with its monstrous family of retired, but still practicing, slaughterhouse workers; the underprivileged devil worshipers of *Race with the Devil* (1975); and the revolutionary army of *Assault on Precinct 13* (1976).

3. *Other cultures.* In the '30s the monster was almost invariably foreign; the rebellious animal-humans of *Island of Lost Souls* (though created by the white man's science) on one level clearly signify a savage, unsuccessfully colonized culture. Recently, one horror film, *The Manitou* (1978), identified the monster with the American Indian (*Prophecy* [1979] plays tantalizingly with this possibility, also linking it to urban blacks, before opting for the altogether safer and less interesting explanation of industrial pollution).

4. *Ethnic groups.* *The Possession of Joel Delaney* (1972) links diabolic possession with Puerto Ricans; blacks (and a leader clad as an Indian) are prominent in *Assault on Precinct 13*'s monstrous army.

5. *Alternative ideologies.* The '50s science-fiction cycle of invasion movies are generally regarded as being concerned with the Communist threat.

6. *Homosexuality and bisexuality.* Both Murnau's *Nosferatu* (1922) and Whale's *Frankenstein* can be claimed as implicitly (on certain levels) identifying their monsters with repressed homosexuality. Recent, less arguable instances

The creature wears laborer's clothes in *Frankenstein* (1931).

are Dr. Frank-N-Furter of *The Rocky Horror Picture Show* (1975) (he, not his creation, is clearly the film's real monster) and, more impressively, the bisexual god of Larry Cohen's *Demon* (*God Told Me To*, 1976).

7. *Children*. Since *Rosemary's Baby* (1968) children have figured prominently in horror films as the monster or its medium: *The Exorcist* (1973), *The Omen* (1976), etc. Cohen's two It's Alive films (1974, 1978) again offer perhaps the most interesting and impressive examples. There is also the Michael of *Halloween*'s (1978) remarkable opening.

This offers us no more than a beginning from which one might proceed to interpret specific horror films in detail as well as to explore further the genre's social significance and the insights it offers into our culture. I shall add here simply that these notions of repression and the other afford us not merely a means of access but a rudimentary categorization of horror films in social/political terms, distinguishing the progressive from the reactionary, the criterion being the way in which the monster is presented and defined.

II. Return of the Repressed

I WANT FIRST TO offer a series of general propositions about the American horror film and then to define the particular nature of its evolution in the '60s and '70s.

1. *Popularity and disreputability.* The horror film has consistently been one of the most popular and, at the same time, the most disreputable of Hollywood genres. The popularity itself has a peculiar characteristic that sets it apart from other genres: it is restricted to aficionados and complemented by total rejection, people tending to go to horror films either obsessively or not at all. They are dismissed with contempt by the majority of reviewer-critics or simply ignored. (The situation has changed somewhat since *Psycho* [1960], which conferred on the horror film something of the dignity that *Stagecoach* [1939] conferred on the Western, but the disdain still largely continues. I have read no serious or illuminating accounts of, for example, *Death Line* [*Raw Meat*, 1972], *It's Alive*, or *The Hills Have Eyes* [1977].) The popularity, however, also continues. Most horror films make money; the ones that don't are those with overt intellectual pretensions, obviously "difficult" works like *God Told Me To* (*Demon*) and *Exorcist II: The Heretic* (1977). Another psychologically interesting aspect of this popularity is that many people who go regularly to horror films profess to ridicule them and go in order to laugh, which is not true, generally speaking, of the Western or the gangster movie.

2. *Dreams and nightmares.* The analogy frequently invoked between films and dreams is usually concerned with the experience of the audience. The spectator sits in darkness, and the sort of involvement the entertainment film invites necessitates a certain switching off of consciousness, a losing of oneself in fantasy experience. But the analogy is also useful from the point of view of the filmmakers. Dreams—the embodiment of repressed desires, tensions, and fears that our conscious mind rejects—become possible when the censor that guards our subconscious relaxes in sleep, though even then the desires can only emerge in disguise, as fantasies that are innocent or apparently meaningless.

One of the functions of the concept of entertainment—by definition, that which we don't take seriously, or think about much ("It's only entertainment")—is to act as a kind of partial sleep of consciousness. For the filmmakers as well as for the audience, full awareness stops at the level of plot, action, and character, in which the most dangerous and subversive implications can disguise themselves and escape detection. This is why seemingly innocuous genre movies can be far more radical and fundamentally undermining than works of conscious social criticism, which must always concern themselves with the possibility of reforming aspects of a social system whose basic rightness must not be challenged. The old tendency to dismiss the Hollywood cinema as escapist always defined escape merely negatively as escape *from*, but escape logically must also be escape *to*. Dreams are also escapes, from the unresolved tensions of our lives into fantasies. Yet the fantasies are not meaningless; they can represent attempts to resolve those tensions in more radical ways than our consciousness can countenance.

Popular films, then, respond to interpretation as at once the personal dreams of their makers and the collective dreams of their audiences, the fusion made possible by the shared structures of a common ideology. It becomes easy, if this is granted, to offer a simple definition of horror films: they are our collective nightmares. The conditions under which a dream becomes a nightmare are that the repressed wish is, from the point of view of consciousness, so terrible that it must be repudiated as loathsome, and that it is so strong and powerful as to constitute a serious threat. The disreputability noted above—the general agreement that horror films are not to be taken seriously—works clearly for the genre viewed from this position. The censor (in both the common and the Freudian sense) is lulled into sleep and relaxes vigilance.

3. *The Surrealists*. It is worth noting here that one group of intellectuals did take American horror movies very seriously indeed: the writers, painters, and filmmakers of the Surrealist movement. Luis Buñuel numbers *The Beast with Five Fingers* (1946) among his favorite films and paid homage to it in *The Exterminating Angel* (1962); Georges Franju, an heir of the Surrealists, numbers *The Fly* (1958) among his. The association is highly significant, given the commitment of the Surrealists to Freud, the unconscious, dreams, and the overthrow of repression.

4. *Basic formula*. At this stage it is necessary to offer a simple and obvious basic formula for the horror film: normality is threatened by the monster. I use "normality" here in a strictly nonevaluative sense to mean simply "conformity to the dominant social norms": one must firmly resist the common tendency to treat the word as if it were more or less synonymous with "health."

The very simplicity of this formula has a number of advantages.

a. It covers the entire range of horror films, being applicable whether the monster is a vampire, a giant gorilla, an extraterrestrial invader, an amorphous gooey mass, or a child possessed by the devil, and this makes it possible to connect the most seemingly heterogeneous movies.

b. It suggests the possibility of extension to other genres: substitute for "monster" the term "Indians," for example, and one has a formula for a large number of classical Westerns; substitute "transgressive woman" and the formula encompasses numerous melodramas (Vidor's *Beyond the Forest* [1949] is an especially fine example, as it links woman and Indian as "monsters").

c. Although so simple, the formula provides three variables: normality, the monster, and, crucially, the relationship between the two. The definition of normality in horror films is in general boringly constant: the heterosexual monogamous couple, the family, and the social institutions (police, church, armed forces) that support and defend them. The monster is, of course, much more protean, changing from period to period as society's basic fears clothe themselves in fashionable or immediately accessible garments—rather as dreams use material from recent memory to express conflicts or desires that may go back to early childhood.

It is the third variable, the relationship between normality and the monster, that constitutes the essential subject of the horror film. It, too, changes and develops, the development taking the form of a long process of clarification or revelation. The relationship has one privileged form: the figure of the doppelgänger, alter ego, or double, a figure that has recurred constantly in Western culture, especially during the past hundred years. The locus classicus is Stevenson's *Dr. Jekyll and Mr. Hyde*, where normality and monster are two aspects of the same person. The figure pervades two major sources of the American horror film—German Expressionist cinema (the two Marias of *Metropolis* [1927], the presentation of protagonist and vampire as mirror reflections in *Nosferatu*, the very title of F. W. Murnau's lost Jekyll-and-Hyde film *Der Januskopf* [1920]), and the tales of Poe. Variants can be traced in such oppositions as Ahab / the white whale in *Moby Dick* and Ethan/Scar in *The Searchers* (1956). The Westerns of Anthony Mann are rich in doubles, often contained within families or family patterns; *Man of the West* (1958), a film that relates very suggestively to the horror genre, represents the fullest elaboration.

I shall limit myself for the moment to one example from the horror film, choosing it partly because it is so central, partly because the motif is there partially disguised, and partly because it points forward to Larry Cohen and *It's Alive*: the relationship of monster to creator in the Frankenstein films. Their identity is made explicit in *Son of Frankenstein* (1939), the most intelligent of the Universal series, near the start of which the title figure (Basil Rathbone) complains bitterly that everyone believes "Frankenstein" to be the name of the monster. (We discover subsequently that the town has also come to be called Frankenstein, the symbiosis of monster and creator spreading over the entire environment.) But we should be alerted to the relationship's true significance from the moment in the James Whale original where Frankenstein's decision to create his monster is juxtaposed very precisely with his decision to become engaged. The doppelgänger motif reveals the monster as normality's shadow.

5. *Ambivalence*. The principle of ambivalence is most eloquently elaborated in A. P. Rossiter's *Angel with Horns*, among the most brilliant of all books on Shakespeare. Rossiter first expounds it with reference to *Richard III*. Richard, the "angel with horns," both horrifies us with his evil and delights us with his intellect, his art, his audacity; while our moral sense is appalled by his outrages, another part of us gleefully identifies with him.[14] The application of this to the horror film is clear. Few horror films have totally unsympathetic monsters (*The Thing from Another World* [1951] is a significant exception); in many (notably the Frankenstein films) the monster is clearly the emotional center and much more human than the cardboard representatives of normality. The Frankenstein monster suffers, weeps, responds to music, longs to relate to people; Henry and Elizabeth merely declaim histrionically. Even in *Son of Frankenstein*—the film in which the restructured monster is explicitly designated as evil and superhuman—the monster's emotional commitment to Ygor and grief over his death carries far greater weight than any of the other relationships in the film.

But the principle goes far beyond the monster's being sympathetic. Ambivalence extends to our attitude to normality. Central to the effect and fascination of horror films is their fulfillment of our nightmare wish to smash the norms that oppress us and that our moral conditioning teaches us to revere. The overwhelming commercial success of *The Omen* cannot possibly be explained in terms of simple, unequivocal *horror* at the devil's progress.

6. *Freudian theses*. Finally, I restate the two elementary and closely interconnected Freudian theses that structure this article: that in a society built on monogamy and family there will be an enormous surplus of repressed sexual energy, and that what is repressed must always strive to return.

BEFORE CONSIDERING HOW THE horror film has developed in the past decade, I want to test the validity of the above ideas by applying them to a classical horror film. I have chosen Robert Florey's *Murders in the Rue Morgue* (1932)—because it is a highly distinguished example, and generally neglected; because its images suggest Surrealism as much as Expressionism; and because it occupies a particularly interesting place in the genre's evolution, linking two of the most famous, though most disparate, horror films ever made. On the one hand, it looks back very clearly to *The Cabinet of Dr. Caligari* (1920): the Expressionist sets and lighting, with Karl Freund as cinematographer; the fairground that provides the starting point for the action; the figure of the diabolical doctor, who shows off his exhibit and later sends it to kidnap the heroine; the flight over the rooftops. On the other hand, it looks forward, equally clearly, to *King Kong* (1933): instead of Caligari's sleepwalker, a gorilla, which falls in love with the heroine, abducts her at night and is shot down from a roof. It is as important to notice the basic motifs that recur obstinately throughout the evolution of the horror film in Western culture as it is to be aware of the detailed particularities of individual films. *Murders in the Rue Morgue* responds well to the application of my formula.

a. *Normality*. The film is quite obsessive about its heterosexual couples. At the opening, we have two couples responding to the various spectacles of the fairground; there is a scene in the middle where numerous carefree couples disport themselves picturesquely amid nature. Crucial to the film, however, is Pierre's love speech to Camille on her balcony, with its exaggerated emphasis on purity: she is both a "flower" and a "star"; she is told not to be curious about what goes on in the houses of the city around them ("Better not to know"); she is also prevented from obtaining knowledge of the nature of Pierre's activities in the morgue (a "horrid old place"). Even the usual gay stereotype, Pierre's plump and effeminate friend, fits very well into the pattern. He is provided with a girlfriend, to recuperate him into the heterosexual coupling of normality. His relationship with Pierre (they share an apartment, he wears an apron, cooks the dinner, and fusses) is a parody of bourgeois marriage, the incongruity underlining the relationship's repressive sexlessness. And he underlines the attempts at separating "pure" normality from the pervasive contamination of outside forces by complaining that Pierre "brings the morgue into their home."

   b. *The monster.* Murders in the Rue Morgue has a divided monster, a phenomenon not uncommon in the horror film. (In *The Cabinet of Dr. Caligari* the monster is both Caligari and Cesar; in *Island of Lost Souls* both Dr. Moreau and his creatures.) Here the division is tripartite: Dr. Mirakle (Bela Lugosi), his servant-assistant, and Erik, "the beast with a human soul." The servant's role is small, but important because of his appearance: half-human, half-animal, he bridges the gap between Mirakle and Erik. Scientist and ape are linked, however, in another way: Mirakle himself lusts after Camille, and Erik (the animal extension of himself) represents the instrument for the satisfaction of that lust. Together, they combine the two great, apparently contradictory, dreads of American culture as expressed in its cinema: intellectuality and eroticism.

The tripartite monster of *Murders in the Rue Morgue* (1932).

c. *Relationship*. The film's superficial project is to insist that purity/normality can be separated from contaminating eroticism/degradation; its deeper project is to demonstrate the impossibility of such a separation. In the opening sequence, the couples view a series of fairground acts as spectacles (the separation of stage from audience seeming to guarantee safety): an erotic dance by "Arabian" girls, a Wild Red Indian show, and finally Erik the ape. The association of the three is suggestive of the link between the horror film and the Western—the link of horror, Indians, and released libido. In each case the separation of show and audience is shown to be precarious: Pierre's sidekick asks his girl if she "could learn to do that dance" for him; two spectators adopt the name "Apache" to apply to the savages of Paris; the audience enters the third booth between the legs of an enormous painted ape, where its phallus would be. Dr. Mirakle's introduction uses evolutionary theory to deny separation: Erik is "the darkness at the dawn of Man." His subsequent experiments are carried out to prove that Erik's blood can be "mixed with the blood of man"—and as the experiments all involve women, the sexual connotations are plain.

Though not obvious, the "double" motif subtly structures the film. It comes nearest to explicitness in the effeminate friend's remark that Pierre is becoming fanatical, "like that Dr. Mirakle." But Pierre and Mirakle are paralleled repeatedly, both in the construction of the scenario and through the mise-en-scène. At the end of the balcony love scene, Florey cuts from the lovers' kiss to Mirakle and Erik watching from their carriage. Later, the juxtaposition is reversed, the camera panning from Mirakle-Erik lurking in the shadows to Pierre-Camille embracing on the balcony; it is as if the monster were waiting to be released by the kiss. Mirakle sends Camille a bonnet; she assumes it is from Pierre. After Pierre leaves her at night, there is a knock at her door. She assumes it is Pierre come back and opens; it is Mirakle. Bearing in mind that Mirakle and Erik are not really distinct from one another, one must see Pierre and this composite monster paralleled throughout as rival mates for Camille, like Jonathan and Nosferatu, or like David Ladd and the underworld man of *Death Line*. (The motif's recurrence across different periods and different continents testifies to its importance.) At the climax Pierre and Erik confront each other like mirror images on the rooftop, and Erik is shot down by Pierre; the hero's drive is to destroy the doppelgänger who embodies his repressed self.

Murders in the Rue Morgue is fascinating for its unresolved self-contradiction. In the fairground Mirakle is denounced as a heretic, in the name of the biblical/Christian tradition of God's creation of man; the whole notion of purity/normality clearly associates with this—explicitly, in the very prominent, carefully lit crucifix above Camille's bed. Yet Mirakle's Darwinian theories are also obviously meant to be correct. Erik and humanity are not separable; the ape exists in all of us; the "morgue" cannot be excluded from the "home."

THE HORROR FILM SINCE the '60s has been dominated by five recurrent motifs. The list of examples offered in each case begins with what I take to be the decisive source-film of each trend—not necessarily the first, but the film that, because of its distinction or popularity, can be thought of as responsible for the ensuing cycle. I have included a few British films that seem to me American derived (*Death Line*, arguably the finest British horror film, was directed by an American, Gary Sherman); they lie outside the main British tradition represented by Hammer Productions, a tradition very intelligently treated in David Pirie's book *A Heritage of Horror*.[15] The lists are not, of course, meant to be exhaustive.

    a. *The monster as human psychotic or schizophrenic*: *Psycho* (1960), *Homicidal* (1961), *Repulsion* (1965), *Sisters* (1972), *Schizo* (1976).

    b. *The revenge of nature*: *The Birds* (1963), *Frogs* (1972), *Night of the Lepus* (1972), *Squirm* (1976), *Day of the Animals* (1977).

    c. *Satanism, diabolic possession, the Antichrist*: *Rosemary's Baby* (1968), *The Possession of Joel Delaney* (1972), *The Exorcist* (1973), *The Omen* (1976), *God Told Me To* (*Demon*, 1976), *The Car* (1977), and *Race with the Devil* (1975), which, along with *High Plains Drifter* (1973), interestingly connects this motif with the Western.

    d. *The terrible child (often closely connected to the above)*. To the first three films in (c) add: *Night of the Living Dead* (1968), *Hands of the Ripper* (1971), *It's Alive* (1974), *Cathy's Curse* (1977); also, although here the "children" are older, *Carrie* (1976) and *The Fury* (1978).

    e. *Cannibalism*: *Night of the Living Dead*, *Raw Meat*, *The Texas Chainsaw Massacre* (1974), *The Hills Have Eyes* (1977), *Frightmare* (1983).

The Birds (1963): An example of the revenge-of-nature horror theme.

These apparently heterogeneous motifs are drawn deeper together by a single unifying master figure: the family. The connection is most tenuous and intermittent in what has proved, on the whole, the least interesting and productive of these concurrent cycles, the "revenge of nature" films; but even there, in the more distinguished examples (outstandingly, of course, *The Birds*, but also in *Squirm*), the attacks are linked to, or seem triggered by, familial or sexual tensions. Elsewhere, the connection of the family to horror has become overwhelmingly consistent: the psychotic/schizophrenic, the Antichrist, and the child-monster are all shown as products of the family, whether the family itself is regarded as guilty (the "psychotic" films) or innocent (*The Omen*).

THE "CANNIBALISM" MOTIF FUNCTIONS in two ways. Occasionally members of a family devour each other (*Night of the Living Dead*, and *Psycho*'s Mrs. Bates is a metaphorical cannibal who swallows up her son). More frequently, cannibalism is the family's means of sustaining or nourishing itself (*The Texas Chainsaw Massacre*, *The Hills Have Eyes*). Pete Walker's revoltingly gruesome and ugly

British horror film *Frightmare* deserves a note here, its central figure being a sweet and gentle old mother who has the one unfortunate flaw that she can't survive without eating human flesh, a craving guiltily indulged by her devoted husband.

If we see the evolution of the horror film in terms of an inexorable "return of the repressed," we will not be surprised by this final emergence of the genre's real significance—together with a sense that it is currently the most important of all American genres and perhaps the most progressive, even in its overt nihilism—in a period of extreme cultural crisis and disintegration, which alone offers the possibility of radical change and rebuilding. To do justice to the lengthy process of that emergence would involve a dual investigation too complex for the framework of this article into the evolution of the horror film and into the changing treatment of the family in the Hollywood cinema. I shall content myself here with a few further propositions.

1. The family (or marital) comedy in which the '30s and '40s are so rich, turns sour (*Father of the Bride* [1950], *The Long, Long Trailer* [1953]) in the '50s and peters out; the family horror film starts (not, of course, without precedents) with *Psycho* in 1960, and gains impetus with *Rosemary's Baby* and *Night of the Living Dead* toward the end of the decade.

2. As the horror film enters into its apocalyptic phase, so does the Western. *The Wild Bunch* appeared in 1969, the year after *Rosemary's Baby*. And *High Plains Drifter* fused their basic elements in a Western in which the hero from the wilderness turns out to be the devil (or his emissary) and burns the town (American civilization) to the ground after revealing it as fundamentally corrupt and renaming it Hell.

3. The family comedies that seemed so innocent and celebratory in the '30s and '40s appear much less so in retrospect from the '70s. In my book *Personal Views* I pointed to the remarkable anticipation in *Meet Me in St. Louis* (1944) of the terrible child of the '70s horror film, especially in the two scenes (Halloween, and the destruction of the snow people) in which Margaret O'Brien symbolically kills parent figures.[16] What is symbolic in 1944 becomes literal in *Night of the Living Dead*, where a little girl kills and devours her parents—just as the implications of another anticipatory family film of the

early '40s, *Shadow of a Doubt* (1943), becomes literally enacted in *It's Alive* (the monster as product of the family).

4. The process whereby horror becomes associated with its true milieu, the family, is reflected in its steady geographical progress toward America.

a. In the '30s, horror is always foreign. The films are set in Paris (*Murders in the Rue Morgue*), in Middle Europe (*Frankenstein* [1931], *Dracula* [1931]) or on uncharted islands (*Island of Lost Souls*, *King Kong*); it is always external to Americans, who may be attacked by it physically but remain (superficially, that is) uncontaminated by it morally. The designation of horror as foreign stands even when the "normal" characters are Europeans. In *Murders in the Rue Morgue*, for example, the young couples, though nominally French, are to all intents and purposes nice clean-living Americans (with American accents); the foreignness of the horror characters is strongly underlined, both by Lugosi's accent and by the fact that nobody knows where he comes from. The foreignness of horror in the '30s can be interpreted in two ways: simply, as a means of disavowal (horror exists, but is un-American), and, more interestingly and unconsciously, as a means of locating horror as a "country of the mind," as a psychological state: the films set on uncharted (and usually nameless) islands lend themselves particularly to interpretation of this kind.

b. The Val Lewton films of the '40s are in some ways outside the mainstream development of the horror film. They seem to have had little direct influence on its evolution (certain occasional haunted-house movies like *The Uninvited* [1944] and *The Haunting* [1963] may owe something to them), though they strikingly anticipate, by at least two decades, some of the features of the modern horror film. *Cat People* is centered on the repression of female sexuality in a period where the monster is almost invariably male and phallic. (Other rare exceptions are the panther woman of *Island of Lost Souls* and, presumably, *Dracula's Daughter* [1936], which I have not seen.) *The Seventh Victim* (1943) has strong undertones of sibling envy and sexual jealousy (the structure and editing of the last scene suggesting that Jacqueline's suicide is willed by her "nice" husband and sister rather than by the "evil" devil worshippers), as well as containing striking anticipations of *Psycho* and

Rosemary's Baby; it is also set firmly in America, with no attempt to disown evil as foreign.

ABOVE ALL, *I WALKED with a Zombie* (1943) explicitly locates horror at the heart of the family, identifying it with sexual repressiveness in the cause of preserving family unity. *The Seventh Victim* apart, horror is still associated with foreignness; Irena in *Cat People* is from Serbia, *Zombie* is set in the West Indies, *The Leopard Man* (1943) in Mexico, etc. Yet the best of the series are concerned with the undermining of such distinctions—with the idea that no one escapes contamination. Accordingly, the concept of the monster becomes diffused through the film (closely linked to the celebrated Lewton emphasis on atmosphere, rather than overt shock), no longer identified with a single figure.

Zombie, one of the finest of all American horror films, carries this furthest. It is built on an elaborate set of apparently clear-cut structural oppositions—Canada / West Indies, white/black, light/darkness, life/death, science / black magic, Christianity/ voodoo, conscious/unconscious, etc.—and it proceeds systematically to blur all of them. Jessica is both living and dead; Mrs. Rand mixes medicine, Christianity, and voodoo; the figurehead is both St. Sebastian and a black slave; the black-white opposition is poetically undercut in a complex patterning of dresses and voodoo patches; the motivation of all the characters is called into question; the messenger-zombie Carrefour can't be kept out of the white domain.

c. The '50s science-fiction cycles project horror onto either extraterrestrial invaders or mutations from the insect world, but they are usually set in America; even when they are not (*The Thing*), the human characters are American. The films, apparently simple, prove on inspection often very difficult to "read." The basic narrative patterns of the horror film repeat themselves obstinately and continue to carry their traditional meanings, but they are encrusted with layers of more transient, topical material. *Them!* (1954), for example, seems to offer three layers of meaning. Explicitly, it sets out to cope with the fear of nuclear energy and atomic experiment: the giant ants are mutants produced by the radioactive aftermath of a bomb explosion; they are eventually destroyed under the guidance of a humane and benevolent science embodied in the comfortingly paternal figure of Edmund Gwenn. The fear of Communist infiltration also seems present, in the emphasis on the ants as a subversive subterranean army and on their elaborate communications system. Yet the film continues to respond convincingly to the application of my basic formula and its Freudian implications. The ants rise up from underground (the unconscious); they kill by holding their victims and injecting into them huge (excessive) quantities of formic acid (the release of repressed phallic energy); and both the opening and final climax of the film are centered on the destruction (respectively actual and potential) of family groups.

SINCE *PSYCHO*, THE HOLLYWOOD cinema has implicitly recognized horror as both American and familial. I want to conclude this section by briefly examining two key works of recent years that offer particularly illuminating and suggestive contrasts and comparisons: *The Omen* and *The Texas Chainsaw Massacre*.

One can partly define the nature of each by means of a chart of oppositions:

THE OMEN	THE TEXAS CHAINSAW MASSACRE
big budget	low budget
glossy production values	raw, unpolished
stars	unknown actors
bourgeois entertainment	nonbourgeois "exploitation"
good taste, "good" family	bad taste, "bad" family
the monster imported from Europe	the monster indigenously American
child destroys parents	parent figures destroy "children"
traditional values reaffirmed	traditional values negated

I don't wish to make any claims for *The Omen* as a work of art: the most one could say is that it achieves a sufficient level of impersonal professional efficiency to ensure that the "kicks" inherent in its scenario are not dulled. (I would add here that my description above of *The Texas Chainsaw Massacre* as "raw, unpolished" refers to the overall effect of the film as it seems to be generally experienced. Its mise-en-scène is, without question, everywhere more intelligent, more inventive, more cinematically educated and sophisticated, than that of *The Omen*. Tobe Hooper's cinematic intelligence, indeed, becomes more apparent on every viewing, as one gets over the initial traumatizing impact and learns to respect the pervasive felicities of camera placement and movement.)

In obvious ways *The Omen* is old-fashioned, traditional, reactionary: the "goodness" of the family unit isn't questioned, "horror" is disowned by having the devil-child a product of the Old World, unwittingly adopted into the American family, the devil-child and his independent female guardian (loosely interpretable in "mythic" terms as representing child liberation and women's liberation) are regarded as purely evil (oh, for a cinematic Blake to reverse all the terms).

Yet the film remains of great interest. It is about the end of the world, but the "world" the film envisages ending is very particularly defined within it: the bourgeois capitalist patriarchal establishment. Here "normality" is not merely threatened by the monster, but totally annihilated: the state, the church, the family. The principle of ambivalence must once again be invoked; with a film so shrewdly calculated for box-office response, it is legitimate to ask what general satisfaction it offers its audience.

Superficially, the satisfaction of finding traditional values reaffirmed (even if "our" world is ending, it was still the good, right, true one); more deeply, and far more powerfully, under cover of this, the satisfaction of the ruthless logic with which the premise is carried through—the supreme satisfaction (masquerading as the final horror) being the revelation, as the camera cranes down in the last shot, that the devil has been adopted by the president and first lady of the United States. The translation of the film into Blakean terms is not in fact that difficult: the devil-child is its implicit hero, whose systematic destruction of the bourgeois establishment the

The devil-child invades the American family in *The Omen* (1976).

audience follows with a secret relish. *The Omen* would make no sense in a society that was not prepared to enjoy and surreptitiously condone the working out of its own destruction.

As Andrew Britton pointed out to me, *The Omen* and *The Texas Chainsaw Massacre* (together with numerous other recent horror films) have one premise disturbingly in common: the annihilation is inevitable, humanity is now completely powerless, there is nothing anyone can do to arrest the process.

(Ideology, that is, can encompass despair, but not the imagining of constructive radical alternatives.) *The Omen* invokes ancient prophecy and shows it inexorably fulfilling itself despite all efforts at intervention; we infer near the opening of *The Texas Chainsaw Massacre* that the age of Aquarius whose advent was so recently celebrated in *Hair* has already passed, giving way to the age of Saturn and universal malevolence. Uncontrol is emphasized throughout the film: not only have the five young victims no control over their destiny, their slaughterers (variously psychotic and degenerate) keep losing control of themselves and each other.

This is partly (in conjunction with the film's relentless and unremitting intensity) what gives *Massacre* to such a degree (beyond any other film in my experience) the authentic quality of nightmare. I have had since childhood a recurring nightmare whose pattern seems to be shared by a very large number of people within our culture: I am running away from some vaguely terrible oppressors who are going to do dreadful things to me; I run to a house or a car, etc., for help; I discover its occupants to be precisely the people I am fleeing. This pattern is repeated twice in *Massacre*, where Sally "escapes" from Leatherface first to his own home, then to the service station run by his father.

The application of my formula to *The Texas Chainsaw Massacre* produces interesting results: the pattern is still there, as is the significant relationship between the terms, but the definitions of "normality" and "monster" have become partly reversed. Here "normality" is clearly represented by the quasiliberated, permissive young (though still forming two couples and a brother-sister family unit, hence reproducing the patterns of the past); the monster is the family, one of the great composite monsters of the American cinema, incorporating four characters and three generations, and imagined with an intensity and audacity that far transcend the connotations of the term "exploitation movie." It has a number of important aspects:

1. The image of the "terrible house" stems from a long tradition in American (and Western capitalist) culture (for a fuller treatment of this, see Andrew Britton's magisterial account of *Mandingo* [1975]).[17] Traditionally, it represents an extension or "objectification" of the personalities of the inhabitants. *Massacre* offers two complementary "terrible houses": the once-imposing, now totally decayed house of Franklin and Sally's parents (where we keep expecting

something appalling to happen) and the more modest, outwardly spruce, inwardly macabre villa of the monstrous family wherein every item of decor is an expression of the characters' degeneracy. The borderline between home and slaughterhouse (between work and leisure) has disappeared—the slaughterhouse has invaded the home, humanity has begun literally to "prey upon itself, like monsters of the deep."[18] Finally, what the "terrible house" (whether in Poe's "The Fall of the House of Usher," in *Psycho*, in *Mandingo*, or here) signifies is the dead weight of the past crushing the life of the younger generation, the future—an idea beautifully realized in the shot that starts on the ominous gray, decayed Franklin house and tilts down to show Kirk and Pam, dwarfed in long shot, playing and laughing as they run to the swimming hole, and to their doom.

2. The contrast between the two houses underlines the distinction the film makes between the affluent young and the psychotic family, representatives of an exploited and degraded proletariat. Sally's father used to send his cattle to the slaughterhouse of which the family are products.

3. The all-male family (the grandmother exists only as a decomposing corpse) also derives from a long American tradition, with notable antecedents in Ford's Westerns (the Clantons of *My Darling Clementine* [1946], the Cleggses of *Wagonmaster* [1950]) and in *Man of the West* (1958). The absence of woman (conceived of as a civilizing, humanizing influence) deprives the family of its social sense and social meaning while leaving its strength of primitive loyalties largely untouched. In *Massacre*, woman becomes the ultimate object of the characters' animus (and, I think, the film's, since the sadistic torments visited on Sally go far beyond what is necessary to the narrative).

4. The release of sexuality in the horror film is always presented as perverted, monstrous, and excessive (whether it takes the form of vampires, giant ants, or Mrs. Bates), both the perversion and the excess being the logical outcome of repression. Nowhere is this carried further than in *The Texas Chainsaw Massacre*. Here sexuality is totally perverted from its functions into sadism, violence, and cannibalism. It is striking that there is no suggestion anywhere that Sally is the object of an overtly sexual threat: she is to be tormented, killed, dismembered, eaten, but not raped. Ultimately, the most terrifying thing about the film is its total negativity; the repressed energies—represented most unforgettably

by Leatherface and his continuously whirring phallic chainsaw—are presented as irredeemably debased and distorted. It is no accident that the four most intense horror films of the '70s at "exploitation" level (*Night of the Living Dead*, *Raw Meat*, and *The Hills Have Eyes* are the other three) are all centered on cannibalism, and on the specific notion of present and future (the younger generation) being devoured by the past. Cannibalism represents the ultimate in possessiveness, hence the logical end of human relations under capitalism. The implication is that "liberation" and "permissiveness," as defined within our culture, are at once inadequate and too late—too feeble, too unaware, too undirected to withstand the legacy of long repression.

5. This connects closely with the recurrence of the "double" motif in *Massacre*. The young people are, on the whole uncharacterized and undifferentiated (the film's energies are mainly with its monsters—as usual in the horror film, the characteristic here surviving the reversal of definitions), but in their midst is Franklin, who is as grotesque, and almost as psychotic, as his nemesis Leatherface. (The film's refusal to sentimentalize the fact that he is

The release of sexuality is always presented as perverted and monstrous in the horror film (*The Texas Chainsaw Massacre*, 1974).

An Introduction to the American Horror Film - 99

crippled may remind one of the blind beggars of Buñuel). Franklin associates himself with the slaughterers by imitating the actions of Leatherface's brother, the hitchhiker: wondering whether he, too, could slice open his own hand, and toying with the idea of actually doing so. (Kirk remarks, "You're as crazy as he is.") Insofar as the other young people are characterized, it is in terms of a pervasive petty malice. Just before Kirk enters the house to meet his death, he teases Pam by dropping into her hand a human tooth he has found on the doorstep; later, Jerry torments Franklin to the verge of hysteria by playing on his fears that the hitchhiker will pursue and kill him. Franklin resents being neglected by the others, Sally resents being burdened with him on her vacation. The monstrous cruelties of the slaughterhouse family have their more pallid reflection within "normality." (The reflection pattern here is more fully worked out in *The Hills Have Eyes*, with its stranded "normal" family besieged by its dark mirror image, the terrible shadow family from the hills, who want to kill the men, rape the women, and eat the baby.)

6. Despite the family's monstrousness, a degree of ambivalence is still present in the response they evoke. Partly, this is rooted in our sense of them as a family. They are held together—and torn apart—by bonds and tensions with which we are all familiar, with which, indeed, we are likely to have grown up. We cannot cleanly dissociate ourselves from them. Then there is the sense that they are victims, too—of the slaughterhouse environment, of capitalism—our victims, in fact. Finally, they manifest a degraded but impressive creativity. The news reporter at the start describes the tableau of decomposing corpses in the graveyard (presumably the work of the hitchhiker, and perhaps an homage to his grandparents: a female corpse is posed in the lap of a male corpse in a hideous parody of domesticity) as "a grisly work of art." The phrase, apt for the film itself, also describes the artworks among which the family live, some of which achieve a kind of hideous aesthetic beauty: the lightbulb held up by a human hand, the sofa constructed out of human and animal bones surmounted by ornamental skulls, the hanging lamp over the dining table that appears to be a shrunken human head. The film's monsters do not lack that characteristically human quality, an aesthetic sense, however perverted its form; also, they waste nothing, a lesson we are all taught as children.

7. Central to the film—and centered on its monstrous family—is the sense of grotesque comedy, which in no way diminishes (rather intensifies) its nightmare horror: Leatherface chasing Sally with the chainsaw, unable to stop and turn, skidding, wheeling, like an animated character in a cartoon; the father's response to Leatherface's devastations, which by that time include four murders and the prolonged terrorization of the heroine ("Look what your brother did to that door"); Leatherface dressed up in jacket and tie and fresh black wig for formal dinner with Grandpa; the macabre farce of Grandpa's repeated failures to kill Sally with the hammer. The film's sense of fundamental horror is closely allied to a sense of the fundamentally absurd. The family, after all, only carry to its logical conclusion the basic (though unstated) tenet of capitalism, that people have the right to live off other people. In twentieth-century art, the sense of the absurd is always closely linked to total despair (Beckett, Ionesco, etc.). The fusion of nightmare and absurdity is carried even further in *Eaten Alive* (*Death Trap*, 1972), a film that confirms that the creative impulse in Hooper's work is centered in his monsters (here, the grotesque and pathetic Neville Brand) and is essentially nihilistic.

The Texas Chainsaw Massacre, unlike *The Omen*, achieves the force of authentic art, profoundly disturbing, intensely personal, yet at the same time far more than personal, as the general response it has evoked demonstrates. As a "collective nightmare" it brings to a focus a spirit of negativity, an undifferentiated lust for destruction, that seems to lie not far below the surface of the modern collective consciousness. Watching it recently with a large, half-stoned youth audience who cheered and applauded every one of Leatherface's outrages against their representatives on the screen was a terrifying experience. It must not be seen as an isolated phenomenon: it expresses, with unique force and intensity, at least one important aspect of what the horror film has come to signify, the sense of a civilization condemning itself, through its popular culture, to ultimate disintegration, and ambivalently (with the simultaneous horror / wish-fulfillment of nightmare) celebrating the fact. We must not, of course, see that as the last word.[19]

III. The Reactionary Wing

I SUGGESTED EARLIER THAT the theory of repression offers us a means toward a political categorization of horror movies. Such a categorization, however, can never be rigid or clear-cut. While I have stressed the genre's progressive or radical elements, its potential for the subversion of bourgeois patriarchal norms, it is obvious enough that this potential is never free from ambiguity. The genre carries within itself the capability of reactionary inflection, and perhaps no horror film is entirely immune from its operations. It need not surprise us that there is a powerful reactionary tradition to be acknowledged—so powerful it may at times appear the dominant one. Its characteristics are, in extreme cases, very strongly marked.

Before noting them, however, it is important to make one major distinction between the reactionary horror film and the "apocalyptic" horror film. The latter expresses, obviously, despair and negativity, yet its very negation can be claimed as progressive: the "apocalypse," even when presented in metaphysical terms (the end of the world), is generally reinterpretable in social/political ones (the end of the highly specific world of patriarchal capitalism). The majority of the most distinguished American horror films (especially in the '70s) are concerned with this particular apocalypse; they are progressive in so far as their negativity is not recuperable into the dominant ideology, but constitutes (on the contrary) the recognition of that ideology's disintegration, its untenability, as all it has repressed explodes and blows it apart. *The Texas Chainsaw Massacre, Sisters, Demon* are all apocalyptic in this sense; so are Romero's two Living Dead movies. (Having said that, it must be added that important distinctions remain to be made between these works.)

Some of the characteristics, then, that have contributed to the genre's reactionary wing:

1. *The designation of the monster as simply evil.* In so far as horror films are typical manifestations of our culture, the dominant designation of the monster must necessarily be "evil": what is repressed (in the individual, in the culture) must always return as a threat, perceived by the consciousness as ugly, terrible, obscene. Horror films, it might be said, are progressive precisely to the degree that they refuse to be satisfied with this simple designation—to the degree that,

whether explicitly or implicitly, consciously or unconsciously, they modify question, challenge, seek to invert it. All monsters are by definition destructive, but their destructiveness is capable of being variously explained, excused, and justified. To identify what is repressed with "evil incarnate" (a metaphysical, rather than a social, definition) is automatically to suggest that there is nothing to be done but strive to keep it repressed. Films in which the "monster" is identified as the devil clearly occupy a privileged place in this group; though even the devil can be presented with varying degrees of (deliberate or inadvertent) sympathy and fascination—*The Omen* should not simply be bracketed with *The Sentinel* (1977) for consignment to merited oblivion.

2. *The presence of Christianity* (in so far as it is given weight or presented as a positive force) is in general a portent of reaction. (This is a comment less on Christianity itself than on what it signifies within the Hollywood cinema and the dominant ideology.) *The Exorcist* is an instructive instance—its validity is in direct proportion to its failure convincingly to impose its theology.

3. *The presentation of the monster as totally nonhuman.* The "progressiveness" of the horror film depends partly on the monster's capacity to arouse sympathy; one can feel little for a mass of viscous black slime. The political (McCarthyite) level of '50s science-fiction films—the myth of Communism as total dehumanization—accounts for the prevalence of this kind of monster in that period.

4. *The confusion (in terms of what the film wishes to regard as monstrous) of repressed sexuality with sexuality itself.* The distinction is not always clear-cut; perhaps it never can be, in a culture whose attitudes to sexuality remain largely negative and where a fear of sex is implanted from infancy. One can, however, isolate a few extreme examples where the sense of horror is motivated by sexual disgust.

A very common generic pattern plays on the ambiguity of the monster as the "return of the repressed" and the monster as punishment for sexual promiscuity (or, in the more extreme puritanical cases, for any sexual expression whatever: two teenagers kiss; enter, immediately, the Blob). Both the Jaws films (1975, 1978) (their sources in both '50s McCarthyite science fiction and all those beach-party / monster movies that disappeared with the B feature) are obvious recent examples, Spielberg's film being somewhat more complex, less blatant, than Jeannot Szwarc's, though the difference is chiefly one of ideological sophistication.

I WANT TO EXAMINE briefly here some examples of the "reactionary" horror film in the '70s, of widely differing distinction but considerable interest in clarifying these tendencies.

David Cronenberg's *Shivers* (1975, formerly *The Parasite Murders*) is, indeed, of very special interest here, as it is a film single-mindedly about sexual liberation, a prospect it views with unmitigated horror. The entire film is premised on and motivated by sexual disgust. The release of sexuality is linked inseparably with the spreading of venereal disease, the scientist responsible for the experiments having seen fit (for reasons never made clear) to include a VD component in his aphrodisiac parasite. The parasites themselves are modeled very obviously on phalluses, but with strong excremental overtones (their color) and continual associations with blood; the point is underlined when one enters Betts, the Barbara Steele character, through her vagina. If the film presents sexuality in general as the object of loathing, it has a very special animus reserved for female sexuality (a theme repeated, if scarcely developed, in Cronenberg's subsequent *Rabid* [1977]). The parasites are spread initially by a young girl (the original subject of the scientist's experiments), the film's Pandora whose released eroticism precipitates general cataclysm; throughout, sexually aroused, preying women are presented with a particular intensity of horror and disgust. *Shivers* systematically chronicles the breaking of every sexual-social taboo—promiscuity, lesbianism, homosexuality, age difference, finally incest—but each step is presented as merely one more addition to the accumulation of horrors. At the same time, the film shows absolutely no feeling for traditional relationships (or for human beings, for that matter): with its unremitting ugliness and crudity, it is very rare in its achievement of total negation.

The Brood (1979), again, is thematically central to the concept of the horror film proposed here (its subject being the transmission of neurosis through the family structure) and the precise antithesis of the genre's progressive potential. It carries over all the major structural components of its

Shivers (1975) views sexual liberation with unmitigated horror and disgust.

two predecessors (as an auteur, Cronenberg is nothing if not consistent): the figure of the scientist (here psychotherapist) who, attempting to promote social progress, precipitates disaster; the expression of unqualified horror at the idea of releasing what has been repressed; the projection of horror and evil onto women and their sexuality, the ultimate dread being of women usurping the active, aggressive role that patriarchal ideology assigns to the male. The film is remarkable for its literal enactment, at its climax, of the Freudian perception that, under patriarchy, the child becomes the woman's penis substitute—Samantha Eggar's latest offspring representing, unmistakably, a monstrous phallus. The film is laboriously explicit about its meaning: the terrible children are the physical embodiments of the woman's rage. But that rage is never seen as the logical product of woman's situation within patriarchal culture; it is blamed entirely on the woman's mother (the father being culpable only in his weakness and ineffectuality). The film is useful for offering an extremely instructive comparison with *Sisters* on the one hand and *It's Alive* on the other.

In turning from Cronenberg's films to *Halloween* (1978) I do not want to suggest that I am bracketing them together. John Carpenter's films reveal in many ways an engaging artistic personality: they communicate, at the very least, a delight in skill and craftsmanship, a pleasure in play with the medium, that is one of the essential expressions of true creativity. Yet the film-buff innocence that accounts for much of the charm of *Dark Star* (1974) can go on to combine (in *Assault on Precinct 13*) *Rio Bravo* (1959) and *Night of the Living Dead* without any apparent awareness of the ideological consequences of converting Hawks's fascists (or Romero's ghouls, for that matter) into an army of revolutionaries. The film buff is very much to the fore again in *Halloween*, covering the film's confusions, its lack of real thinking, with a formal/stylistic inventiveness that is initially irresistible. If nothing in the film is new, everything testifies to Carpenter's powers of assimilation (as opposed to mere imitation): as a resourceful amalgam of *Psycho*, *The Texas Chainsaw Massacre*, *The Exorcist*, and *Black Christmas* (1974), *Halloween* is cunning in the extreme.

The confusions, however, are present at its very foundation, in the conception of the monster. The opening is quite stunning both in its virtuosity and its resonances. The long killer's-point-of-view tracking shot with which the film begins establishes the basis for the first murder as sexual repression: the girl is killed because she arouses in the voyeur-murderer feelings he has simultaneously to deny and enact in the form of violent assault. The second shot reveals the murderer as the victim's bewildered six-year-old brother. Crammed into those first two shots (in which *Psycho* unites with the Halloween sequence of *Meet Me in St. Louis*) are the implications for the definitive family horror film: the child-monster, product of the nuclear family and the small-town environment; the sexual repression of children; the incest taboo that denies sexual feeling precisely where the proximities of family life most encourage it. Not only are those implications not realized in the succeeding film, their trace is obscured and all but obliterated. The film identifies the killer with the "bogeyman," as the embodiment of an eternal and unchanging evil, which by definition can't be understood, and with the devil ("Those eyes . . . the devil's eyes"), by none other than his own psychoanalyst, Dr. Sam Loomis (Donald

Pleasence)—surely the most extreme instance of Hollywood's perversion of psychoanalysis into an instrument of repression.

The film proceeds to lay itself wide open to the reading offered by Jonathan Rosenbaum: the killer's victims are all sexually promiscuous, the one survivor a virgin; the monster becomes (in the tradition of all those beach-party monster movies of the late '50s and early '60s) simply the instrument of Puritan vengeance and repression rather than the embodiment of what Puritanism repressed.[20]

Halloween is more interesting than that if only because more confused. The basic premise of the action is that Laurie is the killer's real quarry throughout (the other girls merely distractions en route), because she is for him the reincarnation of the sister he murdered as a child (he first sees her in relation to a little boy who resembles him as he was then and becomes fixated on her from that moment). This compulsion to reenact the childhood crime keeps Michael tied at least to the possibility of psychoanalytical explanation, thereby suggesting that Dr. Loomis may be wrong. If we accept that, then one tantalizing unresolved detail becomes crucial: the question of how Michael learned to drive a car. There are only two possible explanations: either he is the devil, possessed of supernatural powers, or he has not spent the last nine years (as Loomis would have us believe) sitting staring blankly at a wall meditating further horrors. (It is to Carpenter's credit that the issue is raised in the dialogue, not glossed over as an unfortunate plot necessity we aren't supposed to notice; but he appears to use it merely as another tease, a bit of meaningless mystification.) The possibility this opens up is that of reading the whole film against the Pleasence character: Michael's "evil" is what his analyst has been projecting onto him for the past nine years. Unfortunately, this remains merely a possibility in the material that Carpenter chose not to take up: it does not constitute a legitimate (let alone a coherent) reading of the actual film. Carpenter's interviews (see, for example, the quotation that opens Tony Williams's essay in *The American Nightmare*)[21] suggest that he strongly resists examining the connotative level of his own work; it remains to be seen how long this very talented filmmaker can preserve this false innocence.

At first glance, *Alien* (1979) seems little more than *Halloween* in outer space: more expensive, less personal, but made with similar professional skill

Michael's killings lead to his fixation on Laurie as a substitute for his sister (*Halloween*, 1978).

and flair for manipulating its audiences. Yet it has several distinctive features that give it a limited interest in its own right: it clearly wants to be taken, on a fairly simple level, as a "progressive" movie, notably in its depiction of women. What it offers on this level amounts in fact to no more than a pop feminism that reduces the whole involved question of sexual difference and thousands of years of patriarchal oppression to the bright suggestion that a woman can do anything a man can do (almost). This masks (not very effectively) its fundamentally reactionary nature.

Besides its resemblance to *Halloween* in general narrative pattern and suspense strategies (Where is the monster hiding? who will be killed next?—When?—How?), *Alien* has more precise parallels with *The Thing*. There is the enclosed space, cut off from outside help; the definition of the monster as both non- and superhuman; the fact that it feeds on human beings; its apparent indestructibility. Most clearly of all, the relationship of Ash, the robot science officer, to the alien is very close to that of Professor Carrington to the Thing; in both films, science regards the alien as a superior form of life to which human life must therefore be subordinate; in both films, science is initially responsible for bringing the monster into the community and thereby endangering the latter's existence.

What strikingly distinguishes *Alien* from both *Halloween* and *The Thing* (and virtually every other horror movie) is the apparently total absence of sexuality. Although there are two women among the spaceship's crew of seven, there is no "love interest," not even any sexual banter—in fact, with the characters restricted exclusively to the use of surnames, no recognition anywhere of sexual difference (unless we see Parker's ironic resentment of Ripley's domineeringness as motivated partly by the fact that she is a woman; but he reacts like that to all displays of authority in the film, and his actual phrase for her is "son of a bitch"). Only at the end of the film, after all the men have been killed, is female sexuality allowed to become a presence (as Ripley undresses, not knowing that the alien is still alive and in the compartment). The film constructs a new "normality" in which sexual differentiation ceases to have effective existence—on condition that sexuality be obliterated altogether.

The term "son of a bitch" is applied (by Ripley herself) to one other character in the film: the alien. The cinematic confrontation of its two "sons of bitches" is the film's logical culmination. Its resolution of ideological contradictions is clear in the presentation of Ripley herself: she is a "safe threat," set against the real threat of the alien. On the one hand, she is the film's myth of the "emancipated woman": "masculine," aggressive, self-assertive, she takes over the ship after the deaths of Kane and Dallas, rebelling against and dethroning both "Mother" (the computer) and father (Ash, the robot). On the other hand, the film is careful to supply her with "feminine," quasimaternal characteristics (her care for Jones, the cat) and gives her, vis-à-vis the alien, the most reactionary position of the entire crew (it is she who is opposed to letting it on board, even to save Kane's life). She is, of course, in the film's terms, quite right; but that merely confirms the ideologically reactionary nature of the film in its attitude to the other.

If male and female are superficially and trendily united in Ripley, they are completely fused in the alien (whose most striking characteristic is its ability to transform itself). The sexuality so rigorously repressed in the film returns grotesquely and terrifyingly in its monster (the more extreme the repression, the more excessive the monster). At first associated with femaleness (it begins as an egg in a vast womb), it attaches itself to the most "feminine" of the crew's males (John Hurt, most famous for his portrayal of Quentin Crisp) and enters him through the mouth as a preliminary to being "born" out of his stomach. The alien's phallic identity is strongly marked (the long reptilian neck); but so is its large, expandable mouth, armed with tiers of sharp metallic teeth. As a composite image of archetypal sexual dreads it could scarcely be bettered: the monstrous phallus combined with vagina dentata. Throughout the film, the alien and the cat are repeatedly paralleled or juxtaposed, an association that may remind us of the panther / domestic cat opposition in *Cat People* (the cats even have the same surname, the John Paul Jones of Jacques Tourneur's movie reduced here to a mere "Jones" or "Jonesey"). The film creates its image of the emancipated woman only to subject her to massive terrorization (the use of flashing lights throughout *Alien*'s climactic scenes strikingly recalls the finale of *Looking for Mr. Goodbar* [1977]) and enlist her in the battle for patriarchal repression. Having destroyed the alien, Ripley can become completely "feminine"—soft and passive, her domesticated pussy safely asleep.

It is not surprising, though disturbing and sad, that at present it is the reactionary horror film that dominates the genre. This is entirely in keeping with the overall movement of Hollywood in the past five years. Vietnam, Nixon, and Watergate produced a crisis in ideological confidence that the Carter administration has temporarily resolved; *Rocky* (1976), *Star Wars* (1977), *Heaven Can Wait* (1978)—all overwhelming popular successes—are but the echoes of a national sigh of relief. *Sisters, Demon, Night of the Living Dead, The Texas Chainsaw Massacre* in their various ways reflect ideological disintegration and lay bare the possibility of social revolution; *Halloween* and *Alien*, while deliberately evoking maximum terror and panic, variously seal it over again.

(1978)

DER ERLKÖNIG

The Ambiguities of Horror

THE INCLUSION, IN AN anthology on the American horror film, of an essay on a musical setting by Schubert of a poem by Goethe requires explanation but not apology. One of the aims of this book and the retrospective it accompanies is to stress the centrality of the horror film to our culture, and "our culture" means more than "North America, now." There is always of course a cultural moment, a here and now with its own detailed specifics; but that here and now grows out of, and to a great extent continues to incorporate, a history to which it is as impossible to assign a beginning as it is a predictable end (no one, hopefully not even Godard himself, seriously believes in the practicality of a cultural "return to zero"). To relate the basic structures of the American horror film to a literary/musical composition from another age and place is not to confuse two obviously disparate cultural moments (the Germany that produced Goethe and Schubert with the America that produced Hooper and Romero) but to insist on continuities within the development of Western patriarchal civilization: we shall find the step from "Der Erlkönig" to, say, *The Curse of the Cat People* (1944) and *The Exorcist* (1973) a surprisingly easy one to make. The inclusion of this essay signifies a further, related, intention: the desire to rescue the horror film from the "film buffs," that species who collect movies the way others collect stamps or butterflies, thereby depriving them of their contextual significance. An interest in one art form should presuppose an interest in art generally and its functions within our culture.

Why Schubert's setting, rather than simply the poem itself? First, because that is how I know it, and I cannot separate the two; second, because it is in that form that it will be most widely familiar; third, because Schubert's magnificent realization both intensifies the poem's force and very precisely underlines implications on which I wish to dwell.

The Plot

THE STORY OF GOETHE'S poem is itself but one example from a tradition of horror/fairy tales that goes right back through patriarchal history (which is to say, the known history of mankind). A man is riding home "through night and wind," carrying his small son in his arms. The child believes he sees and hears the Erl-king; the father explains the vision away in terms of natural phenomena. The Erl-king tries to lure the child to him, with various temptations, and eventually threatens force. The father reaches the house and apparent safety, but the child is dead in his arms.

The Dominant Reading

SUPERFICIALLY, WE HAVE A simple, traditional tale enacting the normality/monster opposition quite straightforwardly, the terms virtually synonymous with good/evil: the good, protective father; the security of home; the innocent child; the evil Erl-king / devil / bogeyman first insidiously luring, then tyrannically seizing, the helpless boy. This is how I understood the song when I first encountered it about twenty-five years ago; it is probably how most people "read" it; it is also how most singers interpret it (e.g., the justly celebrating renderings by Dietrich Fischer-Dieskau use every means of vocal signification to underline the Erl-king's evil, the sinister nature of his seductiveness). It is also, in a sense, the "correct" reading, endorsed by both poet and composer: Goethe stresses the child's terror of the Erl-king, his pain when seized, the Erl-king's selfish cruelty; Schubert achieves that magnificent and unforgettable stroke at the conclusion, moving to an apparent resolution in the major on the penultimate line (the seemingly safe arrival home), the headlong, galloping accompaniment slowing to a standstill, before the abrupt, devastating revelation of the child's death. No irony beyond the obvious one seems intended.

The dominant discourse (the joint discourse of poet and composer within, and determined by, patriarchal ideology) permits one alternative reading that already begins the process of opening out the song: the Erl-king can be read as a figment of the child's imagination rather than an actual supernatural being, the boy literally scaring himself to death. Such a reading immediately and inevitably raises a crucial question: in this case, what forces have produced this "figment"?

Psychoanalysis

EVEN THE SIMPLEST ANSWER to that question presupposes a use of psychoanalysis, in however primitive and rudimentary a form (the "psychological insights" familiar from even pre-Freudian literary criticism). Today, twentieth-century developments fused with a radical political position transform an apparently simple song into a complex of shifting ambiguities whose signifying potential this account will certainly not exhaust. The very simplicity and baldness of the text (both Goethe's and Schubert's), its lack of psychological elaboration, its reduction of its characters to archetypes, its spare precision of action combined with reticence about motivation make possible a multiplicity of interrelated readings.

Psychoanalysis must start by rigorously rejecting the supernatural: gods, demons, monsters, bogeymen become manifestations of inner forces. To define the Erl-king as "the repressed" leads directly to the question "Whose repressed? The father's? The child's? Both?" By way of partial, tentative answer, one may recall that certain theories of dream maintain that all the characters (and other elements) of a dream embody different, conflicting aspects of the self. We all contain within us our own child, father, and Erl-king, loosely corresponding to the Freudian ego, superego, and id. A systematic examination of some of the song's constituent elements will help clarify its rich suggestiveness.

The Setting—the Journey—the House

GOETHE ESTABLISHES THE SETTING succinctly as "night and wind"; Schubert responds with a minor key accompaniment that evokes both the galloping of the horse and a generalized, ominous tumult. Darkness and turbulence combine as a powerful representation of the disturbed unconscious within which the repressed forces lurk. Otherwise, the landscape is evoked only by a few stray details ("a streak of mist," "the wind rustling in dry leaves," "the old grey willow") that, with their connotations of decay, desolation, sterility, and colorlessness, contrast strongly with the "pretty flowers," "river bank," "golden robe," games, and company promised by the Erl-king.

The goal of this frantic journey through night, wind, and wilderness is the house: in dreams, frequently a symbol for the personality, in this context also a symbol of security and order—security above all from the Erl-king, whom the house would finally exclude and deny. The house can be read both as an extension of the father (what culture regards as the "mature," finished, ordered personality) and as an image for the order within which the father will enclose the child: in Lacanian terms (were the journey successfully completed), the child's entry into the Symbolic, at once the surrender to and acquisition of patriarchal law (itself a kind of death).

The Father

EVEN ON THE MOST superficial level, the father's role is characterized by ambiguities. It is not clear whether: (a) he is actually unaware of the Erl-king and really believes the child is hallucinating or imagining (his suddenly revealed fear at the end can be read as fear for the terrified child rather than fear of the Erl-king); (b) he recognizes his adversary but struggles to protect his child from the knowledge, deliberately (if with the best intentions, like so many parents) deceiving him and denying his perceptions; or (c) he gradually comes to share the child's vision as the song proceeds, in doubt from the beginning, finally capitulating toward the end. Schubert's setting of the father's words to me suggests uncertainty and a desire to deny what is feared may be there (but responses to music are notoriously subjective). All three interpretations work very well but carry somewhat different inflections. In psychoanalytic terms, it is a matter of degrees of repression, of how completely all that the Erl-king represents has been repressed in the father. What is unambiguously clear, on the other hand, is the father's determination to deny and suppress his child's knowledge of the Erl-king.

We may note that Goethe himself generalizes the figure: he is from the outset, not "a father," but "the father," the patriarch, the heterosexual male, the ideologically dominant figure of our culture, whose continuing dominance depends upon the maintenance and transmission of repression. The Erl-king—the figure in the darkness—is also a father and, as king, the supreme patriarch: the clearest psychoanalytic reading would be in terms of what I have described as the privileged instance of the normality/monster relationship, the doppelgänger. Father and Erl-king take their place in a chain that passes through and connects all patriarchal societies, and whose links include the traditional good father / ogre of fairy tales, Jonathan/Nosferatu, Dr. Jekyll / Mr. Hyde, the police detective / revolutionary god of *God Told Me To* (*Demon*, 1976) . . . The father's protectiveness ("He clasps him safe and holds him warm") finds its sinister echo in the Erl-king's desire to possess—possession finding its logical culmination in death, since only the inanimate can be totally possessed. According to this reading, it is the father who creates the desolation of the landscape by repressing the Erl-king: the ambivalence with which the monster is viewed, the inextricable fusion of positive and negative connotations, arises from the complexity of the doppelgänger relationship, the "double" simultaneously reflection and opposite. The hammering, repeated chords of Schubert's accompaniment (bare octaves or harsh dissonances) are quite amazingly evocative in connection with the father, suggesting tremendous energy perverted toward repression instead of creativity, violent, insistent, obsessive, unresolved, tied to endless repetition.

The Child

THE CHILD'S AGE IS not mentioned, but the phase of his psychic development is very precisely defined: the Erl-king is still a potent reality for him (he hasn't reached "the house"), but he has learned to regard him (both rightly and wrongly) as an object of terror. If the Erl-king represents what is repressed in the father, he also represents what is in process of being repressed in the son, whose true innocence is being converted into the false, desexualized innocence recognized by patriarchal culture. The dual function should not be found confusing: what is the history of patriarchy but the history of the transmission of repression? If the relationship father/Erl-king emphasizes the monster's negative aspects, the relationship child/Erl-king (despite the boy's terror) emphasizes the positive: the Erl-king as the realm of imagination, eroticism, and play. What the child justifiably fears is the Erl-king's tyrannical possessiveness, his aspect of monstrous father; what is attractive is the lure of sensuality and relaxation. When the Erl-king speaks and only then (and progressively, as the song continues) does the piano accompaniment relax and escape that reiterated hammering, modulating into the major. Yet the child's responses invariably return the music to the minor key, panic, and obsession: he is already under his father's domination, and the Erl-king can only win him by killing him.

The Erl-king

THE THEORY OF REPRESSION helps to explain the often-noted phenomenon that in the works of our culture "evil" is always more interesting than "good." Audiences go to horror movies to see, not Frankenstein but the monster, not Dr. Jekyll but Mr. Hyde, not a nice young girl but a child spouting filth (both literal and metaphorical) over authority figures when "diabolically" possessed. The restoration of "normality" and destruction of the monster at the end of horror movies has always produced at least as much resentment as relief: certainly, films that forego such reassurance (*It's Alive* [1974], *The Omen* [1976], *Halloween* [1978], etc.) have not forfeited the genre's popularity. The reasons for this fascination are complex: the monster is the source of true energy; it represents the breaking of taboos, the transgression against patriarchal authority that a part of everyone responds to; it is also, by its very nature, the most complex and ambivalently viewed component of the horror syndrome.

The Erl-king of Goethe and Schubert is a remarkably rich creation (given the succinctness of the work—a song lasting scarcely more than four minutes). The folklore figure itself carries multiple and contradictory connotations, which poet and composer emphasize rather than suppress. The *Oxford Dictionary* defines him as "Bearded, golden-crowned giant of Teutonic folklore who lures little children to the land of death"; the German name means "alder-king," carrying suggestions of a fertility god (Goethe has the father explain away his son's vision of the Erl-king's daughter as a willow tree); this, in turn, is a mistranslation of the original Danish *eller-konge*, "king of the elves," a title with somewhat different connotations of a less terrible and destructive world of magic (the desire of Oberon for the changeling boy in *A Midsummer Night's Dream* is clearly related). All these aspects are palpably present in the song: the Erl-king is ambiguously destroyer and savior, terrible father and playmate, death and life; the menace that Schubert underlines in his setting of the king's last line ("If you won't come willingly, I'll use force") doesn't obliterate the irresistible lilt of the dance melody that expresses his attempts at seduction. (The rhythmic complexity of the song, it should be noted, is largely Schubert's: Goethe's poem is firmly metrical, in regular stanzas, the composer supplying both the minor-major modulation and the corresponding transformation of rhythm that add so much force to the Erl-king's positive connotations.)

The song opposes two forms of energy: the strife of repression, the relaxation of play and dance. The Erl-king's invitation is plainly sexual and involves the offer of both himself and his daughters: it carries implications of child sexuality, bisexuality (since the boy is expected to find both offers attractive), and pedophilia. The Erl-king's negative connotations (the desire to possess through violation) are clearly attached to this last; they are also what make him a sinister reflection of the father. There is no reason to suppose that pedophilia (literally, simply the love of children, though in common usage the term always carries connotations of erotic attraction) need necessarily be one-sided and exploitive, but in our culture it is likely to be, because the patriarchal family system associates it closely with repression and because of the false innocence imposed on children. The current prosecution of *Body Politic* (Toronto's gay newspaper) for publishing an innocuous (if somewhat sentimental and question-begging) article on the subject testifies to our society's hysterical fear of the whole issue (and of course the related issue of child sexuality). The phenomenon remains wrapped in mystery and danger (anything that can't be discussed becomes dangerous by virtue of that suppression), but it seems clear that the dread it arouses is closely bound up with the repression of parent-child eroticism: the Erl-king's desire to violate is the reverse side of the father's protectiveness and denial of the other's existence.

One may find already implicit in "Der Erlkönig" what is perhaps the central question of the horror film today: the question of the extent to which it is possible to conceive of and create a "positive" monster. The repressed cannot be released with impunity. If it didn't constitute a threat, it wouldn't have been repressed in the first place; and to repress a drive is to some degree to distort and pervert it. Any attempt to create a positive monster must steer a perilous and perhaps impossible course between the Scylla of sentimentality and the Charybdis of fascism, dangers one might represent by (among recent distinguished examples) Romero's *Martin* (1978) and Badham's *Dracula* (1979), respectively. It is a problem that reaches out far beyond the horror genre and the cinema: its resolution is central to the future of our civilization.

(1979)

THE DARK MIRROR

Murnau's *Nosferatu*

It is difficult to talk other than tentatively about the work of F. W. Murnau. He directed twenty-two films, of which a number are apparently lost. Of the remainder, all but a few exist only in prints in inaccessible archives. But three of the films still in intermittent circulation seem to me among the cinema's greatest achievements—which is why it is necessary to make some attempt at discussing Murnau despite the handicaps.

Nosferatu (1922), *Sunrise* (1927), and *Tabu* (1931) are not merely remarkable individually. One senses between them a fascinatingly complex relationship of likeness and opposition. The three are widely separated in time and space: Murnau shot *Nosferatu*, his tenth film, in Germany in 1922; *Sunrise* in Hollywood in 1927; *Tabu* in the Pacific islands in 1930 (it was his last film). Oddly, it is *Nosferatu* and *Tabu*, the furthest separated in time, that reveal at once the deepest affinities and the strongest contrasts.

What, in simple terms, have these three obviously very different films in common? *Sunrise* and *Tabu* are easy to relate in that both are single-mindedly concerned with the couple, with the sense of the marriage relationship as having prime and central significance in human life. Beyond this, both films share what one might call the romantic attitude to nature—a life close to nature, based on "natural" simplicities, being upheld against the corruption and artificiality of the city (*Sunrise*) and of white civilization (*Tabu*)—though nature in both films is shown to have a dark, terrible aspect beneath its surface appearance of sunshine and health. But *Nosferatu* is an early version of *Dracula*, antedating Tod Browning and Terence Fisher; its most striking, and apparently central, figure is the vampire count; the film is for the most part a fairly straight retelling of Bram Stoker's familiar narrative that for most people nowadays, at first viewing anyway, seems to live (if at all) by virtue of certain arresting images and compositions, of which the shot of Nosferatu against sky and rigging from the hold of the ship may stand as an example. What has such a horror-fantasy to do with universal concepts like "nature" and "the couple"? The answer is, in Murnau's hands, everything.

The introductory caption might alert us to what is essential in the film: it mentions the Bremen plague, then tells us that "at its origin and its climax were the innocent figures of Jonathan Harker and his young wife Nina." I am going to argue that in *Nosferatu* we have one of the cinema's finest and most powerfully suggestive embodiments of what I call the "descent myth"—one of those universal myths that seem fundamental to human experience. Reduced to its simplest essentials, the descent myth shows characters existing in a state of innocence who by a process of (often literal) descent are led to discover a terrible underlying reality of whose existence they had scarcely dreamed. They either are destroyed by the experience or emerge from it sadder and wiser.

The myth is perhaps fundamental to all civilized existence, suggesting the darker depths beneath our civilized appearances; it also has an odd and ambiguous connection with the Garden of Eden myth. The classic Greek rendering is the myth of Persephone, where it is linked to nature and the seasons, with the Orpheus myth as a variant. But the main lines of the myth recur repeatedly in Western culture and probably in all cultures. In English literature one of its supreme embodiments (as my reference above will have suggested) is the "Ancient Mariner"; but its presence is at least equally striking in Conrad's *Heart of Darkness*. In the cinema it can be seen as activating much of Hitchcock's work: *Psycho* (1960) is one of the great descent films. Recent Bergman, especially *Persona* (1966) and *Face to Face* (1976), can be explored in relation to such a myth. It is common in fairy tales and horror films; its outlines can be discerned, in an emasculated form, lurking in the background of *Chitty Chitty Bang Bang* (1968); its most powerful recent embodiment is in Gary Sherman's *Death Line* (1972, or *Raw Meat*, as the mutilated American-release version was retitled).

The vampire myth and Bram Stoker's development of it easily coalesce with the Descent myth. Indeed, it could be argued that almost everything I am seeking to demonstrate in *Nosferatu* is inherent in vampire mythology. Yet this in no way diminishes the film's stature. Through the power and suggestiveness of his imagery, Murnau really does justice to the rich potentialities of material that (with the notable exception of Dreyer's *Vampyr* [1932]) has generally been merely debased and exploited. It is the quality of the director's response to his material that matters, and I am not concerned with the precise degree to which Murnau was conscious of the implications his film can be seen to have. *Nosferatu* remains itself a myth, with figures who are more archetypes than psychologically rounded characters; Murnau doesn't himself seek to explain the myth, but to embody it in images. What I am forced for the sake of clarity to spell out is in the film a matter of suggestive resonances arising from the intensity with which Murnau *feels* his material, rather than clear-cut allegory.

When Persephone was carried off by Pluto, the god of the underworld, she was gathering flowers in the spring meadows. *Nosferatu* begins with Jonathan gathering flowers for his wife—whom we first see leaning over a flower-filled window box to play with a kitten. Murnau very simply establishes an innocent, almost oversweet, idyllic relationship—though even at the outset a distinction is suggested between the two characters: the young man seeming complacent and overconfident, while a look of sadness and tenderness comes over Nina's face as he gives her the flowers. Jonathan is sent to negotiate a property sale, and early in the film we are shown the house in question, a great derelict building evoking decay and desolation. It is immediately opposite Jonathan and Nina's house—like a mirror, but a mirror in which there is as yet no clearly defined reflection; its position is made much of, visually, in the film's climactic sequences.

Nature is the real subject of *Nosferatu*. The "nature" suggested by Nina's flowers—the daytime nature of sunlight and harmony—is referred to at several points as the film progresses: in the shots of horses moving across a hillside in early morning sunshine, in the shots of the sea sparkling in the sun. Behind this, as it were, is the nighttime nature, the terrible underworld into which Jonathan descends and whose forces he releases. Nosferatu is consistently associated with nature throughout the film. His castle, on its first appearance, is like a natural continuation of the rock, an outcrop. He is identified with the jackal prowling the woods at night—the jackal that startles and unsettles the horses—during the scene at the inn where the landlord warns Jonathan against continuing his journey. Nosferatu's first appearance suggests a nocturnal animal emerging from its lair (the cave-like vault). His movements are not those of a human being; he seems to move silently, with a skulking, sidling motion. His ears are long and pointed and have hair growing on them; his hands and fingernails are like talons or claws; his teeth are fangs.

This "nature" motif is taken up more explicitly elsewhere in the film, notably in Professor Van Helsing's lecture. The caption tells us that "Professor Van Helsing was giving a course on the secrets of nature and their strange correspondences to human life." The lecture we watch is concerned with the venus flytrap and a carnivorous polyp. After it, we see Renfield, Nosferatu's agent in the city, catching and eating flies in his madman's cell; and slightly later he fascinatedly watches spiders devouring their victims in a web. In the sequences of his escape and pursuit Renfield seems to revert to an animal level, swinging down from rooftops like an ape, crouching behind a rotting tree stump, hopping like a frog or toad. These scenes suggest the continuity between the nature the film depicts and human nature—between the exotic venus flytrap, the commonplace spider, and Renfield, and by implication between Nosferatu and ourselves.

The film postulates, then, a duality in nature. Below the surface of sunlight, flowers, and innocence, a terrible undernature, precariously repressed, awaits its chance to surge up and take over. Horses (traditionally the friend of man) belong to the daytime nature; and this gives particularly macabre overtones to the sinister hooded horses that draw the vampire's coach. The transition from the horses that draw Jonathan's coach from the inn to the vampire's horses underlines the symbolism of the crossing of bridges: "And when he had crossed the bridge; the phantoms came to meet him."[22]

Repression imagery dominates the film. Nosferatu emerges from his cave-vault as from under the ground, like a horribly perverted version of D. H. Lawrence's snake driven down into its dark hole. When Jonathan descends into the crypts to find Nosferatu's coffin, he passes under a huge oppressive overhang of rock that also forms part of the castle's structure. The arch is a visual leitmotif in the film. Murnau uses it particularly to characterize the vampire as a repressed force who is always emerging from under arches or arch shapes that seem to be trying unsuccessfully to press down upon him, often forming a background of darkness. That the image is again inherent in vampire mythology is suggested by its recurrence in most vampire films; the traditional setting of Gothic castle inevitably includes arches in association with the other traditional elements of vaults, crypt, coffin, etc. But Murnau's compositions with arches have such striking pictorial force that few will question the validity of finding a more than incidental (though not necessarily fully conscious) significance in them.

The arch is used also to link Nosferatu with Jonathan. There is an arch over the bed in which Jonathan sleeps in the inn—the first effectual appearance

The vampire is a repressed force always emerging from under arches (*Nosferatu*, 1922).

of the image—as he nears the vampire's domain. At their first meeting, Nosferatu emerges from one arch, Jonathan from another, as if he were walking out to meet his reflection. The scene ends with Nosferatu leading the young man down into the darkness of his arched vault—a perfect "descent" image, and one that in its context calls to mind the descent of Cocteau's Orpheus into the underworld via mirrors (i.e., a descent into himself).[23] At the end of the dinner scene, where Nosferatu is roused by the blood from Jonathan's cut finger, the arch structure is very like that from which he first emerged, an alternate patterning of light and darkness. When Jonathan wakes up the next morning, at sunrise, contemptuously dismissing the marks on his neck as of no significance, he is still beneath an arch structure formed by the decor and shadows. He walks out into the open through an arched doorway in long shot, and then under a dark arch that oppressively fills the entire foreground of the image, to write a letter to Nina under the arches of a small pavilion. In the letter he again dismisses the marks on his throat and his bad dreams; the Nosferatu arches comment on his confidence. Jonathan's movement under a series of arch shapes here is later "mirrored" in Nosferatu's nocturnal visit to his bedroom to suck his blood.

The richness of the film's suggestiveness can be seen as the product of a synthesis of a number of traditional or cultural elements fused within the particular sensibility of Murnau: the repressive arches of Gothic fiction and cinema; vampire mythology; the "descent" myth; the notion of the double or doppelgänger, which Lotte Eisner sees as a central motif of Expressionist cinema ("the haunted screen") but which has obvious antecedents in nineteenth-century literature (Poe's "William Wilson," Wilde's *Dorian Gray*).[24] Of Murnau's lost German films, the one that most particularly arouses curiosity (the more so in that it stars the remarkable Conrad Veidt) is *Der Januskopf* (1920), a version of *Dr. Jekyll and Mr. Hyde* that antedates *Nosferatu* by two years.

The linking image of the arch is not the only way in which a parallel is established between Jonathan and Nosferatu. I have already suggested that the house opposite, which Jonathan looks at with such fear, is a mirror awaiting a reflection—a gap that will ultimately be filled by the vampire as he stares across beseechingly at Nina. Nosferatu becomes a kind of demonic alternative husband for Nina, one she must accept with ambiguous desire and revulsion.

The explanatory caption to the contrary, it is not Jonathan who "hears" Nina in the scene of telepathic communication when she interrupts Nosferatu's nocturnal visit to his prey. Jonathan makes no response whatever; it is the vampire who hears Nina, looks up, and moves away, not so much prevented from sucking the man's blood as distracted by a greater, more necessary pull.

André Bazin's opinion that "in neither *Nosferatu* nor *Sunrise* does editing play a decisive part" is even more perverse than his rejection of the view that "the plasticity of Murnau's images has an affinity with a certain kind of expressionism."[25] The elaborate intercutting of Jonathan's and Nosferatu's journeys, and Nina's ambiguous expectation, is crucial to the film's meaning. Jonathan travels by land, the vampire by sea; Nina, awaiting her husband, looks out to sea all the time, from a seashore dotted with crosses that associate her with Christian redemption and death. The hero and his released double reach the city simultaneously, Nosferatu scurrying surreptitiously through the shadows with his coffin as Jonathan rides in. Above all, there is the disturbingly weird incident of Nina's sleepwalking along a parapet, arms outstretched to the darkness. She calls out as she collapses, "He's coming, I must go to meet him." But Murnau has cut to this (and the editing seems here to be consistent in all extant versions of the film), not from Jonathan's ride, but from Nosferatu's inexorable progress by ship.

Jonathan can't destroy Nosferatu—can't even *attempt* to destroy him. Even when the vampire is lying helpless in his coffin during the daytime, all Jonathan can do is recoil in horror. Significantly, it seems to be Jonathan's impotence that gives Nosferatu the power and freedom to leave his environment, shut away from civilization in inaccessible forests and wilds, to rise and spread like a pestilence over the civilized world. Only after Nosferatu has been released in this way can Jonathan summon up his forces for pursuit and combat—though in fact he never does provide any effective opposition to the vampire. Near the end of the film, when Nina makes Jonathan look at the house opposite and begins to tell him, "Every night, in front of me . . . ," he can again do nothing but recoil helplessly and collapse on the bed. He seems not to want to know what Nina sees clearly.

From the moment of Nosferatu's release, Murnau emphasizes the growth of his power. The ship is consistently photographed in ways evoking power,

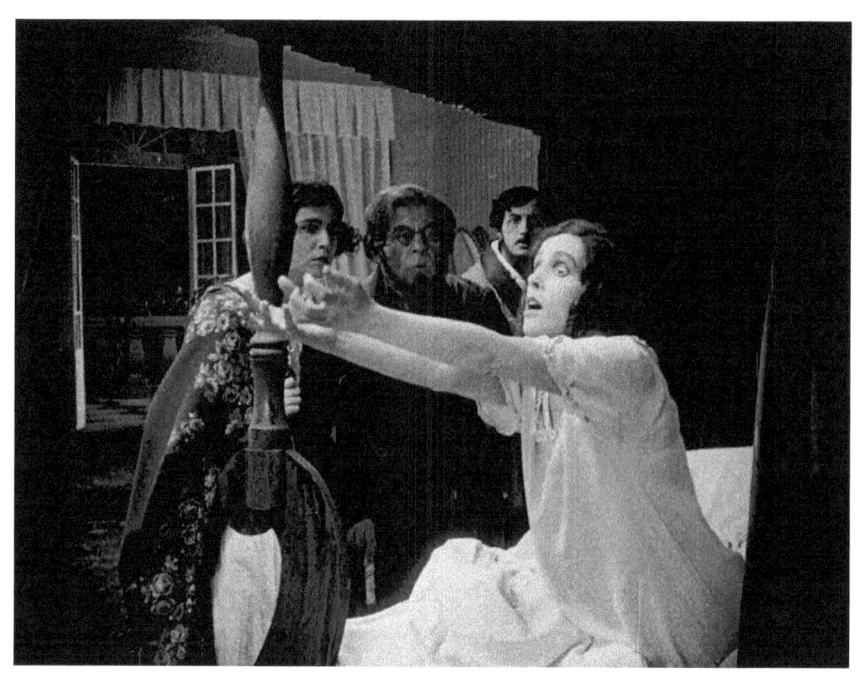

Nina's ambiguous cry that "he's coming" (*Nosferatu*, 1922).

sweeping across the screen so that, instead of being neatly framed and "fixed," it seems to burst into and out of the image; or with the camera on deck behind the prow as it pushes ahead through the waves. At first the ship is guided and controlled by normal human means, normal human consciousness, with Nosferatu hidden away in the hold in his coffins, an unknown presence (the repression motif again). Earlier, the supernaturally opening door—no catch and no lock—into Jonathan's chamber resembled a coffin lid, with the vampire exactly fitting in the door space like a body in a coffin; the resemblance links the film's main repression images, the door having the characteristic arch shape. Gradually, on the ship, the vampire rises up and takes over, undermining and destroying the whole crew, until the ship has become an extension of his power, supernaturally propelled by his mysterious energies. The culminating image here is the one I have already alluded to: Nosferatu, filmed from the hold, seeming immensely tall from so low an angle, moving around the deck against a background of sky and rigging. It's an unforgettable power image.

The sea and its associations are very important in these scenes. The sea should be a barrier, a protection; our sense of security is undermined by the images of the boat bearing Nosferatu sweeping irresistibly across it. The sea is traditionally associated with purity, or purification (as in late Shakespeare), and the suggestion of Nosferatu's power spreading across it intensifies our sense of contamination. The inexorability of his progress is conveyed in another unforgettable shot (and one Murnau was to use again with similar effect in *Tabu*)—in which the ship glides in from the side of the frame completely to fill an image previously occupied by quiet river and quay and sleeping town. Our sense of Nosferatu's power is intensified by the fact that the ship is deserted and is moving without human agency, and by the fact that it is still full-rigged as it slides toward the quay. He enters the town like fate, like a doom.

In the scenes of his progress, his identity as a force of nature, or the underworld of nature, is again implied and strengthened. There are the rats with which he is repeatedly associated, swarming out from the black coffin interiors in which they have been breeding in darkness, then out from the hold when

The low-angle shot of the vampire as he takes control of the ship (*Nosferatu*, 1922).

the ship is in the city; there is also the plague, with which the rats are connected. The exact nature of the plague is left ambiguous; it is spread by the rats, yet the vampire's marks are on the victims' necks, as if Nosferatu had visited each personally. The ambiguity is essential to the film's symbolism, allowing us to view the plague as the eruption both of universal natural forces and of repressed energies in the individual. In this context the thrice-recurring image of the rats swarming out from their coffined darkness is powerfully evocative.

The plague is a means of universalizing the whole idea of the film. Nosferatu is not only in Jonathan, in the marriage, he is in civilization itself. And at about this point Murnau begins to put more emphasis on the animal-like Renfield, who was present in the midst of society from the start, an extension of his "master." We see the impotence of society to combat the forces that have been released in the scenes of the hysterical pursuit of Renfield, where the baffled pursuers vent their fury on a scarecrow.

Nosferatu's real opponent is not Jonathan but Nina. The film endows her, as it does the vampire, with a superhuman force. Just as Nosferatu telepathically controls Renfield at long distance, so Nina is able telepathically to save Jonathan, at the moment when the vampire may destroy him. In the last scenes of the film the sexual overtones inherent in the vampire myth (and exploited throughout the recent British Dracula cycle) become explicit. The window from which Nosferatu watches, like a sinister reflection in a mirror, is opposite the couple's bedroom. It is Nina the vampire wants, from the moment he sees her miniature; and the intercutting of Jonathan's and Nosferatu's journeys—intercut also (as we have seen) with Nina's ambiguous expectations—suggests that the struggle is essentially for *her*. Nina embodies the film's most apparent positive values, the civilized human existence for which human nature, in the form of Nosferatu, has been repressed. Her sacrifice of herself is ambiguously motivated. From her window she watches the procession of coffins down the street and gives herself to remove the plague from the world. But the film also makes clear that she is giving herself to save Jonathan: at her moment of decision, she is stitching a sampler that says, "Ich Liebe Dich." Her sacrifice thus carries Christian overtones more complex and powerful than the hold-up-the-cross-and-splash-him-with-holy-water tactics of most vampire films.

But one must beware of emphasizing this at the expense of the sexual meaning of the last scenes. One is tempted toward a straight psychoanalytical interpretation: Nosferatu is the symbol of neurosis resulting from repressed sexuality (repressed nature); when the neurosis is revealed to the light of day it is exorcised, but the process of its emergence and recognition has been so terrible that positive life (Nina) is destroyed with it. The real energies displayed in the film belong to the vampire. Or another way of looking at it: if one accepts my implication that Jonathan and Nosferatu are really the same character, then Nina must accept in her husband what he himself can't confront or control. At the same time, there is in the images and the acting a suggestion that Nina secretly and ashamedly desires the vampire. It is worth repeating at this point that the film, in the form of myth rather than psychological drama, is by no means restricted to a single allegorical interpretation. Evil (if one can call Nosferatu simply evil) is destroyed; but good is destroyed with it. The ultimate effect, for all the uplift of the final shot of the vampire's shattered castle in the sunlight, is of a tragic pessimism.

Yet this is still to make the ending too simple. I haven't taken into account the very striking change in Murnau's presentation of the vampire in the closing sequences. After building up his monster into a figure of terrible power, Murnau finally presents him as essentially pathetic, helpless, a victim. When he at last appears in the position of a reflection, at the opposite window, he seems suddenly a pitiful old man at Nina's mercy. The image arouses powerfully ambivalent feelings toward the repressed animal nature Nosferatu represents, and the film's most disturbing final effect arises from this. Our sense that the greatest energies in the film are Nosferatu's intensifies the poignance of his helplessness and his destruction; and we cannot entirely evade the feeling that Nosferatu is, in a way, an important part of ourselves. Our attitude to Nina, to Christian sacrifice, to the centuries of "Christian" repression that have made such sacrifice necessary, undergoes subtle modification.

I threw out earlier a comparison with D. H. Lawrence's "Snake."[26] Both the parallel and the difference are very striking. In Lawrence's poem, the snake, like Nosferatu, comes out of a dark hole to become a symbol of all that civilized society disowns and rejects; and the poet, driven by what he calls the "voice of his education," drives it back into the subterranean darkness by casting a log at it. But to Lawrence, the snake, though venomous, is essentially beautiful and pure; he calls it a "god," a "king uncrowned in the underworld, now due to be crowned again," "one of the lords of life"; he is ashamed of the "pettiness" provoked by his "accursed human education," a pettiness he feels he must now "expiate." If one must simply choose, it is perhaps more realistic to see all that civilization has repressed through the centuries emerging as a Nosferatu rather than Lawrence's pure and uncorrupted snake. But few will deny, I hope, that Lawrence's image and the vital positive faith it exemplifies have their validity too—are given it, indeed, by the convincing presence in Lawrence's own work of just those energies the snake symbolizes. To depict our repressed animal natures, our sensuality, solely as a Nosferatu, while opposing to him the somewhat bloodless Nina, cannot but strike us as unhealthy.

The unhealthiness is not only Murnau's; it derives in large measure from the film's background in German Expressionism. If one takes *The Cabinet of Doctor Caligari* (1920) as the Expressionist film par excellence, then one will see that even as early as *Nosferatu* the Expressionist tendencies were already becoming modified and muted in Murnau's work. The chief distinguishing feature of Expressionist style (from which its name derives) is the deformation or distortion of reality for the sake of direct expressive effect. Little in *Nosferatu* corresponds *precisely* to such a description; there is nothing in it like the fantastic, twisted, hallucinatory decors of *Caligari*. On the contrary, one is continually struck by the context of reality given to the horror-fantasy by the use of real locations (doubtless, as Raymond Durgnat has suggested, one of the things that so attracts Georges Franju to Murnau's film)[27]: the wild mountains, the forests, the sea; even the city scenes were largely shot in the streets of Hamburg. Normally, one would stress the film's surprising freedom from Expressionist mannerisms. Nevertheless, Expressionist influence pervades the film. The first shot of the vampire's castle jutting up from the rock, the strange geometrical patterning of arch forms out of which Nosferatu emerges to meet Jonathan, the use of "unnatural" camera angles as in the shot from the hold of the ship, the trick effects, the huge shadow as Nosferatu ascends the stairs to Nina's room, the shadow of his fingers clenching into a fist upon her heart—these are only the more obvious manifestations of the Expressionist manner.

Expressionist design in *The Cabinet of Dr. Caligari* (1920).

But Expressionism in the German cinema was more than a style; it was an atmosphere and an ethos. Among its salient characteristics were an oppressive sense of doom or fate, and an obsessive association of sensuality with evil. By identifying its "doom" figure with repressed sensuality *Nosferatu* makes perfect sense of the coexistence of these characteristics; if it is partly limited by the movement that produced it, it can also be seen as the fulfillment of that movement. And for the film to make sense, it is obvious that Nina *must* be what she is, pallid, emaciated, seeming drained of blood even from the outset, her face at times almost a death's head, in the last scenes agonized and exalted like Christ on the cross. She is the inevitable corollary of the repressed Nosferatu.

Such tendencies are still present in *Sunrise*, again associated with the stylistic characteristics of Expressionism: the hero's wife strikes one as quite sexless, while sensuality (in the person of the Woman from the City) is willfully destructive and evil. Only in *Tabu*—under the complex influences of America, Robert Flaherty, and the Pacific islands—was Murnau able to achieve a healthier, more positive, and integrated attitude toward the body. Significantly, only fleeting traces of Expressionist style remain in that film; and I doubt if one would call them that if one were not alerted by knowledge of Murnau's background.

(1976)

Sisters

I have argued that horror films can be profitably explored from the starting point of applying a simple all-purpose formula: "Normality is threatened by the monster." The formula offers three variables with which to go to work on the analysis of individual films: the definition of "normality," the definition of the "monster," and, crucially, the definition of the relationship between the two. As a general rule, the less easy the application, the more complex and interesting the film, though no horror film is entirely simple (i.e., with the monster as purely external threat). Take *The War of the Worlds* (1953) as an example of the horror film at its simplest (as far as meaning is concerned). There, on surface level, normality = humans, the monster = Martians; this covers (not very concealingly) a second level where normality = the "free world" and the monster = Communism (the news bulletins in the film name every major country but Russia as the victim of "Martian" invasion, an absence that leaves the audience to make a simple deduction). Yet even here the threat only *appears* purely external. The topical fear of Communist invasion in its turn covers a more fundamental fear, and the true subject of horror films, the fear of the release of repressed sexuality: the Martian machines are blatantly phallic, with their snakelike probing and penetrating devices; it is the monogamous heterosexual couple (classical Hollywood's habitual basic definition of "normality") who are centrally threatened; and the film ends with God and nature combining, at the very moment when the whole "world" (i.e., normality) is in imminent danger of destruction, to reunite the couple, annihilate the invaders, and restore repression. The film is also crudely sexist—lip service is paid to female equality, the heroine being supplied with an MA in technological science, but once that's been established all the film gives her to do is scream every time a Martian phallus pokes in through her window. *The War of the Worlds*, then, to which the formula applies very simply, is (like thousands of other films) reducible to the simplest and crudest patriarchal ideology.

The great horror movies demand a far more complex application of the formula. For example, *I Walked with a Zombie* (1943) is structured on a complicated set of oppositions (crudely reducible to normality/monster) that the film systematically undermines until everything is in doubt; in *Psycho* (1960) "normality" and "the monster" no longer function even superficially as separable opposites but exist on a continuum which the progress of the film traces. *Psycho* is clearly a seminal work, definitively establishing (if hardly inventing) two concepts crucial to the genre's subsequent development: the monster as human psychotic/schizophrenic and the revelation of horror as existing at the heart of the family. The continuum is represented not only by the transition from Marion Crane to Norman Bates, but by the succession of references to parent-child relationships that starts with Marion's mother's picture on the wall overseeing the "respectable" steak dinner and culminates in Mrs. Bates. The relevance of *Psycho* to *Sisters* (1972) scarcely needs spelling out, the film being on one level Brian De Palma's conscious homage; its thematic content is in fact very different.

Since *Psycho*, and particularly in the '70s, the horror film has established itself as the major characterizing genre of the period: the two most interesting American directors to emerge in the '70s seem to me Brian De Palma and Larry Cohen, both of whom have gravitated to the horror genre and both of whom pay regular homage in their work to Hitchcock. Here, and in other distinguished modern horror films, the definition of "normality" becomes increasingly uncertain, questionable, open to attack; accordingly, the "monster" becomes increasingly complex.

The force and complexity of *Sisters* (still, I feel, De Palma's finest achievement, and one of the great American films of the '70s) can be demonstrated through the ways in which it responds to the formula. Traditional normality no longer exists in the film as actuality but only as ideology—as what society tries, at once unsuccessfully and destructively, to impose. Specifically, it is what Grace Collier's mother wants to do to Grace (Jennifer Salt) and what Emil Breton (William Finley) wants to do to Danielle/Dominique (Margot Kidder). Grace's mother speaks condescendingly of her daughter's journalism career as her "little job," regards it as a phase she is going through, looks forward to her marrying, and proposes an appropriate suitor; Emil's obsessive project has been to create Danielle as a sweet, submissive girl at the increasing expense of Dominique (eventually provoking Dominique's death). "Normality," therefore, is still marriage, the family, and patriarchy—all that the monster of the horror movie has always implicitly threatened; but whereas in the traditional horror film there had to be an appearance of upholding normality, however sympathetic and fascinating the monster, in *Sisters* normality is not even superficially endorsed. If the monster is defined as "that which threatens normality," it follows that the monster of *Sisters* is Grace as well as Danielle/Dominique: a point the film acknowledges in the climactic hallucination/flashback sequence wherein Grace becomes Dominique, joined to Danielle as her Siamese twin, the film's privileged moment on which its entire significance hinges. Simply, one can define the "monster" of *Sisters* as women's liberation; adding only that the film follows the time-honored horror film tradition of making the monster emerge as the most sympathetic character and its emotional center.

Sisters analyzes the ways in which women are oppressed within patriarchal society on two levels, which one can define as the professional (Grace) and the psychosexual (Danielle/Dominique). Grace's progress in the film can be read as a depiction of how women are denied a voice. At times this can be taken

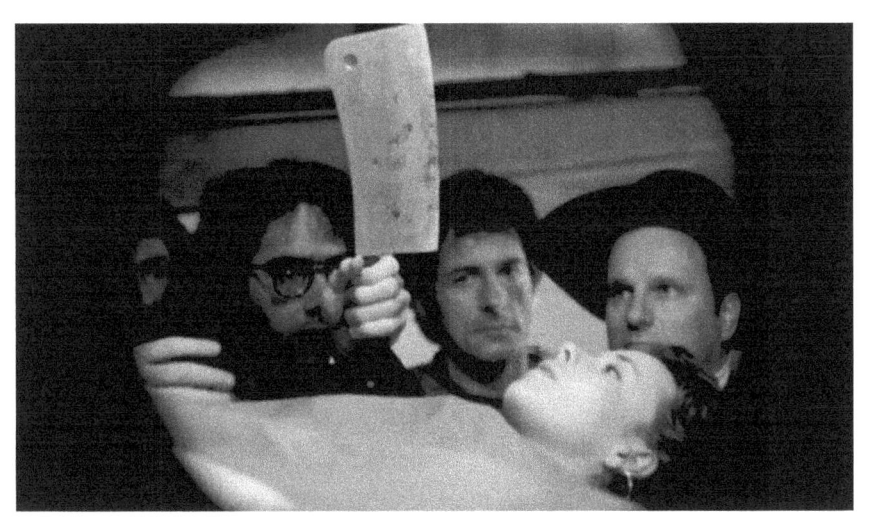

The hallucination sequence is punishment for usurping the gaze (*Sisters*, 1972).

literally: the police inspector denies Grace the right to ask questions or to make verbal interventions; in the asylum she is prevented from using the phone, her attempts to assert her sanity (and even her own name) are overruled, and she is silenced by being put to sleep. More widely, her professional potency is frustrated at every step: the police refuse to believe her story; her editor habitually gives her ludicrous assignments such as the convict who has carved a model of his prison out of soap; her mother tries to make her "normal"; even when she gets permission to pursue her investigations, it must be under the guidance of a (male) private detective (Charles Durning); the detective rejects her spontaneous ideas in favor of the methods he has been taught in school. Finally, rendered powerless by a drug, she is given her words by Emil Breton: all she will be able to repeat when she wakes up is "There was no body because there was no murder." At the end of the film she is reduced to the role of child, tended by her mother, surrounded by toys, herself denying the truth of which she once alone had possession.

Also—and this is where the Hitchcock/De Palma fascination with voyeurism becomes incorporated significantly in the film's thematic structure—Grace transgresses by her desire to usurp the male prerogative of the look. The opening of *Sisters* succinctly establishes the gaze as another means of male dominance: Danielle is blind; not only does Philip watch her begin to undress, but we, the cinema audience (thus defined by identification as male) also watch. This is of course immediately and brilliantly undercut: we discover that, having allowed ourselves to be drawn into the voyeuristic act, we have identified ourselves less with Philip than with the lewd and philistine panel (with male and female members) of a particularly mindless TV show. But, having established "looking" as a theme at the outset, De Palma can take it up again later. There, it is Grace who aspires to the "look" of dominance, the look that will give her knowledge, and it is for this that she is most emphatically punished—the hallucination sequence is introduced by Emil's telling her that, as she wanted to see, she will now be forced to witness everything, and it is punctuated by huge close-ups of her terrified eye. What Grace "sees" is the ultimate subjugation (castration) of woman by man.

When Danielle/Dominique murders Philip, her attack is on the two organs by which male supremacy is most obviously enforced, the phallus and the voice (the shot of the knife being driven into his mouth, as a shadow on the wall, seems to be missing from all British prints, presumably removed by the censor); the logic of the film perhaps would also demand that she blind him. Through the presentation of Danielle/Dominique the theme of women's oppression is given another dimension, an altogether more radical level. Crucial to it is the opposition the film makes between "freaks" and mad people. Freaks are a product of nature; the insane are a product of society ("normality"). The two mad people we see are simply carrying to excess two of society's most emphasized virtues, tidiness and cleanliness: the man obsessively trimming hedges with his shears in the night, the woman with her cleaning cloth terrified of the germs that can be transmitted through telephone wires; both pervert the "virtue" into aggression. (One might note here that the detective's van assumes two disguises in the course of the film, first that of a housecleaning firm, later that of "Ajax Exterminators"). Freaks, on the other hand, are natural: it is "normality" that names, degrades, rejects, or seeks to remold them (see Danielle's horror, in the hallucination sequence, not of being a freak but of being named as one). The morality of using real freaks (the photographs of genuine Siamese twins in the videotape Grace is shown, the various freaks discernible in the hallucination sequence) may be touched on here, and the essential point made by comparing De Palma's use of them with Michael Winner's in the worst (most offensive and repressive) horror film of the '70s, *The Sentinel* (1977). Winner, with his usual taste and humanity, uses real freaks, unforgivably, for their (socially defined) ugliness, to represent demons surging up out of hell. De Palma uses them, in a film that consistently and subversively undercuts all assumptions of the "normal," to symbolize all that "normality" cannot cope with or encompass. To object, in this context, to the association of women's liberation with "freaks" would be simply to endorse "normality's" definition. "Freaks" only become freaks when "normality" names them; to her mother, as to the police inspector, Grace is clearly a "freak," hence the mother's appearance with a camera in the hallucination sequence, where Grace becomes Dominique. Danielle/Dominique function both literally and symbolically: literally, as "freaks" whom "normality" has no place for, must "cure," hence destroy; symbolically, as a composite image of all that must be repressed under patriarchy (Dominique) in order to create

Sisters - 137

the "nice," "wholesome," submissive female (Danielle). Dominique's rebellion against patriarchal normality took the extreme but eloquent form of killing Danielle's (unborn) baby with garden shears after which Emil killed her by separating her from her twin. What is repressed is not of course annihilated: Dominique continues to live on in Danielle. Further, the point is made (and underlined by repetition: the speech of the priest in the videotape that recurs during the hallucination sequence) that Danielle's sweetness depends on the existence of Dominique, on to whom all her "evil" qualities can be projected. Equally, Dominique is Danielle's potency: the scar of separation, revealed by the slow zoom-in to her body as she and Philip make love, is also the "wound" of castration. Having deprived Danielle of her power (creating her as the male ideal of the "sweet" girl), Emil can realize a union with her only when she (or the "repressed" Dominique), in turn, has castrated him, signified by his pressing their clasped hands into the blood of his wound.

The intelligence (and radicalism) of the film is manifested in its refusal to produce a scapegoat, in the form of an individual male character who can be blamed. Philip is an entirely sympathetic figure, Emil ultimately a pathetic one (he loves Danielle in precisely the way ideology conditions men to love women). He is also one of De Palma's hopeless romantic lovers, played by William Finley who was to fill the same role a year later in *Phantom of the Paradise* (1974).

Philip, moreover, provides a further extension of the oppression theme in being black. The film at no point presents his color as an "issue" but shows it as an issue for white-dominated "normality" (his prize for his TV appearance is dinner for two in The African Room; the police sergeant's comment is that "those people [i.e., blacks] are always stabbing each other"). The amiable private investigator asserts his authority over Grace because he is placed in that position. The final image of him (last shot of the film), up a telegraph pole by a tiny railway depot somewhere in remote Quebec, watching the sofa containing Philip's body, which there is nobody left alive to collect, is at once funny and poignant. The assertion of male dominance in the film is shown everywhere as destructive; nowhere as successful; variously misguided, disastrous, and futile.

One must not, however, look to *Sisters* for any optimistic portrayal of liberation. If the horror film of the '70s has lost all faith in "normality," it simultaneously sees all that "normality" repressed (the monster) as, through repression, perverted beyond redemption. In its apocalyptic phase, the horror film, even when it is not concerned literally with the end of the world (*The Omen* [1976]), brings its own world to cataclysm, refusing any hope of positive resolution (see, to name three distinguished and varied examples, *The Texas Chainsaw Massacre* [1974], *Carrie* [1976], and *God Told Me To* [1976]). The most disquieting aspect of *Sisters* is that the two components of its composite "monster," Grace and Danielle/Dominique, are in constant and unresolved antagonism. They operate on quite distinct levels of consciousness: Danielle tells Philip near the beginning of the film that she is not interested in women's liberation; Grace clearly is, but only on the professional level. Even when forced together (as Siamese twins) they are constantly straining apart. The deeper justification for the use of split screen (which also works brilliantly on the suspense level) is that it simultaneously juxtaposes and separates the two women, presenting them as parallel yet antagonistic.

The question whether *Sisters* is really "about" the oppression of women or is "just" a horror movie is one that I decline to discuss. It is, however, illuminating to place it beside a Hollywood film whose concern with women's liberation is conscious and overt, *Alice Doesn't Live Here Anymore* (1974). *Alice* (a charming, indeed disarming, film) is a perfect example of what Roland Barthes calls "inoculation": ideology inoculates itself with a small dose of criticism in order to distract attention from its fundamental evils.[28] The opening of the film (after the childhood prologue) depicts an impossible marital situation, wherein the woman is ignored, taken for granted, or maltreated, her role as wife and mother being assumed to be all she needs. The end of the film unites her with a man who will treat her well, permit discussion, and perhaps allow her to pursue her own career on the side: the patriarchal order is restored, suitably modified. *Sisters* is beyond such inoculation. On the one hand, ideology can always render anything safe by labelling it: to label *Sisters* a "horror film" is to place it beyond serious discussion. On the other hand, it is only under the disguise of being "just entertainment" (a disguise that may fool the filmmakers as much as the public) that really subversive films can be made in Hollywood. *Sisters* may be the only really radical feminist film Hollywood has given us since the heyday of Dietrich and Sternberg.

(1979)

World of Gods and Monsters

The Films of Larry Cohen

It can be no accident that three of the most interesting directors to emerge in the Hollywood cinema of the '70s—Brian De Palma, Tobe Hooper, and Larry Cohen—have all gravitated to the horror film. Or, to approach the same phenomenon from another viewpoint, no accident that it is within the horror genre that the most interesting work is currently being produced. I have argued that the evolution of the American horror film can be read in terms of the evolution of a national collective unconscious.[29] The 1970s have seen the raw materials of the horror film develop to the point where their significance and implications (concealed earlier by the insistence on the exotic, the bizarre, the foreign, and by notions of "entertainment" and "escapist fantasy") are at last fully recognizable: the "double" motif, the definition of the monster as the product of the normality it threatens (the return of what normality represses), the location of horror at the heart of the bourgeois-capitalist family.

What the horror film now insists upon is the impossibility (not just undesirability) of a society founded upon monogamy and family and their inherent repressiveness. The horror film has entered its apocalypse phase (sometimes literally, as in the two Omen films [1976, 1978] or *Holocaust 2000* [*The Chosen*, 1977]). In the characteristic '70s horror film, the stress is on powerlessness and uncontrollability, and nothing can be saved; "good" is destroyed with "evil." The monster can no longer be repressed, but neither can it be conceived in positive terms. If the energies it represents were once positive—and the energies of many contemporary "monsters," such as De Palma's Danielle/Dominique (in *Sisters* [1972]) and Carrie, have strong positive connotations—they have been perverted, turned destructive, by the length and thoroughness of the repression.

Without getting drawn into useless questions of what is conscious and what unconscious in an artist's work, one can suggest that different degrees or levels of consciousness are demonstrable, in general terms, in different oeuvres. It may be only through a consciousness of issues (as opposed to plot, characterization, emotional effect, etc.) that the horror film can develop beyond its present apocalyptic despair. Any work of construction demands analysis as its starting point.

The work of Larry Cohen is clearly enough circumscribed within the syndrome I have described. It does not offer an alternative, except by implication, to a society perceived as locked in the processes of its self-destruction. But the particular distinction of *It's Alive* (1974) and *God Told Me To* (1976) can partly be defined by saying that they could only have been made by someone aware of the issues. This does not affect my argument that horror films represent our collective nightmares and depend for their existence on a certain relaxation of consciousness. The play between conscious and unconscious (which can take an infinite number of forms) is central to the phenomenon we call art.

The material of Cohen's films, however personal (and I shall show how consistent his work to date has been), is also central to the evolution of the horror film; his films, like those of other filmmakers, are the product of a given culture at a given phase of history. But the artist—any artist—is not entirely helpless or determined; anyone who has attempted to analyze his own dreams (which will inevitably bear a significant relationship to the dreams of others within the same culture) will know that it is possible to achieve a certain degree of dominance over them. The conscious artist—the conscious part of any artist—does not so much invent dreams as inflect the available ones, pointing their significance, perhaps redirecting them.

Cohen and De Palma

An attempt to define Cohen's work can profitably begin by comparing it with De Palma's; their careers to date offer remarkable parallels that serve to illuminate the differences. In their early works, both directors use blacks as a threat to white supremacy, a variant on the "return of the repressed" theme: De Palma in the extraordinary "Be Black, Baby" section of *Hi, Mom!* (1970) (and, although not presented as a threat, Philip in *Sisters* is relevant here);

Cohen in *Black Caesar* (1973), *Hell Up in Harlem* (1973), and, very impressively, in *Bone* (1972). Both directors have attempted overtly experimental works early in their careers, disrupting the conventions of realist narrative (*Greetings* [1968], *Hi, Mom!*; *Bone*). Both have returned repeatedly to the horror film *(Sisters, Carrie* [1976], *The Fury* [1978]; *It's Alive, God Told Me To, It Lives Again* [1978]). Both have abandoned their early experimentalism, temporarily at least, to express an obviously genuine (not merely commercial) allegiance to the Hollywood tradition. Thus De Palma "remakes" *Phantom of the Opera* (1925, 1943) as *Phantom of the Paradise* (1974), *Psycho* as *Sisters*, *Vertigo* (1958) as *Obsession* (1976), in each case producing a valid variation rather than imitation. In the case of Cohen, the allegiance is expressed less specifically (though *Black Caesar* very consciously transposes the structures of the '30s gangster film, drawing particularly on *Little Caesar* [1931] and *Scarface* [1932]) but seems even stronger.

One form it takes is Cohen's extensive use of Hollywood old-timers: Sylvia Sidney and Sam Levene in *God Told Me To*, and most of the cast of *The Private Files of J. Edgar Hoover* (1977) (Broderick Crawford, Dan Dailey, Celeste Holm, June Havoc, Jose Ferrer). The choice of Miklos Rozsa to score *Hoover* is also relevant here, Cohen using his "stirring" end music with splendid irony. Cohen also wanted Rozsa for *God Told Me To*; Rozsa has been quoted as saying that he saw the movie and God told him not to, a smart line that unfortunately rebounds.

The most obvious link is the common debt to Alfred Hitchcock (who, with *Shadow of a Doubt* [1943], *Psycho* [1960], *The Birds* [1963], and *Marnie* [1964], might reasonably be called the father of the modern horror film). Here one should include Tobe Hooper as well: the buildup to the first killing in *The Texas Chainsaw Massacre* (1974) is worthy, shot by shot, of the master in the sophistication of its suspense devices, its play with suggestion, expectation, relaxation, the subtle discrepancies between the characters' awareness and the audience's. The influence is most obvious in De Palma because deliberately flaunted, an aspect of the signified, but it is clear enough in Cohen, in the overt homage of the staircase assault in *God Told Me To* and more pervasively in the suspense techniques (including subjective camera) of *It's Alive*. Most specifically, there is the use both directors have made of Bernard Herrmann, who composed the scores for *Sisters*, *Obsession*, and *It's Alive*, and to whom *God Told Me To* is dedicated; he also receives a posthumous credit for the score of *It Lives Again*.

De Palma's work has achieved great commercial success and widespread (though still insufficient) critical attention; Cohen's has achieved neither. *It's Alive* did well enough at the box office, but *Bone*, *God Told Me To*, and *Hoover*—all very difficult box-office propositions requiring careful and intelligent handling—have been thrown away. Cohen's work is scarcely referred to by critics, though *It's Alive* was summarily dismissed in a recent *Film Comment* as a *Rosemary's Baby / Exorcist* rip-off (I think it is more intelligent than either and owes them about as much as *Rio Bravo* [1959] owes *High Noon* [1952]).[30] It can be argued that Cohen has not yet achieved the brilliance of *Sisters*, but his oeuvre to date strikes me as easily the more satisfying and consistent of the two. Why, then, this neglect?

One might start with the word "brilliance," which for me always carries a hint of possible pejorative overtones: *Carrie* and *The Fury* are also "brilliant," and arouse a fear that the showman in De Palma is going to take over completely, that the interest of his films is becoming submerged beneath the desire to dazzle with an ever more flamboyant rhetoric and effects out of all proportion to meaning. Cohen, on the other hand, never attracts attention to himself; his work relates back beyond the director-as-superstar era to the classical Hollywood tradition of directorial self-effacement. I would find it difficult to describe a Cohen visual style that would clearly distinguish his work from the mainstream of contemporary cinema; like a Hawks or a McCarey he is content so far to work within the anonymity of generally accepted stylistic-technical procedures. Indeed, if his work stands out stylistically from a cinema given more and more to forcing itself on the spectator, it is precisely because of a frequent refusal to underline effects or insist on points. One tiny example: in *God Told Me To* the protagonist, visiting the woman who turns out to be his mother in her old people's home, is instructed by the overcasual nurse to take the first door on the left; he takes, correctly, the first door on the right. The point is given no emphasis whatever, whether in acting (gestures of hesitation), editing (a "significant" track-in or zoom). At that stage of the narrative, it seems without any meaning. It is only subsequently that we register it (if we remember it at all) as the first hint of the protagonist's supernatural powers.

The peculiar distinction of De Palma's work lies in its disturbing and paradoxical fusion of an extreme passionate romanticism with an equally extreme self-consciousness and obtrusive technical sophistication. Both are foreign to Cohen, who consistently refuses his audiences both the visual kicks of split screen and slow motion and the satisfaction of emotional identification with a central figure that largely accounts for *Carrie*'s commercial success. On the one hand, we regard his protagonists more critically, from a greater distance; on the other, we see them as people (however fallible) more capable of choice, of thinking and learning. De Palma is the readier simply to surrender to, express, and reinforce the prevailing desperation of the modern American cinema; Cohen's work, while offering no "solutions," is far more critical and analytical. There is the sense that he, his protagonists, and his audience, have more freedom, more space to breathe.

Cohen as Auteur

IF IT IS DIFFICULT to define Cohen as yet in terms of stylistics, it is relatively easy in terms of theme and structure. It is worth noting here that all of the Cohen films to date are "written, produced, and directed by Larry Cohen"; all are original screenplays, not adaptations; all are Larco productions. Insofar as it can be said of anyone, he is in complete control of his own work.

Two structural features, closely interconnected, dominate his films:

1. The refusal of the "hero." No one in Cohen's films is "right," no one is glorified, no one is exonerated. Not only is there no character with whom the spectator can identify (as distinct from "feel sympathy for"), there is no "correct" position offered within the action in relation to its conflicts, the resolution in every case leaving a sense of dissatisfaction, uncertainty, or loss. The inherent but conventionally suppressed ambivalence of the hero-villain, hero-monster dichotomy is here brought to the surface, made explicit, in a dialectic in which neither term is endorsed (though neither is simply denounced or designated evil). Implicit in this is a radical (rather than liberal) critique of Western capitalist culture. There is never a suggestion that things can be put right, solutions be found, within the system; the conflicts are presented as fundamental and unresolvable, short of a total rethinking.

2. Central to the Cohen structure is the figure of the double, which I have suggested is the privileged form of the "return of the repressed" in horror

movies: the recognition of the monster not as external threat but as other side of the coin, normality's mirror image. The films' recurring structure can be rendered in terms of a formula: the protagonist learns to recognize his identity with the figure he is committed to destroying. As with my horror film formula—"Normality is threatened by the monster"—the intention is not at all to collapse all the films into a single, simple meaning, but to provide a starting point from which their individual complexities can be explored. There has been to date no repetition in Cohen's work. Each film constitutes a significant variation on this basic structure (which is more obviously central to some, namely the horror films, than to others), as the notes that follow will attempt to show.

Bone (*Beverly Hills Nightmare, Dial Rat for Terror, Housewife*)

THIS IS THE FILM about which I must be most tentative. It is Cohen's most obviously difficult work, an example of that generally doomed phenomenon, the attempt by an American director at the equivalent of a European art-house movie (compare *Puzzle of a Downfall Child* [1970], *Mickey One* [1965], and *Images* [1972], which I list in what I believe to be descending order of artistic merit), though it is much less anxious than its fellows to impose its signifiers of "artisticness." And it is virtually inaccessible. (I have seen it only once, at a screening specially arranged for me in the Museum of Modern Art, in the middle of which two security guards attempted to evict me from the auditorium, despite the fact that I was the only person present and the film was presumably being projected for someone. I lost about ten minutes, and concentration was seriously hindered.) *Bone* is the only Cohen film to date that is not easily classifiable within a genre. If it reminds one of any other movie, it is *Weekend* (1968), to which its opening seems to pay homage. As in Godard's film, the action is loosely centered on the desire of husband and wife to destroy each other, money greed being the chief motivation.

The film opens with an executive from a car company (Andrew Duggan), microphone in hand, giving what appears to be a TV commercial. The camera zooms out to reveal that he is in a junkyard and that the cars are all wrecks; subsequent shots show that they are filled with bloody corpses. It is important that the level of "reality" here is never defined (as nightmare, fantasy, or whatever). Unlike *Weekend*, the main body of the film operates in terms of a heightened naturalism; the action, however unpredictable, is plausible enough within a mode of caustic satire. But no level of "reality" is maintained consistently, so that the viewer's illusionist involvement is continually threatened and at times undermined. The film allows its audience no security whatever.

The action proper begins with the executive and his wife beside their Beverly Hills swimming pool; a rat emerges from the drain, as succinct an image for the return of the repressed as one could ask for. (There is a thesis to be written on the significance of the rat in contemporary cinema, from *Willard* [1971] and *Ben* [1972] up through *Straw Dogs* [1971]—"Rats is life"—to *Last Tango in Paris* [1972] and Dusan Makevejev's *Switchboard Operator* [*Love Affair, or the Case of the Missing Switchboard Operator*, 1967].) A phone call to the pool-servicing company produces nothing but indifference; but Bone (Yaphet Kotto) materializes abruptly beside the pool as if in answer to it, kills the rat, and proceeds to take over the household, keeping the wife (Joyce van Patten) under threat of rape and murder while the husband goes into town to draw ransom money. The latter, however, meets Jeanie Berlin in the bank and decides to leave his wife to her fate. She, realizing she has been abandoned, enlists Bone in a plot to kill her husband—and the two couples become mirror images of each other. At first, the Berlin character's kookiness seems to be offered as a positive: bourgeois eccentricity against bourgeois conformism. Subsequently, it is revealed as the mere cover of neurosis.

Two issues become central:

1. Bone as a symbol of the forces white capitalist society represses. Although the film's nearest approach to a "positive" character, he is presented as involved in the same processes, the same value system, as the white oppressors. The killing of the rat is itself an ambiguous action: Bone has the power to do what the corrupt and affluent whites are incapable of; yet the rat (Liberty Valance to Bone's Tom Doniphon?) is a symbol of the energies bourgeois civilization represses. Bone's challenge to the supremacy of the white world is more apparent than real. When he attempts to carry out the threatened rape of the wife, he is impotent; they make love later when she wants him. Like the protagonist

of *Black Caesar*, his impulse is to reverse the terms rather than change them. The film never suggests that he is the answer to anything.

2. The hypocrisy of bourgeois-capitalist marriage/family. The couple are held together purely by money; when that tie proves illusory (the husband is in up to his ears and has been secretly swindling his wife), their essential hatred of each other surfaces. Their beloved son is supposed to be a prisoner in Vietnam (a myth they have almost convinced themselves is true); in fact, he is in a Spanish jail for dope smuggling—his parents could have used their money to buy him out but the sacrifice was too great. The end of the film intercuts the mother battering the father to death on a vast sand bank with the son laughing hysterically in his cell; Bone, having no force that can offset the entrapment in familial guilt, vanishes as abruptly as he appeared.

Bone might be regarded as Cohen's *Mickey One*; I am not sure how successful it is, though it clearly lacks the vagueness and sentimentality that flaw Penn's film. At the least, it makes explicit Cohen's ambition, a characteristic that the modest genre frameworks of *Black Caesar* and *It's Alive* (films no less ambitious, in their implications) conceal. The "double" motif is less obvious here than in any of the other films; in a sense, it is diffused through the whole structure, all the characters mirroring each other in their entrapment in a process. But a local instance is provided in the husband's acceptance that he is the man who molested Jeanie Berlin in a cinema when she was thirteen—an acceptance based less on any certainty that he is than on a feeling that there is no reason why he shouldn't be.

Black Caesar

COHEN'S ANALYTICAL INTELLIGENCE IS immediately manifested in the way in which he rises to the challenge of a blaxploitation movie with Fred Williamson. Characteristically, he rigorously rejects what appeared to be one of the genre's basic conditions: the celebration of the black hero. The film is deliberately modeled on the '30s gangster films evoked by its title and inherits their ambivalence toward the gangster protagonist. Here, however, the violence—whether that of the oppressive white world or that of black retaliation—is never exhilarating (as it is, for example, in *Scarface*), never accompanied by any sense of release or satisfaction.

The film takes as premise the protagonist's humiliation in youth, as a delinquent shoeshine boy, at the hands of a white police detective, and his desire for revenge on the white world in general and the policeman in particular. Its point is that, sharing the world's ideological entrapment, its materialistic values, his imagination cannot rise above the aim of reversing its terms without changing them. His purchase of the high-rise apartment where his mother works as maid (complete with its white owners' furnishings, pictures, clothes, etc.) in order to install her in it, merely destroys her sense of role without replacing it, leaving her lost and empty amid luxuries that continue to intimidate and oppress her. He himself can find nothing to do with all the expensive clothes but fling them from the high balcony in a gesture of grandeur and futility. The film moves logically to the scene that stamps it as Cohen's: with the policeman at last in his power, the protagonist blacks his victim's face with shoe polish before killing him. The psychological motivation is to repeat, in reverse, the initial act of humiliation; for the movie audience, the two become mirror images, equally monstrous, locked in a common process whose only resolution is the acknowledgment of futility.

The ending of the film, with the protagonist returning to his childhood slum tenement (now half demolished, but with no sign of any rebuilding) to die, is quite different in effect from the moralistic endings of *Little Caesar* and *Scarface*: not the reimposition of established values but a reminder of the social roots of the evil and an acknowledgment that nothing has been achieved. The overt expression of a revolutionary commitment is still impossible within the Hollywood system, and there is no evidence that Cohen would wish to offer it. But it is implicit in all the films that the revolutionary position—on all levels, social, political, sexual, personal—is the only tenable one.

Hell Up in Harlem

Hell Up in Harlem (the instant sequel) is much less successful: one suspects at its basis a battle between Cohen and the star persona Fred Williamson was beginning to develop. The presentation of the central figure (carried straight over from the previous film, *Hell*'s first ten minutes borrowing lavishly from its footage and rewriting its ending, with the protagonist saved from death and hospitalized in a sequence directly anticipating *It's Alive*) is less secure, more ambiguous, his monstrousness compromised by a tendency to glorification. The film looks as though it were thrown together in a great hurry, the narrative is incoherent, the sequences very uneven in interest. There are a number of characteristic moments: the scene where Williamson and his gang force the white leaders of a drug organization to eat "soul food" and sing "The Star-Spangled Banner"; the brilliant use of an airport baggage collection area in a climactic scene of violence (with the brutal but unobtrusive irony of a sign saying "No live animals" as a body is pushed down a delivery chute); the final reversal of a black man lynching a white (a variant on the shoe-polish climax of *Black Caesar*). Cohen undercuts the attempts to build the Williamson character into a conventional blaxploitation hero in several ways: the theme of his moralistic crusade against drug traffic is simply dropped; interest is deflected from him to his father (Julius W. Harris), who becomes the film's emotional center, the theme of his destruction by his own son carried over and developed from the previous film; the apparently optimistic ending (Williamson's rescue of his child) is countered with a chilling irony ("I'll love you like I loved my father"). But for all the film's crude energy the final effect is stalemate.

It's Alive

THE RELATIONSHIP OF *It's Alive* to the Satanist cycle is more that of intelligent comment than of "rip-off." What is crucial to the film—and profoundly characteristic of Cohen—is its difference from all the other "monstrous child" movies of the past decade, notably in its resolute refusal of any Christian-metaphysical explanation and/or solution. Unlike *The Exorcist* (1973), it does not reimpose repression at the end (the destruction of the baby is by no means regarded as positive). And unlike *Rosemary's Baby* (1968) and *The Omen*, it does not present the birth as the inevitable outcome of ancient prophecy, its consequences beyond anyone's control. Cohen's films never repress the possibility of imagining that the world might be changed; indeed, they implicitly encourage it.

The film takes up from *Bone* the concern with the family, though the scathing tone of the earlier film here gives way to sympathy and compassion. The opening offers Frank Davis (John Ryan), his wife (Sharon Farrell), and son as the model American nuclear family, affectionate, humorous, warm, relaxed—except that no one is really relaxed, and the tension in retrospect is not entirely accountable for by the fact that Lenore is about to give birth to another child. Frank chews gum all the time and has a curiously aggressive-humorous way of awakening his son (applying the family cat to the back of the boy's neck). The sweetness and light of the family relationship begins to appear an artificial construction, imposed above all by the father, epitomized by the wallpaper above Chris's bed which loudly advertises the word "LOVE." Before the departure for the hospital, Frank pauses proudly in the doorway of the new nursery, in the attitude of creator-proprietor, and we note that the walls are blue; in the car, Lenore tells Chris that they'll phone to tell him if he's got "a baby sister or a baby brother." The lies on which the relationship is built are represented for us later by the casual hypocrisy of Frank's claim that he has generously taken a vacation for Lenore's sake (he has in effect been laid off from his public relations job, against his will and despite his protests, because of the "scandal" of the new baby). Nevertheless, the film gains strength from the sense that the Davises represent the bourgeois-capitalist family at its best rather than (as in *Bone*) its worst: we are not allowed to dissociate from them as a "special case."

The monster-child is never explained by the film, though two possible explanations are hinted at. The first, made fairly explicit in the scene in the

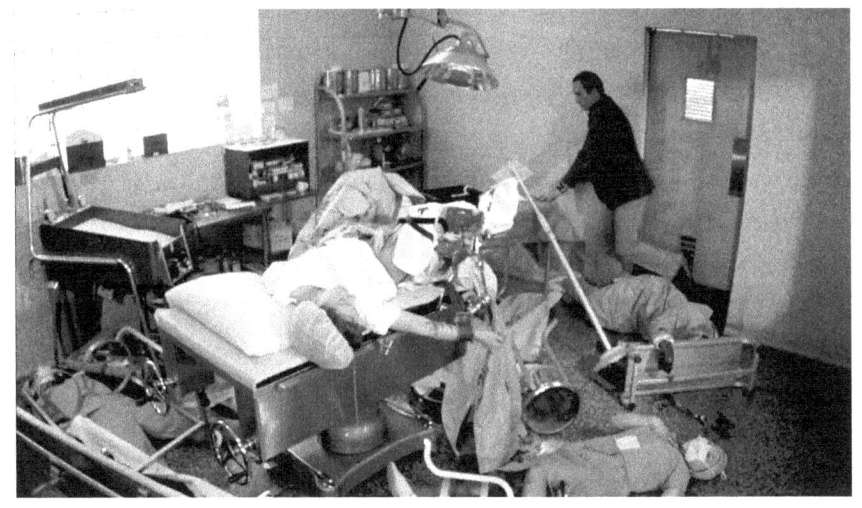

Carnage in the delivery room in *It's Alive* (1974).

hospital waiting room before the birth, is ecological: the child is the product of man's pollution of his own environment. The second, implicit but much more pervasive, is that the child is actually the logical product of the family itself. The two explanations are not incompatible. Frank's role as head of the patriarchal-capitalist family is not distinct from his work role as public-relations man; in both, he is a complacent and typical member of the social order, committed to and dependent upon its continuance. The concept of pollution becomes as much metaphorical as literal.

The film is centered on the process whereby Frank moves from rejection to acceptance of the child as his own. Around the midpoint of the film he reminisces about the movie-going experience of his youth: he always thought "Frankenstein" was the name of the monster, not the creator. The reference is crucial, giving point both to the film's title (the phrase "It's alive!" echoes down through the horror film, of course, but the strongest association, and presumably its source in the sound film, is James Whale's *Frankenstein* [1931]) and to the protagonist's christian name. Who, ultimately, is the more monstrous, creator or creature, progenitor or progeny—when the latter is, in both cases, the embodiment of what is repressed in the former? The climactic line of Frank's speech ("Somehow, the identities get all mixed up, don't they?") might stand as epigraph for all Cohen's films to date.

The action of the film alternates between the child's inexorable progress home to demand recognition by the family (via the school playroom of the "good" son, the theme of brotherhood extending the "double" motif), and Frank's development from disowning his offspring (to the point of wishing himself to be the one to kill it) to passionately accepting and defending it in the Los Angeles sewers to which (like the giant ants of *Them!* [1956]) society has driven it. The ending of the film (the child's destruction, followed immediately by the announcement that another has been born elsewhere), besides offering the opening for a sequel, extends and generalizes its theme: not just this family—any family.

God Told Me To (Demon)

For me, God Told Me To is Cohen's most fascinating film to date, and the most ambitious in theme (while characteristically modest in budget and treatment).

Frank (John P. Ryan) at first disavows his monstrous child (*It's Alive*, 1974).

Its subject is no less than the repression of bisexuality within Christian patriarchal culture. The film strikes me as somewhat less than completely realized: its science-fiction aspects are cumbersome, its narrative sometimes awkward, and one wants almost everything in it developed more fully. It should be seen, perhaps, as a sketch for the great movie Cohen may make one day.

A police detective (Tony Lo Bianco), reared a strict Catholic, but with both a wife (Sandy Dennis) and a lover (Deborah Baffin), investigating a series of apparently random and motiveless killings by various assassins, traces them to the inspiration of a young god, born of a human virgin impregnated by light from a spacecraft. He also discovers, however, that he is himself another such "god," though in him the supernatural force has been repressed by his Catholic-orthodox upbringing. He kills (or seems to kill) his unrepressed "brother," and ends up convicted of murder, repeating as explanation of his motive the phrase used earlier by each of the assassins: "God told me to."

The god is conceived as both beautiful and vicious. Like the snake of D. H. Lawrence's famous poem,[31] he is associated with danger, energy, and fire—with forces that society cannot encompass and therefore decrees must be destroyed. His disruption of the social order is arbitrary, involving a series of meaningless sniper killings, the devastating of the St. Patrick's Day Parade, and the annihilation of a family by its father; yet the imagery associated with him (the dance of light and flame) gives him stronger positive connotations than any other manifestation of the return of the repressed in Cohen's work, or indeed in any other contemporary horror film.

Crucial to the film is the god's dissolution of sexual differentiation: apparently male, he has a vagina, and invites the protagonist to father their child. The new world he envisages is, by implication, a world in which the division of sexual roles will cease to exist. What is proposed is no less than the overthrow of the entire structure of patriarchal ideology. The two god-inspired assassins whom the film presents in any detail are strongly characterized in terms of sexual ambiguity: the first (played by the actor who originated the role of the homosexual in *A Chorus Line*) is clearly meant to be taken as gay, the other (the young father who has murdered his wife and children) is also given culturally recognizable signifiers of gayness. Against all this is set the tangle and misery of the protagonist's sexual life under Christian culture, characterized by possessiveness, secrecy, deception, and denial. Significantly, what first arouses him to open violence is the young father's sense of release and happiness after he has destroyed his family.

Like Cohen's other films, *God Told Me To* proposes no "solution." If its god was ever pure, his purity has been corrupted through incarnation in human flesh and the agents he is forced to use (the disciples are businessmen and bureaucrats, the possessed executants are merely destructive). Yet, unlike the use of Catholicism in *The Exorcist*, the restoration of repression at the end of the film is not allowed to carry any positive force, uplift, or satisfaction—only a wry irony. It is not even certain that the god is dead: the narrative says he is; the images, editing, and implications question it. We last see him (after he appears to have been buried in the collapse of a derelict building) rising up in flames, his native element. Nothing clearly connects the protagonist to the god's destruction, so we must assume that his conviction for murder rests on his own confession; we may infer that he has confessed in order to reassure himself that his antagonist/brother double is really dead. In fact, the ending is left sufficiently open for one to wonder whether, had the film achieved any commercial success, Cohen would have written and directed a sequel to it rather than to *It's Alive*. Certainly, the issues it opens up are both immense and profound, and absolutely central to our culture and its future development.

The Private Files of J. Edgar Hoover

"We soon found ourselves besieged on all sides with no political group to spring to our defense."

—Larry Cohen

THE PRIVATE FILES OF J. Edgar Hoover is perhaps the most intelligent film about American politics ever to come out of Hollywood. I cannot speak for its historical accuracy, or for the justice of its speculative audacities: that Clyde Tolson was Deep Throat; that Hoover may have been implicated in the assassination of Bobby Kennedy—a possibility the film, keeping just the safe side of libel, allows us to infer rather than states. But the film would be no less intelligent were its entire structure fictional. It is a question, not of whether what the spectator sees on the screen is "objective truth," but of the relationship between the spectator and narrative.

The revealing comparison is with *All the President's Men* (1976). The overall effect of Alan Pakula's film is complicated by the pervasive urban paranoia of film noir, a dominant element that makes the film's relationship to Pakula's *The Parallax View* (1974) less clearly one of simple contrast than the director seems to have intended. Nevertheless, it offers its audiences satisfactions that Cohen's film rigorously eschews, notably in its suspense-thriller format and its hero-identification figures. *Hoover* offers no equivalent for Robert Redford and Dustin Hoffman; there are no heroes on whom we can rely to have everything put right at the end. No "correct" position is dramatized in the film with which the spectator might identify, by which he might be reassured. As there is no hero to uncover, be threatened by, and finally rectify the corruption, there can be no suspense, only analysis. Beside the obvious thriller brilliance of *All the President's Men*, the sobriety and detachment of *Hoover* might be mistaken for flatness. In fact, the narrative's ellipses and juxtapositions demand a continual activity on the part of the spectator very different from, and incompatible with, the excitements of "What happens next?"

In the famous *Cahiers du cinéma* analysis of *Young Mr. Lincoln* (1939), the editors claim that the film eventually produces Lincoln as a "monster," both castrated and castrating.[32] What is arguably implicit (or repressed) in John Ford's film is the explicit subject of Cohen; applied to his *Hoover*, the *Cahiers* description is exact, word for word. Two points are made about the "purity" that Hoover attempts to bring to his work: that it is at all stages compromised by the corruptions of the system, and that it is itself artificial, an act of will growing out of a denial of the body. The film translates into overtly political terms the dialectic of its predecessors: neither the purity nor the corruption is sanctioned; they are presented as two aspects of the same sickness. As in *It's Alive*, the monster is the logical product of the capitalist system.

Here, the "double" motif is made verbally explicit in the scene with Florence Hollister (Celeste Holm). Hoover has been responsible for the death of John Dillinger (whom he wanted to kill in person) and has since obsessively preserved his death mask and collected relics. Mrs. Hollister tells Hoover that he would secretly like to be Dillinger, and the context links this to Hoover's sexual repression. Having destroyed Dillinger, Hoover has internalized his violence, converting it into a repressive, castrating "morality."

Essential to the repression theme is the film's treatment of Hoover's alleged homosexuality, and his relationship with Clyde Tolson. The presentation of Hoover as monster rests on the notion that his repression is total, that he is incapable of acknowledging a sexual response to anyone, male or female. The desolate little scene where he sits in semidarkness and long shot, listening to a tape of erotic love play of a politician he has bugged, suggests less a vicarious satisfaction than his sense of exclusion from an aspect of life as meaningless to him as a foreign language. Elsewhere, he can "innocently" reminisce about the time when Bobby Kennedy, as a child, sat on his lap and asked if he was "packing a gun"; for the audience, the line evokes Mae West, yet it is clear that for Hoover the obvious implication (that the boy's proximity had given him an erection) simply does not exist.

The Tolson-Hoover relationship is treated with great delicacy and precision; out of it develops the film's culminating irony. Hoover wants publicly to repudiate the press's "slanders"; Tolson quietly advises him just to leave things alone. Tolson, in other words, is perfectly aware of what Hoover can never face: the real nature of their relationship. For a time, it looks as if the film is going to produce Rip Torn as the politically aware (and heterosexual) hero who sets things right; but it is Tolson who acquires the private files, in his determination to vindicate his friend, after which the film is content enigmatically to inform us that Watergate happened a year later and Hoover couldn't have done a better job.

The film's point is that Watergate was made possible, not by the altruistic endeavors of a couple of heroic seekers after truth, but by the unfulfilled personal commitment of one man to another. Hoover's one "pure" achievement, that is, grows inadvertently and apolitically, after his death, out of a relationship he could never even recognize for what it was. If the film celebrates anyone it is Tolson, but he is scarcely presented as any kind of answer. *All the President's Men* communicates (at least on surface level) that the system may be liable to corruption but will always right itself; *Hoover* views such a belief with extreme skepticism.

It's Alive II (originally *It Lives Again*)

(NOTES MADE IN COLLABORATION with Richard Lippe and Andrew Britton within three hours of viewing the film.) We expected a "run for cover" movie (after the commercial disaster of *God Told Me To* and the protracted problems over even getting *Hoover* a release); we got what appears (in the immediate excitement of discovery) one of the richest horror movies of the '70s and a decisive confirmation (if any were still needed) of Cohen's intelligence, consistency, and capacity for significant development. (Its critical reception, insofar as there has been one, has been predictably stupid and ignorant—see, for example, the review in *Variety*.)[33] It proves the ideal film on which to end not only the present article but the work on the horror film of which it forms a part. We feel unable to do more, under the circumstances, than offer rough notes which a subsequent article might develop.

1. The film is deeply rooted in the entire American horror tradition, evoking (without ever appearing imitative or eclectic) *Frankenstein*, *King Kong* (1933), *The Thing from Another World* (1951), *The Birds* (1963), *Rosemary's Baby*. It thereby confirms the basic unity of horror-movie material, however heterogeneous the particular examples may appear, and however significant the individual inflections.

2. The general tendency of Cohen's work has been to lead the spectator toward a recognition and qualified acceptance of the "otherness" of the monster that is impossible for the characters (clearest in *God Told Me To*). *It Lives*

Again takes up and substantially develops from the end of *It's Alive* the possibility of dramatizing this recognition within the film, through the responses to the monster of the characters. Hence it is among the most humane and progressive of all horror films, but never at the cost of sentimentalizing the monster or diminishing its dangerousness.

3. With *Hoover* and *It Lives Again* Cohen's films are noticeably growing in stature, developing from rough sketches into fully realized works, becoming more reflective and elaborated, the mise-en-scène more considered, the narrative more complex.

4. The implications of the monster-baby (here babies) are worked out and followed through much more thoroughly than in *It's Alive*, the children being both savage and destructive and (perhaps) superior beings, a new stage of evolution. (This development, together with the thread of religious imagery—Frank Davis as the Annunciation, the male and female babies named Adam and Eve, the climactic reunion of a new "holy family"—provides an important link between *It's Alive* and *God Told Me To*). This gives rise to a number of richly suggestive ambiguities: a) The baby is at different points in the film identified with both rattlesnake and pigeon: the dual aspects of nature kept rigorously separate in Murnau's *Nosferatu* (1922) are united in Cohen's monster-child. b) The cyclical nature of the beginning and end: the father (at both points) is ambiguously compensating for his complicity in the death of his own child and willing a similar child onto another couple. c) The audience's ambivalent attitude to both baby and parents, dramatized in the constant reversals of their behavior, oscillating between acceptance and rejection. d) The disturbing use of subjective shots for the child's point of view (carried over from *It's Alive* but here much more meaningful), placing the spectator abruptly in the position of the other. Two rhyming moments stand out: the child's focally distorted first sight of its father (to whose viewpoint we have been fairly close up to that moment); the climactic subjective shot (derived perhaps from *Spellbound* [1945]) when the father shoots his baby by firing directly into camera.

5. The tensions between the parents are developed far more explicitly here than in *It's Alive*. The birth of the baby provokes in the wife a sexual revulsion and terror (which her mother partly stimulates) that appear to be on the verge of resolution in the "family reunion" scene (surely one of the most moving

scenes in any horror film) where she persuades her husband to accept the child but are only actually resolved when he shoots it (the only time subsequent to the birth when the couple embrace).

Postscript

AFTER SOME HESITATION, I have decided to leave the last section of this essay as we wrote it, qualifying it with some additional comments rather than attempting a revision; it was an honest response to our immediate experience of the film, and the points it makes are (if incomplete) mostly valid. It is the third of the notes on *It's Alive II* that most demands qualification, the proposition that it is a "fully realized" work, more reflective and elaborated, the mise-en-scène more considered, being contradicted more than confirmed by reviewing. In fact, my description of *God Told Me To* as "a sketch for the great movie Cohen may make one day" might stand, to varying degrees, for all his films so far. The reasons for the apparent sketchiness and haste are probably complex and not to be accounted for simply in economic terms of low budgets and short shooting schedules (relevant as such conditions clearly are). The realization of the films sometimes testifies to bad habits acquired from television and never quite cast off (useful, no doubt, in the saving of time and money). The conventional, at times perfunctory, ping-pong crosscutting of dialogue scenes (Hitchcock's phrase "photographs of people talking" springs to mind) suggests a filmmaker whose ambitions don't entirely transcend expectations of casual viewing and immediate disposability (the general critical response to Cohen, if it can be said even to exist, would scarcely encourage him to think beyond that). It may be, however, that these are the conditions in which Cohen operates most spontaneously and effectively—the urgency and intensity of the films may be partly dependent on the speed with which they are tossed off (I once heard Cohen speculate about the film he could make with the budget De Palma had for *The Fury*—"Or rather," he added, "the three or four films . . ."). Tony Williams's complaint (in his essay on *Assault on Precinct 13* [1976]) that John Carpenter lacks intellectual awareness of the implications of his material seems to me (though not without validity) problematic.[34] The richness of an artist's work often arises from the dramatization of tensions and contradictions that intellectual awareness may actually inhibit and impoverish. In Cohen's case, such tensions are centered on attitudes to the family: the thematic thread connecting all his films is the "monstrous" child's striving for recognition by his parents and the impossibility of such recognition within existing familial codes and structures. It does not seem to me clear that his work would necessarily improve were he given more time to prepare and reflect, more time to shoot, and more money to spend. Which is not, of course, to say that one would not be extremely interested to see the results . . .

The fascination and importance of Cohen's work lies primarily, then, at the conceptual level. Many people are puzzled that I value the It's Alive films above *Halloween* (1978). Yet the pleasures of *Halloween* are not of the kind that (in D. H. Lawrence's words) "lead the sympathetic consciousness into new places, and away in recoil from things gone dead."[35] *Halloween*, in fact, does nothing new, but does it with extreme cinematic sophistication and finesse. Cohen, on the contrary, extends the boundaries of the genre to breaking point. The intelligence behind the It's Alive films drives its thinking to the point where the horror movie becomes impossible and must logically give way to some form of revolutionary movie; to the point at which the monstrousness of "normality" is explicitly recognized. *It's Alive II* is surely the first horror film in which the suspense derives as much from attempts to protect the monster as from the menace it represents. The traditional concept of horror on which the genre rests can scarcely survive such a development. But any responsible celebration of achievements within the genre should contain the acknowledgment that what we are striving toward is a civilization in which it could no longer exist—in which, in fact, its very premises would become strictly meaningless.

Apocalypse Now

Notes on the Living Dead

NIGHT OF THE LIVING DEAD (1968) and *Dawn of the Dead* (1979) are the first two parts of a trilogy that Romero plans to complete later with *Day of the Dead*. They are among the most powerful, fascinating, and complex of modern horror films, bearing a very interesting relationship both to the genre and to each other. What I want to examine here is their divergence: together, they demand a partial redefinition of the principles according to which the genre usually operates; and they are more distinct from each other—in character, tone, and meaning—than has generally been noted (*Dawn of the Dead* is much more than the elaborate remake it has been taken for).

The differences—both from other horror films and between the two films—are centered on the zombies and their function in relation to the other characters. The zombies of *Night* answer partly to the definition of the monster as the "return of the repressed"—but only partly: they lack one of the crucial defining characteristics, energy, and carry no positive connotations whatever. In *Dawn*, even this partial correspondence has almost entirely disappeared. On the other hand, the zombies of both films are not burdened with those actively negative connotations ("evil incarnate," etc.) that we have seen as defining the reactionary horror film. The earlier films to which the living dead movies most significantly relate are both somewhat to one side of the main development of the horror film: *The Birds* (1963) (*Night* more than *Dawn*), and *Invasion of the Body Snatchers* (1956) (*Dawn* more than *Night*). The strategy that connects all four films (and at the same time distinguishes them from the most fully representative specimens of the genre) is that of depriving their monsters of positive or progressive potential in order to restore it to the human characters. From this viewpoint,

Dawn of the Dead emerges as the most interesting of the four films (which is not to say that it is "better"—more complex, more suggestive, more intelligent—than *The Birds* [1963]).

MUCH HAS BEEN MADE of the way in which *Night of the Living Dead* systematically undercuts generic conventions and the expectations they arouse: the woman who appears to be established as the heroine becomes virtually catatonic early in the film and remains so to the end; no love relationship develops between her and the hero. The young couple, whose survival (as future nuclear family) is generically guaranteed, are burnt alive and eaten around the film's midpoint. The film's actual nuclear family are wiped out; the child (a figure hitherto sacrosanct—even in *The Birds* children sustain no more than superficial injuries, and this is the same year as *Rosemary's Baby* [1968]) not only dies but comes back as a zombie, devours her father, and hacks her mother to death. In a final devastating stroke, the hero of the film and sole survivor of the zombies (among the major characters) is callously shot down by the sheriff's posse, thrown on a bonfire, and burnt.

But the film's transgressions are not just against generic conventions: those conventions constitute an embodiment, in a skeletal and schematic form, of the dominant norms of our culture. The zombies of *Night* have their meaning defined fairly consistently in relation to the family and the couple. The film's debt to *The Birds* goes beyond the obvious resemblances of situation and imagery (the besieged group in the boarded house, the zombies' hands breaking through the barricades like the birds' beaks): the zombies' attacks, like those of the birds, have their origins in (are the physical projection of) psychic tensions that are the product of patriarchal male-female or familial relationships. This is established clearly in the opening scene. Brother and sister visit a remote country graveyard (over which flies the stars and stripes: the metaphor of America as graveyard is central to Romero's work, the term "living dead" describing the society of *Martin* [1978] as aptly as it does the zombies). Their father is buried there, and the visit (a meaningless annual ritual performed to please their mother) is intensely resented, actively by the man, passively by the sullen woman. They take their familial resentments out on each other, as (the film indicates) they have always done; the man frightens his sister by

Night of the Living Dead (1968) systematically undercuts generic convention.

pretending to be a monster, as he used to do when they were children; the first zombie lurches forward from among the graves, attacks them both, and kills the man. At the film's climax, when the zombies at last burst into the farmhouse, it is the brother who leads the attack on his sister, some obscure vestige of "family feeling" driving him forward to devour her.

In between, we have the film's analysis of its "typical" American nuclear family. The father rages and blusters impotently, constantly reasserting a discredited authority (the film continuously counterpoints the disintegration of the social microcosm, the patriarchal family, with the cultural disintegration of the nation, the collapse of confidence in authority on both the personal and political level). The mother, contemptuous of her husband yet trapped in the dominant societal patterns, does nothing but sulk and bitch. Their destruction at the hands of their zombie daughter represents the film's judgment on them and the norm they embody.

The film has often been praised for never making an issue of its black hero's color (it is nowhere alluded to, even implicitly). Yet it is not true that his color is arbitrary and without meaning: Romero uses it to signify his difference from the other characters, to set him apart from their norms. He alone has no ties—he remains unconnected to any of the others, and we learn nothing of his family or background. From this arises the significance of the two events at the end of the film: (a) he survives the zombies, (b) he is shot down by the posse. It is the function of the posse to restore the social order that has been destroyed; the zombies represent the suppressed tensions and conflicts—the legacy of the past, of the patriarchal structuring of relationships, "dead" yet automatically continuing—which that order creates and on which it precariously rests.

ALMOST EXACTLY HALFWAY BETWEEN the two Living Dead films, and closely related to both, is *The Crazies* (1973), an ambitious and neglected work that demands parenthetical mention here for its confirmation of Romero's thematic concerns and the particular emphasis it gives them. The precredits sequence is virtually a gloss on the opening of *Night of the Living Dead*, with brother and sister as young children and the acting out of tensions dramatized within the family. Again, brother teases sister, pretending to be a monster coming to kill her; abruptly, their game is disturbed by the father, the first "crazy" of the title, who has already murdered their mother and is now savagely destroying the house. The subsidiary family of the main body of the film (here father and daughter), instead of killing and devouring each other, act out the mutual incestuous desire on whose repression families are built. In general, however, the film moves out from *Night*'s concentration on the family unit into a more generalized treatment of social disintegration (a progression *Dawn* will complete).

The premise of the film is similar to that of Hawks's *Monkey Business* (1952) (that the same premise can provide the basis for a crazy comedy and a horror movie is itself suggestive of the dangers of a rigid definition of genres, which are often structured on the same sets of ideological tensions): a virus in a town's water supply turns people crazy, their craziness taking the form of the release of their precariously suppressed violence, its end result either death or incurable insanity. The continuity suggested by the opening between normality and craziness is sustained throughout the film; indeed, one of its most fascinating aspects is the way the boundary between the two is continuously blurred. In the first part of the film, after the declaration of martial law and the attempt to round up and isolate all the town's inhabitants, the local priest finds his authority swept aside and the sanctuary of his church brutally repudiated. He becomes increasingly distraught, and publicly immolates himself. We never know whether or not he is a victim of the virus (acting, in his case, on a desire for martyrdom). Once such a doubt is implanted, it becomes uncertain what instigates the uncontrolled and violent behavior of virtually everyone in the film. The hysteria of the quarantined can be attributed equally to the spread of contagion among them or to their brutal and ignominious herding together in claustrophobically close quarters by the military; the various individual characters who overstep the bounds of recognizably normal behavior may simply be reacting to conditions of extreme stress. The "crazies," in other words, represent merely an extension of "normality," not its opposite. The spontaneous violence of the mad appears scarcely more grotesque than the organized violence of the authorities.

THE END OF *NIGHT of the Living Dead* implies that the zombies have been contained and are in process of being annihilated; by the end of *Dawn of the Dead* they have apparently overrun everything and there is nothing left to do but flee. Yet *Dawn* (paradoxically, though taking the cue from its title) comes across as by far the more optimistic of the two films. This is due partly to format (bright colors, against *Night*'s grainy and drab black and white), partly to setting (garish and brilliantly lit shopping mall, against shadowy, old-fashioned farmhouse), partly to tone (in *Night*, the zombies are never funny, the film's black humor being mainly restricted to the casual brutalism of the sheriff's posse). But these are only the outward signs of a difference that is basically conceptual. Both films are built upon all-against-all triangular structures, strikingly similar yet crucially different:

NIGHT

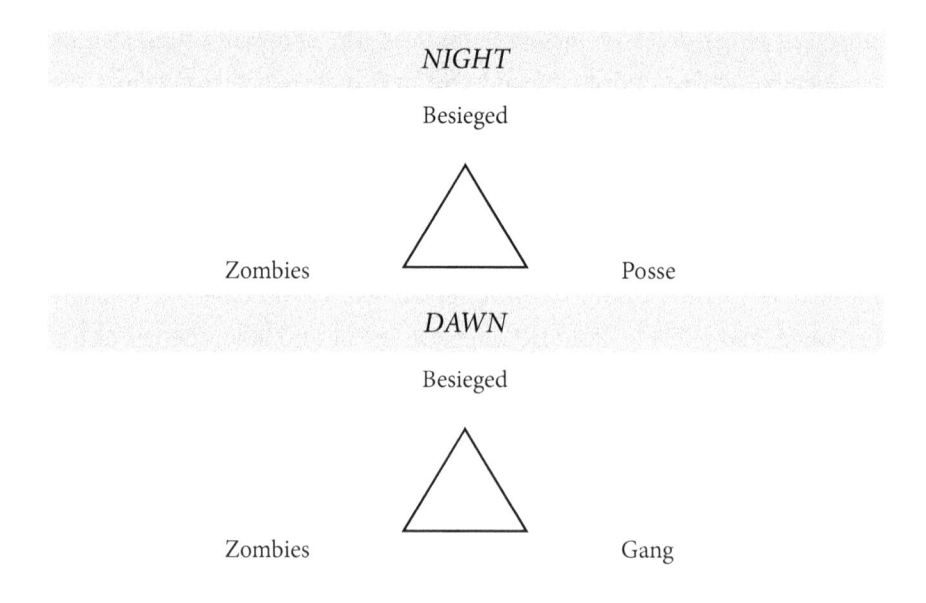

Besieged

Zombies △ Posse

DAWN

Besieged

Zombies △ Gang

(*The Crazies* essentially repeats the pattern of *Night*, with "crazies" instead of zombies and the military in place of the posse.)

The functions of the sheriff's posse in *Night* and the motorcycle gang in *Dawn* are in some ways very close: they constitute a threat both to the zombies and to the besieged (even if, in *Night*, inadvertently, by mistaking the hero for a zombie); more importantly, both dramatize (albeit in significantly different ways) the possibility of the development of fascism out of breakdown and chaos. The difference is obvious: the purpose of the posse is to destroy the zombies and restore the threatened social order; the purpose of the gang is simply to exploit and profit from that order's disintegration. The posse ends triumphant, the gang are wiped out.

The premise of *Dawn*, in fact, is that the social order (regarded as in all Romero's films as obsolete and discredited) can't be restored; its restoration at the end of *Night* simply clinches the earlier film's total negativity. The notion of social apocalypse is succinctly established in *Dawn*'s TV-studio prologue: television, the only surviving medium of national communication whereby social order might be maintained, is on the verge of closing down; as a technician tells Fran, "Our responsibility is at an end." The characters of *Night* were still locked in their responsibility to the value structure of the past; the characters of *Dawn* are at the outset absolved from that responsibility, they are potentially free people, with new responsibilities of choice and self-determination. Since the zombies' significance in both films depends entirely on their relationship to the main characters, it follows that their function here is somewhat different. They are no longer associated with specific characters or character tensions, and the family as a social unit no longer exists (it is only reconstituted in parody, when the injured Roger becomes the baby in the pram, wheeled around the supermarket by his "parents" as he shoots down zombies with childish glee). The zombies instead are a "given" from the outset; they represent, on the metaphorical level, the whole dead weight of patriarchal consumer capitalism, from whose habits of behavior and desire not even Zen Buddhists and nuns are exempt, mindlessly joining the conditioned gravitation to the shopping mall.

As in *The Crazies*, the seemingly clear-cut distinctions between the three groups are progressively undermined (aside from the obvious visual differentiation between zombies and humans). The motorcycle gang's mindless delight in violence and slaughter is anticipated in the development of Roger; all three groups are contaminated and motivated by consumer greed (which the zombies simply carry to its logical conclusion by consuming people). All three groups,

In *Dawn of the Dead* (1978) the zombies represent the whole dead weight of consumer capitalism.

in other words, share a common conditioning: all are predators. The substance of the film concerns the four characters' varying degrees of recognition of, and varying reactions to, this fact. Two become zombies, two (provisionally) escape.

In place of *Night*'s dissection of the family, *Dawn* explores (and explodes) the two dominant couple relationships of our culture and its cinema: the heterosexual couple (moving inevitably toward marriage and its traditional male/female roles) and the male "buddy" relationship with its evasive denial of sexuality (the pattern is anticipated in the central triangle relationship of the three principles of *The Crazies*). Through the realization of the ultimate consumer-society dream (the ready availability of every luxury, emblem, and status symbol of capitalist life without the penalty of payment) the anomalies and imbalances of human relationships under capitalism are exposed. With the defining motive—the drive to acquire and possess money, the identification of money with power—removed, the whole structure of traditional relationships, based on patterns of dominance and dependence, begins to crumble.

The heterosexual couple (an embryonic family, as Fran is pregnant) begin as a trendy variation on the norm: they are not legally married, and the woman is allowed a semblance of independence through her career; but as soon as the two are together the conventional assumptions operate. It is the man who flies the helicopter and carries the gun, the film's major emblems of sexual/patriarchal authority. At various points in the narrative Fran nostalgically re-enacts the role of female stereotype, making up her face as a doll-like image for the male gaze, skating alone on the huge ice rink—woman as spectacle, but without an audience. But in the course of the film she progressively assumes a genuine autonomy, asserting herself against the men, insisting on possession of a gun, demanding to learn to pilot the machine. The pivotal scene is the parody of a romantic dinner, the white couple, in evening dress, cooked for and waited on by the black, with flowers and candlelight, the scene building to the man's offer and the woman's refusal of the rings that signify traditional union.

The closest link between *Night* and *Dawn* is the carry-over of the black protagonist—his color used again to indicate his separation from the norms of white-dominated society and his partial exemption from its constraints. Through the developing mutual attachment between him and Roger, the film takes up and comments on the "buddy" relationship of countless recent Hollywood movies and its implicit sexual undercurrents and ambiguities. Neither man shows any sexual interest in the woman, yet both are blocked by their conditioning from admitting to any in each other. Hence the channeling of Roger's energies into violence and aggression, his uncontrolled zest in slaughter presented as a display for his friend. The true nature of the relationship can be tacitly acknowledged only after Roger's death, in the symbolic orgasm of the opening of a champagne bottle over his grave.

Both the film's central relationships are broken by the death of one of the partners. The two who die are those who cannot escape the constraints of their conditioning, the survivors those who show themselves capable of autonomy and self-awareness. The film eschews any hint of a traditional happy ending, there being no suggestion of any romantic attachment developing between the survivors. Instead of the restoration of conventional relationship patterns, we have the woman piloting the helicopter as the man relinquishes his rifle to the zombies. They have not come very far, and the film's conclusion rewards them with no more than a provisional and temporary respite: enough gasoline for four hours, and no certainty of destination. Yet the effect of the ending is curiously exhilarating. Hitherto, the modern horror film has invariably moved toward either the restoration of the traditional order or the expression of despair (in *Night*, both).

Dawn is perhaps the first horror film to suggest—albeit very tentatively—the possibility of moving beyond apocalypse. It brings its two surviving protagonists to the point where the work of creating the norms for a new social order, a new structure of relationships, can begin—a context in which the presence of a third survivor, Fran's unborn child, has its significance. Romero has set himself a formidable challenge, and it will be interesting to see how the third part of the trilogy confronts it.

(1979)

The American Family Comedy

From *Meet Me in St. Louis* to *The Texas Chainsaw Massacre*

I would like to address myself to the question: What became of the American family comedy? There is one simple answer that I shall dispense with quickly, finding it unsatisfactory though in some respects interesting: that it migrated to the TV domestic-comedy series. The answer demands simply a slight modification of the question: What became of the *distinguished* American family comedy? The TV comedy series can be regarded as the rough equivalent of the Hardy family or Jones family films; it cannot be regarded as the equivalent of *You Can't Take It with You* (1938) and *It's a Wonderful Life* (1946), or of *Meet Me in St. Louis* (1944) and *Father of the Bride* (1950), or of *Alice Adams* (1935) and *I Remember Mama* (1948) or even of *Margie* (1946) and *Life with Father* (1947). All of these have their thematic or motivic TV equivalents—what has happened, in general, is the reduction of once-vital material to formula.

Before discussing specific films, I find it necessary to define, however crudely, a context of general ideas about the family as an institution. First, let me introduce two words that may prove crucial: "containment" and "repression." I do not want to suggest that the two are interchangeable, since containment operates on a more or less conscious level, repression, by definition, on an unconscious. What I have in mind is the Freudian thesis that in a society built on monogamy and family there will be an enormous surplus of sexual energy that will have to be repressed and that what is repressed must always strive to return. Containment, then, implicitly accepts monogamy and family as natural and inevitable, and refers to the ways in which excess energies can be dealt with. Ford's films, in which the affirmation of family as a value is so often a central concern, are very much preoccupied with this: containment assumes various forms of discipline (the cavalry), work (the building of civilization), the communal dance, and comic horseplay. Generally (both in Ford and in classical Hollywood cinema), it is *male* energy that must be contained, channeled, or given a safe outlet; excessive female energy must be chastised and subjugated by the male, either by dumping it in a Tombstone horse trough or dragging it halfway across Ireland by its arm.

Ideology, and its embodiment in myth (in Barthes's sense)[36] can be seen as having two closely related major functions: to naturalize as eternal assumptions that are in fact cultural/historical; to render it impossible to imagine radical alternatives. To detach oneself from the dominant ideology one needs a perspective, even if an arbitrary one. If one provisionally accepts as a hypothesis Norman O. Brown's assertion in *Life Against Death* that the defining characteristic of man is neurosis,[37] one can pass on to see the family as the central medium for the transmission and perpetuation of neurosis in our culture. The institution on which the family in bourgeois capitalist society depends—legal marriage—appears flagrantly neurotic, its sole function being to make it more difficult for couples to separate if they are miserable. The justification of that function is of course the family, that hotbed of neurosis on which our civilization is founded. The ideological prohibition against imagining radical alternatives is still largely operative, though the positive force of the notion of family has been drastically weakened. The couples I know tend either not to be legally married or to wish they weren't; yet all my friends, gay or straight, tend to gravitate toward the patterns and assumptions of monogamy/family; so do I, despite continual resistance.

Society, even at its more sophisticated levels and despite a great deal of theorizing, does not yet seem capable of producing models for practical radical alternatives, only liberal modifications. It is a case of what Barthes calls "inoculation": ideology accepts limited criticism the better to safeguard itself against radical criticism.[38] One of the nearest approaches to a distinguished contemporary family comedy, *Alice Doesn't Live Here Anymore* (1974), provides a precise and exemplary reflection of this. At the start of the film (after the childhood prologue), Alice is shown as trapped in an intolerable marital familial situation with a male-chauvinist pig who at best ignores, at worst maltreats, her. He is killed in an accident; Alice sets off on a journey of self-discovery and self-definition, at the end of which is Kris Kristofferson, waiting to restore patriarchy with suitable modifications (the couple will now talk things over, and Alice is at liberty to pursue her career if she wishes—a career the film has shown to be meaningless). The pattern (complete with precocious offspring and unsatisfactory alternative lover en route) is almost exactly repeated in *An Unmarried Woman* (1978), a "coincidence" that would seem to confirm its significance as a means of recuperating the feminist threat.

An attempt, then, to explain the existence of the family comedy (which was always affirmative on the overt level), as against the family melodrama (which was always much more equivocal, to say the least): even if we always really knew that the family was a monstrous institution, we had to love it and laugh at it—we were stuck with it, as an act of God and law of nature, sanctified by religion.

So what *did* become of the family comedy? Crucially, if the imagining of alternatives is still difficult, the necessity for *trying* to imagine them has become far more pressing. Central to this is the "delayed action" of Freud. Obviously, his was one of the most radical minds of Western civilization, but the radicalism was to some extent circumscribed within the ideology of his time and place: one can take from Freud the assumption that the process of repression and sublimation is necessary and inevitable, which leaves one the choice between containment and despair. Within our lifetime, Freud has been reread and in the process has become a living force for change; the work of R. D. Laing, Morton Schatzman, Juliet Mitchell, and Norman O. Brown has, in various ways, undermined and attacked the ideological assumption of monogamy/family, repression/sublimation, as an inalterable fact of nature. It is basically the findings of psychoanalytical theory that validate the more direct political force of such contemporary, vital, irrepressible, and revolutionary (hence antifamily) movements as feminism and gay liberation. The overt and unqualified celebration of family (a condition of the family comedy's functioning on a conscious level) has become impossible, except at the lower levels of mechanically repeated formulae.

From such a vantage point, the classical Hollywood family comedy looks somewhat different from how it was received (and presumably intended) at the time. In terms of a rereading of '30s and '40s family comedies, the importance of the feminist consciousness should particularly be stressed. The films allow that the perpetuation of the family involves certain strains and sacrifices. Yet it is habitually the male who is presented as the victim of domesticity; the assumption is that for woman, monogamy and family are sufficient fulfillment. That Mary Astor in *Meet Me in St. Louis*, Donna Reed in *It's a Wonderful Life*, Joan Bennett in *Father of the Bride*, are just as trapped and constricted as, respectively, Leon Ames, James Stewart, and Spencer Tracy, may or may not be implicit in the film's subconscious, but it never reaches explicit statement.

There is an interesting contradiction here in American ideology, which finds its inevitable reflection in the opposition of two Hollywood genres. On the one hand, it is commonly held that Western capitalist society is patriarchal; on the other, American society is often referred to as a matriarchy: the "American mother," from, say, Mary Boland in *Ruggles of Red Gap* (1935) (even if her only child is her husband) to Mrs. Bates in *Psycho* (1960), is an almost proverbial figure, always associated with dominance, tyranny, the castration of the male. The seeming paradox is not difficult to resolve: the matriarch's power exists solely within the confines of the home and can be seen as her reward for her enslavement. In the larger world outside, the world of money and the law, she has no voice, no potency. The male, on the other hand, offers himself (give or take a few grumbles) for castration within the home, on condition that his potency outside suffers no interference or challenge.

The genres I have in mind are the domestic comedy and the domestic melodrama (or "woman's picture"). Without suggesting that there are no exceptions, it seems generally true that the former is built on the entrapment of the male, the latter on that of the female. The question of why the subject of male entrapment produces comedy while that of female entrapment demands melodrama or tragedy (the dividing line between the two being notoriously difficult to define) has sociological implications too broad to be adequately covered here. The crux is the ideological concept of woman as the heart of the family (and of civilization). Male entrapment (hence potential rebellion) can be treated as a joke, but the recognition of female entrapment can produce only tension and catastrophe. The domestic comedy depends for its very existence on the repression of any sense that the wife/mother could be other than blissfully content, completely fulfilled by her role. The ideological contradictions do occasionally come into direct conflict within a specific film: see, for example, McCarey's *Good Sam* (1948), a domestic comedy that continually threatens to become domestic melodrama. But McCarey's work, because of his commitment to anarchic individualism, produces conflicts and ambiguities every time it touches on the family. See, above all, *Make Way for Tomorrow* (1937), but also the astonishing domestic comedies of Laurel and Hardy made under his close supervision: the cinema offers no more ruthless deconstruction of domestic life than *Brats* (1930).

As a supreme example of the American family comedy, I want to focus on *Meet Me in St. Louis*. In its time it was widely acclaimed as a celebratory film; in retrospect from the '70s, it can more convincingly be read as a relentless study of the psychopathology of the family. It is a period film, but I don't think that affects the issue seriously. Its conscious Victoriana aspects simply facilitate its ostensible celebration of a family structure that is essentially repeated in *Father of the Bride*, which has a contemporary setting.

Central to the film is the notion of the sacrifice (castration) of the father. Mr. Smith, in the great American tradition, wants progress, advancement, success; his family wants to stay in St. Louis; they win. Essentially, this is presented as a triumph of the women: mother, four daughters, and maid, all wish to remain in St. Louis, conceived of as "home." If the film acknowledges at all that the principle (or joke) of American matriarchy is in fact built on the ideological imprisonment of the woman within the home, it can do so only surreptitiously, by a kind of elision. Tootie (Margaret O'Brien), the youngest daughter, plays obsessively with dolls. Her games consist of attributing to the dolls morbid illnesses and finally death (she buries them). The child's play with dolls represents, notoriously, her acting out of transmitted maternal attitudes: one may deduce that Tootie is reproducing, unconsciously, her mother's equally unconscious desire that Tootie die and become the subject of self-justifying sentimental sorrow. More generally, the notion of the home as prison is pervasively present in Minnelli's use of decor, and this is by no means restricted to the males.

Virtually every sequence in the film is built on tension, constraint, and repression within the family. The musical numbers, in the tradition of the

Hollywood musical, provide a partial release from this, but it is never more than partial or temporary: even the famous "Trolley Song" is structured on the separation of the lovers, their eventual union on the trolley characterized by extreme embarrassment rather than romantic fulfillment. All the film's sexual relationships (on which much of its humor is based)—which in 1944 seemed quaint and funny, a trifle old-fashioned, yet familiar, Victorian exaggerations of our own familial experiences—in 1978 look pathological.

The ostensible harmony—the celebratory level of the film—is particularly disrupted by two scenes centered on Tootie and the "killing" of parent figures. The first is the now-famous Halloween sequence, which MGM wanted cut from the film as irrelevant to the narrative (which on the simple level of linearity it is). The whole sequence draws lavishly on the iconography of the horror film. It is introduced by a shot of the Smith home that turns it (with the aid of darkness and thunder) into the old dark house of the horror film—or the Bates house of *Psycho*—a figure that, recurring in American fiction, both prose and film, from "The Fall of the House of Usher" to *Mandingo* (1975) and *The Texas Chainsaw Massacre* (1974), seems primarily to signify the terrible weight of the past, the legacy of repression. It is the night when children are allowed full license; some of them are dressed as devils. Tootie undertakes the "killing" of the terrible Mr. Brockhoff (by throwing flour in his face): a classic horror film sequence, dark street, eerie music, sinister house, isolated and vulnerable figure, wind, blowing leaves. Given the introductory image of the Smith house, it is perhaps not too fanciful to see the Brockhoff house as a dream displacement.

The later scene may be argued to confirm this reading and is even more disruptive of the celebratory tone, partly because it is central to the narrative, not, like the Halloween sequence, parenthetical: it can't stand as an isolated set piece but is the product of the tensions generated throughout the film. Immediately after Judy Garland sings to her "Have Yourself a Merry Little Christmas," within the Minnellian entrapment of a window frame, Tootie dashes out into the snow in her nightdress to hack down her snow people, ostensibly because she can't take them with her to New York. The snow people are dressed in adult coats, hats, and scarves, recognizably parent figures. Father watches from an upstairs window. Wisely, he decides to accept his castration and stay in St. Louis.

The Halloween scene in *Meet Me in St. Louis* (1944) anticipates the shift from family comedy to family horror.

The end of the film has been considered puzzling, because it is such a letdown. The whole action has built toward the grand opening of the fair, and we expect a big, lavish production number, clinching the sense of celebration. All we get is the family and its guaranteed perpetuation in the young lovers (Judy and her narcissistic fantasy figure, the boy next door) gazing at some bright lights and concluding that life has nothing more to offer. They are right, of course: sublimation and fantasy fulfillment (however emotionally cheating) represent the only option open to them. The ending strikingly anticipates that of Hollywood's supreme sublimation movie of all time, *Close Encounters of the Third Kind* (1977), where, under the sign of the castrated mountain, Richard Dreyfuss is literally transported by bright lights St. Louis never dreamed of.

What happened to the American family comedy? There is a third answer. During the '50s the genre turns sourer and peters out: *Father of the Bride* could almost be *The Indiscreet Charm of the Bourgeoisie*. In 1960, *Psycho* was released, and the great age of the American horror film was inaugurated. The American

The Texas Chainsaw Massacre (1974): Another great family comedy.

family didn't disappear from the screen: it simply moved into the genre where it had always rightly belonged. Virtually every distinguished American horror film since *Psycho* has been centered on the family. In 1944 Tootie symbolically hacks down her parents with a spade; in 1968 a little girl, surprised in the act of eating Daddy's hand, literally hacks down her mother with a builder's trowel (*Night of the Living Dead* [1968]). The Halloween demons of *Meet Me in St. Louis* become the literal devil-children of *The Exorcist* (1973) and *The Omen* (1976). The long-protracted legacy of sexual repression erupts in Carrie's telekinesis, destroying the good along with the evil—one of the major characterizing features of '70s horror.

I want to end, then, by pointing the reader to another great American family comedy, *The Texas Chainsaw Massacre*, a film for which my respect increases on every viewing. I have written on this film at length already,[39] and it would be pointless to repeat here what I say there (the article is in many ways complementary to this one and should be read in conjunction with it). *Meet Me in St. Louis* is a comedy with intermittent horror-film overtones; *The Texas Chainsaw Massacre* is a horror film with more than intermittent overtones of comedy all which are centered on its monstrous family ("Look what your brother did to that door"). What is important is the difference between the nature of comedy in *Meet Me in St. Louis* and in *The Texas Chainsaw Massacre*, in relation to the two films' images of family: the question of what we are laughing at and why. *Meet Me in St. Louis* was a comedy of containment: we laugh at its accumulating horrors of family life in order to find them acceptable and to feel affectionate toward them. By the 1970s such containment is no longer possible, though ideology continues to repress the imagining of constructive social alternatives. *The Texas Chainsaw Massacre* is a comedy of despair: as everything is hopeless, there is nothing left to do but laugh.

(1979)

Neglected Nightmares

Last year, for the Toronto Film Festival, Richard Lippe and I organized a sixty-film retrospective of the American horror film called "The American Nightmare" and brought out a book of essays under the same title. The aim of both the retrospective and the book was to further the responsible reading of the horror film as an important phenomenon within our culture, since the genre, and particularly its finest specimens, offer (it seems to us) the material for a radical and diagnostic reading of the culture itself. One of the by-products of the venture was the discovery of a number of remarkable works hitherto unknown to us and generally denied either critical or popular recognition. The present article offers a survey of these discoveries and should be regarded as an addendum to the book: many of its ideas and valuations have developed out of discussions between Richard Lippe and me, and I would not want his contribution to go unacknowledged.

I want to glance (somewhat perfunctorily—some of the films I was able to see only once, none more than twice) at the work of Wes Craven and Stephanie Rothman; at Bob Clark's *Night Walk* (*Night Walker*, *Dead of Night*, 1974); and at the lesser-known films of George Romero. Craven, Rothman, and Romero all appeared at the retrospective (as did Brian De Palma and David Cronenberg), and all three were extremely articulate about their work. The usual gulf that separates the artist's perception of her/his work from the critic's was on these occasions almost nonexistent (though it was wider than ever with De Palma).

Wes Craven

If I begin with *The Last House on the Left* (1972), it is partly because it has achieved at least a certain underground notoriety (unlike, say, *Night Walk* or *Jack's Wife* [1972]) and surfaced briefly in the pages of *Film Comment* as one of Roger Ebert's "Guilty Pleasures." I had better say that the "Guilty Pleasures" feature seems to me an entirely deplorable institution. If one feels guilt at pleasure, isn't one bound to renounce either one or the other? Preferably, in most cases, the guilt, which is merely the product of that bourgeois elitism that continues to vitiate so much criticism. The attitude fostered is essentially evasive (including *self*-evasive) and anticritical: "Isn't this muck—to which of course I'm really so superior—*delicious*?"

Ebert's "Guilty Pleasure" (which may be *Last House*'s only recognition so far by a professedly serious critic) is brief enough to quote in full:

> The original *Keep repeating—It's Only a Movie!!!* movie. The plot may sound strangely familiar. Two young virgins go for a walk in the woods. One is set upon by vagabonds who rape and kill her. The other escapes. The vagabonds take their young victim's clothes and set on through the wood, coming at last, without realizing it, to the house of the victim's parents. The father finds his daughter's bloodstained garments, realizes that he houses the murderers, and kills them by electrifying the screen door and taunting them to run at it, whereupon they slip on the shaving cream he's spread on the floor, fall into the screen, and are electrocuted.
>
> Change a few trifling details (like shaving cream) and you've got Bergman's *The Virgin Spring* ([1956]). The movie's an almost scene-by-scene ripoff of Bergman's plot. It's also a neglected American horror exploitation masterpiece on a par with *Night of the Living Dead* ([1968]). As a plastic Hollywood movie, the remake would almost certainly have failed. But its very artlessness, its blunt force, make it work.[40]

Pleasure or not, Ebert has plenty here to feel guilty about.

1. The virginity of one of the girls (Phyllis) is very much in question. The relationship between them is built on the experienced/innocent opposition (as in Bergman's original, the plot of which, by the way, was also a "scene-by-scene ripoff" of a medieval ballad), though the innocence of Mari (the nice bourgeois family's daughter) is also questioned: she is a flower child with an ambiguous attraction to violence.

2. The girls meet the "vagabonds" in the latter's apartment in the city; they are on their way to a concert by a rock group noted for its onstage violence and

pause to try to buy some dope from the youngest of the gang, who is lounging about on the front steps.

3. Ebert is decently reticent about the "vagabonds" (their background, relationships, sex, and even their number); his association of them with "the wood" deprives them of the very specific social context that Craven in fact gave them. There are four: an escaped killer, his sadistic friend Weasel, their girl Sadie, and the killer's illegitimate teenage son Junior.

4. I am not clear which girl Ebert thinks "escapes." Phyllis gets away briefly but is soon recaptured, tormented, repeatedly stabbed, and (in the original, though Craven himself wonders if a print survives anywhere with this in) virtually disemboweled. (The abridged version leaves no doubt that she is dead.) Mari staggers into the water to cleanse herself after she is raped, and she is repeatedly shot; her parents later find her on the bank, and she dies in their arms.

5. The "vagabonds" do not take Mari's clothes. Her body, which they presume dead, is drifting out in the middle of a large pond. The mother (as in Bergman), searching the men's luggage after overhearing some semi-incriminating dialogue and one of the gang calling out in his sleep, finds the "peace pendant" her husband gave Mari at the start of the film and blood on the *men's* clothes.

6. No one in the film dies from electrocution; the father spreads shaving cream outside the upstairs bedroom door to slow his victims down and electrifies the screen door to prevent their escaping by it. The gang are disposed of as follows: the nice bourgeois mother seduces Weasel out in the dark by the pond where Mari was raped, fellates him, and bites off his cock as he comes; the killer contemptuously persuades his son Junior to blow out his own brains; the mother cuts Sadie's throat outside in an ornamental pond while her husband dispatches Junior's father with a chainsaw—presumably decapitating him and thereby completing the parallel between the simultaneous actions (though this is about the only thing that Craven doesn't show).

That Ebert's plot synopsis sets a new record in critical inaccuracy (combined with characteristic critic-as-superstar complacency) says less about him personally than about a general ambience that encourages opinion mongering, gossip, guilty pleasures, and similar smartassery—and, as an inevitable corollary, actively discourages criticism and scholarship. What does it matter whether he gets the plot right or not? Hell, it's only a movie, and an exploitation movie at that, albeit an "American horror exploitation masterpiece on a par with *Night of the Living Dead*"—which Ebert mercilessly slammed when it came out. (Is this supposed to be his public retraction?)

What I mean by bourgeois elitism could as well be illustrated from the writings of John Simon or even Pauline Kael. What the critic demands, as at least a precondition to according a film serious attention, is not so much evidence of a genuine creative impulse (which can be individual or collective, and can manifest itself through any format) as a set of external signifiers that advertise the film as a work of art. No one feels guilty about seriously discussing *The Virgin Spring*, though the nature of Bergman's creative involvement there seems rather more suspect than is the case with *Last House*. What is at stake, then, is not merely the evaluation of one movie but quite fundamental critical (hence cultural, social, political) principles—issues that involve the relationship between critic and reader as well as that between film and spectator.

The relation of *Last House* to *The Virgin Spring* is not, in fact, close enough to repay any detailed scrutiny—though one might remark that, if the term "ripoff" is appropriate here, it is equally appropriate to the whole of Shakespeare, the debt being one of plot outline and no more. The major narrative alterations—the transformation of Ingeri into Phyllis and of the child goatherd into the teenage Junior, the killing of *both* girls, the addition of Sadie, the mother's active participation in the revenge, the destruction of Junior by his own father—are all thoroughly motivated and in themselves indicate the creative intelligence at work.

The most important narrative change is that of overall direction and final outcome. Bergman's virgin is on her way to church, and the film leads to the somewhat-willed catharsis of her father's promise to build a new church, and the "answer" of a spurious and perfunctory miracle. Craven's virgin is on her way to a rock concert by a group that kills chickens on stage and, as the recurrent pop song on the soundtrack informs us, "the road leads to nowhere." The last image is of the parents, collapsed together in empty victory, drenched in blood.

But the crucial difference is in the film-spectator relationship, especially with reference to the presentation of violence. Joseph Losey saw Bergman's film

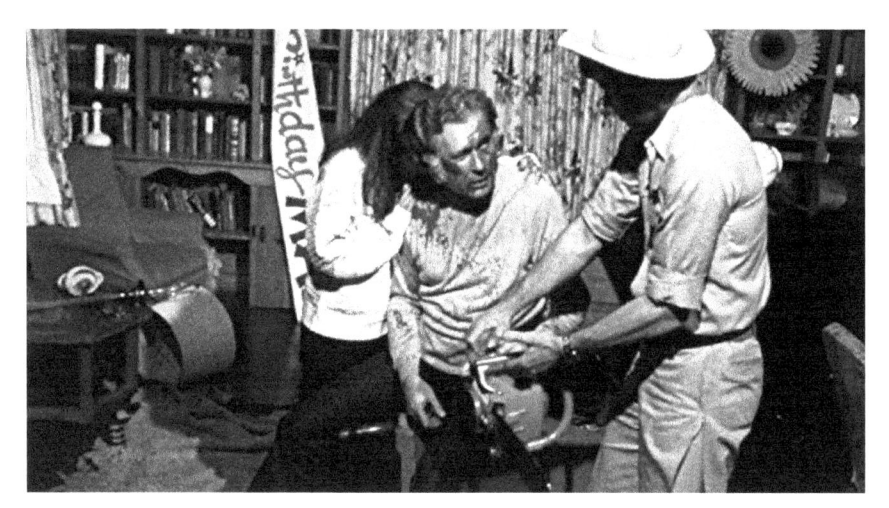

The Last House on the Left (1972): The final image of the parents collapsed together in empty victory.

as "Brechtian," but I think its character is determined more by personal temperament than aesthetic theory: the ability to describe coldly and accurately, without empathy—or, perhaps more precisely, with an empathy that has been repressed and disowned. If there is something distasteful in the film's detailing of rape and carnage, it is because Bergman seems to deny his involvement without annihilating it and to communicate that position to the spectator.

The Virgin Spring is art; *Last House* is exploitation. One must return to that dichotomy because the difference between the two films in terms of the relationship set up between audience and action is inevitably bound up with it. I use the terms art and exploitation here not evaluatively, but to indicate two sets of signifiers—operating both within the films as "style" and outside them as publicity, distribution, etc. that define the audience-film relationship in general terms. As media for communication, both art and exploitation have their limitations, defined in both cases (though in very different ways) by their inscriptions within the class system. Both permit the spectator a form of insulation from the work and its implications: art by defining seriousness in aesthetic terms implying class superiority (only the person of education and refinement can appreciate art, i.e., respond to that particular set of signifiers); exploitation by denying seriousness altogether. It is the work of the best movies in either medium to transcend, or transgress, these limitations—to break through the spectator's insulation.

In organizing the horror-film retrospective, Richard Lippe and I also set out to transgress. We wanted (through the book and the seminars, which only a very small proportion of our audience attended) to cut through the barriers bourgeois society erects as protection against the genre's implications—defenses that take many forms: laughter, contemptuous dismissal, the term "schlock," the phenomenon of the late-night horror show, the treatment of the horror film as camp.

In a way, *Last House* succeeded where we failed. A number of our customers—even in the context of a horror retrospective, even confronted by a somewhat bowdlerized print—gathered in the foyer after the screening to complain to the theater management that the film had been shown at all. Clearly, the film offers a very disturbing experience, its distinction lying in both the degree and nature of the disturbance. It is essential to this that its creation was a disturbing experience for Craven himself, a gentle, troubled, quiet-spoken ex-professor of English literature. The exploitation format, the request from the producer to "do a really violent film for $50,000," seems to have led him to discover things in himself he scarcely knew were there—which is also the effect it has on audiences.

"I found that I had never written anything like this," Craven said, "and I'd been writing for ten to twelve years already. I'd always written artistic, poetic things. Suddenly, I was working in an area I had never really confronted before. It was almost like doing a pornographic film if you'd been a fundamentalist. And I found that I was writing about things that I had very strong feelings about. I was drawing on things from very early in my own childhood, things that I was feeling about the war, and they were pouring into this very simple B-movie plot."

That extraordinary linking of "things from very early in my childhood" to "things that I was feeling about the war" is the kind of central perception about a film that criticism strives for and often misses. The connection between Vietnam and the fundamental structures of patriarchal culture is one I shall return to in discussing *Night Walk*.

The reason people find the violence in *Last House* so disturbing is not simply that there is so much of it, nor even that it is so relentlessly close and

186 - Neglected Nightmares

immediate in presentation. (Many, myself included, have come to praise films for being "Brechtian," but it should also be acknowledged that distanciation is not the only valid aesthetic method.) I want to draw here on ideas derived from an admirable book, *Violence in the Arts*, whose author, John Fraser, was a valuable contributing participant in our seminars. The book is one of the rare treatments of this subject that manages to be intelligent and responsible without ever lapsing into puritanism, hypocrisy, or complacency. Its weakness is, I think, a failure to argue clearly as to whether violence is innate in "the human condition" or a product of specific social structures or a combination of the two—to speculate, that is, as to the degree to which violence would disappear within a truly liberated society.[41]

Violence, whether actual or implicit, is so powerfully and obstinately inherent in human relationships as we know them (structured as they are on dominance and inequality) that the right to a "pure" denunciation of it must be a hard-won and precarious achievement. It is difficult to point to such an achievement in the cinema: perhaps Mizoguchi (the brandings and cutting of the tendon in *Sansho the Bailiff* [1954]), perhaps Fritz Lang (the scalding of Gloria Grahame in *The Big Heat* [1953])—but even there, what feelings are aroused by her eventual retaliation? As for myself, I am a committed pacifist who has experienced very strong desires to smash people's faces in and who can remember incidents when I joined in the persecution of those in an inferior position and took pleasure from it; I have also, not infrequently, been a victim, and my greatest dread is of total helplessness at the mercy of tormenters. It is these three positions—the position of victim, the position of violator, the position of righteous avenger—and the interconnections among them that *The Last House on the Left* dramatizes. Its distinction lies in the complex pattern of empathies that it creates.

To empathize exclusively with the victims is to see the violators as strictly other, nonhuman, to erect a clear-cut boundary between one's own humanity and the inhumanness of someone "out there"; it is the grave error Michael Cimino makes in the Vietnam sequences of that nonetheless great movie *The Deer Hunter* (1978). On the other hand, to empathize exclusively with the violators is to adopt the position of the sadist, seeing the victims as mere objects; it is a position to which Tobe Hooper's *The Texas Chainsaw*

Massacre (1974) comes perilously close, in its failure to endow its victims with any vivid, personalized aliveness. *Last House* involves the spectator, simultaneously and inescapably, in the experience of both violator and victim.

How does one recognize the aliveness of characters in a movie? What I am pointing to is not merely a matter of subjective impression; nor is it a matter of those "rounded," "complex" characters beloved of critics whose aesthetic criteria are derived from the psychological novel. What is crucial is the suggestion of common intimate experience shared between character and spectator, particularly the suggestion of vulnerability. It is there in the nervous, darting glances of the Viet Cong tormenter in *The Deer Hunter*—though not sufficiently to offset the film's horrified repudiation of him. It is there much more strongly in *The Texas Chainsaw Massacre*, especially in the little scene (echoed in *Eaten Alive* [1976] with Neville Brand) where Leatherface is seen alone and appears at a loss what to do next, but also in his curiously endearing dressing-up for the family dinner, complete with curly wig. In Hooper's films, however, such moments are reserved for the monstrous figures. The young people are scarcely more than objects, capable of nothing beyond a completely generalized and stereotypical display of pain and terror.

In *Last House*, all the major characters are allowed these moments of particularized vulnerability (except perhaps the father, the center of Bergman's film, relatively peripheral in Craven's). As the two girls rest in the woods on their way to the concert, Mari talks shyly and hesitantly to Phyllis about her sense of awakening womanhood, her developing breasts, her awareness of her own sexuality. The moment involves the spectator in an intimate relationship with her that makes objectification impossible. Yet her counterpart Sadie is equally alive, always groping toward an awareness that is beyond her grasp: she is acquainted with "Frood," and knows that a telegraph pole is "not just a telegraph pole but a giant phaylus"; she has also been brushed by feminism, to the extent that she can sum up one of the men who pushes her around as a "male chauvinist dog."

The men, corrupt and brutalized, never cease to be recognizably human: Weasel's horrendous castration nightmare, wherein the father, as dentist, prepares to knock out his front teeth with hammer and chisel, attests to a continuing capacity for Oedipal guilt. As for Junior, we have his embarrassed, puzzled, troubled reaction to the extraordinary moment where Mari, in a desperate attempt to seduce him into a relationship with her and break through the gang's objectification of her, confers upon him the name Willow and proceeds to offer to steal him a fix from her father's house.

One incident in Craven's original version clearly dramatized the breakdown of objectification; it must have been the most disturbing moment in this most disturbing of films, bringing home the common humanity of violators and victim. It may have been cut from all prints, but we have Craven's account of it.

> The killing of Phyllis is very sexual in feeling, and ended with her being stabbed not only by the men but by the woman repeatedly. Then she fell to the ground and Sadie bent down and pulled out a loop of her intestines. They looked at it and that's where it all stopped. That's when they realized what they had done, and they looked at each other and walked away. They were disgusted at what they had done. It was as if they had been playing with a doll, or a prisoner they thought was a doll, and it had broken and come apart and they did not know how to put it back together again. Again, there were parallels with what I was seeing in our culture, where we were breaking things that we did not know how to put back together.

The film offers no easily identifiable parallels to Vietnam (in the somewhat opportunistic, though eminently well intentioned, manner of *Little Big Man* [1970]). Instead, it analyzes the nature and conditions of violence and sees them as inherent in the American situation. Craven sees to it that the audience cannot escape the implications. We are spared nothing in the protracted tormenting of the two girls—our having to share the length of their ordeal is part of the point—and we cannot possibly enjoy it. They are us. Yet we also cannot disengage ourselves from their tormenters: they are us, too. We can share the emotional and moral outrage of the parents, yet they take hideous revenge on characters we have entered into an intimate relationship with, and we are kept very much aware that it is the revenge of the "haves" on the "have nots"—that the gang's monstrousness is the product of the inequalities and power structures of a class system into which all the characters are bound. No act of violence in the film is condoned, yet we are led to understand every act as the realization of potentials that exist within us all, that are intrinsic to our social and personal relationships.

The domination of the family by the father, the domination of the nation by the bourgeois class and its norms, the domination of other nations and other ideologies, more precisely, attempts at domination that inevitably fail and turn to mutual destruction—the structures interlock, are basically a single structure. My Lai was not an unfortunate occurrence out there; it was created within the American home. No film is more expressive than *Last House* of a(n) (inter)national social sickness, and no film is richer in Oedipal references—an extension, in its widest implications, of the minutiae of human relations under patriarchal-capitalist culture. Craven is fully aware of this macrocosm/microcosm relationship; I leave the last word to him, adding merely that these concerns are taken up (with great intelligence, a higher budget, more polish, but less disturbing intensity) in *The Hills Have Eyes* (1977), a work that, while it has not to my knowledge received serious critical treatment, is scarcely unknown.

> The family is the best microcosm to work with. If you go much beyond that you're getting away from a lot of the roots of our own primeval feelings. Let's face it, most of the basic stories and the basic feelings involve very few people: Mommy, Daddy, me, siblings, and the people in the other room. I like to stay within that circle. It's very much where most of our strong emotions or gut feelings come from. It's from those very early experiences and how they are worked out. I grew up in a white working-class family that was very religious, and there was an enormous amount of secrecy in the general commerce of our getting along with each other. Certain things were not mentioned. A lot of things were not spoken of or talked about. If there was an argument it was immediately denied. If there was a feeling it was repressed. As I got older I began to see that as a nation we were doing the same thing.

Stephanie Rothman

Throughout the series of directors' seminars that formed part of "The American Nightmare," one question recurred: what was the filmmaker's attitude to the possibility of social change, and did s/he feel a responsibility in that direction? The responses of the five directors we interviewed seem closely relevant to their work—indeed, almost deducible from it, though such correspondences are not as common as one might logically expect.

For Brian De Palma, the cultural situation is beyond any hope, social change impossible, and all one has left is to enjoy the fascinating spectacle of corruption and disintegration as best one can; generally, he wanted to discuss his films as formal exercises (invoking Hitchcock as precedent), disclaiming much interest in what they were about. David Cronenberg's attitude was, roughly, that as we all die in the end anyway, what does it matter? He resisted any social analysis of his films in favor of a metaphysical reading (they are about "mortality"). George Romero gave what was at once the most equivocal, guarded, and complex answer. He by no means rejected notions of social engagement but didn't think of his work primarily in such terms; the desire to change society might be present but was not a primary, conscious motivation. Only Stephanie Rothman and Wes Craven gave unequivocal affirmative answers on the subject of the artist's responsibility; both wished to make films that engaged directly and progressively with social issues.

I certainly don't wish to attribute any absolute authority to an artist's view of her/his own work; but my growing distrust of De Palma's work, my hatred of Cronenberg's, and my increasing interest in and respect for that of the other three directors all received support from their statements. Equally, of course, one must resist any simplistic equation between conscious social engagement and artistic merit: it is the work that confers significance on the artist's statement, not vice versa.

The interest of Stephanie Rothman's films has been signaled in a number of places—in the work of feminist critics and in a *Film Comment* article by Terry Curtis Fox.[42] Only one of her films (*The Velvet Vampire* [1971]) belongs within the horror genre, though we also screened *Terminal Island* (1973) for its treatment of violence as a response to oppression.

Rothman's work embodies a vitality, inventiveness, and general likability that suggest a potential far beyond the films' actual achievement. I have not seen a Rothman film for which I would stick out my neck, as I would for Larry Cohen's *Demon* (*God Told Me To*, 1976), De Palma's *Sisters* (1972), Romero's *Dawn of the Dead* (1978), or *The Last House on the Left*. But perhaps the absence from her work to date of the fully convincing, fully realized film should not be seen in personal terms or even in terms of the specific production setups (with obvious deficiencies of budget, casting, and shooting schedules) of each film.

Rothman's films—and particularly *The Velvet Vampire*—raise the question of whether a feminist intervention in heavily male-dominated and traditionally sexist genres can be more than disruptive, can produce more than sketchy, fragmented and self-contradictory texts. De Palma's *Sisters* (cowritten by Louisa Rose) suggests that a coherent feminist horror movie is possible, though only in negative terms: the systematic analysis of the oppression of women, the annihilation of any movement of revolt. It is Rothman's desire to offer more positive statements that makes her films at once so sympathetic and so problematic. *Group Marriage* (1973), for example, is one of the only American films actually to propose alternatives to the battered ideological tradition of monogamous relationships, but it evades most of the problems it raises under the alibi of being a light comedy.

The inclusion of *Terminal Island* in the retrospective foregrounded, among other things, the perennial quandary of genre movies with ulterior motives. For me, the film, though invigorating and effective (unlike Terry Curtis Fox, I don't sense any inhibitions whatever in Rothman's treatment of violence), is too clear-cut, too pared down to the bare lines of a thesis; a message movie is a message movie, even if one likes the message. Yet, to judge from the reactions of our audience, most people respond only to the generic signifier and miss the message altogether. Despite all the work on genre and "entertainment" that has been done in film education, reactions to films remain largely determined by the spectator's cultural position. To recognize a film as exploitation, etc. is instantly to know how to respond to it, and all local particularities and inflections become obliterated.

As a "fable for our time," *Terminal Island* works beautifully. To save the taxpayers' money, convicts who would otherwise be subject to the death

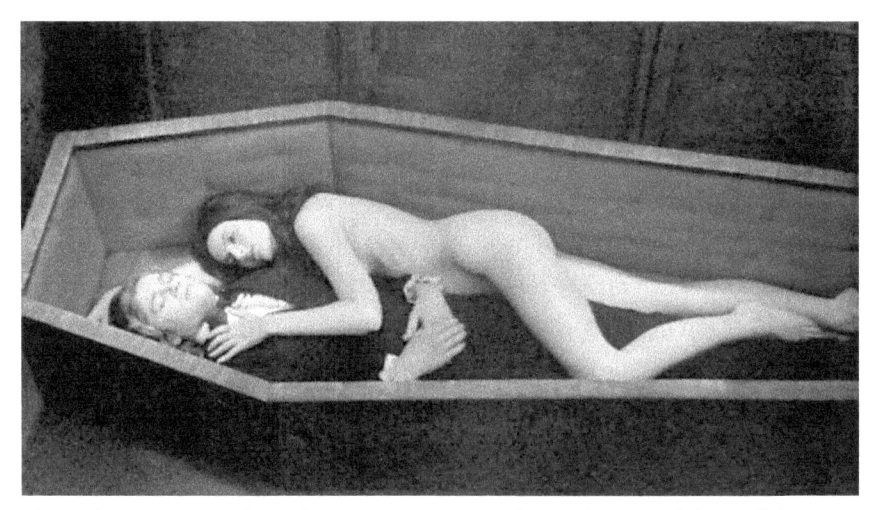

The Velvet Vampire (1971) raises questions about the possibility of feminist intervention in the traditionally sexist genre of horror.

penalty or life imprisonment are released to fend for themselves on a small island off the coast of California. The action begins and ends with the arrival of the boat that periodically deposits new islanders. The woman who arrives at the start finds a state not without parallels in the real world: on the one hand, a primitive quasifascist dictatorship based on force and terrorization, in which women are prostitutes ignominiously servicing the men; on the other, a band of guerrillas, disruptive and violent but ultimately impotent and disorganized. The women escape to the guerrillas, help overthrow the dictatorship, and exert their new power to create a free democracy based on true equality (including of course full sexual equality). When the boat arrives at the end, it brings a new murderess and a pardon for the doctor convicted of euthanasia. The doctor decides not to leave—not, as in the traditional genre movie, because he has fallen in love, but because he recognized the superiority of the new order to the "civilized" world that awaits him; and the new woman is welcomed into the order by her sisters.

The film works partly because the action-movie format permits the simplification of the issues and problems arising from the contemporary crisis in male and female roles. But the film's limitations are not, I think, solely explicable in terms of generic determinants. Rothman's work suggests that she is more a liberal feminist than a radical feminist; the key issue of bisexuality is repeatedly evaded or refused recognition as an issue. The statement that *Terminal Island* seems to be making is that men and women should collaborate and accept each other on equal terms. Fine, of course, as far as it goes; but it leaves undisturbed the fact that the terms "men" and "women" are themselves culturally defined and defined in terms of specific roles.

The group in *Group Marriage* explicitly rejects bisexuality; on the periphery of the group hovers a gay couple conceived in terms of the most blatant sexual stereotyping. The film does not treat them unkindly; they are permitted to join the group wedding ceremony at the film's climax, but as a couple who tag along, not as full members. Rothman's feminism never wants to acknowledge that the male and female roles of our culture are built upon the repression of bisexuality and the resultant separation and reinforcing of masculinity and femininity. She wants men and women to be equal—but without ceasing to be men and women as our culture defines and conditions them.

Bisexuality is allowed far greater freedom in *The Velvet Vampire* but is treated very equivocally. Both the release and the equivocation are characteristic of the horror genre. I find the film very difficult to come to terms with: it is imaginative and audacious, gaining a strong impetus from Rothman's interest in Surrealism (in her seminar she expressed a debt to and great admiration for Jean Cocteau and Georges Franju), but riven by contradictory impulses and confusions.

The feminist inflection actually intensifies the genre's unresolvable quandary—a problem developed in various ways by Andrew Britton, Richard Lippe, and me in our essays in *The American Nightmare*. To wit: if one accepts that the "monster" of the horror film is the embodiment of all that our culture represses, and that (as a direct consequence of this) the monster of almost every "progressive" horror film is necessarily the most sympathetic character, isn't any attempt to find a positive resolution to the conflicts doomed to failure by the inescapable connotations of evil inherent in the genre's basic premises? Larry Cohen's *It's Alive* (1974) and *It Lives Again* (1978) drive the notion of the "positive" monster as far as it can be driven; George Romero's *Night of the Living Dead* and *Dawn of the Dead* sidestep the problem by removing all positive connotations from the monsters and restoring them to the human beings.

Both directors reach the point where, logically, the genre would have to be abandoned altogether. *The Velvet Vampire* never progresses beyond confusion, but its internal contradictions are very interesting.

They are centered, of course, in the vampire Diane herself. The plot concerns her shifting relationship with a "normal" young couple (quasiliberated, i.e., bourgeois-trendy) whom she picks up at an art exhibition and invites to her desert retreat, where she seduces them both (thereby anticipating *The Rocky Horror Show* [1975] by several years). Logically, she should represent a deeper level of sexual liberation than the young couple have hitherto experienced, and this meaning does seem to be intermittently present. This reading is undermined, however, by the fact that Diane's most obvious connotations link her to decadence and perversity. Rothman, in other words, equivocates with her very much as Bernardo Bertolucci equivocates with the Dominique Sanda character of *The Conformist* (1970).

The issue is obfuscated further by the fact that Diane is obsessively tied to a husband (apparently one of those "real men" who, once bedded, is never forgotten), to whom she is faithful, in her fashion; the husband is long dead, so necrophilia enters in as well. By the end of the film, the character, in terms of the values she is meant to embody, seems quite unreadable. Rothman produces a splendid climax, with Diane destroyed in the Los Angeles sunshine by an impromptu lynch mob of young people mindlessly waving at her crosses snatched from a souvenir stall: repression restored by the permissive young having a ball. But the kind of liberation Diane embodies—if indeed she can be said to embody any at all (but if she doesn't, then what is the film about?)—is by this time so unclear that the spectator scarcely knows how to react.

Bob Clark

THE GREAT PERIOD OF the American horror film was the period of Watergate and Vietnam: the genre required a moment of ideological crisis for its full significance to emerge, the immediate cultural breakdown calling into question far more than a temporary political situation. It is scarcely a coincidence that both Wes Craven and George Romero see certain of their films—*The Hills Have Eyes* and *The Crazies* (1973), respectively—as deliberate, if oblique, commentaries on Vietnam and its impact on the structures of American society. The reference of Bob Clark's *Night Walk* (also known, in the manner of commercially dubious propositions, by several aliases: *Deathdream* and *Dead of Night*) is more direct. The film, made in 1972, seems to have been almost entirely buried; it is certainly worth digging up again. It shares with Clark's subsequent films (*Black Christmas* [1974], *Murder by Decree* [1979]) a certain laboriousness at the level of mise-en-scène, an overanxiety that points be clearly made. But the concept is remarkable and rigorously worked out; the film accumulates tremendous force by the time its climactic sequences are reached.

Its premise is that a young man, killed in Vietnam, is willed home by his mother (Lynn Carlin). He returns as a zombie, able to sustain himself only on human blood and driven by a desire for revenge on the society that sent him to war. The film's resonances develop out of the three-way connection set up among the raw materials of the horror film, the family, and Vietnam. Its anticipations are very striking: not just the basic concept (the monster as product of the family) but whole sequences evoke *It's Alive* and Romero's *Martin* (1978). The coincidental proximity of these three distinguished films, without any direct connecting links or influence, greatly strengthens the argument that to study the evolution of a genre is to study the evolution of a national (un)consciousness.

Few horror films have been so explicit about the monstrousness of patriarchal family structures. Within the home, the mother rules—the reward for her

Black Christmas (1974): A certain laboriousness at the level of mise-en-scène.

196 - Neglected Nightmares

exclusion from the world of money, power, and politics. She devotes her frustrated energies entirely to the perpetuation of patriarchy, in the shape of her obsessively adored son, relegating her daughter to unconsidered subordination and an impotent and furtive complicity with the ineffectual father (John Marley). The family is seen as a structure of relationships based on hate masquerading as love; everything is to be sacrificed for the son, the future patriarch, the most "loved," hence most resented, of the family group. Of Andy, the son, the film offers (by presentation and implication) a double image: nice, unremarkable boy and devouring ghoul—a figure quite inadequate to sustain the ideological burden he is meant to carry. The film never falls into the simplistic trap of innocent boy corrupted by horrors of war. It was not Vietnam alone that produced Andy's monstrousness.

The dinner scene near the start of the film, before Andy's return, establishes the theme succinctly. The roast is brought in, and the mother insists that the father carve it; she loves to watch the head of the family carve. Andy has already learned to carve beautifully, as befits a future head of a future family. It is the symbol of his position and the duties that go with it—duties that clearly extend to "serving his country," killing, and being killed. Imperialism begins at home. So the father carves, very awkwardly and badly, as his wife watches admiringly.

The film builds logically from that moment to a climax of sustained hysteria: the mother frantically driving her vampire son to the grave he has prepared for himself, before he can wreak further destruction on the community and the family. The film's ultimate insight is remarkable: that, under patriarchy, the patriarch suffers as much as anyone and from the very assumptions that enthrone him as an ideologically privileged figure. The film is also a useful reminder that a radical statement about Vietnam must be a statement about much more.

George Romero

Anyone happening today upon earlier articles I wrote for *Film Comment* in 1978 on the horror film must be aware of an absence so glaring as to appear a major critical aberration: aside from a few casual references to *Night of the Living Dead*, George Romero was ignored, and neither the nature nor the scope of his achievement was given recognition.[43] In my defense, I must therefore point out that, at that time, *Dawn of the Dead* had not been completed, *Martin* had not been released in Canada, and both *Jack's Wife* and *The Crazies* appeared entirely inaccessible. What reputation they had did nothing to suggest that they might be worth the effort of tracing. I assumed, then, that *Night of the Living Dead* represented a one-shot success that its director had feebly tried (with *The Crazies*) to repeat. The news that Romero was currently "remaking" it provoked little beyond a raised eyebrow.

I have made some amends in *The American Nightmare*. Clearly, Romero's work demands extended treatment, and in the space available here I can do no more than indicate the lines that exploration might take. To remedy at once, however, the deficiencies of those earlier articles: Romero has already produced a rich, coherent, and substantial oeuvre, an achievement matched, in the '70s horror genre, only by Larry Cohen; none of the films merely repeats or "remakes" others; the neglected works, far from being negligible, add important dimensions to our knowledge of Romero as an artist and deserve a general rediscovery; *Dawn of the Dead* seems to me among the half dozen best American movies of the 1970s.

The five Romero films I have now seen (his comedy, *There's Always Vanilla* [1971], remains inaccessible[44]) divide clearly into two groups: on the one hand, *Night*, *Dawn*, and *The Crazies*; on the other, *Jack's Wife* and *Martin*. Within each group the films can be seen as complex variations on one another; what I want to consider briefly here is the relationship between the two groups. But both groups also stand in an interestingly eccentric relationship to the mainstream horror film (Cohen's work, while not superior, is much more central), and this needs to be defined first.

Romero's zombies carry none of the positive connotations of a "return of the repressed." Their most obvious antecedent is the pod people of *Invasion of the Body Snatchers* (1956), though they lack the unresolved and unprofitable ambiguity (Commies or capitalists?) of Don Siegel's film. The zombies can be read as representing the heritage of the past from which the protagonists must struggle to free themselves. Their most obvious characteristic is their need—apparently their sole need—to consume. They represent, that is, the logical end result, the reductio ad absurdum and ad nauseum, of capitalism; the fact that they consume flesh is but a literal enactment of the notion that under capitalism we all live off other people. *Dawn* makes this meaning explicit in the zombies' gravitation, from force of habit, to the shopping mall, and also spells out the relationship of the zombies to the surviving humans ("They are us") whose behavior patterns they reflect and parody.

All three films relate this theme of consumerism to the major relationship structures of capitalist society, but with significantly different emphases. The main focus of *Night* (the most "traditional" of the three) is on the family, with the zombies acting out the repressed aggressions between brother and sister, child and parents. *The Crazies*, thematically as well as chronologically, occupies a midway position between the two Dead films, reflecting the earlier film's concern with the family (though the precredits sequence is the only close recapitulation) and anticipating elements of *Dawn of the Dead*.

Dawn abandons the family to juxtapose the two dominant "couple" relationships of our culture and our cinema: heterosexual marriage, in a society where the sexes are not equal; and the male buddy relationship, where the price of equality is the repression of sexuality. The tentative, provisional optimism of the end—the (temporary) escape by helicopter of the surviving partners of the two relationships, between whom there is never any question of any kind of coupling—is given added point by the presence of a third passenger, the woman's unborn baby, and by the final use the film makes of its two emblems of male authority: the man relinquishes his rifle to the zombies, and the woman is piloting the helicopter.

Jack's Wife and *Martin* counterpoint the progression represented by these three films. Certain oppositions between the two groups help define their relationship. The three films in the first group are built on events, the two in the second (as their titles indicate) on the development and fate of individual protagonists. The first group are about the disintegration of the established order, the second are about people trying to define themselves within it and ultimately being defeated or destroyed by it. The implications of Romero's work are that the total disintegration of society is the necessary prerequisite for new growth. For *Jack's Wife* and for *Martin*, even the heavily qualified optimism of *Dawn of the Dead* is impossible.

The society symbolized in fable or parody form by the zombies is realistically dramatized in *Jack's Wife* and *Martin*; the structures and values of high and low bourgeoisie (respectively) are presented as equally constricting and demoralizing. The two films are perfect companion pieces: the feminist concern with the oppression of women that counterpoints the main plot of *Martin* is the dominant issue of the earlier work. Central to both films is the protagonist's

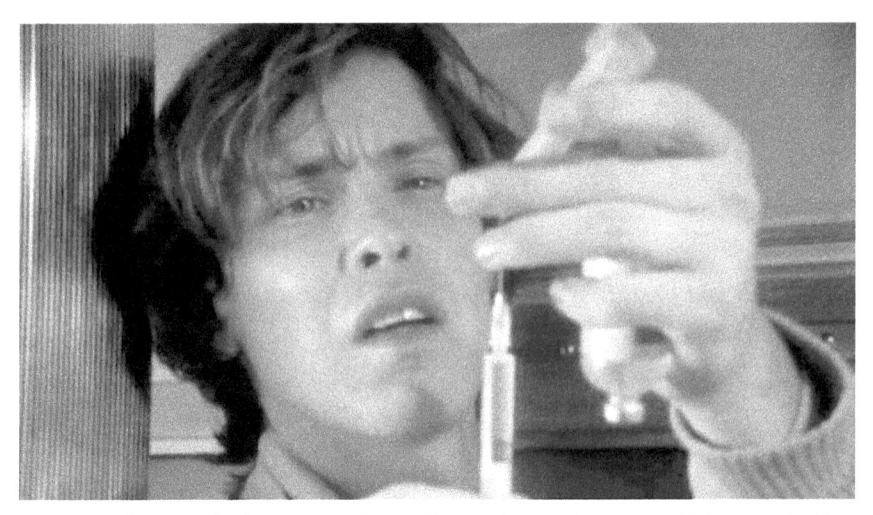

Martin (John Amplas) imagines himself as a doomed vampire (*Martin*, 1978).

sense of ignominy, of having no respect or recognition as a person. Jack's wife is simply that; she is defined exclusively in relation to the male. Martin's sensitivity and particularity are accorded no value; he is treated as a mental defective, pushed around, reduced to the status of errand boy. So Joan becomes a witch and Martin becomes a vampire (in his case, a ready-made identity, an aspect of his ethnic inheritance). Being a witch gives Joan the illusion of power; Martin's fantasies present him to himself as a charismatic, doomed romantic hero desired by women, hunted down by the society whose codes he transgresses.

But, as Martin himself realizes, "there is no magic." He is not a romantic vampire but a sexually disturbed boy who cuts the veins of his drugged victims with razor blades. Joan isn't a witch but an isolated woman moving from one servitude to another; her opening dream of being her husband's dog is echoed at the end when, as part of her initiation into the coven, she is led on a leash.

Romero must be perfectly aware that the only answer, within the world he creates, is revolution—and the problem of how a revolutionary filmmaker continues to work within a commercial entertainment medium is likely to become more and more pressing. Meanwhile, he is the producer of an impressive body of work within which no individual film is superfluous. Each throws light on all the others, and it is important that *The Crazies* and *Jack's Wife* be rescued from oblivion.

(1980)

"Art" and Alligators

The revelation that the Canadian Film Development Corporation helped finance *My Bloody Valentine* (1981) raised a few eyebrows and provoked a few protests (gentle, of course, because after all, the film did make money—though not much—and for that the priests of capitalism are ready to absolve practically any sin). My impulse is to join the protesters (the film is neither the most inept nor the most offensive of the *Halloween* spin-offs, unlike *Don't Go into The House* [1979], but it has nothing positive to offer on any level worth considering). Yet I hesitate. To such protests there is usually a corollary, explicit or implicit: "Why do they support films like *My Bloody Valentine*?" tends to be followed in the next breath by "Why don't they help set up more films like *Les Bons Débarras* [1980]?"

That word "like" is quite a problem. "Films like *My Bloody Valentine*" doesn't just mean *bad* films, and films "like *Les Bons Débarras*" doesn't just mean *good* films (though that is probably what such critics think they mean). In fact, beyond a very superficial level, no film is really "like" any other film: to stick to the Halloween cycle, there is a world of difference between *Don't Go in the House* (1979) and *He Knows You're Alone* (1980), in sophistication, awareness, intelligence, and sensitivity. It seems fair to say that, in relation to *Valentine* and *Débarras*, "like" refers to certain categories of films which—objectively considered—carry no guarantees of quality one way or the other. The valuing of one category over the other is determined by the contingencies of class position and bourgeois aesthetics.

The high esteem with which *Les Bons Débarras* is generally regarded (many think it's the sort of film by which Canada might be proud to be internationally represented) is dependent on a number of factors commonly mistaken for positive qualities:

1. Crucially, it's a film that wants to resist generic classification. It's about a "pioneer" family (of sorts), yet it clearly isn't a Western; it has a monstrous

child, but no one will mistake it for a horror movie; it contains the odd incursion into opera, but it certainly isn't a musical. To classify it as "family melodrama" (which is accurate, in terms of basic subject matter), goes against the film's wishes: it would find such terms demeaning.

2. So what does the film want to be? Clearly, "realistic," a "slice of life." Genre movies are, almost by definition, not "realistic," though some try to be (e.g., some Westerns are commonly regarded as more "realistic," i.e., better, than others). The currency and prestige this word continues to command, despite the prolonged and dedicated assaults of structuralists and semiologists, is amazing. In fact, it should by now be clear that "realism" in the arts implies no more than an aesthetic preference for one set of codes over others and carries no evaluative validity whatever.

3. Genre films have stereotypes, *Les Bons Débarras* has "real people" (like us): the signifiers of real-icity with which the film is so loaded are particularly evident in the acting.

4. Since the film is about "real life" and "real people," it follows that it has, of course, no ideological position: it is simply "truth."

What all this adds up to—in terms of bourgeois aesthetics—is "art" (which is, somehow, despite the common linguistic root, mysteriously distinct from and even opposed to "artifice" and "artifacts"). The film offers—by providing this contact with reality in an apparently unmediated form—a rich emotional experience conceived as being somehow valuable as such. In fact, the film could be taken as representative of bourgeois "art" at its most insidious (and most intractably and irreducibly bourgeois), using the alibis of "real life" and "individual psychology" to conceal and validate the most reactionary position. Directed by one male from a book by another, the film is centrally posited on the incompetence and malice of the female deprived of (or perversely rejecting) male guidance. At a time when the media generally conceal or downplay the serious social problem of the sexual harassment of little girls by heterosexual males (in order to define pedophilia as a specifically gay phenomenon) the film reinforces the myth that little girls really like to be molested and to invent malicious stories about it. At a time when more and more women are struggling to define themselves outside marriage (the institution of oppression par excellence), the film posits the disaster of the fatherless family: the confusion of the mother, the evil of the daughter (insufficiently controlled and conditioned). Has anyone noticed that the particular bit of opera playing on the truck radio in the scene of the brother's suicide *just happens*—as this is a "realistic" movie it must just have been on at the time—to be Puccini's "O My Beloved Daddy"?

The term "genre" being notoriously loose we can, after all, tentatively redefine the genre to which *Les Bons Débarras* belongs, in two ways: (a) It belongs, though in an oblique way (through the *absence* of a generically central male figure), to that current cycle of films that invite us to feel endless compassion for the suffering and noble endurance of our patriarchs who have to bear such a huge burden (the burden, especially, for being represented by the women they have been oppressing for so many centuries); a cycle ranging from the pseudorespectable *Ordinary People* (1980) to the transparently despicable *Middle Age Crazy* (1980). (b) Less obliquely, but more vaguely, the film belongs to that genre that might be defined as "films that are taken seriously by the journalist-reviewers of the bourgeois press and win awards."

Around the time when *My Bloody Valentine* and *Les Bons Débarras* were earning money and prestige, respectively, a little American horror movie called *Alligator* (1980) slipped in and out of Toronto, earning neither. No one, I suppose (least of all its makers), is going to claim that it is a great movie: in fact it is quite a trivial piece. But it strikes me as at least more honest, neither cynically exploiting and manipulating its audience nor inviting them to mistake it for "reality." Instead, it invites them to play with generic conventions, managing (in a way that recalls Hawks's classic *The Thing from Another World* [1951]) both to enhance its own sense of generic fantasy and to remain very exciting. Its premise is magnificent: a little girl on vacation with her mother visits a safari park where she watches an attendant almost get his leg bitten off by an alligator; she immediately acquires a pet baby alligator. In the next scene we see why: her bombastic and repressive father comes home and (objecting to his daughter's possession of the phallus) flushes it down the toilet. It retreats to the sewers where, in the course of the credits and the next twelve years, it grows to thirty-six feet and (in the words of the splendid poster) is "about to break out." The film never quite fulfils its feminist promise, but it does produce an attractively Hawksian male-female relationship based on equality and independence, and it does permit the alligator (before its obligatory destruction) to kill off all the more offensive father figures in the cast.

Whether *Alligator* is a "better" film than *Les Bons Débarras* is not an easy question. It is certainly more progressive socially, it displays a sophisticated and intelligent use of the mainstream cinema's methods of representation instead of trying to conceal them, and it draws on a whole tradition of accumulated generic meaning. Unpretentiousness, however, can function as a limitation as well as a virtue. By contrast, thoroughly as I dislike Francis Mankiewicz's film, I have to admit that the aesthetic assumptions of our culture encouraged him to take his own work seriously. It is worth suggesting, however, that the question "Why aren't there more Canadian films like *Les Bons Débarras*?" is no more pertinent than the question "In popular Canadian cinema, why are there no *Alligators*, but only an endless procession of prom nights, bloody valentines, cries in the night, and happy birthdays to me?"

(1981)

BURYING THE UNDEAD

The Use and Obsolescence of Count Dracula

"Oh my God, what have we done to have this terror upon us?"
    Bram Stoker, *Dracula*

THE IMMENSE CULTURAL SIGNIFICANCE of Count Dracula (and associated vampire mythology) cannot be doubted; it is attested to by the fictional persistence of the count within our culture and especially underlined by the fact that there have been at least five major film versions of Bram Stoker's 1890 novel: those by F. W. Murnau (1922), Tod Browning (1931), Terence Fisher (1958), Werner Herzog (1979), and John Badham (1979). In addition, a distinguished television version with Louis Jourdan appeared in 1978—not to mention minor versions, sequels, spin-offs, and related movies on vampire themes. It is not farfetched to claim that Count Dracula offers himself as a privileged focus for any inquiry into the possibilities of liberation within Western civilization.

Dracula mythology has various historical sources and literary precedents, but its major cultural importance clearly begins with Stoker's novel. As a figure of popular myth in Western culture, Dracula is the product of Victorian sexual repressiveness; over ninety years later, we are still trying to exorcise him.

My objective in the following essay is to explore the implications of this situation through a consideration of the differences and similarities between Stoker's novel and the films of Murnau and Badham, respectively the earliest and the most recent major film treatments, as well as the two most distinguished, challenging, and intelligent of the lot. Specifically, I shall begin by establishing the most important variants in the three versions; then I will take a closer look at Stoker's novel; and finally I will return to the two film versions to identify what seems to be their essential contribution to the Dracula mystique.

The clearest way of setting forth the major variants is to examine in turn each of the five main characters. In Stoker's novel, Renfield is explicitly insane, an inmate of Dr. Seward's asylum; in Murnau's film, he is the estate agent who sends Jonathan to Transylvania and plans Dracula's invasion of civilization; in Badham, he is Dracula's servant/assistant from the outset. The novel explains why Dracula chooses Renfield as an assistant and is able to manipulate him: he is zoophagous and hence prone to vampiristic tendencies; but Stoker does not account for the basis of his carnivorous appetites nor define precisely what they might entail. Murnau provides no explanation whatsoever, and while this might seem to be a weakness, it can be argued to be a strength; for what Dracula (called Nosferatu) represents is something that already exists—albeit in a feebler form—at the heart of civilization.[45]

Of all the five major characters, Jonathan undergoes the least change (perhaps because he is the least interesting, the obligatory "leading man" whose function is taken for granted). The first part of Murnau's film follows the first part of the novel quite closely; Badham denies Jonathan even the quasiheroic status of the trip to Transylvania and the personal confrontation with Dracula in his castle. Whereas Stoker wants Jonathan read as the conventional "noble hero" and Badham reduces him to a conventional nonentity, Murnau emphasizes his impotence before the terrible forces, creating Dracula as Jonathan's repressed double through a complex and systematic use of mirror images. His precise relationship to the woman changes somewhat from work to work: in Stoker they are engaged and marry during the course of the novel; in Murnau they are married from the outset; in Badham they are only engaged and never marry. Only Badham suggests that they indulge in premarital intercourse, thereby significantly weakening the connotations of Dracula as the product of sexual repression, a change of emphasis crucial to the meaning of the film: the opposition becomes that of the ordinary guy vs. the sexual superman.

Much more complex, in this comparativist respect, is the figure of Van Helsing, for here the crucial changes involve the novel's three central characters, and one quickly realizes that a change in one necessitates a modification of the others, so intricate and essential are the interconnections.

Dracula (1979): The vampire as sexual superman.

In the novel, Van Helsing is one of the three major characters; he and Dracula battle for possession of the woman (the outcome viewed as her damnation/salvation). Murnau, however, demotes Van Helsing to an amiable old fuddy-duddy who lectures on venus flytraps but achieves nothing whatever; Badham preserves the central conflict in Stoker but totally transforms, or reinterprets, the implicit attitudes and sympathies.

As for the female protagonist, here we have first to clear up some confusing name changes—the reason why hitherto I have referred to the heroine as "the woman" rather than by a name. In Stoker, Lucy is the weaker girl who becomes vampirized by Dracula and begins to prey on others; Mina—the major character of the two—is at first engaged to Jonathan and subsequently marries him; Dracula assaults her, and the men have to struggle to rescue her from his power. Murnau reduces Lucy to insignificance (all but eliminating her from the film) and changes Mina to Nina, making her the vampire's antagonist and destroyer (the reason, obviously, for the demoting of Van Helsing). Badham—confusingly—reverses the two names, seemingly a result of his decision to make the first, weaker woman Van Helsing's daughter (in the novel, Van Helsing, like Dracula, is not related to anyone): Van Helsing is Dutch, and Lucy is not a Dutch name, but Mina could be short for Wilhelmina. The facility of this name change, however, may also point to the recognition that, despite the way in which Stoker insistently *contrasts* the characters, the women are to some degree interchangeable—or two aspects of a composite figure.

The distinction in characterization between the two women is simple and obvious—and carried over from Stoker to Badham fairly consistently. Stoker's Lucy is a lightweight, frivolous figure—"girlish," as the term is popularly used; his Mina is stronger, more solid, more intelligent, more determined. Yet both are repeatedly described as feminine ideals (though sexually mature women, both are called "little girls" by their menfolk), so to see them as two sides of the same coin is entirely appropriate. Taken together, they can be seen as exemplifying a deep-seated Victorian unease about womanhood which (as the Badham version demonstrates) our culture has still not resolved nearly a hundred years later. Stoker's Lucy embodies the more obvious Victorian ideal of what a woman should be: helpless, rather silly, irresistibly pretty, in urgent need of the protection and leadership of a good, strong, noble man. Yet there lingers the constant sense that a woman who is strong, intelligent, clear sighted (but still, of course, irresistibly pretty—or here should one say "beautiful"?—and still, somehow, totally dependent on the male) would be even better. But what to do with such a type? She scarcely needs that male protection and thereby constitutes an implicit threat to male supremacy. By actually improving on the ideal, she raises problems.

In any case, all the three versions have one crucial recognition in common: it is the woman that the work is really about.[46] This is especially clear in the Badham film (wherein much of the fascination lies in its efforts to cope with feminism), but it is equally true of the novel, or at least its second half, to which Mina is absolutely central and in which Dracula appears only intermittently. A similar claim can be made for the Murnau film, where, as we have seen, Nina is raised to the status of the vampire's true antagonist.

Before leaving the female roles, I should indicate one further important difference between Stoker and Badham. In the novel, Mina has no parents and Lucy's are very minor figures. Dr. Seward, head of the asylum, is one of Lucy's three suitors, the other two (a British lord and a rich American—shades of Henry James!) being dropped from (as far as I know) all the film versions but the Louis Jourdan television adaptation. It is the Badham version that, very interestingly, makes Mina Van Helsing's daughter and Lucy Dr. Seward's—the paralleling of the two women echoed in the paralleling of the two fathers, with the weak woman having the strong father and vice versa.

Dracula himself also undergoes striking transformations from version to version. In the book, he is an old man when Jonathan encounters him in Transylvania, and he is rejuvenated in England by fresh blood. But he is never as grotesque as Max Schreck (Murnau) nor as romantically attractive as Frank Langella (Badham): the two films "exaggerate" him in precisely opposite directions. It should also be pointed out that, after the Transylvania prologue, Dracula virtually disappears from the surface action of the novel, reappearing only in occasional fleeting glimpses. There is nothing in the novel corresponding to Murnau's account of Dracula's journey, nor to the scenes between Dracula and Lucy in Badham's version. To account for this situation, let us turn now to a consideration of the implications of Stoker's narrative technique.

Obviously the diary/journal/letter format employed by Stoker makes for an extremely cumbersome and frequently implausible narrative. How fortunate that so many of the characters keep diaries, and of such inordinate length and detail, often reporting entire conversations verbatim—or entire speeches in broken English by the interminable Van Helsing! How do they find the time, patience, and inclination, with so many extraordinary things going on around them? About the midpoint of the book, furthermore, there comes a time when, for the narrative to continue, it becomes necessary for all the characters to read each other's diaries, so that they may catch up with the reader, in the intervals of congratulating each other (their other major occupation) on their extraordinary goodness and nobility. The insistence on goodness and nobility is itself significant, far exceeding the requirements of Victorian courtesies: one way of describing the book today might be to say that it is about the price at which all that goodness and nobility must be bought.

Also significant, I think, is that the diary form is a means of excluding from any apparent control over the narrative the two most powerful presences of the novel: Count Dracula himself and Bram Stoker. The author, who conceived Dracula, must absolve himself of all responsibility and guilt for that conception; with his (superficial, profoundly hypocritical) commitment to the "good" and the "noble," he must never be seen to describe Dracula himself, in his own person, and above all must never appear to enter into the count's mind. The corollary is that Dracula must never be allowed a voice, a discourse, a point of view: he must remain the unknowable, whom the narrative is about, but of whom it simultaneously disowns all intimate knowledge. All the presented discourses are those of the good and the noble; it is only through their voices that their author must be seen to speak. It is up to the reader to supply the discourse of Dracula, from the manifold hints the book offers.

Another important aspect of this disowning of Dracula has to do with his foreignness. The remoteness and inaccessibility of his Transylvanian fastness are repeatedly stressed. The first pages of the novel introduce the motif of the crossing of bridges—a piece of symbolism vividly taken up by Murnau and his screenwriter ("And when he had crossed the bridge, the phantoms came to meet him"). The book also has Jonathan cross the "Mittel Land" into regions where language ceases to be recognizable or clearly identifiable. The only intermediaries between Dracula and civilization are those upon whom he depends for transport: the Szgany, gypsies, traditionally regarded as outside civilization, deeply suspect and dangerous, and possessors of magical powers. Dracula himself is descended from Attila and the Huns, the traditional enemies of the civilized world. He is also, of course, associated insistently with the animal kingdom, especially nocturnal animals such as wolves and bats.

The other attribute given to Dracula and Transylvania is that they are dreamlike and are, in fact, the characters' dreams, the nightmares of the good and noble, who at various points in the book are said to rub their eyes in the expectation of waking up. It is worth mentioning here that, according to the testimony of their creators, all three of the archetypal works to which virtually all our horror literature and cinema can be traced back—*Frankenstein* (1818), *Dr. Jekyll and Mr. Hyde* (1886), and *Dracula* (1897) itself—had their origins in nightmares. As Bram Stoker's nightmare, then, Count Dracula cannot be so easily disowned, just as we, living in the post-Freudian age, cannot be so innocent about nightmares as was possible for Mary Shelley, Stevenson, and Stoker.

The monstrous figures from our dreams are our images of our repressed selves, and thus Transylvania, by extension, becomes the land of the unconscious, an interpretation which is thoroughly continued by Stoker's imagery. There is the whole nightmare-like account of Jonathan's journey to the castle at the opening, with its wolves and mysterious lights hovering on the verge of impenetrable darkness; and consider this, from near the close, as the party returns to Transylvania to hunt Dracula down: "It is a wild adventure that we are on. Here, as we are rushing along through the darkness, with the cold from the river seeming to rise up and strike us; with all the mysterious voices of the night around us, *it all comes home*. We seem to be drifting into unknown places and unknown ways; into a whole world of dark and dreadful things" (emphasis added).[47] For all the emphasis on "unknown" places, "it all comes home": the sense of terrible familiarity, combined with the sense of helplessness suggested by "drifting," must be read not only in terms of the repetition of past experience but as referring to the familiarity of nightmares, the familiarity of a disowned self that insists upon recognition.

Approached from such a psychoanalytic perspective, and in terms of not only his novelistic but also his various cinematic incarnations, the meanings he has accrued since 1890, Dracula becomes a remarkably comprehensive amalgam of our culture's sexual dreads. But first I should deal briefly with one interpretive problem (actually, it seems to me a nonproblem and can be settled quite simply).

The question has been raised as to whether Dracula is really about sexuality and sexual repression or about the human fear of death, compensated for in the vampire's immortality (an aspiration that must, however, be chastised at the close). The simple answer is that if it is about the former, it must be also about the latter; and one can appeal here to the Freudian theory of the conflict between the pleasure principle and the reality principle. We are born with the pleasure principle—the naïve expectation of the immediate and unqualified satisfaction of our desires—and our development grows out of the collision between this and the reality principle, the realization that our desires cannot all be totally and immediately gratified. The ultimate, irresistible reality, the ultimate and final interruption of pleasure, is plainly death. If Dracula, then, is to embody the potential triumph of the pleasure principle, he must be potentially immortal. Further, it is important to distinguish between different kinds of "reality" that impede the untrammeled functioning of the pleasure principle. Death is a metaphysical reality; we cannot change it. But many of the so-called realities that get in the way of the satisfaction of desire are social realities, that is to say not "realities" at all but products of a specific cultural situation, ideological constructs, hence susceptible to challenge and change. It is to these "realities" (to all that Marcuse, following Freud, defines as "surplus repression") that Dracula provides one of the supreme challenges in our art and entertainment.[48]

What, then, gives the figure of the vampire count such comprehensive potency? In light of the Victorian England that conceived and nurtured this monster (though perhaps things have not changed as much as we would like to think), the answers seem to be:

1. *Irresistible power; physical strength; supernatural magnetic force*—easily translatable into imagery of sexual potency. For this was a time when the fact of sexuality was regarded as in itself a great pity, even within the sanctification of marriage.

2. *Nonprocreative sexuality*. For the Victorians, the sole legitimate *aim* of sex was procreation; if one equates Dracula's blood-sucking with sexual pleasure (made horrifying in order to be designated as evil and disowned), it is clear that, whatever it is, it is not going to produce offspring. (The heavily signified *contagion* of vampirism is a very different thing.)

3. *Promiscuity or sexual freedom*. Though Dracula is shown to have a passion for particular women and to value some women over others, his attachments are clearly not exclusive. He transgresses against the principle of monogamy—for Victorians, the only legitimate *form* of sexuality.

4. *"Abnormal" sexuality*. However we interpret the blood-sucking, it is clearly other than "normal" copulation (for Victorians, the only legitimate method of sexuality). The stunning climactic moment in the novel when the men break into the bedroom to find Mina with the count is eloquently suggestive here: Dracula has gashed open his chest, and Mina is kneeling on the bed and sucking his blood, while her husband lies in a trance beside her. The suggestion of fellatio is obviously very strong; one can easily apply the same principle in reverse to Dracula's sucking of women.

These components of the Dracula mystique are strongly established and fairly obvious. Two others are all but suppressed in the novel but are hinted at sufficiently to be regarded as present there and are more fully developed in (respectively) the Murnau and Badham versions:

5. *Bisexuality*. Dracula's attraction to blood, although generally focused on women, crosses the boundary of gender: when Stoker's Jonathan cuts himself shaving, Dracula wants to "suck" him. This homosexual element is played up strongly in Murnau's film—not surprisingly, given the director's homosexuality—in Dracula's nocturnal visit to Jonathan's bedchamber. True, the vampire is interrupted and diverted by Nina's telepathic communication (and henceforth she, not the male, becomes his obsessive, goal). Yet the bedchamber scene is played, unmistakably, for its potential perverse sensuality, with Jonathan prostrate on the bed (his attitude suggests a kind of desperate surrender) and the monster advancing and enfolding him with a lascivious longing.

6. *Incest*. In the book this remains ambiguous and uncertain, but Stoker describes one of the three female vampires who haunt Dracula's castle (and have presumably been vampirized by him) as bearing a striking physical resemblance to him: we must, I think, take her as a close relative, probably a sister. The Badham version takes up the incest hint strongly, transferring it to father and daughter: Mina's attempted seduction of Van Helsing in the vaults beneath the graveyard, which is "answered" by her father's plunging a phallic stake into her.

The violation of one further taboo—perhaps the one that still arouses the most horror and resistance—is suggested in the novel but has not, as far as I know, been taken up in any film version except the Jourdan television film:

7. *Child sexuality*. All of Lucy's victims are children; the strong suggestion is not only that she (the Victorian child-woman) likes children but, even more shockingly, that the children have enjoyed the experience and want more.

It should be added that the novel (which is probably more "perverse" than any film version has dared to be, despite—or perhaps because of—its insistent dedication to the cause of the good and the noble) symbolically enacts in its "good" characters, under cover of the most admirable intentions, something of the "forbidden" that Dracula represents: after Lucy has been sucked by the vampire, all three of her suitors, and later Van Helsing himself, give their blood to her in transfusions. Not only can this be read in terms of all three (or four) men "having" her, it also realizes the novel's suppressed but quite insistent homosexuality, the men mingling their blood with each other's. (We know now that Stoker was himself homosexual, which on the one hand supports this reading and on the other highlights the oppressiveness of the novel's surface, its "conscious" level of meaning: its dedication to the good and the noble of Victorian society is not merely oppressive but self-oppressive.)

The simplest way of looking at the novel is to see it as resolving into the classic Freudian struggle between the superego (Van Helsing) and the id (Dracula) for possession of the ego (Mina). It is the product of a culture wherein superego and id can never possibly be reconciled and where no compromise is conceivable: one must annihilate the other. Within the Freudian terms themselves, such an account must be immediately qualified: superego and id are not simply different, diametrically opposed forces but are intimately related, closely involved with one another. According to Freud, all energy derives from the id; in the course of human development, some of this energy becomes siphoned off (through the processes of repression) and converted into the *repressive* energy of the superego; the psyche's warring elements have a single origin. This is dramatized throughout horror (and other) fiction in the figure of the double—a figure too complex to be reduced to a single generalized meaning, but which always carries overtones (at least) of the superego/id dichotomy.

Such a meaning lurks just beneath the narrative surface of Stoker's novel and is reproduced (in one form or another, the form depending on the changes I outlined earlier) in the various film versions. Why, we must ask, must Van Helsing be foreign—the only foreign character of any consequence beside Dracula himself? Because the good and noble British (and the American) cannot cope with Dracula—to cope with him requires access to knowledge that would threaten their innocence, and that innocence must be preserved at all costs. Van Helsing has possession of that knowledge; the novel also gives him connections as close to Dracula as Budapest.

But Van Helsing is related to Dracula not only in being foreign. The two characters are linked by one very striking physical characteristic: both are described as having bushy eyebrows that meet over their noses. Above all, Van Helsing is given one of the most remarkable and revealing Freudian slips in literature.[49] The passage comes the morning after Dracula and Mina have been discovered together in the bedroom; the men are discussing, in Mina's presence, the means of trapping Dracula in his London hideout (it is Jonathan's narration):

> So I started up crying out: "Then in God's name let us come at once, for we are losing time. The count may come to Piccadilly earlier than we think."
> "Not so!" said Van Helsing, holding up his hand.
> "But why?" I asked.
> "Do you forget," he said, with actually a smile, "that last night he banqueted heavily, and will sleep late?"
> Did I forget? shall I ever—can I ever! Can any of us ever forget that terrible scene! Mina struggled hard to keep her brave countenance; but the pain overmastered her and she put her hands before her face, and shuddered whilst she moaned. Van Helsing had not intended to recall her frightful experience. He had simply lost sight of her and her part in the affair in his intellectual effort. When it struck him what he had said, he was horrified at his thoughtlessness and tried to comfort her. "Oh, Madam Mina," he said, "dear, dear Madam Mina, alas! that I of all who so reverence you should have said anything so forgetful." (p. 276)

It is not only the relish evident in Van Helsing's gloating words ("last night he banqueted heavily, and will sleep late"), but the fact that they are spoken "with actually a smile" that suggest the character's vicarious enjoyment of what Dracula has done. With Mina present to hear, the words become a reenactment of her violation, illuminating the close relationship between exaggerated "reverence" and the desire to rape. The relationship between repressor and repressed, superego and id, can never be pure, never one of simple and absolute opposition.

But the superego-ego-id account leaves undiscussed what I have already signaled as the crucial issue of the novel and both film versions: the centrality of the woman to the fiction, whether Mina, Nina, or Lucy. The ultimate horror of the novel is horror at the possibility of the arousal of female sexuality. The virtuous Victorian woman was, after all, supposed not to enjoy sex but to endure it, perhaps praying to pass the time and distract her mind from the inherent disgustingness of the operation. Sexuality is also energy, power, activity: sublimated, it is the source of all creativity, pleasurable work, achievement. If women became sexual beings, who knows where it might all end? Only two options could be permitted: women must be either asexual, passive, and pure, or sexual and degraded. Stoker enlists Mina as an accomplice in her own continued repression: she is horrified at her own "contamination" by Dracula and actually makes the men, including her adoring husband, promise to cut off her head and drive a stake through her heart if they cannot prevent her from becoming a vampire.

Stoker's mise-en-scène for the final climax is expressively magnificent (if horrifying in ways quite beyond anything of which we can assume him to have been conscious): Dracula destroyed by the three younger men under Van Helsing's supervision, as Mina watches from a hill, secure within a circle drawn by pieces of holy wafer, the woman surveying and assenting to her own castration. The problem Mina represents is posed, as I suggested earlier, by her actually improving on the Victorian ideal of insipid and submissive girlhood: she has, as Van Helsing says at one point, "the mind of a man" (p. 221); she participates in the male knowledge and abilities of writing, typing, and shorthand; she is strong and determined. So, above all, she must be shown to submit voluntarily to the patriarchal order, to the (supposedly) benign domination of all these good and noble, strong and brave, and above all manly men. The purpose of this submission is revealed on the book's very last page in a brief, perfunctory, yet crucial epilogue: the child, male of course, who bears the names of all the virtuous male figures. Stoker makes it explicit that the child is born on the anniversary of the death of the American suitor Quincey Morris; he does not make explicit (though the reader cannot but recall) the far more significant fact that this is also the anniversary of the destruction of Dracula.

As for patriarchy, its rights, and its true source of strength and endurance, there is a marvelous giveaway in Mina's own journal—the irony clearly inadvertent on the part of both character and author, but no less telling for that:

"Oh, it did me good to see the way that these brave men worked. How can women help loving men when they are so earnest, and so true, and so brave! And, too, it made me think of the wonderful power of money! What can it not do when it is properly applied" (p. 332). It is a passage to delight the heart of any Marxist-feminist—the economic base of male dominance so nakedly exposed. Elsewhere, Mina's husband puts it even more brutally: "Judge Money-bag will settle this case, I think" (p. 312).

There remains to consider briefly some of the significant variants worked on these themes in the two film versions.

In Murnau, the first, and still the greatest, adaptation, all of the changes are guided by a sure creative intelligence. (I have elsewhere analyzed the film at length and will not repeat the details of my interpretation here.)[50] What is most fascinating is the most drastic change, the promotion of Nina to status of chief antagonist. The use of Nina throughout the film is amazing: Stoker's implication that Jonathan and Dracula represent alternative husbands for her is greatly developed, and the decision is made hers. The intercutting of the journeys of Jonathan and Dracula is among the film's finest inspirations (and a sequence that makes nonsense of Bazin's extraordinary assertion that "in neither *Nosferatu* nor *Sunrise* does editing play a decisive part").[51] Through the editing, the two men are exactly paralleled as Nina's two husbands; Nina sits by the shore (among gravestones in a cemetery in the dunes) looking out to sea, ostensibly for Jonathan, whose mode of travel is by land; in the sleepwalking scene she exclaims, "He is coming! I must go to meet him!" after a shot, not of Jonathan, but of the vampire's ship.

Nina herself, emaciated and bloodless, ambiguously resembles both vampire and Christian martyr; at once Nosferatu's destroyer and potential mate, her ecstasy and terror are both religious and sensual. The film's background is of course German Expressionism, with its characteristic awareness of repressed forces but its simultaneous viewing of them as horrifying, bestial, and overwhelmingly powerful. Nina's sacrifice of herself again enlists the woman in the battle for patriarchy, but the nature of the sacrifice is profoundly ambiguous, and the price of victory is her own destruction, so that patriarchy is left empty, without the ratification of the adoring woman to venerate the brave, strong, pure men. Unlike Stoker's novel, therefore, Murnau's film cannot possibly move toward the birth of the child "whose bundle of names links all our little band of men together" (p. 352). Indeed, the film casts grave doubt on the virtues of courage, strength, and purity, Jonathan becoming completely impotent at all points when he is confronted with the vampire, who in turn symbolizes his repressed self.

We may turn, then, to a film in which Dracula receives a totally different embodiment, and ask how far, in fact, have we progressed in the last half century? Badham's movie has been gravely underestimated, by critics and public alike: in many ways it is quite remarkable, and as an interpretation of the novel extremely audacious. *Sight and Sound*, in one of its inimitable capsule reviews, went so far as to call it a straightforward adaptation that did not try to interpret, an observation that must go down in history as one of the most startling critical aberrations of all time.[52] For a start, this appears to be the first Dracula movie with a happy ending (of sorts) and the first in which it is Van Helsing, not Dracula, who is transfixed through the heart with a stake (minor details that presumably escaped the *Sight and Sound* reviewer). Its key line is perhaps Van Helsing's earlier "If we are defeated, then there is no God"; they are defeated.

The film is very much preoccupied, in fact, with the overthrow of patriarchy in the form of the father, Van Helsing, of whom God the Father is but an extension. The ending is the triumph of not merely Dracula (who, progressively undaunted by garlic and crucifixes in the course of the film, finally flies off, burnt, battered, but still alive and strong, into the sunlight) but of Oedipus, who, having carried off the woman, kills the father and flies away. The film makes clear that Lucy is still his, even though she cannot join him until the sequel (which, in view of the poor box office response, will now never be made). Indeed, the editing suggests quite strongly that it is Lucy who gives Dracula the strength to escape. It would be nice simply to welcome the film on those terms and leave it at that. Unfortunately, the matter is not so clear-cut, and the film seems to me, though very interesting and often moving, severely flawed, compromised, and problematic. Its chief effect, perhaps, is to remind us that we live in an age not of liberation but of pseudoliberation.

The film's problems are again centered on the woman, now Lucy (the superb Kate Nelligan), and on the difficulties of building a positive interpretation

Dracula (1979) is unable to liberate vampire mythology from connotations of evil.

on foundations that obstinately retain much of their original connotations of evil. The result is a film both confused and confusing. In response to our popular contemporary notions of feminism, Lucy's strength and activeness are strikingly emphasized and contrasted with Mina's weakness, childishness, and passivity. Dracula insists that Lucy come to him of her free choice: the film makes clear that he deliberately abstains from exerting any supernatural or hypnotic power over her, as he did over Mina. The film thus ties itself in knots in first presenting Lucy as a liberated woman and then asserting that a liberated woman would freely choose to surrender herself to (of all people) Dracula. Badham wants to present the Dracula-Lucy relationship in terms of romantic passion, a passion seen as transcending everyday existence; yet he cannot free the material of the paraphernalia of Dracula mythology, and with it the notion of vampirism as evil. With its romantic love scenes on the one hand, and the imagery that associates both Dracula and Lucy with spiders on the other, the film never resolves this contradiction.

Although it pays a lot of attention to the picturesque details of Victoriana, Badham's movie seems far more Romantic than Victorian in feeling and owes a lot to a tradition that has always had links with Dracula mythology: the tradition of *l'amour fou* and Surrealism. It is a tradition explicitly dedicated to liberation, but the liberation it offers (lacking any theories of feminism or of bisexuality) proves usually to be very strongly male centered, with an insistent emphasis on various forms of machismo. From *Wuthering Heights* (1847) through *L'Age d'Or* (1930) to Badham's *Dracula*, *l'amour fou* is characteristically built on male charisma, to which the woman surrenders. The film's emphasis on heterosexual romantic passion actually diminishes the potential for liberation implicit in the Dracula myth: the connotations of bisexuality are virtually eliminated (Dracula vampirizes Renfield purely to use him as a slave, not for pleasure, and he does so in the form of a bat; Jonathan's visit to Transylvania is foregone, so there is no possibility of any equivalent for the castle scenes in Murnau); and the connotations of promiscuity are very much played down, with Dracula vampirizing other women almost contemptuously, his motivation centered on his passion for Lucy. Under cover of liberation, then, heterosexual monogamy is actually reinstated.

More sinister (though closely related) is the film's latent fascism. Dracula and Lucy are to be a new king and queen; the "ordinary" people of the film—Jonathan, for example, and Mina—are swept aside with a kind of brutal contempt. Between them, Dracula and Lucy will create a new race of superhuman who will dominate the earth. Dracula's survival at the end—with Lucy's complicity—is a personalized "triumph of the will," the triumph of the superman over mere humans.

What Badham's film finally proves—and it is a useful thing to have demonstrated—is that it is time for our culture to abandon Dracula and pass beyond him, relinquishing him to social history. The limits of profitable reinterpretation have been reached (as Frank Langella's Dracula remarks, "I come from an old family—to live in a new house is impossible for me"). The count has served his purpose by insisting that the repressed cannot be kept down, that it must always surface and strive to be recognized. But we cannot purge him of his connotations of evil—the evil that Victorian society projected onto sexuality and by which our contemporary notions of sexuality are still contaminated. If the "return of the repressed" is to be welcomed, then we must learn to represent it in forms other than that of an undead vampire-aristocrat.

(1983)

Returning the Look

Eyes of a Stranger

Confronted over the past few years with the proliferation of escalating violent and gruesome low-budget horror movies centered on psychopathic killers, one may take away the impression of one undifferentiated stream of massacre, mutilation, and terrorization, a single interminable chronicle of bloodletting called something like *When a Stranger Calls After Night School on Halloween or Friday the Thirteenth, Don't Answer the Phone and Don't Go into the House Because He Knows You're Alone and Is Dressed to Kill.* In fact, the films are distinguishable both in function and in quality, and however one may shrink from systematic exposure to them, however one may deplore the social phenomena and ideological mutations they reflect, their popularity (especially—indeed, almost exclusively—with youth audiences) suggests that even if they were uniformly execrable they should not be ignored; an attempt both to understand the phenomena and discriminate among the films seems valid and timely.

The films can be seen to fall into two partially distinguishable categories, answering to two partially distinguishable cultural "needs": the "violence-against-women" movie (of which Brian De Palma's *Dressed to Kill* [1980] is the most controversial—as well as the most ambitiously "classy"— example) and what has been succinctly dubbed the "teenie-kill pic" (of which the purest—if that is the word—examples are the three Friday the 13th movies [1980, 1981, 1982]). The distinction is never clear-cut. The two cycles have common sources in Tobe Hooper's *The Texas Chainsaw Massacre* (1974) and John Carpenter's *Halloween* (1978) (which in turn have a common source in *Psycho* [1960]); the survivor in the teenie-kill movies—endurer of the ultimate ordeals, terrors, and agonies—is invariably female; the victims in the violence-against-women films are predominantly young. But the motivation for the slaughter, on both the dramatic and ideological levels, is somewhat different: in general, the teenagers are punished for promiscuity, and the women are punished for being women.

Both cycles represent a sinister and disturbing inversion of the significance of the traditional horror film: there the monster was in general a "creature from the id," not merely a product of repression but a protest against it, whereas in the current cycles the monster, while still "produced by" repression, has become essentially a superego figure, avenging itself on liberated female sexuality or the sexual freedom of the young. What has not changed (making the social implications even more sinister) is the genre's basic commercial premise: that the customers continue to pay, as they always did, to enjoy the eruptions and depredations of the monster. But where the traditional horror film invited—however ambiguously—an identification with the "return of the repressed," the contemporary horror film invites an identification (either sadistic or masochistic or both simultaneously) with punishment.

On the whole, the teenie-kill pic seems the more consistently popular of the two recent cycles, and one can interpret this as a logical consequence of a "permissive" (as opposed to liberated) society. The chief, indeed almost the only, characteristic of the film's teenagers (who are obviously meant to be attractive to the youth audience as identification figures) is a mindless hedonism made explicit by a character in Steve Miner's *Friday the 13th Part III*, who remarks (without contradiction) that the only things worth living for are screwing and smoking dope. The films both endorse this and relentlessly punish it; they never suggest that other options might be available. (After all, what might it not lead to if young people began to think?) What is most stressed, but nowhere explicitly condemned, is promiscuity—the behavior that consumer capitalism in its present phase simultaneously "permits" and morally disapproves of.

The satisfaction that youth audiences get from these films is presumably twofold: they identify with the promiscuity as well as the grisly and excessive punishment for it. The original *Friday the 13th*, directed by Sean S. Cunningham, dramatizes this very clearly: most of the murders are closely associated with the young people having sex (a principle that reaches ludicrous systematization in the sequels, where one can safely predict that any character who shows sexual interest in another will be dead within minutes); the psychopathic killer turns out to be a woman whose son (Jason) drowned because the camp counselors who should have been supervising him were engaged in intercourse. In the sequels Jason himself returns as a vaguely defined mutant monster, virtually indistinguishable from Michael of the Halloween films, introducing another indispensable component of the cycle, the monster's unkillability: the sexual guilt that the characters are by definition incapable of analyzing, confronting, or understanding can never be exorcised.

THE VIOLENCE-AGAINST-WOMEN MOVIES HAVE generally been explained as a hysterical response to 1960s and 1970s feminism: the male spectator enjoys a sadistic revenge on women who refuse to slot neatly and obligingly into his patriarchally predetermined view of "the way things should naturally be." This interpretation is convincing so long as one sees it as accounting for the intensity, repetitiveness, and ritualistic insistence of these films, and not for the basic phenomenon itself. From *The Cabinet of Dr. Caligari* (1920) to *Psycho* and beyond, women have always been the main focus of threat and assault in the horror film.

There are a number of variously plausible explanations for this. As women are regarded as weak and helpless, it is simply more frightening if the monster attacks them; the male spectator can presumably identify with the hero who finally kills the monster, the film thereby indulging his vanity as protector of the helpless female. That he may also, on another level, identify with the monster in no way contradicts this idea; it merely suggests its inadequacy as a *total* explanation. Second, as men in patriarchal society have set women up on (compensatory) pedestals and, thereby, constructed them as oppressive and restrictive figures, they have developed a strong desire to knock them down again.

As in every genre, the archetypal male-constructed opposition of wife-whore is operative. In the traditional horror film the women who got killed were usually whore figures, punished for "bringing out the beast" in men; the heroine who was terrorized and perhaps abducted (but eventually rescued) was the present or future wife.

The ideological tensions involved here are still central to our culture. The films obliquely express what Alfred Hitchcock's films, for example, consistently dramatized: the anxiety of the heterosexual male confronted by the possibility of an autonomous female sexuality he cannot control and organize. But the key point is that in the traditional horror film, the threatened heroine was invariably associated with the values of monogamous marriage and the nuclear family (actual or potential): the eruption of the Frankenstein monster during the preparations for his creator's wedding in the 1931 James Whale movie was the locus classicus. What the monster really threatened was the repressive, ideologically constructed bourgeois "normality." Today, on the other hand, the women who are terrorized and slaughtered tend to be those who resist definition within the virgin-wife-mother framework. As with the teenie-kill movies, the implications of the violence-against-women films are extremely disturbing.

The dominant project of these overlapping, interlocking cycles is, then, depressingly reactionary, to say the least. However, as both can be shown to have their sources in contemporary ideological tension, confusion, and contradiction, both also carry within them the potential for subverting that project. There is, for example, no inherent reason why a filmmaker of some intelligence and awareness should not make a teenie-kill movie that, while following the general patterns of the genre, analyzes sexual guilt and opposes it: it would chiefly require characters who are not totally mindless, for whom both filmmaker and spectator could feel some respect. The recent *Hell Night* (1981), directed by Tom De Simone, in which sorority pledges brave a haunted house, shows vestiges of such an ambition—it at least produces an active and resourceful heroine (Linda Blair) capable of doing more than screaming and falling over—but in general the apparently total complicity of the youth audience in these fantasies of their own destruction has licensed a corresponding mindlessness in the filmmakers.

Feminists (of both sexes) have, on the other hand, been quite vociferous on the subject of violence against women, and this can be credited with provoking various degrees of disturbance in recent specimens of the genre, ranging from vague uneasiness to an intelligent rethinking of the conventions. In *Dressed to Kill* the violence to women is consistently countered by a critique of male dominance and an exposure of male sexual insecurities; it is among the most complete expressions of De Palma's obsessive concern with castration, literal or symbolic. Armand Mastroianni's *He Knows You're Alone* (1980), in which a maniac stalks brides-to-be, is finally very confused but makes a highly sophisticated attempt (through a very conscious, intermittently reflexive play with narrative) to analyze violence against women in terms of male possessiveness and the fear of female autonomy. It is certainly worth discriminating between it and Joseph Ellison's *Don't Go in the House* (1979), which may be taken as representing the cycle at its most debased: the latter is a film in which the most disgusting violence (a pyromaniac flays his victims alive with a blowtorch) is significantly juxtaposed with some unusually strident dialogue about "faggots" in a way that can be seen as indicating, however inadvertently, some of the sexual tensions that motivate the cycle as a whole.

Ken Wiederhorn's *Eyes of a Stranger* (1981) strikes me as the most coherent attempt to rework the conventions of the violence-against-women cycle so far. Although the film doesn't escape contamination (the generic patterns are to some degree intractable), it does come closest to embodying a systematic critique of the dominant project. Disgracefully mishandled and thrown away by its distributors, it seems to have come and gone virtually unnoticed on both sides of the Atlantic (apart from some predictable abuse from journalist-critics incapable of distinguishing between different uses of the same generic material). The film follows the basic rules of the cycle faithfully, so the necessary synopsis can be brief. A psychopath is terrorizing women (obscene phone call, followed by rape and murder); a television news reporter (Lauren Tewes) comes—correctly—to suspect a man in the apartment opposite her own; she endangers her own life by searching his apartment for evidence while he is out; he discovers who is harassing him and, in the climactic scene, invades her apartment in return, assaulting her younger sister (Jennifer Jason Leigh), who is blind, mute, and deaf from the shock of being raped and beaten when she was a child. I shall restrict analysis to three aspects, representing the major components of the subgenre.

Eyes of a Stranger (1981): An attempt to rework the gendered conventions of the horror film.

The psychopath, the "look." Much has been made of the strikingly insistent use (in both teenie-kill and violence-against-women movies) of the first-person camera to signify the approach of the killer, perceived by many critics as an invitation to sadistic indulgence on the part of the spectator. There is a simple alternative explanation for the device: the need to preserve the secret of the killer's identity for a final "surprise." The second motivation might be seen merely as supplying a plausible alibi for the first: the sense of indeterminate, unidentified, possibly supernatural or superhuman menace feeds the spectator's fantasy of power, facilitating a direct spectator-camera identification by keeping the intermediary character, while signified to be present, as vaguely defined as possible. In *Eyes of a Stranger* the psychopath's identity is revealed quite early in the film: a rather ordinary-looking, confused, ungainly, unattractive man who strongly evokes memories of Raymond Burr in *Rear Window* (1954). The point-of-view shots of strippers, naked women, and so on (surprisingly infrequent for the genre) are always attached to an *identified* figure: so that if the male spectator identifies with the point of view, he is consistently shown precisely whose it is. Hence, although the film is posited on the terrorization of women (and, during its first half, certainly gets too much mileage out of that for its own good), this is never presented with simple relish, and the sadism can never be simply enjoyed. It is difficult to imagine audiences cheering the murders—a not uncommon phenomenon within this cycle—deprived as they are of all possible perverse "glamour."

The other male characters. The two "attractive" young men—potential hero figures, though one is murdered very early in the film—are both associated with the killer on their first appearances (a device also employed, though less strikingly, in *He Knows You're Alone*). The first frightens the first victim by appearing in her doorway wearing a grotesque mask that resembles the killer's face under its concealing stocking (meanwhile, the killer is already hiding in her apartment); the second (Tewes's lover, the film's apparent male lead) leaps on her violently in bed in a parody of sexual assault. Male aggression is thus generalized, presented as a phenomenon of our culture; the lover, significantly, is trying throughout the film to circumscribe Tewes within his values and his apartment. Consistently, the men in the film are either unhelpful or uncomprehending, or they are active impediments. The police refuse to investigate the first victim's reports of harassment in time to save her because Tewes's (fully justified) warning newscast has provoked an epidemic of obscene calls that turn out to be "jokes," like the lover's pretended assault. The lover refuses to accept Tewes's evidence (circumstantial but persuasive, and strongly supported by that "intuition" that men like to see as the prerogative of the female so that they can condescend to it) until it is too late, because of his commitment, as a lawyer, to one of the dominant institutions of patriarchy. Tewes's attempts to express her concern on television are met by her fellow newscaster with bland indifference; the film is very shrewd in pinpointing the tendency of television to cancel out and reassure, Tewes's warning to women being immediately followed by the determinedly comic antics of the (male) weather reporter.

The women. The film is consistently woman centered. Our identification figures are exclusively female, and the temptation to produce a male hero who springs to the rescue at the last moment is resolutely resisted, the women handling everything themselves. Tewes and Jennifer Jason Leigh are both presented (in their different ways, and within the limitations of the generic conventions) as strong, resourceful, and intelligent. Here, too, comparison with *Rear Window* is interesting. In Hitchcock's film, Grace Kelly invades the murderer's apartment to demonstrate her courage to a man; Tewes's motivation, in the corresponding scene of *Eyes of a Stranger*, is a genuine and committed social concern. It is true that this is shown to have roots in personal psychology (her feeling for her younger sister and a largely irrational guilt about what happened to her), but the film strongly suggests that this has become generalized into a concern about the victimization of women in contemporary society. Crucial to the film is its reversal of the patterns of male domination: the turning point is the moment when Tewes phones the killer to persuade him to turn himself in, but also to let him know what it feels like to be on the receiving end of an anonymous phone call.

The conclusion of the film is particularly satisfying by virtue of its play on the "look," and the way in which it "answers" the beginning. The opening images show a man photographing marine life along the Florida coastline who suddenly finds himself photographing a woman's body: the "look," innocent enough on the personal level, is symbolically established as male, the "looked-at" as female (and passive). The psychosomatically blind sister's recovery of her sight during the murderer's assault—dramatically predictable and, if you like, "corny" (I find it, like many "obvious" moments in the cinema, very moving)—takes on corresponding symbolic significance in relation to this, and to the film's play on "looking" throughout (from its title onward).

Leigh's regaining of her sight, and her voice, can be read in terms of pop psychology (the reliving of a traumatic experience); the film also makes clear that she sees at the moment when she finally realizes that she has to fight for her life. The regaining of sight represents the renunciation of the passivity into which she had withdrawn: immediately, the power of the look is transferred to the power of the gun with which she shoots the murderer, the reappropriation of the phallus. In accordance with current convention, he is not really dead, and Tewes, returning just in time, has to shoot him again; unlike Michael and Jason, however, he is by no means signified as indestructible. The contemporary horror film has, typically, two possible endings (frequently combined): the "heroine" survivor alive but apparently reduced to insanity; the suggestion that the monster is still alive. (Like so much else in these twin cycles, the endings were initiated by *The Texas Chainsaw Massacre* and *Halloween*, respectively.) *Eyes of a Stranger* ends with the murderer, definitively dead, slumped ignominiously in the bathtub, his eyes closed, his glasses still perched incongruously on his nose: an unflattering reflection for any male who relished the sadistic assaults.

(1983)

CRONENBERG

A Dissenting View

THERE CAN BE NO doubt that, after many years of critical neglect and disfavor, David Cronenberg is now "in": the film retrospectives, the growing number of adulatory articles, the high seriousness increasingly attributed to the Cronenberg "vision" all attest to it. Certainly, Cronenberg deserves recognition: he is perhaps the one authentic auteur of English-speaking Canadian cinema; he has several of the distinguishing marks of the authentic artist—thematic obsessiveness, combined with a remarkable tenacity that has enabled him to develop his career in the teeth of general critical reaction and without any substantial box-office endorsement (if his films have not on the whole been commercial failures, they have not been huge successes either). When I attacked Cronenberg's films five years ago in *The American Nightmare* (also published in relation to a Toronto Festival of Festivals retrospective) I had no sense that I was doing anything outrageous, or even particularly controversial: the controversy, in fact, has largely developed since, with the steadily growing claims made for Cronenberg's work. I accepted the present editor's invitation to reiterate the attack initially with great reluctance. The original attack has been the object of numerous counterattacks, but as far as I am aware it has not been effectively answered: no one, that is, has been able to demonstrate that Cronenberg's films do something substantially different from what I said they do. True, at that time I had seen only three of Cronenberg's eight feature films (two had not yet been made), but (I had better make clear at once, to avoid any false expectations) my position has not basically changed, and I shall not be offering any fresh revelations. On a cruder level, I was also deterred by the daunting prospect of sitting through at least some of the films again in order to reassess them. Two considerations overcame this reluctance. I agreed with the editor that at least one dissenting voice should be heard within the book, and (such is the degree of Cronenberg's present "in"-ness) mine was apparently the only one that could be found. More important, however, was the realization that far more is at stake than the evaluation of a specific group of films: the real issue is one of critical position. The counterattacks I spoke of by Cronenberg himself and by John Harkness don't content themselves with disagreeing with me about the value of the films: they question my right to attack them from the position I hold.[53] The basis of this is not entirely clear to me: at times the implication appears to be that my own political position is rigid and dogmatic, at times that it is radical positions generally that are unacceptable, at times that you shouldn't mix aesthetics with politics at all. What I wish to defend is the legitimacy of a politicized criticism.

First, however, I should point out that the distaste I feel for Cronenberg's films is not the product of my current political position. I was introduced to his work in the early '70s when I saw *Shivers* (1975) at the Edinburgh Film Festival and discussed it briefly in a festival report for *Film Comment*.[54] That still belongs to the period when I was producing what Mr. Harkness is kind enough to call my "classics of bourgeois humanist criticism": indeed, throughout that period I was set up as the "enemy" (by *Screen* and its followers) and was writing explicitly anti-Marxist articles. (At that time, in my naïveté, I continued to swallow most of the bourgeois capitalist myths about Marxism and assumed that the only possible form of Marxist criticism was hard-line semiotics.) Further, my reaction to the film would have been the same ten years earlier. It is a fallacy to assume that a change in one's political position automatically necessitates a change in one's whole system and habit of evaluation (the relationship between aesthetics and politics, though very intimate, is not a simple one). The films that I took, in my "bourgeois humanist" period, to represent the peak of cinematic achievement—for example, *La Regle du jeu* (*Rules of the Game*, 1939), *Letter from an Unknown Woman* (1948), *Vertigo* (1958), *Ugetsu monogatari* (1953), *Tokyo Story* (1953), *Rio Bravo* (1959)—still seem to me to do so, though I am now able to understand them much better, perceiving in them whole dimensions to which the blinkers of "bourgeois humanism" rendered me completely blind.

On these grounds I must take strenuous exception to Harkness's remark about the "ideological tunnel vision" of my present position in contrast to (apparently) the wider vision of my early work (89). Precisely the opposite seems to me to be the case. Since my work became politicized I have, as a direct consequence, enormously extended both my areas of interest and my sympathies. My sections of *The American Nightmare* would have been unthinkable to me prior to this: I had no tools with which to grapple with such material and in general adopted an attitude of elitist intellectual superiority to it. Harkness continues to do this now when he tells us that "the science element" in Cronenberg's work lifts it "above the realm of exploitation horror films"—as neat an example of "ideological tunnel vision" as you could wish for, occurring, ironically enough, in the very sentence in which he uses the phrase of me. Similar examples proliferate throughout Harkness's minidiatribe, alongside gross distortions and simplifications of my position. Consider the following set of notions attributed to me (the final clause presumably gives us Harkness's view): "Politically correct filmmakers who attack the notions of bourgeois normality (Craven, Romero, Tobe Hooper, Stephanie Rothman) are by definition better than conservative directors like Brian De Palma and David Cronenberg, who by almost any critical standard are better filmmakers than the aforementioned directors" (88).

First, I have no idea what Harkness means by lumping together Craven, Romero, Hooper, and Rothman as "politically correct." I have written about all four with varying degrees of appreciation, and I think have made some careful discriminations between them (and within their respective bodies of work). I am not at all sure what, in terms of aesthetics, is "politically correct," but I would not use the term for any of these directors. Second, the categorization of De Palma as a "conservative" director (although apparently attributed to me) is entirely Harkness's, and I wish to dissociate myself from it totally. In fact, I devoted one of the essays in *The American Nightmare* to defending the proposition that *Sisters* (1972) is one of the most authentically radical horror films ever to come out of Hollywood. I'm not sure whether Harkness has forgotten this, didn't read that far, or simply failed to follow the argument (his grasp of the book's general thesis is decidedly shaky). As for Harkness's last clause, the only "critical standard" according to which the superiority of De Palma's and Cronenberg's films to, say, *The Last House on the Left* (1972), *Terminal Island* (1973), *The Texas Chainsaw Massacre* (1974), and *Night of The Living*

Dead (1968) is obvious would appear to be the long-discredited bourgeois criterion of the "well-made film": it amounts to little more than the fact that De Palma and Cronenberg have had (since quite an early stage in their careers) much higher budgets to work with.

Cronenberg's own comments on my recent work are equally full of distortions—not to mention downright misrepresentations. One remark that Cronenberg appears to be attributing to me is "Unfortunately this is reactionary and should be suppressed" (122). I have never suggested anywhere that any film should be suppressed; on the contrary, for the past five years I have been (intermittently—I don't see it as my life's work) at the forefront of the campaign to abolish film censorship in Ontario, and I think Cronenberg must be aware of this. During the horror-film retrospective that *The American Nightmare* accompanied, we screened two of Cronenberg's films and invited him to discuss them: a curious form of suppression. In fact, I believe that any film is potentially useful as a means to understanding our culture. I cannot, however, see that "understanding" in academic or neutral terms: to try to "understand" our culture is to attempt to sort out, evaluatively, what is progressive from what is reactionary. Cronenberg's work has value, for me, precisely in that it crystallizes some of our society's most negative attitudes—to physicality, to sexuality, to women, to all ideas of progress. The existence of the films helps make such traits accessible to examination.

I am also credited with the opinion that "despite the fact that this piece of film of Larry Cohen's is awful, it is admirable and should be seen because it proposes what I think is right for human beings to do in society" (192). I had better say at once that I can think of no film of Cohen's that "proposes what I think is right for human beings to do in society"; leaving aside that I have no dogmatic views of "what I think is right for human beings to do," I have certainly never discussed Cohen's work in such simplistic terms. Neither have I made, anywhere in my work, any such separation between the aesthetic and ideological aspects of films. I am puzzled by the view apparently attributed to me here that Cohen's films are "awful" (one or two of them are certainly not very good). I suspect that Cronenberg thinks they are awful; that this then becomes a "fact"; that since it is a "fact" then I must think so, too. If I continue to prefer *It's Alive* (1974) to *The Brood* (1979) it is because it seems to me so much more complex: so many more things are going on in it, so that it becomes the site of a genuinely rich and disturbing intersection of ideological conflicts.

Cronenberg goes on to imply that what I want is some form of propaganda; worse, he implies that this is what is demanded by any critics "interested in exploring the underlying ideology and patterns that are at work in the cinema" (192). Films I have written on positively in the last few years include *Taxi Driver* (1976), *The Deer Hunter* (1978), and *Cruising* (1980). I don't really see that any of these can be reduced to "propaganda," and certainly not to the kind of propaganda Cronenberg assumes I would be interested in promoting. But Cronenberg seems anxious, everywhere, to reduce the complex issue of the role of ideology in art to something that could be isolated as "propaganda" in order to be rejected. Hence he can produce the astonishing observation that he doesn't "base [his] life's value or [his] work's value in any ideology" (192): surely the statement is a logical impossibility for anyone who knows what the term really *means*.

In Defense of Political Criticism

IN A SENSE, ALL criticism is political: every piece of critical writing, like every work of art, is rooted in a particular ideological position, is implicated in the dominant ideology of our culture. The position may be heavily disguised, and the writer (or artist) may be entirely unaware of its existence; but it is always, inevitably, there, and susceptible to analysis. (My early remarks, sketchy as they were, will have sufficiently indicated the ideological position underlying the writings of John Harkness.) The difference with which we are concerned, then, is not so much between "political" and "nonpolitical" criticism, but between criticism that knows it is political and criticism that doesn't.

This corresponds, broadly, to a distinction between conservative and radical criticism. I am using the term "conservative" here very loosely: not with reference to party politics (from this standpoint, all the parties that offer themselves for our votes are conservative), but to make a brutal and basic distinction between those who are committed to the continuance of the present economic/social/sexual organization (improved by whatever "reforms") and those who are not. Roland Barthes in *Mythologies* discusses bourgeois ideology's resistance to being "named,"[55] and my own experience has amply confirmed this perception.

If one uses terms like "patriarchal," "bourgeois," and "capitalist," one is usually greeted (if that is the word) with uneasy and embarrassed laughter: to use such words is either absurd or reprehensible. Yet how else (without resorting to cumbersome periphrases) can one describe the dominant ideology under which we all live? The words are there, they exist, they have meaning, they correspond to verifiable material phenomena. Yet patriarchal-bourgeois-capitalist critics resolutely refuse to use them (unless to ridicule an alternative critical practice their readers will automatically recognize—alerted by a certain tone of voice—as beyond serious consideration: a strategy of which I have been the frequent victim in recent years). "Patriarchal-bourgeois-capitalist ideology"—ha-ha! Of course it doesn't exist, the words sound so silly. (They "sound so silly" because that is how patriarchal bourgeois capitalism makes them sound: of course no one is really patriarchal, bourgeois, or capitalist, that is just a Marxist myth: we are all simply people.)

It would be extremely interesting to find a patriarchal-bourgeois-capitalist critic who was willing to "come out" (I have not found one yet who is). The implicit assumption runs something like: "They have an ideology; we have truth" (or "common sense," which is patriarchal bourgeois capitalist ideology's favorite masquerade). Bourgeois criticism rests upon shared ideological assumptions that neither writer nor reader is encouraged to examine or challenge. Radical criticism, of course, has its ideological assumptions also (no thought, no mental activity of any kind, can exist outside of ideology), but they are of a different order: because they are oppositional to the status quo the kind of inertia that characterizes most bourgeois criticism becomes impossible, and the "assumptions" become consciously held beliefs that must be argued. Where bourgeois criticism masks its assumptions (and is frequently unaware of them), the assumptions of radical criticism are of necessity defined and foregrounded.

Before attempting to define the assumptions that underlie my current work (which necessarily influence, but do not determine, my attitude to the films of Cronenberg), I am forced to take a detour into areas of my personal life. What makes the detour obligatory is that both Cronenberg and Harkness raise the issue and raise it in order to invalidate my work. According to Cronenberg, the purpose of my criticism is that of "justifying [my] own sexuality": "I think that's exactly what he's doing. When your work becomes an apology for an event or turn in your life, then I think you have invalidated yourself as a serious critic" (192). According to Harkness, "It is possible to argue seriously that Wood was a better critic when he was repressing his homosexuality" (89). (In fact, I never "repressed" it: I simply didn't act on it, which is not at all the same thing.)

Of course, like anyone else, I cannot vouch for what goes on in unconscious levels of my psychic life; consciously, I am certainly not aware that my sexuality needs "justifying." I am, as the phrase has it, "glad to be gay"—not because I consider homosexuality intrinsically superior to heterosexuality, but simply because it is a relief to be outside the appalling strains, tensions, power struggles, mutual oppressions that appear to characterize most heterosexual relations in the present phase of social evolution. It is certainly true that coming out as gay had a decisive influence on my development as a critic; though equally decisive was the introduction into critical theory about the same time of concepts of ideology (I shall always be very grateful for the challenge and indirect support represented by the work of *Screen*). To identify oneself as gay is openly to acknowledge one's membership of an oppressed minority group. This consciousness of oppression is unlikely to stop there: it leads logically to an awareness of oppression as a central and characterizing fact of our culture, and ultimately to a view of our culture as a system of interlocking structures of oppression/domination (class, wealth, gender, race, sexual orientation . . .) that bourgeois ideology strives to conceal or disguise. It would be accurate, then, to see my "coming out" as the starting point for the development of a political position; what Harkness and Cronenberg make of that, however, strikes me as somewhat unscrupulous. Harkness adds a further distortion when he writes that the tone of my recent work "suggests that we should ignore that earlier phase of his criticism" (89)—that is, the phase of "bourgeois humanist classics." Naturally, I have to view it with ambivalence and suspicion. Certainly, for example, I would want readers to be aware of the strain of unconscious sexism that runs throughout *Hitchcock's Films*—a striking example of the "ideological tunnel vision" of that earlier phase, when I had no awareness whatsoever of the ways in which women are oppressed within our culture.

Against the bourgeois critic's (usually automatic) commitment to established "norms," "common sense," etc., I would therefore set an overt, commitment to the various radical movements that have sought to draw attention to the oppressiveness of our culture, the deceptions of its dominant ideology, and hence to increase the possibility of change: especially radical feminism, Marxist theory, and the political use of psychoanalytical theory. This last has been of immense importance in recent years in tying everything together: it offers a convincing explanation of how the human being is constructed as a subject within ideology, of the construction of those clear-cut gender roles that serves the interests of patriarchal capitalism, through (especially) the repression of constitutional bisexuality (which Freud showed to be our "natural" heritage).

Politics and Aesthetics

THE RELATION OF THE political position I have defined to the criticism of specific films is not simple, though it is often made to appear so: the parodic version (with which I am repeatedly confronted) reduces it to something like: "Any film that does not perfectly correspond to these ideological presuppositions (i.e., is not 'politically correct') should be rejected and if possible suppressed." The function of this kind of parody is obvious: it reduces a disturbing and complex issue to something so simple, so silly, and so monstrous, that it needn't trouble us any further. The whole business of evaluation strikes me, frankly, as quite bewilderingly complex: every new work of art of any real significance or force demands a reconsideration of one's premises. I can, however, offer a few basic principles:

1. A total and uncompromising opposition to censorship. In view of the current escalation of increasingly violent pornography, this is becoming an increasingly difficult and beleaguered position. But it seems to me that the healthy and profitable response to what offends us is not suppression but active engagement and protest. Pornography/violence/degradation are not the sickness but the symptoms: we can't diagnose the social disease if the symptoms are obliterated.

2. The refusal to proscribe has as complement the refusal to prescribe. The routes of art are devious and unpredictable. Any reader who takes the trouble to peruse my work will not, I believe, find anywhere in it statements to the effect that, "Such films should be made." It is certainly one of my ambitions

to help create a social climate in which certain kinds of art are encouraged above others: if I can do anything to affect the present desperate situation in which a *Heaven's Gate* (1980) becomes a "debacle" and a *Return of the Jedi* (1983) a "triumph," I would like to do it.

3. Evaluation. The critic's job is to examine and discuss what is produced; s/he cannot do that without evaluating, and evaluation depends upon criteria that in turn are developed out of his/her position within, and in relation to, culture. All critics, like all artists, are engaged (whether they know it or not) in ideological struggle. It is quite impossible that there should be a single set of criteria that all critics could apply; when Cronenberg tells us it is a "fact" that Larry Cohen's films are "awful," he is, quite simply, talking nonsense. Certain criteria appear to be universally sharable: significantly, they can only be defined by abstract terms such as "intelligence," "sensitivity," "creativity," detached from any precise relationship to social/historical realities. As soon as they attempt to give such abstractions a concrete and specific application, conservative and radical critics will immediately part company. What, after all, is "intelligence" in relationship to cultural product? Certainly not something you can measure in terms of IQ. I am sure, for instance, that Steven Spielberg's IQ is extremely high, but I would never dream of describing his films as "intelligent." *It's Alive* seems to me a far more intelligent film than *E.T.: The Extra-Terrestrial* (1982); to most bourgeois reviewers it is a senseless piece of crap. "Intelligence" can only be discussed in terms of the artist's engagement with the social/political realities of his culture, and conservative and radical critics will probably be unable to agree as to what those realities are, let alone agree on an attitude toward them.

For me, the major criterion (it encompasses all the others) is usefulness; and again, inevitably, one's view of what is useful will depend upon one's position. Films can be useful in a number of ways, which I shall now attempt to indicate:

1. Pleasure. One of the basic and dominant purposes of art has always been to give pleasure. "Pleasure" is, of course, another deeply problematic concept: as subjects constructed within ideology, we cannot simply take our pleasure for granted. I recently found myself "enjoying" *Return of the Jedi*: I was excited, I laughed, I cried, all right on cue. The experience did not, however,

lead me to think very highly of the film: I am all too aware of the nature of my pleasure (pleasure can be reactionary, too) as arising out of a specific social conditioning. "Pleasure" in our culture is all too often assumed to be passive, even infantile (the baby's mouth finds the lost breast once again). There are other, finer forms of pleasure, in which intellectual activity and an active and critical emotional engagement play a part.

2. Understanding. This is by no means separable from the foregoing: understanding is one of the finest forms of pleasure. What I have in mind here is specifically understanding the culture in which we live and our positions within it. From this viewpoint, all films, all artifacts, are potentially useful. To take again *Return of the Jedi* as a convenient example; a critical examination of the film will reveal something of the fundamental Oedipal/imperialist structures on which patriarchal culture is based (precisely why we are excited, laugh, and cry); something of the contemporary need for reassurance, in the form of fantasy in which we can simultaneously (on different levels) believe and disbelieve; and something of the bankruptcy (both, economic and spiritual) of contemporary capitalism, which has endlessly to dazzle us with spectacle and "special effects" to keep us happily bemused. This is not, obviously, to attribute any very high value to the film: precisely the same information can be gleaned from hundreds of others. As with "pleasure," however, higher levels are possible. I think particularly of films that (without necessarily having any overtly "progressive" viewpoint) dramatize and foreground the strains, tensions, and contradictions that our culture produces. In this category, the work of Scorsese seems to me exemplary and outstanding. It is also from this viewpoint that a left-wing case might perhaps be argued for Cronenberg. I don't wish to undertake this myself, but I would be very interested in reading it.

3. Progressiveness. One thing (not the only thing) the radical critic will look for in films is the way in which they dramatize the major conflicts within our culture (especially those centered on class/wealth and gender). On certain levels, every work produced within our culture must necessarily be "about" these conflicts, whatever the particularities of the individual subject. If one believes in the possibility of a liberated society (as the only viable alternative to universal annihilation), then one will necessarily be drawn toward elements, signs, pointers in films that hint (perhaps quite inadvertently) at a progressive

tendency, that engage with those major conflicts in a progressive way. It should be clear, on the one hand, that this has nothing to do with a demand for "propaganda," and, on the other, that it is not cleanly separable from the type discussed above, of which Scorsese was suggested as a salient example.

I shall close this introduction by saying that the North American film of the past few years that seems to me uniquely to fulfil this whole complex of the "useful" is *Heaven's Gate*; and that my problem with Cronenberg's films is that the use I have been able to make of them has been minimal.

In Defense of Cronenberg

BEFORE REITERATING MY ATTACK on Cronenberg (and I'm afraid I can promise little more than reiteration), it seems worth attempting to define his distinction: what it is that makes his work not negligible. Confronted with, say, the Friday the 13th movies, the critic need really do no more than try to define their function within contemporary culture; Cronenberg's work, on the contrary, demands careful attention and even, in a certain limited sense, respect.

I suggested the major concession at the opening of this article: Cronenberg's work has artistic authenticity, guaranteed by thematic and stylistic consistency, the creation on film of a personal "world." It also has integrity. In recent years, Scorsese with *Raging Bull* (1980) and *The King of Comedy* (1982), Ridley Scott with *Blade Runner* (1982), Cimino with *Heaven's Gate*, have earned respect for their stubbornly oppositional stance in relation to the mainstream of cultural and cinematic development; I think that Cronenberg should be added to this list, without at all committing myself to any proposition that his achievement is qualitatively comparable. To offer *Videodrome* (1983) to a public that appears to want nothing but more Lucas and Spielberg is an action that commands a certain admiration. The last thing Cronenberg could be accused of offering is mindless reassurance.

Intimately bound up with this is the films' evident neuroticism: the obsessive repetition of themes and imagery, the pervasive fascination with forms of perverse sexuality. To offer this as a (potential) positive feature may seem at best a backhanded compliment, but it's not meant to be: some of the most distinguished bodies of work in the cinema are centered on a similarly obtrusive neuroticism: Hitchcock, von Sternberg, and Scorsese come immediately to

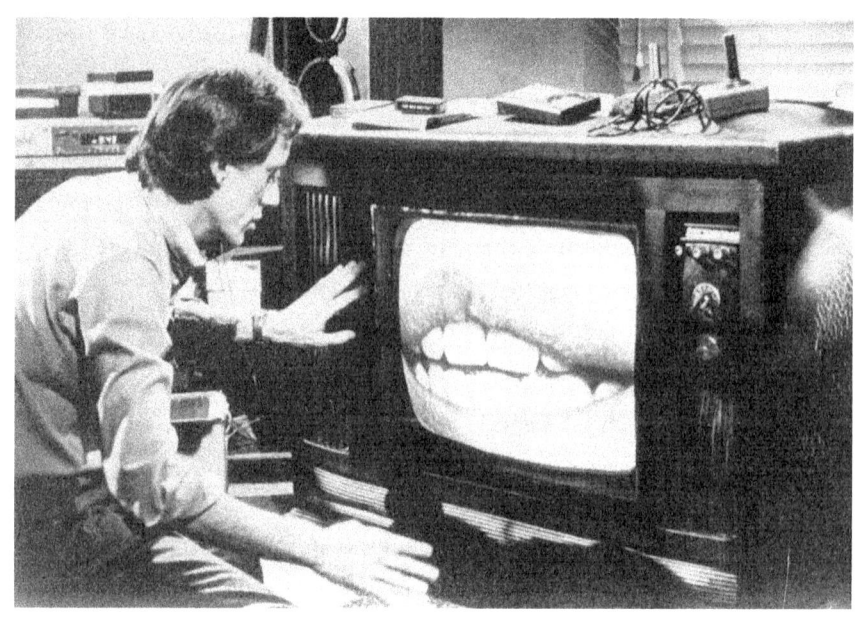

Mindless reassurance is hardly David Cronenberg's aim in *Videodrome* (1983).

mind. Neurotic symptoms (like the monster of the traditional horror movie) can be read as at once the product of repression and a protest against it; they may therefore, in the context of a "normality" built on a system of interlocking oppressions, acquire strong positive (positively disruptive) force—under the right conditions. One does not, of course, value Hitchcock's or von Sternberg's or Scorsese's work for the neuroticism itself, but for what it produces when brought into contact (or collision) with other factors, other material: a *Vertigo*, a *Scarlet Empress* (1934), a *Raging Bull*. For this reason it might be considered a pity that Cronenberg so completely dominates his own work, writing as well as directing: there is little room for fruitful collision, interaction, permutation. It will be interesting to see what he makes of *The Dead Zone* (the novel being very interesting in itself).

There is one way in which Cronenberg's work may be extremely interesting to which I (as a mere immigrant) may not be properly attuned: the argument that it is peculiarly Canadian, that it crystallizes a particular national angst. This has a certain credibility: Canada has, on the one hand, a continual dread of cultural colonization by the United States and, on the other, the pervasive American dread (being already effectively colonized) of any alternative form of social organization other than patriarchal capitalism. One can well see that a response to this might logically be the impotence, negativity, fear of change but contempt for the status quo of Cronenberg's films. It does not, however, seem a very helpful response (though, again, viewed in this way the films take on a certain value as documentation).

A Joyless World

IT IS INTERESTING THAT Cronenberg's work has received so much critical attention and recognition during a period in which it is so alien to the cinema's dominant trends: interesting, because the vicissitudes of bourgeois criticism can generally be explained, not in terms of any "critical objectivity," or set of established, time-hallowed aesthetic criteria, but in relation to the changing social climate. Why, in the age of Lucas and Spielberg, the age of a willing regression to infantilism, the age of reassurance and the restoration of the Father, is Cronenberg—whose films seem to be the precise opposite of such a cinema—suddenly a name to be reckoned with?

When I first saw *Shivers* (under its original title, *The Parasite Murders*) at the Edinburgh Film Festival about ten years ago, the unanimous reaction among people I talked to was disgust. Edinburgh has traditionally been the left-wing film festival; it was dominated at that time by *Screen* magazine, who organized seminars that were right at the forefront of contemporary theory. We were still in the aftermath of May '68 and its related events over the Western world. Even "bourgeois humanists" like myself were beginning to become politicized and ideologically aware. We believed not only that a "liberated society" was possible, but even that it might be within sight. Now, a decade later, a few of us are still trying to cling on to a radicalism the society around us (predominantly cynical and reactionary) appears to regard as increasingly ridiculous.

My point is that opposites are often, also, complementary. If Cronenberg's films were the contrary of *E.T.*, the Rocky series, the Star Wars series, they are also the other side of the coin. Our dominant cinema tells us that we shouldn't wish to change society because it's just great as it is; Cronenberg's movies tell us that we shouldn't want to change society because we would only make it even worse. From a political viewpoint, we are confronted not with opposites but with two variants on the reactionary. If Spielberg is the perfect director for the '80s, so, in his way, is Cronenberg. What follows is a recapitulation, with additions, of what I wrote in *The American Nightmare*: the additions are a paragraph on *Rabid* (1977) and a brief account of the modifications occasioned by viewings of the five films I had not then seen. I want to preface this with one retraction. In *The American Nightmare* my remarks on Cronenberg were followed by a passage on *Halloween* (1978) that began by suggesting that John Carpenter is a more interesting and engaging artist than Cronenberg. Carpenter's subsequent work has revealed this as a critical aberration: the confusions I noted in his early work have never been resolved or interestingly developed, and his work overall conspicuously lacks precisely that "artistic authenticity" I have acknowledged in Cronenberg's. Faced with the choice of reseeing *Videodrome* or any of Carpenter's movies, I would choose *Videodrome*.

SHIVERS, RABID, AND THE Brood were the films with which I got to know Cronenberg's work, and it remains convenient to begin with them: they are so closely connected, sharing an identical basic plot structure, as to be seen as a loose trilogy. Their basis is this: a man of science invents something (an aphrodisiac, a new technique of skin grafting, a new method of psychotherapy) that he believes will benefit mankind and promote social progress (in *Shivers* and *The Brood*, explicitly a form of liberation); he uses a woman as the (chief or sole) guinea pig for his experiments; the results are unpredictably catastrophic, escalate way beyond his control, and eventually produce a kind of mini-apocalypse. (*Scanners* [1981] and *Videodrome* share much of this plot structure, confirming its centrality to the Cronenberg oeuvre, but introduce two important modifications, both of which serve to make the films less actively objectionable: the chief experimentee/victim is no longer a woman, and the form of science involved, the ambition of the scientist, has far less progressive connotations, so that the "awful warning" the films offer is less unacceptable.)

Shivers can be read as Cronenberg's response to the notion of sexual liberation.[56] As the parasites proliferate through the apartment building, all the taboos of bourgeois sexual morality—promiscuity, female aggressiveness, age difference, homosexuality (both male and female), incest—are systematically overthrown. The film identifies this with the spread of disease and views it with unmitigated horror and disgust. The parasites themselves combine strong sexual and excremental overtones: shaped like phalluses (and one invades a woman in a bath via her vagina), they are colored like turds. Disgust is indeed the film's dominant and pervasive tone: by the end it has colored the presentation of every human physical activity, becoming a kind of obsessional aversion therapy for such things as kissing and eating. Cronenberg (in the 1979 panel discussion at the Festival of Festivals) claimed that this disgust is not really sexual—it is disgust with "mortality" itself, with the fact that the human body is prone to disease, grows old, decays. As an "explanation" of the films, that strikes me as fairly ludicrous: it totally fails to account for the sexual nature of their imagery, and it merely substitutes another form of negative and unhelpful morbidity for the one the films insistently project. I pointed out the oddity of the ending of *Shivers* long ago, in my *Film Comment* report from Edinburgh: when all the apartment dwellers have succumbed to the parasites and set out to infect the rest of the world, all signs of disease have disappeared. No reason is given for this; of course, the author of a work of horror or science fiction has every right to ask us to accept a fantastic premise, but I think she or he is then obliged to follow its logic and not arbitrarily alter its data. The absence of disease can, however, give rise to the question of what, then, is finally so terrible about this invasion? If these people are now neither sick nor unhappy, why can't what they are offering the world be seen as liberation after all? What is even odder than this anomaly is that Cronenberg now seems ready to argue that this is a legitimate reading of the film: it can, of course, only be a reading against it, the specific signifiers and generic pressures combining to express a totally unambiguous horror at what is happening. And what, in any case, could we possibly make of a film that dramatized liberation like that?

Perhaps I should make it clear (in view of Cronenberg's suggestion that my dislike of his work is somehow bound up with "justifying my sexuality" [192]) that I am not in the least accusing *Shivers* of being antigay or antilesbian: it is antieverything, and if there is one thing it cannot be accused of, it is discrimination. One may feel, however, that the film reserves a special frisson of horror for the release of an active, aggressive female sexuality, and this is pursued much further in *Rabid*. Here, as the result of a skin-graft experiment, Marilyn Chambers develops an all-purpose sexual organ in her armpit: a vagina that opens to let out a nasty sharp little phallus that drains her victims' blood and gives them rabies. The sexual connotation of her encounters is, I think, quite obvious: she is seeking release or satisfying a "hunger." It is true that the film presents her as a victim (and the victim of a misguided male), but I don't think that radically affects the issue: the horror the film is playing on is the dread of the release of what Freud called the woman's "masculinity," which our culture is so concerned to repress.

If *Shivers* evokes *Invasion of the Body Snatchers* (1956), *Rabid* evokes *Night of the Living Dead* (1968) (at the same time anticipating, in its urban settings, *Dawn of the Dead* [1978]) even down to its final images of Marilyn Chambers's body being thrown into a garbage truck. The comparison is instructive. Both films show social breakdown, with human beings converted into predatory monsters; both are entirely pessimistic. But there is an essential difference between the premises of the two films, with marked ideological consequences. Romero's ghouls are the embodiment of established values / dominant norms; from the beginning of the film, and consistently throughout, they are linked specifically to the tensions and conflicts within the bourgeois-patriarchal family. The problem for the survivors, then—merely implicit in *Night of the Living Dead* but magnificently developed in the sequel—is to extricate themselves from these values and create new ones, new forms of relating. Nothing comparable is even implicit in *Rabid*, where the catastrophe is caused by an attempt at progress and takes the form of released female activeness, dramatized as horrific and disgusting. It is important to distinguish clearly between pessimism and negativity, two very different phenomena that are often confused. Our current social/political situation gives one few grounds for optimism, and it is scarcely surprising that many of the finest contemporary works of art (the operas of Sallinen, for example) are deeply pessimistic (though not at all negative).

The Brood develops this attitude to female activeness ("masculinity") much more explicitly; it is also interesting in that "science" here becomes psychotherapy, directly concerned with the release of repressed energies. Again, the central victim/predator is a woman, Nola (Samantha Eggar); again, the film engages with one of our culture's major radical issues and treats it in the most reactionary and negative way possible. Cronenberg's defense of the film (that he saw Nola as just an individual character, not an archetype) strikes me as merely another instance of his extraordinary ideological innocence (181). It is impossible to make a film without involving oneself in the network of contemporary social relations and without revealing one's own position within that network. The choice of "individual case" that one makes is, precisely, the dramatization of that position. *The Brood* is concerned with the oppression of women, the repression of the woman's "masculinity," the secret, internalized rage that this repression produces. It then proceeds to attribute this not to patriarchy but to the fact that Nola's father was weak: it was all the fault of an aggressive mother. The implication is clear: patriarchal dominance is "natural," any deviation from it will result in disaster. The misguided psychotherapist (of course) succeeds only in making things much, much worse: he finds a means whereby the repressed rage can be externalized and released, in the form of Nola's monstrous, murderous children. The scene of childbirth gives us one of Cronenberg's most remarkable images: the unborn child, a huge excrescence on Nola's body, has the appearance of an enormous penis, a vivid literal enactment of Freud's perception that, under patriarchy, the child is the woman's substitute phallus. The implication, again, is quite clear (and highlighted by the film's immediate historical context of the growth of

Woman's repressed rage is released as monstrous children in *The Brood* (1979).

radical feminism): at all costs, women's repressed "masculinity," activeness, and rage must remain repressed—their release would be catastrophic.

If Cronenberg's films are reactionary, they are so in a quite unusual way: they are not reactionary in the simple, easily comprehensible way of *Rocky*, *E.T.*, or *Poltergeist* (1982), they do not reaffirm "establishment" values—except perhaps negatively, by default. When what we call "normality" appears in the films, it is presented as unattractive and joyless. In fact, the films seem unable to affirm anything, and unable, at the same time, to offer any very helpful analysis of the oppressiveness of our social institutions. It seems very odd that Harkness should describe him as a "visionary" (96): in the sense in which I have always understood the term—the "vision" of a Blake or a Janáček, in which the furious protest against oppression is accompanied by intimations of a possible transcendence, the coming of the New Jerusalem, or the "transfigured city" of the Janáček "Sinfonietta"—Cronenberg is as far from being a visionary as any artist one can think of. The world of his films is not only a world without joy, it is a world in which there is no potential for joy. The films lack any sense of the tragic (though Marilyn Chambers in *Rabid* achieves a certain pathos): nothing of value is lost, because nothing has value. It is this total negativity that gives the films their interest (I would describe it as a "clinical" interest), but it is also their crippling limitation. It accounts for the uniform drabness, the lack of energy, the fact that, while frequently repulsive, the films are almost never exciting or frightening (which perhaps explains the rather meager box-office response).

IT REMAINS TO DISCUSS the modifications to this view of Cronenberg necessitated by viewing his other five feature films: the two early "experimental" movies (*Stereo* [1969] and *Crimes of the Future* [1970]); the would-be "commercial" *Fast Company* (1979) (it was in fact an unmitigated box-office disaster); and the two films released since *The American Nightmare* was published. The modifications are slight.

Fast Company can be disposed of very quickly. No one (as far as know) makes any claims for it whatever, and it is indeed utterly conventional. Indeed (some nudity, sexual explicitness, and coarse language apart, plus the fact that it is in color), it seems virtually indistinguishable from the numerous B movies I used to see when I was a kid, in the '30s and '40s: one feels, nostalgically, that it should have starred Richard Arlen, Wayne Morris, and Barton MacLane. On that level, it's not bad. Its interest within the Cronenberg oeuvre lies in its professional competence. This is not, of course, to suggest that Cronenberg's other films are incompetent, which would be silly. What *Fast Company* does is prove that he can make a decent, ordinary little movie. The term "conventional" can have connotations that are not necessarily negative: if *Fast Company* has a certain energy that the typical Cronenberg films lack, this doubtless derives precisely from the conventions of classic Hollywood cinema. The existence of the film underlines the fact that the peculiar distinction of the "real" Cronenberg films—their very peculiar flatness and drabness—is a matter of artistic choice. Accordingly, the film increases one's respect for Cronenberg—one's awareness of the authenticity of his work.

The two "avant-garde" movies, on the other hand, come initially as something of a shock. Not that they are by any means incompatible with the subsequent films (indeed, *Crimes of the Future* should be seen as their prototype); what is startling is their explicit and pervasive homoeroticism. Cronenberg (in the interview in this book) attributes this to the presence in both films of Ron Mlodzik (167–68); yet, according to the credits, Cronenberg himself wrote, directed, and edited both films (Mlodzik is credited solely as an actor). If one switched off the soundtrack of *Crimes of the Future* (the loss would not be great), one might easily assume that the main body of the film had no ambition beyond chronicling a series of somewhat kinky gay pickups, with the participants perversely interested in each other's feet: one is interrupted by a jealous lover, another is brought to a halt by the second man, who is understandably pissed off by the extremely limited manner of intercourse.

Stereo should perhaps be read as marking, at the outset of Cronenberg's career in feature films (I have not seen the shorts that precede it), a crucial moment of hesitation. The Cronenberg structure (the attempt at progress that goes disastrously wrong) is already there embryonically. Yet the film has an openness and uncertainty that I don't find in any of the subsequent works. What is especially remarkable is the way it moves toward (a) an explicit lecture on "omnisexuality" of quite extraordinary radical import (heterosexuality and homosexuality are both "perversions," extended bisexuality—with socially constructed masculinity and femininity quite broken down—the preferred and logical norm) and (b) the one scene in Cronenberg (the "conventions" of *Fast Company* excepted) where people actually appear to enjoy eroticism—the bisexual "threesome" with two men and a woman. I don't want to make any great claims for the film (the Cronenbergian enervation is already the dominant feature); but I think it does suggest a direction his work might have taken and didn't.

Crimes of the Future is much more insistently homoerotic, but it contains no equivalent to the three-way-lovemaking scene of *Stereo*: here, already, sexuality has become perverse, pleasureless, and associated with disgust and disease. It is symptomatic that Ron Mlodzik, who is quite an attractive presence in the earlier film, is here completely devitalized. The two films' chief claim on the attention of aficionados of the "experimental" film is doubtless their play with words and images: the verbal narration and the visual representation seldom neatly coincide—the spectator has to work to piece things together. But it seems uncertain whether the things in question can really be pieced together in any satisfactory way: the science-fiction pretensions of the soundtrack often seem more a pretext for the visual kinkiness than an intellectual justification of it. This sense of discrepancy seems to me to recur, in slightly different forms, in the later films also. Mr. Harkness (whose assessment of my intelligence appears roughly to coincide with mine of his) reprimands me for not noticing that Cronenberg's films are "about science" (88). If one manages to reach this perception, apparently, it becomes unnecessary to examine their tone and imagery. In fact, there seems to me throughout Cronenberg's work a dislocation between the intellectual pretensions (what the films say they are about) and the repulsive and obsessional imagery (what they actually do). The gulf between the two is far from being breached in *Videodrome*.

Two developments (in relation to the preceding "trilogy") need to be noted in *Scanners*:

1. The woman moves from the film's center to its periphery (with the result that Jennifer O'Neill, who played so wonderfully for Hawks, Mulligan, and Visconti, is here completely wasted). Cronenberg, in the interview, shows a certain sensitivity to feminist attacks on his work, and perhaps this change is his tacit acknowledgment of its vulnerability on this score. The dread of

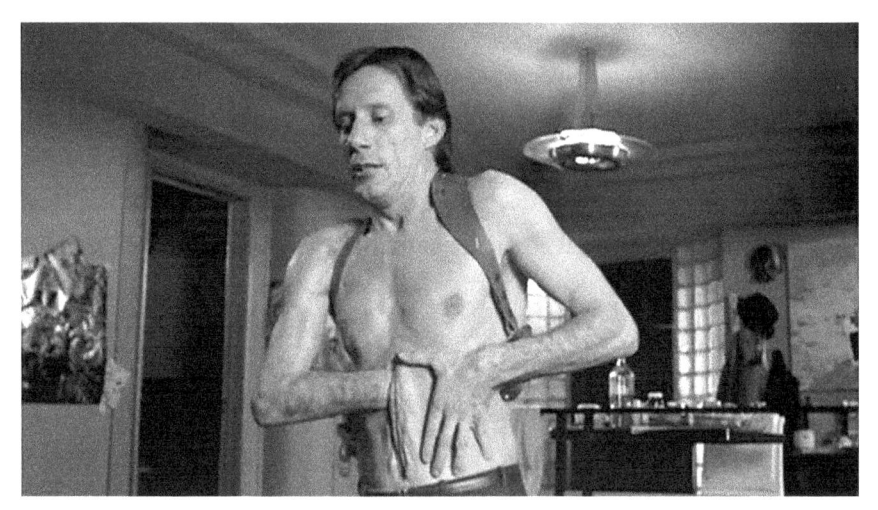

Max Renn (James Woods) develops a vaginal orifice in *Videodrome* (1983).

female activeness, which seemed so potent in the three previous films, here quite disappears.

2. Arguably—I am really uncertain about this—this relegation of women to the margins of the film makes way for the return of the homoeroticism that seemed to disappear after *Crimes of the Future*, in a hideously perverse form: the climax of the film has two men systematically destroying each other's bodies through an exertion of will, a process presented with much relish.

Videodrome is interesting in respect to this, as its imagery once again plays with bisexuality, again in a quite repulsive way: one might say that the phallus that Marilyn Chambers developed in her armpit in *Rabid* gets its echo and "answer" in the vagina James Woods develops in his stomach in *Videodrome*. I think the general consensus that it is Cronenberg's best film to date is probably correct: its science-fiction premise is more interesting than usual, and more interestingly developed. There remains the question of identifying the real impulse behind the film, the problem of the "excessive" imagery—with its marked sexual overtones, which the premise neither demands nor justifies. The film wraps itself in so many ambiguities that it is very hard to read (a number of critics have adopted the line of "I don't understand it, but I love it"): ambiguities centered especially on the two women and on the question of the "New Flesh" into which James Woods may or may not be about to be reborn when he commits suicide at the end of the film. It is presumably this "New Flesh" that is taken by Harkness to justify the term "visionary"; yet the film offers one absolutely no grounds for reading it positively. The treatment of human physicality throughout the film continues to suggest revulsion as the dominant attitude, and the whole paraphernalia of means by which the "New Flesh" is to be produced (if it is) carries entirely negative, sinister connotations.

I have suggested that—all the way from *Stereo* to *Videodrome*—Cronenberg's work is haunted by the specter of bisexuality. It takes many different forms: the feminized men of *Crimes of the Future*, the horrified fantasies of transplanted sexual organs in *Rabid* and *Videodrome*, the dread of female activeness. Only in *Stereo* (which gives the impression of being much more a collaborative enterprise than the subsequent films, with the actors given an unusual degree of freedom) is bisexuality allowed any positive connotations. It has been a major tendency of psychoanalytical theory since Freud to suggest that it is on the repression of our innate, constitutional bisexuality that the gender roles (the clear-cut division of "masculinity" and "femininity") that oppress us all are constructed. Conceived positively, the "New Flesh" could only be androgynous.

(1983)

King Meets Cronenberg

The appearance of David Cronenberg's film version of Stephen King's novel *The Dead Zone* raises issues far too complex to be dealt with adequately in this column: King's novels as a cultural phenomenon; the various and distinctive cinematic adaptations; the critical controversy surrounding Cronenberg's work (of which I may legitimately claim to be at the center); the questions *The Dead Zone* (1983) poses with regard to the auteur theory, the relation of the film both to Cronenberg and to King (not to mention the contributions of the screenwriter, Jeffrey Boam, and the strong and assertive producer, Debra Hill). There is matter here for a fascinating PhD thesis; I shall attempt simply to sketch out how some of these issues interrelate.

King's novels deserve more respect than the press in general is willing to accord them. Almost every film reviewer seems to find it necessary to preface a review of the latest adaptation with disparaging remarks about King, in which the word "hack" is likely to figure prominently. With its connotations of cynical commercialism, it is a singularly infelicitous term; one of the main reasons why King is so compulsively readable is that he is such a compulsive writer. Doubtless his commercial success encourages him, feeds his energy (I don't mean *just* the money: also the sense of being widely read, of being *needed* by large numbers of people), but it is impossible to read the books without becoming aware that they are the product of an inner necessity. King's prose is verbose, overheated, "sensationalist," frequently erupting into the "pulp" rhetoric of one-word paragraphs and sentences in block capitals; I prefer it, in its raw energy, its force and honesty, to much that currently passes for fine writing, and I never skip a word of his books. Let me admit unashamedly that I read the novels not primarily for their sociological interest, which, especially in view of their popularity, is enormous, but because I enjoy and admire them, especially the later ones, from *The Dead Zone* on: *Firestarter* and *Cujo* are particularly fine; I have not yet read *Christine*.

The squeamishness of reviewers is exacerbated not only by the uncouthness of King's prose, but by his repeated offences against the criterion of "good taste"—offences that are crucial to his interest. Though his work is obviously crammed with, and the product of, neurotic conflicts, in one sense it is markedly unneurotic: he has no inhibitions, he is never afraid to go all the way. It takes a special kind of genius (often called nerve) to dare to imagine something like *Apt Pupil*, the second of the four novellas that make up *Different Seasons*, in which the healthy all-American boy becomes obsessed with fascism and the extermination camps, and ends up a mass murderer. King's greatest weakness—that he seems largely unaware of what his fictions actually do, of the forces that drive them—is also arguably his greatest strength; were he *more* aware, he might no longer be able to permit himself the freedom that makes possible the appalling resonances of his best work.

What gives King's work its interest is the fundamental disturbance that is the source of that inner necessity: disturbance intimately related to his essential Americaness. It has two interrelated aspects, social/political and sexual. On the one hand, there is the evident pervasive unease at what American civilization has become, the proneness of the system to corruption and decadence; on the other, a disturbance concerning the family, heterosexual relations, and female sexuality. King's work is characterized by a chronic, so-far unresolved, perhaps unresolvable, tension between this radical disturbance and the liberal inability to imagine radical alternatives: America may have become crass, corrupt, exploitative, even monstrous, but there remains some vague, unformulated ideal America which is what America ought to be; the patriarchal nuclear family may be built on tension and oppression, but there remains some equally vague good family which is what the family ought to be. The novels' pervasive, uneasy homophobia doubtless points the way to a psychoanalytical reading of this ideological paralysis. At present, King seems quite incapable of the imaginative leap that would expose the evils as inherent in the very structures and systems of "democratic" capitalism, rather than as an unfortunate and deplorable corruption of those structures and systems explainable only in terms of individual abuses or aberrations.

I wrote on Cronenberg at length in *The Shape of Rage*, the book published to coincide with the retrospective of his films in the last Toronto Film Festival.[57]

In "absolute" terms, clarity is a virtue and confusion a fault; yet I far prefer the rich confusion of King to the impoverished clarity of Cronenberg. Where King's work bears an ambiguous relationship to the dominant ideology, he is decidedly and explicitly not a radical, yet his novels have particular interest and resonance viewed from a radical position; Cronenberg's relationship to it is basically very simple: he is against everything. If his previous films, which he conceived, wrote and directed, are unambiguously reactionary, they are so in a very peculiar way: while they cannot possibly be appropriated for radical or progressive use, they are equally recalcitrant to appropriation within traditional humanist values. They present a world without joy and without value, and proceed to demonstrate that any attempt to improve it can only make things much worse. The films are stylistically very distinctive, the mise-en-scène economical and disciplined yet curiously flat. Often notoriously repulsive, they are seldom exciting or genuinely frightening, partly because there is little possibility of emotional involvement with characters who have nothing much to live for anyway.

Superficially, King, with his profligate verbosity and shameless emotionalism, and Cronenberg, with his tightness and frigidity, would seem incompatible. Yet *The Dead Zone* seems to me a quite wonderful movie, the dialectic resulting in a highly idiosyncratic synthesis from which each auteur benefits. Where King can never bring himself to use one word where ten will do, Cronenberg never uses two shots for what can be conveyed in one: the film's disciplined clarity is due more to the precision of his direction than to the inevitable compression of a four-hundred-page novel into a one-hundred-minute screenplay. Scene after scene is exemplary in its economy and control. The use of locations is particularly sensitive, the autumnal-to-wintry landscapes crucial to the tone of the film: this is no commercial chore, or mere opportunistic climb into bigger budgets. On the other hand, King's emotional investment in his characters—a generosity of impulse that remains impressive despite the ideological constraints within which it functions—is carried over into the film (with the aid of a magnificent cast), giving it an aliveness and energy, a power to involve and move, that I have not experienced in any previous Cronenberg film. Adherents of the naïve auteur fallacy that the only thing that matters is the expression of a personal vision (no matter what the vision is, provided it's "personal") will turn up their noses and tell you this is "not a Cronenberg film." The more refined version of auteurism claims importance for the recognizable intervention in a complex, multiply determined project of a defined authorial presence. Here, the engagement with material not his own has enabled Cronenberg at last to escape from the confinement of his own sterile obsessions. He has completely transcended himself: one wonders if he feels a sense of relief.

There are, however, losses in the film's simplification of King's complicated narrative. While it was ingenious and dramatically satisfying to bring back Sarah and her son for the climax (the novel's mother and child are unidentified), it has the unfortunate side effect of undermining the character's intelligence by making her a Stillson campaigner. It also mitigates the characteristic bleakness of King's ending (though less damagingly than in the last three minutes of Lewis Teague's otherwise excellent version of *Cujo* [1983]) by allowing Johnny Smith the satisfaction of being told she loves him before he dies. More serious is the drastic abbreviation of Stillson himself. King's previous novel, *The Stand*, evolved in its disastrous second half into a wildly pretentious allegory about God and the devil. Something of this carries over into *The Dead Zone*, but there it is rendered in much more culture-specific terms: if Johnny

Political candidate Greg Stillson (Martin Sheen) is a disturbingly recognizable devil in *The Dead Zone* (1983).

has overtones of a Christ-figure, he is a very reluctant one, an unremarkable school teacher who sees his supernatural powers as more curse than blessing; if Stillson is a "devil," he is a disturbingly recognizable and human one, a cheap brutalized crook and con man getting into politics over his head, the ironic embodiment of the American-democratic dictum that anyone (even a cheap crook or a second-rate movie actor) can become president. By dropping the novel's detailed characterization of Stillson and its account of his early career (systematically paralleled with Johnny's development), the film returns him to something of *The Stand*'s schematization. Its view of international politics is also more simplistic than King's (which is already not exactly complex): the (possible) end of the world is attributed to the actions of a single crazy individual. King's account of Stillson's possible role is somewhat more circumspect: "If Stillson becomes president, he's going to worsen an international situation that is going to be pretty awful to begin with": words that when the book came out in 1979 already had an ominously familiar, prophetic ring.[58]

(1984)

John Carpenter

It seems to be generally agreed that, after a promising start, John Carpenter's career has been, to date, singularly disappointing: those who hailed *Halloween* (1978) as at once fulfilling the promise of *Dark Star* (1974) and *Assault on Precinct 13* (1976) and definitively establishing Carpenter in the front rank of contemporary American filmmakers cannot but be dismayed and embarrassed by *The Fog* (1980), *Escape from New York* (1981), and *The Thing* (1982). In retrospect, however, the early films seem scarcely more satisfying than their successors, with the reasons for the failure significantly to develop visible from the outset.

The prime attraction of Carpenter's early work lay in its awareness of being rooted in a mainstream Hollywood tradition, its sophisticated play with genres, conventions, references, its delight in skills (learned primarily from Hitchcock) of suspense and manipulation. Both the awareness and the sophistication, however, now look decidedly superficial: a matter of acquiring the skills without acquiring much understanding of what (in Hitchcock's or Hawks's best work) the skills were *for*.

The technical attainment is accompanied by a curious abeyance of thought. Thus, in *Assault on Precinct 13*, Carpenter combines *Rio Bravo* (1959) and *Night of the Living Dead* (1968) without any apparent awareness of the ideological consequences of converting Hawks's fascists and Romero's ghouls into an army of revolutionaries: the film's display of skepticism about established society and celebration of the individualistic outsider is oddly and confusingly juxtaposed with a strikingly reactionary political position. A parallel confusion vitiates *Halloween*: the arresting opening (derived from the Halloween sequence of *Meet Me in St. Louis* [1943] as much as from *Psycho* [1960]) offers us (in line with the major American horror films of the '70s) the monster as the direct product of the psychopathology of the nuclear family. He is subsequently diagnosed (by his own psychiatrist!) as evil incarnate, a horror that cannot be analyzed, only repressed.

Each of Carpenter's films has an interesting premise, but the premise is never satisfactorily followed through, the interest progressively dissipated. *The Fog* offers a rereading of the small town (microcosm of America) as founded, not in the purity of democratic idealism, but in corruption and repression, with "the repressed" returning to exact its revenge; but the realization is curiously half-hearted, the skills of *Halloween* largely absent. Carpenter's reworking of Hawks's 1951 *The Thing* (the original is "quoted" on a television set in *Halloween*) suggests that he has reached a (temporary?) bankruptcy: lacking a single sympathetic (or even interesting) character with whom to identify, the spectator merely waits for the next eruption (admittedly spectacular) of special effects.

Halloween has an undeniable, if scarcely positive, importance in the evolution of the horror film: with Tobe Hooper's greatly superior *The Texas Chainsaw Massacre* (1974), it is the source of the twin cycles that have dominated the genre since the late '70s, the "violence against women" and "slaughter of promiscuous teenagers" movies. It is particularly saddening that Carpenter allowed his name (as producer) to be attached to one of the grossest and most inept of these, *Halloween II* (1981).

(1984)

Dead End

Given the feminist outcry that greeted *Dressed to Kill* (1980) (and of which Brian De Palma was certainly aware), *Body Double* (1984) can only be explained either as a perverse act of defiance and provocation or as the production of irresistible obsession, the murder by razor in the earlier film being capped by the new one's already notorious murder by electric drill. The plea of "dramatic necessity" wears a trifle thin. True, the murders in both films are essential to the development of the plot, but both are shot and edited as "set pieces"; the excessiveness of the violence and the terror of the women is undistanced, detailed, and protracted. The real giveaway is the murder of the prostitute in the train-station washroom in *Blow Out* (1981). It is the one flaw in what is otherwise De Palma's finest, most disciplined, and most authentically disturbing work, and has no dramatic necessity whatever. It is clearly there for its own sake.

De Palma's own line of defense—that he is not interested in what his films are about, for him they are formal structures, exercises in "pure cinema"—can be easily discredited. The thematic obsessions that recur again and again and provide the films' motivating force are clearly not neutral. By arguing such a line, one cannot help thinking, De Palma is not merely defending his films against outside attack, but defending himself against having to seriously confront his own obsessions. Hitchcock did the same thing, but there is an important difference. Hitchcock's apparent attitude of unseriousness was restricted to the peripheries of his work (interviews, the cultivated public persona, the TV series); when it surfaces within the films—in his personal appearances, in the quirky Hitchcock jokes—it is very precisely localized and controlled. The chief exception is *Frenzy* (1972), which is closest to De Palma of all Hitchcock's films in its wavering uncertainty of tone. De Palma's refusal to take the thematic dimension of his work seriously is far more damaging, for it frequently permeates the entire structure and tone of the films. If I find both *Dressed to Kill* and

Body Double insidiously corrupt, it is not because of the violence in itself, but because of the cynicism that pushes the films continuously in the direction of camp, with the implication that the violence is part of the "fun."

De Palma's achievement, then, is very uneven, though his best films—*Sisters* (1972) and *Blow Out*—seem to me among the finest in modern Hollywood cinema. His interest, however, is far more consistent; one might argue that from a certain viewpoint the failed films are the most suggestive, the interest lying partly in De Palma's inability to resolve his own problems. It might be asked whether the films embody the decadence of contemporary civilization or offer a critique of it, whether they exploit violence against women or lay bare its sources. The problem, is, I think, that they do both, and it is virtually impossible to separate one from the other. I don't wish to argue that the feminist anger at De Palma is irrelevant, unfounded, or unjustified. I think, however, that it is inadequate as a reaction to his work, which has extremely interesting implications for feminism.

Psychoanalysis has shown that the source of men's hatred of women in patriarchal culture is castration anxiety. Patriarchy erects, so to speak, the phallus as its symbol of power, domination, and authority; it follows that loss of the phallus (whether literal or symbolic) is its greatest dread. According to Freud, one of the major origins of castration anxiety is the child's discovery of sexual difference. Finding that certain other human beings lack penises, the little boy fears that he may lose his as well. For the little girl, the reverse discovery reveals to her that she is already castrated. Women are caught, then, in a double bind: they are feared and hated by men because (a) they remind them unconsciously of the possibility of literal castration and (b) they may at any moment usurp the symbolic phallus (power and authority) in their demands for autonomy and self-determination (sexual, personal, political, economic).

De Palma's films constitute perhaps the most comprehensive and accessible treatment of castration anxiety the cinema has given us. Most of his films end in castration, either literal (*Sisters, Dressed to Kill*) or symbolic (*Obsession* [1976], *Blow Out, Scarface* [1983]); most of his male protagonists are directly motivated by castration fears. During the first ten minutes of *Body Double* castration—literal and symbolic—is signified in three different ways. We first see the protagonist, Jake (Craig Wasson), in vampire makeup for a scene in

Dressed to Kill (1980): Another example of castration anxiety in the films of Brian De Palma.

his film, which makes him look "feminized," almost like a eunuch. He is then unable to complete the action of the shot because, lying inside a coffin, he is paralyzed by claustrophobia and as a result loses his job. (In the subsequent scene of the acting lesson this is traced back to a childhood experience that rendered him totally incapable of action.) He then returns to his lover's apartment to find her not only delightedly screwing another man but taking the active role, sitting on him and controlling the act of intercourse (Jake's later account of this significantly falsifies it: "She was just lying there . . .").

There are close connections between castration anxiety, voyeurism, and fetishism; the film also connects castration anxiety to pornography. Jake becomes obsessed with watching, through a telescopic lens, a woman perform a strip routine. A favorite male fetish is women's panties: they conceal, but only just, her lack of a penis, therefore they can be taken to disavow that lack (but at that vertiginous moment when the revelation is imminent). Jake's theft of the panties of his new object of desire, Gloria (Deborah Shelton), is followed by another attack of claustrophobia, which is linked to the eruption of the terrifyingly phallic "Indian" who steals Gloria's purse (one of the commonest Freudian symbols for the female sex organ) and pauses to laugh scornfully at Jake's exhibition of incapacity.

Jake and the Indian are systematically paralleled throughout the film. As Jake watches the woman through the telescopic lens in his borrowed apartment, he becomes aware of the other man watching her too; the following sequences are all built on the elaboration of this parallel as both men follow and spy on the unsuspecting Gloria. The culmination of this comes after the murder, when the detective refers to the Indian as Jake's "blood brother" and holds Jake responsible for Gloria's death. Jake is in fact more directly responsible than the detective knows. It is not simply that he has failed to call the police; he calls Gloria, ostensibly to warn her, knowing full well where the telephone is in her apartment and that the Indian (with his monstrous phallic drill) is hiding a few feet away from it. The film's title refers not only to the two interchangeable women, but to Jake and his "blood brother," the alter ego summoned up out of the unconscious to punish, desecrate, and destroy the female body. The horrific excess of the murder scene, quite unmotivated by the progress of the surface narrative, is the whole point of the film's real narrative, the Freudian tale of castration and vengeance.

It is quite false to see De Palma—the artistic personality deducible from the films, who is not necessarily identical with De Palma the individual—as a brutal, roaring macho. The identification figures of his films are either women (*Sisters*, *Carrie* [1976], *Dressed to Kill*, the end of *The Fury* [1978]) or "feminized"—passive, gentle, "castrated"—men. One should see him, I think, as an essentially "feminine" personality who, because he lives and works within a patriarchal culture, is unable to conceptualize his femininity in any terms other than those of castration. *Body Double*, though it is more explicit than its predecessors in its paralleling of hero and monstrous killer, really carries the De Palma dilemma no further. It merely testifies, once again, to the fact that it cannot be resolved within the terms it defines.

(1984)

Cat and Dog

Lewis Teague's Stephen King Movies

WHILE IT LACKS THE idiosyncratic distinction of De Palma's *Carrie* (1970), Kubrick's *The Shining* (1980), or Cronenberg's *The Dead Zone* (1983) (in all of which the Stephen King thematic is conspicuously inflected by the thematic concerns of the filmmaker), Lewis Teague's *Cujo* (1983) is perhaps the most satisfying film version of a King novel to date. Partly this is because the novel is, with *Firestarter* and *The Dead Zone*, one of King's finest; yet the abysmal recent version of *Firestarter* (also faithful to the letter of the book) is sufficient proof that this is no guarantee of cinematic success. Teague's film is the most faithful rendering of a King novel I have seen: given the necessary compression, watching the film was like seeing the novel as I had already "seen" it when reading. Teague is clearly a gifted director, but his "auteur" image remains undefined, and in *Cujo* he has been content brilliantly to realize the original in cinematic terms. When watching *The Shining* one thinks primarily of Kubrick; when watching *Cujo* one thinks primarily of Stephen King. In discussing the work, then, I shall not distinguish between film and novel, except to note their two significant points of divergence; what interests me here is the cultural significance of Stephen King. For the present issue of *CineAction!*, *Cujo* has a particular relevance: it is the one King novel to be centered on an adult woman, and it combines very interestingly certain thematic concerns of the woman's melodrama (sexuality and the family, mother love, adultery, transgression, and punishment) with those of the horror film ("normality" threatened by "the monster").

King prefers to discuss his work (and horror fiction in general) in terms of "universal," "primal" fears: death, darkness, the unknown.[59] One can scarcely deny that such fears are evoked. However, the horrors of King's novels are very firmly rooted in culturally specific disturbances: they belong to a particular phase of American capitalist culture and the sexual and gender relations it has produced. As a context within which to place *Cujo*, I want to begin by defining the major components of the King thematic, the areas of disturbance out of which the novels grow; though I separate them for the sake of clarity, it will be clear that they are intimately interrelated. I should say at the outset that by "King" I understand here a body of work (the novels, the stories, and, with occasional qualifications, the films that have been made from them) rather than a human individual: in a very real sense the "body of work" is the product and expression of a culture (hence both its importance and its popularity). I am interested in psychoanalyzing a group of texts (and through those texts the tensions and struggles within our culture), not the author as person.

1. *Ambivalence about marriage and the family.* The books insistently offer marriage and family as their major positive value, never seeming aware that there is any alternative; this is accompanied by their pervasive and implicit recognition that there are no happy families. There are seemingly happy parent-child relationships, especially fathers and young sons (*Cujo*, *The Mist*, *Pet Sematary*), sometimes fathers and young daughters (*Firestarter*, *Thinner*), but they function best in the absence of the mother and are usually accompanied by fantasies of violence and/or death visited on the child. Several of the novels (*The Shining*, *Cujo*, *Pet Sematary*) can be read as fantasies of the destruction of the family by the father. The simultaneous horror and relish is epitomized near the start of *The Mist* (the opening novella of *Skeleton Crew*): "One of those terrible visions came to me—I think they are reserved exclusively for husbands and fathers—of the picture window blowing in with a low hard coughing sound and sending jagged arrows of glass into my wife's bare stomach, into my boy's face and neck. The horrors of the Inquisition are nothing compared to the fates your mind can imagine for your loved ones."[60] The generalization ("husbands and fathers") is especially interesting in relation to patriarchal culture and the appalling demands and stresses it imposes upon men in the name of authority and "masculinity": women, apparently, are excluded from such "visions." Either they lack the imagination that makes them possible, or they lack the combination of overt anxiety and implicit hatred that gives rise to them.

2. *Male aggression / male masochism*. One would not wish to claim that King is a great creator of characters; his women are particularly colorless (the heroine of *Cujo* the major exception). There are virtually no independent women in his work (the lesbian of *The Stand*—his worst novel—remains a curious anomaly, unconvincingly and uneasily depicted). In the King world, women are wives and mothers, and ideally they are much in need of male protection (if they don't realize it there is something wrong with them). The books cannot attack the institutions of marriage and family to which they are committed (while demonstrating ad infinitum that they don't work); consequently, they repeatedly endorse bourgeois domesticity as right, natural, and inevitable while expressing the most intense resentment of it in the vindictive fantasy. Domesticity is centered on—is essentially for—the woman; hence (despite the repeated assertions of the male's love and need for her), she is resented whether she meekly acquiesces in domesticity or not. If she does (the wife in *The Shining*), she represents everything that traps and emasculates the male; if she rebels (however feebly, like the reluctantly adulterous wife in *Cujo*), she is ungrateful, and the resentment can be visited upon her as monstrous punishment. The resultant rage and frustration (the husband/father monster of *The Shining*, *Cujo* as the embodiment of masculine aggression) has, however, its inevitable corollary in male masochism, the intolerable burden of guilt the aggression brings in its wake and the desire for self-punishment. *Cujo* gives us the ultimate expression of this: the figure of masculine aggression is a rabid dog, disintegrating and dying in protracted agony. On the level on which they are offered—fantasies to get lost in—King's novels obviously imply a male readership and give no space to female pleasure (except to women who are totally complicit in their subordination). The only way in which women (and gays) might get valid pleasure from the novels is by reading them intelligently, as horrifying revelations of what being a heterosexual male within patriarchal culture entails.

3. *Homophobia*. This may seem a marginal constituent of the King world, but it is a crucial one. The reason why it achieves relatively little overt expression is doubtless explainable in terms of inhibition: the enormous progress of the gay movement in the last two decades has made it difficult openly to express hatred and disgust of homosexuals. There are no positive references

to male homosexuals in the King novels, and very few that can be charitably construed as neutral. It is interesting that one narrative thread introduced early in *Firestarter* (the novel that also offers the most positive image of female energy, significantly embodied in a child) is abruptly dropped, never to be taken up again: we are told near the beginning of the book that the man who exactly parallels the little girl's strange, dangerous, and defiantly antiestablishment abilities is a "faggot." The narrative logic is plain: the threat posited by unrepressed female energy is paralleled by that of gay sexuality. It is a logic the King world cannot encompass, and the character is never mentioned again.

The occasional derogatory reference apart, the novels express their homophobia only obliquely, by association. The corruptible pimply fat man in *The Stand* (inevitably named Harold) has been afraid that he might be homosexual; Stillson, the monstrous future president of *The Dead Zone* who may bring about the end of the world, never goes with women and has a constant male companion; one of the supreme horrors witnessed by the little boy (in Kubrick's film by the mother) in *The Shining* is an act of homosexual fellatio; the vampire and his assistant of *Salem's Lot* (significantly masquerading as antique dealers!) are rumored to be a gay couple. The last example is the key one in relation to this aspect of the King novels, as (in its devious way) it is central to the structure of the entire book. The vampires, through their extraordinarily potent and pervasive contagion, essentially construct an alternative world without marriage or family, in which all are equal. The book regards them, of course, with the most extreme horror and revulsion but never finds it necessary to explain why it is so terrible to be one. What it does demonstrate, with King's usual thoroughness, is the wretchedness of the sexual/familial social organization that the vampires destroy.

4. *Repressed/sublimated homosexuality*. Homophobia has no rational motivation—which is what makes that curious affliction so interesting. It can be explained only in psychoanalytic terms. Freud's investigations proved conclusively (at least, I have not seen them convincingly refuted) that the human individual is innately bisexual and that the homosexual side of that bisexuality has to be repressed in order to construct the successfully "socialized" adult, the participant in that "normality" which the King novels so devastatingly dramatize. Homophobia results when that repression is less than completely

successful—when, that is, one's homosexuality is experienced as a constant, if unconscious, threat. In fact, I think it is time to redefine homophobia, which is a far more pervasive mental illness than is commonly recognized (fewer and fewer people are willing to express overt antagonism to gays): homophobia is the inability to accept one's own bisexuality. Masculine violence in our culture (the construction of the male as violent) must be read as the result of the repression of bisexuality. Violence against women: the woman represents the threat of the man's repressed femininity. Violence against other men: the man represents the threat of the arousal of homosexual desire. It is a syndrome magnificently dramatized in Scorsese's *Raging Bull* [1980],[61] one of the few masterpieces of the '80s, in which the essential thematic of the King novels is realized (significantly, outside the Gothic genre) with a coherence and economy of which the novels are never quite capable.

The relationship between repression and sublimation is a complex and difficult one, and it is often hard to see where one ends and the other begins. What is repressed is forced down into the unconscious, inaccessible to consciousness, manifesting itself only in dreams, jokes (Jake LaMotta in *Raging Bull*: "I don't know whether to fuck him or fight him"), and fantasies. Some portion of "surplus" sexual energy, however, can go the way of sublimation, transformed into what our culture calls the "higher" pursuits: pleasurable work, art, creativity. The difficulty of the distinction is evident if one tries to discuss so-called beautiful (i.e., nonsexual) friendships: male camaraderie, the "buddy" syndrome, can be read as the result of part repression, part sublimation. It is hardly surprising that the homophobia of King's novels should be consistently counterpointed by the presence of just such male relationships. Again, *Salem's Lot* provides the prototype (and Tobe Hooper's disappointing 1979 made-for-TV film version at least has the merit, through compression and the elimination of much of the novel's wearisome repetition and superfluous elaboration, of rendering the essentials of the structure with schematic clarity): it is through the "beautiful friendship" of man and adolescent boy that the vampires are finally (though ambiguously) destroyed, an extraordinarily precise account of the enactment of repression.

The precariously repressed homosexuality that pervades King's novels (and our entire culture) rises nearer and nearer to the surface in recent books. *Thinner* (published under the pseudonym of Richard Bachman) can easily be read as a paranoid fantasy about AIDS. The terrible old gypsy with the cancerous nose, when he places his curse, strokes the male protagonist's cheek "like a lover."[62] One of his victims wastes away almost to a skeleton, the second develops scales like an alligator, the third suffers from an eruption of sores all over his body; a major symptom of AIDS is extreme weight loss, and its common consequence is skin cancer. More remarkable still is the introduction to King's latest publication, a collection of short stories published under the title *Skeleton Crew*. It ends: "Grab onto my arm now. Hold tight. We are going into a number of dark places, but I think I know the way. Just don't let go of my arm. And if I should kiss you in the dark, it's no big deal; it's only because you are my love..."[63] As I suggested above, the novels clearly address a male readership.

The most painful aspect in King's work of the homophobia/homosexuality syndrome is that involving male children. Freud is quite clear (though society is still reluctant to understand him) on the subject of infantile sexuality: the infant is polymorphously erotic, capable of enjoying physical contact in diverse forms and with members of either sex. The male child's first homosexual contact is likely to be with his father, a pleasure that "socialization" decrees he must swiftly renounce. The King novels have many moments of father-son intimacy, and they tend to be the moments of greatest happiness. *Pet Sematary* is especially eloquent on this:

> It was a moment with his son that Louis never forgot. As he had gone up and into the kite as a child himself, he now found himself going into Gage, his son. He felt himself shrink until he was within Gage's tiny house, looking out of the windows that were his eyes...
>
> "Kite flyne!" Gage cried out to his father, and Louis put his arm around Gage's shoulders and kissed the boy's cheek, in which the wind had bloomed a wild rose.
>
> "I love you, Gage," he said—it was between the two of them, and that was all right.[64] (p. 198)

What is disturbing is not at all these privileged moments of perfectly natural man/boy erotic contact (they are among the most touching things in the novels), but the terrible consequences they seem (albeit in narrative terms very indirectly) to entail. It is as if the arousal of the man's erotic feelings for a male child were so troubling that both man and child must be punished for it: the child by being subjected to a whole series of horrors and torments (*Salem's Lot, The Shining, Cujo, The Mist, Pet Sematary*), the man by being identified as monstrous (literally in *The Shining*, by implication in *Pet Sematary*, through a symbolic surrogate in *Cujo*). At times the narrative, while not admitting to any direct cause and effect, makes the connection by close juxtaposition: the very next sentence to the passage from *Pet Sematary* quoted above tells us that Gage has less than two months to live.

THIS ACCOUNT (NECESSARILY, IN the space available, selective and partial—there is far more to be said, but it would need to be said at book length) of King's novels could be mistaken for two things it is not intended to be: a presumptuous attempt to psychoanalyze the author, and an attack on the books. As for the former, it is an old dodge to reduce the analysis of culturally produced texts to the analysis of an individual: the cultural implications of the work, its general relevance to all of us, can then be sidestepped, disowned as the idiosyncrasies of an aberrant individual (albeit a "genius"—the term often operating as a means of just such disownment). I don't find King's work, in relation to the norms of our culture, in the least aberrant. The novels are a battleground on which the central conflict of our civilization (rather than, as King himself might put it, the eternal struggle between good and evil), the conflict between repressive "normality" and the drives that normality seeks to repress, is fought out (and, so far, neither definitively won nor lost—typically in the novels both sides lose). In so far as I am interested in King as a person, it is to admire his courage in daring to offer himself as the medium through which that struggle can be expressed. As for the books, I love them (especially the later ones). On the conscious level—the level at which the author asserts what he means to say, in contradistinction to what the texts he produces say—the novels are, for all their liberal critique of Reaganite America, plainly reactionary. The liberal critique is their least interesting aspect (liberal critiques being invariably impotent, unable to do more than wave their hands in the air and say, "Isn't it terrible?"). But, like much superficially reactionary work (the films of John Ford, for example), the texts generate so many internal tensions and contradictions at such a pitch of intensity that the whole repressive social/ideological structure is blown wide open, its monstrousness revealed. The horrors of the King world are the horrors of our culture writ large, made visible and inescapable.

It must be added that the impressiveness of King's work exists within severe limitations and perhaps could not survive without them. They are precisely the limitations of the Gothic genre,[65] and the unresolvable, appalling stalemate of the novels at once, chicken-and-egg-like, demands that genre for its expression and is perpetually imprisoned within it: the Gothic, one might say, ensures that the battle could never be won, making the victory of repression impossible and the victory of liberation intolerable. I have not yet dealt with the most obvious, and in some ways most impressive, aspect of King's work, that area in the novels that dramatizes "the repressed" and its inexorable return: the Marsten House of *Salem's Lot*, the Overlook Hotel of *The Shining*, the possessed car of *Christine*, the Micmac burying ground of *Pet Sematary*, the gypsies of *Thinner*. The fascination of the novels is clearly the fascination of these potent evocations of the repressed, to which the protagonists and the reader are irresistibly drawn. Yet in the novels, as in the Gothic generally, the energies that give that world its potency can only be depicted as monstrous: they threaten that "normality" to which the books believe themselves to be committed. The impasse of the novels is the impasse of our culture. There are roads beyond it, but they lie necessarily outside the Gothic.[66] To travel them would require a total rethinking of the "return of the repressed" in positive terms: *Firestarter*, the most positive of all King's novels and the one least related to the Gothic genre, suggested that he was about to engage on just such an undertaking, though the subsequent novels have conspicuously withdrawn from it (*Pet Sematary* in particular returning to the Gothic with a vengeance). Centrally, it would involve the full recognition and acceptance of constitutional bisexuality, with all the implications and consequences of such an acceptance: the transformation of male and female roles and heterosexual relations, the rethinking of the family, the positive acceptance of homosexual love as natural rather than aberrant, the overthrow of socially constructed norms of masculinity and femininity, the recognition of infantile eroticism. Meanwhile, the impasse has seldom been dramatized with such compelling intensity as in the novels of Stephen King.

THE CONTEXT CONSTRUCTED ABOVE helps to call into immediate question the simplistic reduction of *Cujo* to yet another violence-against-women movie, subspecies "punishment for adultery." I don't wish to imply that that theme is absent; rather, that it represents only one strand in the text, which is strongly qualified by others. One may point immediately to the simple fact that, while the major emphasis is clearly on the protracted terrorization of Donna Trenton and her son Tad in their stranded car, the three people *Cujo* actually kills are all men: two brutal macho buddies and a policeman.

Again, the necessary compression and stripping down have resulted in the clarification of the novel's structure—or perhaps one should say structures. There is the admirably crafted linear narrative leading to the sustained tour de force of suspense and terror within a severely restricted space (the car itself, the farmyard surrounding it, from any section of which Cujo may emerge) that occupies the second half of both novel and film. This both sustains and is sustained by a complex but much less clearly defined (presumably because less

Donna Trenton (Dee Wallace) and her son Tad (Danny Pintauro) are terrorized out of all proportion to any crime in *Cujo* (1983).

consciously worked) semantic/symbolic structure built on parallels and oppositions. Primarily, there are the two families, both consisting of father, mother, and male child: the "good" family, bourgeois, stable, loving, and respectable (the Trentons); the "bad" family, working-class, disordered, loveless, brutalized by a vicious father/husband (the Cambers, owners of the huge Saint Bernard Cujo). But the goodness of the "good" family is merely apparent: Donna, we make out, is unsatisfied both sexually and by her role as housewife/mother, and is secretly screwing the town stud Steve Kemp. Neither the novel nor film, I think, blames her for this; if Cujo is her punishment, then we experience it as a punishment out of all proportion to any crime, like the shower murder in *Psycho* (1960), and Donna is throughout our main identification figure. The sense of the two families as each other's mirror image is confirmed by a specific inversion: if both are characterized by dissatisfaction and frustration, the primary source of this in the Camber family is the father, in the Trentons the mother. Vic Trenton, professionally successful (in advertising), upwardly mobile, unimaginative, and complacent, shows no signs of dissatisfaction until he discovers Donna's adultery; there is the sense that Charity Camber, who has married beneath her and retains aspirations to gentility, would be perfectly contented as the "good wife" if only she had a good husband. Just as it is Donna's lack of fulfillment that disturbs the Trenton family, it is Joe Camber's frustration (deriving from his debased frontiersman mentality and his failure to "get anywhere") that destroys the Cambers. The opposition has resonances right through the system of the Hollywood genres and the ideological male/female roles they dramatize: Joe, failed as the wanderer-hero of the Western, can't be content with settling; Donna, in the honorable tradition of the woman's melodrama, can't fit happily into her preordained role of supportive housewife/mother. The film systematically parallels the disintegration of the two families, and parallels both with the disintegration of Cujo from amiable pet to rabid monster.

What exactly does Cujo represent? "Exactly," I think, the question is impossible to answer. It is one of the great strengths of realist art that it enables the artist (under cover of "just telling a story") to release his/her fantasies, allowing them partly to escape the vigilant censor (as repressed desires, according to Freud, can be released in dreams). The corollary of this is the frequent difficulty in interpreting realist texts: the components of the fantasy may derive from numerous diverse and perhaps contradictory sources working at different levels, so that no single, coherent meaning is produced—rather, a sum of connotations. In the course of the film, Cujo accumulates the following resonances:

a. During the opening credits sequence, Cujo pursues a rabbit, gets his head stuck in a hole, and is repeatedly bitten by rabid bats. The sequence evokes the most primitive male sexual fears of women: getting stuck in the vagina dentata. I am uncertain how much weight to give this in reading the remainder of the film: its position as starting-point for the narrative (Cujo's monstrousness is the direct result) obviously confers importance on it, yet it seems to me (I may be wrong) not especially illuminating in relation to much of the film's detail.

b. Tad Trenton believes there is a monster in his closet, the door of which swings open by itself at night; subsequently, in the besieged car, he identifies this monster with Cujo. The open closet door seems to correspond to the hole in which Cujo gets stuck, but the monster in this case is clearly male. The simple Freudian explanation would be that Tad, in the Oedipal phase, is fantasizing his punishment for desiring the mother (and we shall see later that Cujo is clearly associated with the vengeful father). In the context of the film, however, one tends to read the incident as dramatizing the child's disturbed, intuitive sense of something secretly wrong at the center of the family: although neither Vic nor the spectator knows this yet, Donna is already conducting her illicit affair with Steve Kemp, and we are soon given various hints of suppressed familial tension. From this association, then, Cujo represents a generalized disturbance within the patriarchal nuclear family—the disturbance produced by the Oedipal tensions the family nurtures and by the woman's dissatisfaction and transgression of its repressive norms.

c. Three of the male characters (Joe Camber, his buddy Gary Pervier, Steve Kemp) are all clearly characterized as brutal, violent, and destructive, and implicitly or explicitly as antagonistic to women. By implication, then, as well as in the juxtapositions of the intricately intercut narrative threads, all are associated with Cujo as figures of masculine aggression. They are also in various ways antagonistic to domesticity, and Cujo as monster can be read as enacting their combined assault on the bourgeois home ("normality") in his assault on mother and child. What does one make (beyond plot convenience), then, of the fact that Gary and Joe are Cujo's first two victims? Within the specific terms of the narrative, not much: it seems one of the aspects of the film that has not been thought through, that fails to achieve resonance. Outside those terms, however, one can point to the social construction of masculinity within our culture, built on the repression of bisexuality and the repudiation of male femininity, which produces violence against men as much as against women: masculinity, gone mad, turns upon itself.

d. In contrast to Joe, Gary and Steve, Vic Trenton is presented as (if unexciting) gentle, decent, and civilized. Yet it is he with whom Cujo is most intimately associated, in the film more clearly than in the novel. One way in which this reading is confirmed is through intertextual association: the scene in *The Shining* in which the wife, motivated primarily by her desire to protect her little boy, swings at her monster husband with a baseball bat is exactly reproduced in *Cujo*, except that here the monster is a dog. Far more explicit is the film's one major improvement on the original narrative: the central climactic scene of violence in which Donna is savaged by Cujo in the car (it looks very like rape), clearly signified as "real," is also Vic's nightmare, Teague cutting abruptly to his appalled awakening. It was Vic, earlier, who most emphatically resisted the notion that monsters exist, yet simultaneously acknowledged their existence by inventing and writing out for Tad the "monster words" ritualistically forbidding them access to the child's bedroom. The paradox has complex resonances with regard to the father-child relationships in the King novels. As soon as Cujo as monster materializes, the "monster words" lose all their supposed efficacy.

The association of Cujo with Vic is of course central to the logic of the narrative: Cujo becomes the instrument, the enactment, of the betrayed husband's revenge. The discrepancy between the human character and the animal surrogate is so extreme—as is the monstrousness of Donna's punishment, inflicted not only on her but on the loved and innocent child—that the fantasy leads one to question the whole basis of male sexual possessiveness. As Donna has no intention of leaving her husband and breaking up the family, why is it so terrible that she enjoys sexual pleasure occasionally with another man?

Why does the act bring down upon her this hideous vengeance? The only plausible answer seems to lie in male sexual anxiety—the other lover may be "better." (The syndrome has been incomparably explored by Hitchcock, most notably in the paralleling of the Cary Grant and Claude Rains characters of *Notorious* [1946].) This in turn raises the question of why our culture has such an obsessive and excessive stake in phallic potency, performance, penis size, etc. The phenomenon explains why Cujo is simultaneously, like the phallus when it is erected (so to speak) into a symbol, both monstrous and pathetic: it is not merely a matter of revenge on an individual transgressing woman, but of an incoherent protest against the demands our civilization places on male potency.

If the invention of Vic's nightmare is a major plus for the film, it is unfortunately countered by a corresponding minus. At the end of the novel, Tad is dead, at the end of the film he has apparently survived, and the final shot is a freeze-frame of father, mother and child reunited on the steps of the Camber house. The film's choice is not, within the context of the specific narrative, illogical, but it is false to the spirit of the King world. Only one King novel, *The Stand*, which is atypical in many ways, ends with the nuclear family intact, and the tensions and contradictions the novels dramatize really forbid the traditional restorative happy ending. (John Carpenter's version of *Christine* [1983]—which also manages totally to destroy the novel's careful ambiguity at a single stroke in the precredit sequence—makes the same error, implying the formation of the heterosexual couple that the novel absolutely rejects.) The psychic discords of the King world are too basic and too shattering to permit the imposition of a harmonious final cadence.

Cat's Eye (1985), while minor (its material is relatively slight, King's stories generally depending on the elaboration of a single gimmick and rarely achieving the resonances of the novels), deserves a brief postscript for its peculiar relationship to *Cujo*. The basis for the film was largely arbitrary and accidental: Dino De Laurentiis had the rights to two (unrelated) stories from *Night Shift*, neither containing a role for a young girl, and he had Drew Barrymore under contract. King was invited to produce a screenplay that would add a new story constructed specifically for Barrymore and find some means of tying the package together. Like *Cujo*, the film is consistently gripping, thanks to Teague's taut direction, once again intelligent without manifesting any strong traits of a definable authorial presence; but its chief interest lies in the solution he and King found to the problem of unification: the presence of the cat as witness that gives the film its title.

Western culture has traditionally associated cats with women. Newcomers to our apartment almost invariably refer to our cat as "she" (and the habit is so strong that some continue to do so after being told that his name is Max); dogs, unless they be poodles or Pekingese, are as commonly referred to as "he." The Hollywood cinema offers a long list of examples of the cat/woman association: *Bringing Up Baby* (1938), *Cat People* (1942), *Bell, Book and Candle* (1958), *Rampage* (1963), *Marnie* (1964), etc. *Cat's Eye* plays on this throughout and also on the cat/dog opposition, opening by establishing a quite explicit link to *Cujo*: the cat is pursued through the alleys and refuse of an urban slum area by an apparently rabid Saint Bernard. If Cujo was masculinity gone mad, the cat represents the feminine viewpoint, a feminine presence even in those sections of the film from which women are absent.

The first story, "Quitters, Inc.," is concerned with the subordination and victimization of women within marriage: the man's "cure" for smoking is the organization's threat to inflict sadistic torments on his wife every time he is caught. Here the cat and the wife are directly paralleled, each in turn subjected to torture by electric shock under the husband's scrutiny, the cat as a demonstration of the punishment, the wife as the punishment itself. The second story, "The Ledge," is again about the monstrousness of masculinity: the two heterosexual males, husband and lover, humiliate and torment each other in turn, exacting mutual revenge. The story's energy derives, again, from the male anxiety that underlies male sexual possessiveness. The woman (we discover that she has been murdered on her husband's orders) is absent from most of the story, but the presence in the film of the cat as witness gives it a perspective the original lacks, a feminine view of masculine behavior.

In the last story the cat becomes the protagonist. Drew Barrymore is assaulted every night by a tiny malignant troll that hides in the woodwork of her nursery. Like Cujo, the troll is somewhat vaguely associated with tensions within the family: the father surreptitiously sides with the daughter against the mother. The father-child relationship that recurs throughout the King novels is not exclusively centered on a male child: *Firestarter* and *Thinner* both extend it to a daughter, though again it typically involves the elimination or absence of the mother (in the last part of *Thinner* the father is actually planning effectively to murder the wife in order to have the daughter all to himself). All this is only embryonically present in *Cat's Eye*; it seems significant, however, in relation to it, that the troll's nocturnal assaults carry strong overtones of rape (he wants to steal the girl's breath by sucking it out of her). The cat, victimized by males throughout the preceding stories, here takes the initiative, defending the child and finally killing the troll; child and cat end up united, the cat now lying on the girl's chest in the troll's position. It looks for a moment as if the film is going to succumb to the usual demand for a gimmicky final twist, with the cat as the new predator, but this is rejected in favor of an unambiguous shared contentment, a mutual pleasure in contact between child and cat.

The association of women with cats has been attacked on occasion as yet another male-constructed myth, designed to link women with the irrational and intuitive in order to imply their inferiority. Yet men have been connected to animals in our culture just as often as women (think of vampire and werewolf mythology, *King Kong* [1933], *Cujo*). One would need to consider each instance on its own terms, examining the particular connotations, but it seems arguable in general that the cat represents the woman's active side, the energies society has traditionally associated with masculinity and has consequently sought to repress in women to construct them as submissive and dependent (as Richard Lippe has pointed out to me, it is especially interesting that in *Bell, Book and Candle* the cat, while clearly an extension of the woman, is emphatically designated as male). The final image of *Cat's Eye*, then, implying the child's possession of and sense of harmony with her active, assertive natural energies, is a very positive one. I have no wish to claim *Cat's Eye* as a major feminist text—its meaning flickers too sporadically, with too many distractions—yet it is of considerable interest in relation to *Cujo* and the King world in general.

(1985)

Notes for a Reading of *I Walked with a Zombie*

With this, the third issue of *CineAction!*, it is becoming clearer that the magazine's position is in certain respects uneasy and problematic. We want, on the one hand, to remain accessible—or at least relatively so (we don't write for people who just want to be entertained). On the other, we want seriously, and we hope formidably, to challenge the current theoretical hegemony, the structuralist/semiotic/Lacanian school. It doesn't take much reflection to realize how difficult it is to do both. Yet the two undertakings are also interdependent: our prime objection to the Lacanian school is its apparently relentless inaccessibility and our sense that it has lost whatever political thrust it once had by becoming increasingly hermetic, self-involved, "academic" in the worst sense. This necessitates a third undertaking, introducing further problems: to rescue from the structuralists (they might prefer "steal") those concepts and aspects of their methodology that we value and try at once to incorporate them in an alternative system and render them comprehensible to intelligent readers who have resisted the structuralist hegemony.

I believe myself that structuralism has revolutionized the analysis—"reading"—of films: simply to ignore the movement is automatically to render oneself obsolete. To be overwhelmed by it, on the other hand, is (as so many cases have demonstrated) to lose one's own voice and much of one's potential audience by adopting a convoluted jargon that frequently has to be translated back into English before it reveals its (often quite simple) meaning.[67] (In certain extremist structuralist/Marxist circles, the desire to preserve one's own voice will be instantly suspect; but I think we need not take very seriously a Marxism that has neither place nor respect for individual utterance and no theorization of its—I was going to write "validity"—necessity. It is precisely when Marxism rejects all intercourse with humanism that it becomes dangerous.) I want in this article to appropriate certain concepts and procedures from the work of Roland Barthes. Strict semioticians will frown upon the appropriation, complaining that I am to some degree diverting the procedures from their original ends, diluting them, and assimilating them into a more traditional aesthetic. But no text, no concept, no procedure is sacrosanct: the critic has the right to appropriate whatever s/he needs from wherever it can be found and use it for purposes perhaps somewhat different from the original ones. And if I, to some degree, transform Barthes, it is at least equally true that Barthes transforms me: it is impossible to adopt his methodology, in however modified a form, without simultaneously modifying (and extending) one's own.

The text that interests me here is *S/Z*. This is far from being the first attempt to apply the "codes of realist narrative" to the reading of a film.[68] I lay no claim to originality, but neither am I merely imitating: both my method and my results are to some degree idiosyncratic. I shall preface the reading of *I Walked with a Zombie* (1943) with my own account of what have come to be known as the "Barthes codes" (though they were his discovery rather than his invention) in the hope of rendering them and the reading accessible to those who have not read *S/Z* (and in the further hope of making the book more accessible too). Those already familiar (perhaps beyond the point of saturation) with Barthes's work can of course skip this, though they may wish to check up on my (mis)representation of this distinguished and important figure.

S/Z

The main body of *S/Z* consists of a reading of Balzac's novella *Sarrasine*. One should first distinguish between "reading" and the more traditional "critical interpretation." The latter usually starts from the critic's sense of what the work in question is, what it is about, what it does; and the interpretation will aim to establish the work's coherence (or criticize its failures to become coherent), supported by quotations of what are regarded as particularly significant passages. A reading, on the other hand, attempts to account for everything and will be more concerned with process (the work of construction) than with establishing a definitive, coherent meaning. (There is of course no guarantee that a reading will not also start from the critic's sense of "what the work in question is.") The reading of Balzac's thirty-three-page novella occupies two hundred pages (not counting the introductory material and the appendices), and every word of Balzac's text is quoted and annotated in the form of "lexias," or units of reading. Barthes attributes to the classical narrative a "limited plurality," and seeks to demonstrate this in his reading of *Sarrasine*. On one level I find this misleading: what finally emerges from the reading is as coherent an overall sense of the novella as any "traditional" interpretation would be likely to produce, largely free from the internal conflicts and contradictions that the promise of a "limited plurality" might seem to suggest. *S/Z* has been widely held to mark a decisive and irreparable break with traditional notions of interpretation; it seems to me that it can just as easily be regarded as demonstrating its continuity and compatibility with them. What *S/Z* uncovers is not so much a plurality of meanings as the intricate and multilayered nature of the activity of reading itself. Here the adoption of the word "text" for any artwork (book, film, painting, piece of music) is important. "Text" suggests "texture," and a texture is composed of many interweaving strands. The analogy with weaving has a further implication, that of an intricate coherence: a texture that did not cohere would simply disintegrate.

The Five Codes

IN HIS READING OF *Sarrasine*, Barthes discovers that the entire novella is constructed (woven) according to the operation of five "codes": "There will be no other codes throughout the story but these five, and each and every lexia will fall under one of these five codes."[69] (In fact, most of the lexias turn out to fall under several simultaneously, and this will also be the case with *I Walked with a Zombie*.) Though Barthes doesn't actually say this, the implication appears to be that all classical narratives are structured upon these five codes and only these. I have accepted this assumption in my reading on the film, but I think the acceptance should only be provisional. As I shall show, there are important differences in function and status among the five codes (so extreme in the case of one that it seems scarcely to belong with the other four, and some alternative form of categorization may prove desirable). It also seems uncertain that the five in themselves account for all the possibilities of classical narrative: the case, for instance, of narratives within narratives, where the "truth" of the internal narrative may be in question, produces problems that cannot be easily resolved within the Barthesian methodology (Ophuls's *Letter from an Unknown Woman* [1948] offers an extreme example, *I Walked with a Zombie* a minor one). I miss particularly the inclusion of an authorial code, that would allow for the annotation of all those points (so important a feature of the "pleasure of the text") where we recognize an author's imprint (whether thematic or stylistic): Barthes was of course committed to a view of art that virtually obliterates the notion of individual authorship, so the omission is understandable if not excusable.

The clearest way to elucidate the codes is by means of examples. I have chosen to concoct my own sentence (to be imagined as the opening of either a story or a chapter of a novel), not because it is beautiful prose but because I can ensure that it exemplifies all five of the codes:

> The day of the picnic, awaited by Max with his usual youthful eagerness, began under the auspices of Phoebus, but little did he guess in what darkness it would end.

As a transition to film, I shall take as second instance the opening shot of *Letter from an Unknown Woman*, chosen because (a) it is probably familiar to most readers and (b) it also happens to exemplify all five of the codes very clearly and precisely.[70] Here, then, are the five codes of realist (or classical) narrative.

1. The *proairetic* code (from the Greek for "actions"): the code that gives us the series of actions upon which the narrative is constructed—in the above sentence, the action of "the picnic." Immediately, we must face a possible objection from those hitherto innocent of semiotics, an objection to the term "code." Everyone knows that a narrative consists of actions and could not exist without them; every schoolchild can follow the actions through a narrative. The term "code" implies the work of decoding, and no such work is necessary here—we are not idiots, thank you. The answer is, first, that the act of decoding is so long ingrained and so familiar as to be entirely automatic, but, second, that such an act does indeed take place. My sentence does not merely convey the fact that a picnic is to take place, it alerts us (because of our familiarity with other narratives) to an implied process of narrative structure: an account of the picnic will follow; it will occupy at the very least a paragraph, probably a chapter, perhaps several chapters (or, if this is the beginning of a story, the entire narrative); the account will probably be subdivisible into numerous stages (preparations,

departure, events on the way, choice of a site, events during the picnic, etc.); eventually we shall be told what happened, the action will be concluded and (if this is part of a novel) will give rise in turn to other actions.

The proairetic code is indeed the fundamental one on which the narrative edifice is built: without actions even the most elementary narrative would be impossible (provided we understand "actions" in the widest sense, to include, for example, the act of thinking or sleeping). What needs to be stressed here is the interweaving of actions in classical narrative: there must be no hiatus, one action must be prepared as one is completed. Even if, as in certain Victorian novels, the action is suspended while the author moralizes, the logical chain will be resumed as soon as the moralizing ceases. Usually, however long the work, there will be a dominant action overarching and encompassing the entire structure. For example, a novel might begin with a ship leaving Southampton and end with it docking in New York: the dominant action would be the "transatlantic voyage." In between the departure and the docking, however, we shall be led through the narrative by a continuous, often overlapping, series of subordinate actions: A and B will fall in love, C will be murdered, D will be unmasked as an enemy agent, the captain will go insane, a giant man-eating spider will be discovered in the boiler-room . . . The typical dominant action of classical narrative (linking *War and Peace* to *The Sure Thing* [1985]) is the construction of the "good" or "normal" heterosexual couple (it is likely that, in our hypothetical novel, this will coincide with the end of the voyage, after all the threats have been systematically eliminated).

The opening shot of *Letter from an Unknown Woman* offers us two actions (one shown visually, the other introduced in the dialogue): the arrival home, the duel. The latter is indeed the dominant action of the film—it has not even been concluded at the end, though we know by then what its outcome will be. The former is the first small, finite action in a proairetic chain—arrival home, preparations for departure, interruption, reading the letter—which will guide us through the film.

2. The *hermeneutic* code (from the Greek for "enigmas"): the proposal, development, and eventual resolution of puzzles, questions, mysteries. In my sentence, "little did he know" immediately presents an enigma, providing the reader with knowledge to which poor, eager, unsuspecting Max does not have access, but not too much knowledge: we know that something frightful will

happen, but we shall have to wait (perhaps for a hundred pages) to find out what. The privileged site of the hermeneutic code is clearly the detective novel: someone is found murdered on page one, and two hundred pages later the great detective expounds the solution, unmasks the culprit. Again, we find a dominant enigma ("Who done it?") encompassing the whole narrative, with a continual play of enigmas (clues, mysterious utterances, anonymous letters, red herrings) interweaving throughout. But every classical narrative plays on suspense and curiosity to some degree. One might certainly argue that the proairetic code, every time an action is introduced, implies an enigma ("What will happen?") automatically. This shows how intimately the two codes are interrelated, but it seems reasonable to follow Barthes in reserving the hermeneutic code for the stronger and more explicit introduction and pursuit of specific enigmas. One might make the distinction by suggesting that, while actions are essential to a narrative, enigmas (in the strict sense) are not, and one might construct a (very boring) narrative without any ("I went for a walk. I met a friend. We talked about the weather. We said good-bye. I went home.").

The *Letter* shot is particularly rich in enigmas, all surrounding the action of the duel: Why is it being fought? Who is the opponent? Will Stefan fight? Will he be killed? All these are answered, but not until the very end of the film, during its closing minutes. This gives us another (almost) absolute principle of the hermeneutic code: just as every action must be concluded, so every enigma must be resolved. (I shall argue that it is one of the distinctions and eccentricities of *I Walked with a Zombie* that one of its enigmas, a crucial one, is left disturbingly unresolved.) We may also notice another common feature of the *hermeneutic chain*, that of apparent but false resolution (I call it "blocking," in preference to the standard translation's "jamming") in order further to postpone the true one: the question as to whether Stefan will stay to fight the duel is apparently answered in the negative in the following scene ("Pack my things. . . . Enough for an indefinite stay."). Typically, this takes the form of a kind of teasing: if we really believed, beyond doubt, that we had already been given the "true" solution, we might be tempted to close the book, walk out of the movie, then and there (compare Hitchcock's audacity, bitterly resented by many spectators, in supplying us with the true solution to *Vertigo*'s [1958] dominant enigma, beyond any uncertainty, two-thirds of the way through the film). In the example from

Letter, we are not really convinced that the film's male protagonist, played by a prominent star, will not fight the duel. We shall encounter excellent examples of "blocking" in *Zombie* (even in the opening credit-title shot).

Clearly, the proairetic and hermeneutic codes belong together: they continually intertwine and supplement each other, their joint task is to push, guide, lure us step by step through the narrative, always focusing our attention on the future ("What will happen?") so that we read on; they are the codes that "tell the story." We can designate them as the linear or horizontal codes (in contradistinction from the other three). In the classical Hollywood cinema (and most postclassical) they are always dominant (audiences go to Hollywood movies "for the story") and on the rare occasions when their dominance is challenged (*Heaven's Gate* [1980]) the work is considered inept. They also represent the level at which the work of producing and reading narratives is likely to be most fully conscious, on the part of both maker and viewer, and also, crucially, on the part of the censorship (literal and symbolic, external and internal). Hence, in the classical Hollywood narrative, the tendency of the linear codes will almost always (there are very few exceptions) be ideologically conservative, leading us, with endless repetition, toward the restoration of the patriarchal-capitalist status quo ("normality") and its attendant value system. (Critics and theorists who dismiss the Hollywood cinema outright habitually reduce Hollywood movies to the operation of the linear codes, ignoring the rest.)

3. The *semantic* code (from the Greek for "meanings"): corresponding roughly to what traditional aesthetics would call the "thematic" level of the narrative. Barthes tells us that this is most commonly attached to characters, and reflection proves him correct (in *Hamlet* and *Macbeth* respectively, the themes of indecision and ambition are clearly introduced and developed through the protagonists). In my sentence, "awaited by Max with his usual youthful eagerness" suggests the themes (or "meanings") of anticipation, youth, innocence: themes that may or may not prove to be important in the total structure of the work, but which are here attached to what may be its main character. The *Letter* example offers most obviously the theme of decadence (the men are returning from some kind of nocturnal debauch, at 2:00 a.m.), attached especially to Stefan (he has been overindulging in cognac, hates getting up in the morning, and is cynical about death and honor). We may notice also, however, the theme

of time (the clock, the men's promise to return at five), which is not a part of the characterization but will be a major preoccupation of the narrative. There will of course be "meanings" that are merely transitory and incidental, dropped as soon as introduced—"meanings" that never become "themes," the defining characteristic of a theme being recurrence. We may say in general that the more frequently a theme recurs from lexia to lexia (perhaps in a variety of forms and modes, from serious to comic, from emphatic statement to glancing allusion), the more important it will prove in the total structure.

4. The *symbolic* code. We are all familiar with the notion of symbolism. Barthes demonstrates very impressively (though the idea is scarcely new to criticism—see, for example, F. R. Leavis's concepts of "symbolic drama" and "dramatic poem"[71]—extended to works of fiction generally) that symbolism is not something applied occasionally to a work like cherries on a cake but a major structuring principle. He shows that the symbolic structure of a work typically organizes itself in terms of oppositions. In my sentence, the obviously "symbolic" use of "darkness" implies one of the fundamental symbolic oppositions of our culture: light/darkness, day/night, happiness/tragedy, good/evil. The *Letter* shot plays on much the same opposition: the night and rain in which the film opens will be replaced in the precisely symmetrical last shot (the carriage drives away from the same gates) by near-dawn and no-rain, expressing the film's progress from confusion to enlightenment, from the dominance of worldliness and corruption to the triumph of spirituality. The symbolic oppositions will not be arbitrary or haphazard: all will relate to all (though the relationship may be complex).

It swiftly becomes clear that, just as the proairetic and hermeneutic codes are more or less inextricably interconnected and interdependent, so too are the semantic and symbolic codes (and more rather than less). The themes of a work will inevitably be drawn into its pattern of oppositions (Hamlet's indecision against the promptness of Laertes, the murderous ambition of the Macbeths against the loyalty of Banquo and Macduff): even within my sentence, Max's eager anticipation has its answer in the threat of disaster, and these correspond to the symbolic opposition of day/night. In *Letter*, Stefan's disillusioned decadence will be answered by Lisa's idealistic purity, and these are taken up in the rain/no-rain, night/near-dawn oppositions. One could of course equally put it the other way around: the symbolic oppositions invariably have a thematic dimension. Consequently, in my reading of *Zombie*, I have not been too scrupulous about distinguishing these two codes: as a theme encounters its opposite I have tended to gather them into the symbolic code and to speak of the film's semantic/symbolic structure as an entity (which does not mean that it is monolithic or free of internal tensions). The relationship of this structure to the linear structure produced by the work of the proairetic and hermeneutic codes can range from the simply supportive (in our more rudimentary narratives) to the highly complex. In general, the semantic/symbolic structure of a work is likely to be far less accessible to consciousness (of the maker, the viewer, the censorship) than the progress of the linear code ("the story"). One can therefore at this stage posit the possibility that the two pairs of codes may develop in a state of permanent tension (perhaps contradiction) rather than in simple cooperation or mutual support. I shall go on to declare that such is indeed the case with a large number of distinguished Hollywood films, and this is why those critics who reduce the films to the progress of the linear codes are quite simply wrong.

5. The *cultural* code (Barthes also calls it the code of reference): reference to shared, familiar knowledge within the culture, such as proverbs, common sayings, mythology, topical events, famous people. In my sentence, we have to know that Phoebus is the Greek sun god if we are to grasp the meaning. Barthes acknowledges that in a sense all the codes are cultural: we have to learn to read narratives, though the learning took place so early in our lives that the process has become entirely naturalized. However, he retains the cultural code for the annotation of specific references. It seems to me that this "code" does not really belong with the other four, its function being entirely different: they are structural codes, this is not (except in so far as the references are drawn into the semantic/symbolic structure, in which case they can be grouped under those codes). Analysis of the cultural code belongs, in fact, to a simpler (though very important) stage in the development of semiotics, that represented by Barthes's earlier *Mythologies*: the exploration of a culture's "myths" through its specific individual artifacts and practices (wrestling, steak and chips, Garbo's face, etc.). As I am concerned in this paper with structure, I have ignored the cultural code as such altogether, preferring to group many of its instances under the canopy of the semantic and symbolic codes. It is probable that all manifestations of the cultural code can be grouped in this way: the obvious one in the *Letter* shot, for

example (the caption "Vienna, about 1900"), immediately evokes not only the music (from Mozart to popular waltzes) that plays so important a part in the film's thematic development and its analysis of class, but also the connotations of "fin de siècle" that attach themselves to the theme of decadence. Or take two striking examples from the decor of Jessica's bedroom in *Zombie*, the harp and Böcklin's painting "Isle of the Dead": both belong within the cultural code (we have to know not only what a harp is but also its association with angels, hence with a certain cultural myth of woman), but they equally belong to the semantic/symbolic structure (the harp standing in opposition to the voodoo drums).

Is It Worth It?

FINALLY, THE READER MAY ask what is gained by a method of analysis that requires such an elaborate exposition. First, quite simply, it helps one to notice (become aware of) so much more: take a sequence from any film with which you believe yourself to be thoroughly familiar, look at it again in relation to the four (or five) codes, and see how many details that previously passed by uncommented suddenly relate, make sense, form patterns with other details across the film. Beyond that, the method greatly heightens one's awareness of structure and the process of structuration. Beyond that again, it makes possible a rigorous and systematic investigation into what has proved by far the most fruitful concept in recent approaches to Hollywood, the concept of ideological tension or contradiction. I hope these claims will be substantiated by the (admittedly skeletal) reading that follows.

To make that skeletal method clear, I close this introduction by showing how the two examples I have used can be succinctly annotated.

My sentence:

> PRO: "picnic" (statement of action)
>
> HER: "little did he guess . . ." (enigma)
>
> SEM: "awaited . . . with his usual youthful eagerness" (themes of anticipation and innocence)
>
> SYM: "auspices of Phoebus," "in what darkness . . ." (opposition of day/night, light/darkness, happiness/disaster)

The *Letter* shot:

> PRO: arrival home; duel (dominant action)
>
> HER: Why is the duel being fought? Who is the antagonist? Will Stefan fight? Will he be killed?
>
> SEM: decadence (cynicism, cognac, "fin de siècle"); time, passing of time (three hours)
>
> SYM: rain and night (answered at end of film by no-rain and near-dawn)

Why *I Walked with a Zombie?*

A COMPLEX OF REASONS. First, I needed a film to which I had easy access (the analysis demanding prolonged and intensive work) and which is in distribution (it has also been repeatedly shown on pay TV) so that interested readers might have access to it also. Second, I wanted an unquestionably distinguished film with a very rich semantic/symbolic structure, but one which nevertheless was securely contained within the bounds of classical Hollywood narrative, a film at once representative and exemplary. Third, I wanted a film as short as possible, for obvious reasons (this article is already lengthy enough—imagine the method applied to *Duel in the Sun* [1946] or *The Deer Hunter* [1978]!). I should add that I have loved *I Walked with a Zombie* for many years: this is not an "objective" academic exercise carried out upon a film whose title was produced out of a hat (an exercise of which I think I would be absolutely incapable).

The Reading

THIS IS AN ATTEMPT to outline the basis for a complete reading of a specific classical Hollywood narrative (one of great distinction) and to suggest, at the same time, how classical Hollywood narratives work, the process of their construction. The major omission is a very serious one: there is no adequate attention to the operation of the "codes specific to film"—camera placement, camera movement, camera angle, editing, lighting, framing, etc.—but to attempt this as well would make the exercise virtually interminable!

The film, just under seventy minutes long, consists of 509 shots. I have broken it down into forty-six segments, roughly along the lines of Metz's Grande Syntagmatique.[72] In most cases the "autonomy" of the segment is clearly marked (change of location, time lapse, cinematic punctuation such as fades or dissolves); in a few cases my divisions are more questionable, especially that between segments 28 and 29 (which occurs in the middle of a shot). The great majority of the segments are, in Metzian terminology, either "scenes" or "ordinary sequences," and I have not bothered to specify these, noting only the more unusual types.

The figures in brackets denote the number of shots in each segment (I have tried for perfect accuracy, but there may be errors).

1 [1]. Title, Credits, Opening Shot

Diegetic ambiguity:[73] though seemingly "realistic," the shot has no logical place within the narrative. Purely "poetic" status?

TITLE:

>PRO: the walk (specific reference to cane-field sequence?)
>
>HER: the zombie

VISUAL:

>PRO: the walk (an impossible one)
>
>HER: the zombie (blocking of enigma: the zombie referred to in the title is Jessica, not Carrefour)
>
>SEM: freedom, space; harmony between races (deception)
>
>SYM: land/sea (the figures walking along the boundary between); black/white (race, clothing—the black cape)

NOTE: Beginning of Betsy's narration.

The opening shot (1).

2 [7]. The Office

Establishing shot: "Parish and Burden"

> SEM: Connotations of religion and slavery

THE SCENE:

> PRO: the interview (completed here); the journey (i): announcement; the job (continued to end of film)
>
> HER: Who is Betsy's employer? Nature of wife's illness? Question about witchcraft?
>
> SEM: Betsy as nurse (service, dedication, purity); Betsy's rationalism (witchcraft); Betsy's romantic aspirations (fantasy of West Indies); dominant position of male, submissive position of female
>
> SYM: Canada / West Indies, medicine/witchcraft, rationalism/superstition.

3 [13]. The Ship

> PRO: journey (ii): the ship; the relationship between Paul and Betsy (beginning—the dominant action of the film?)
>
> HER: Why does Paul behave like that?
>
> SEM: bitterness, destruction of illusions (Paul's character); deceptiveness of appearances; romantic aspirations (beauty, the ladder, the stars); death ("Everything dies here"); dominance (male over female, master over workers, white over black)
>
> SYM: development of semantic connotations into structure of oppositions: Canada / West Indies, white/black, master/slave, male/female, illusion/reality, life/death, beauty/horror

NOTE: Betsy's reaction to Paul ("Clean, honest") will be echoed in segment 33 by Paul's words to Betsy ("Clean, decent thinking").

4 [3]. Disembarkation

> PRO: journey (iii): arrival at St. Sebastian
>
> HER: Paul's absence (SEM: aloofness)
>
> SEM: cultural difference

5 [5]. The Carriage

The carriage ride (5).

294 - Notes for a Reading of *I Walked with a Zombie*

PRO: journey (iv): driving to Fort Holland

SEM: cultural difference; Betsy's rationalism ("You mean a figurehead"); domination and oppression (linked especially to the name "Holland," hence indirectly to Paul, not Wesley); deceptiveness of appearances ("If you say, Miss . . .") again linked to "beauty"; black subservience

SYM: white/black (race); rationalism/superstition; power/oppression

NOTE: Ti-Misery introduced as emblem of oppression and black ("his black face").

6 [13]. Fort Holland

The sequence is unclassifiable within Metz's categories as it moves from chronological narrative into an achronological "descriptive syntagma" and back again, the transitions linked by Betsy's narration. The three subsections are:

a. Characterized by Betsy's POV (seven shots)

PRO: journey (concluded): arrival

SEM: rationalism undermined in this new world ("like a dream")

SYM: Ti-Misery / St. Sebastian, uniting white/black, Christian / non-Christian

b. "Descriptive syntagma": the rooms (three shots linked by dissolves)
c. Return to chronology: Betsy preparing for dinner (three shots)

PRO: dinner (i): preparation

SEM: shadow patterns, evoking notions of uncertainty, ambiguity, confusion; deceptiveness of appearances (sinister shadow is merely the servant announcing dinner)

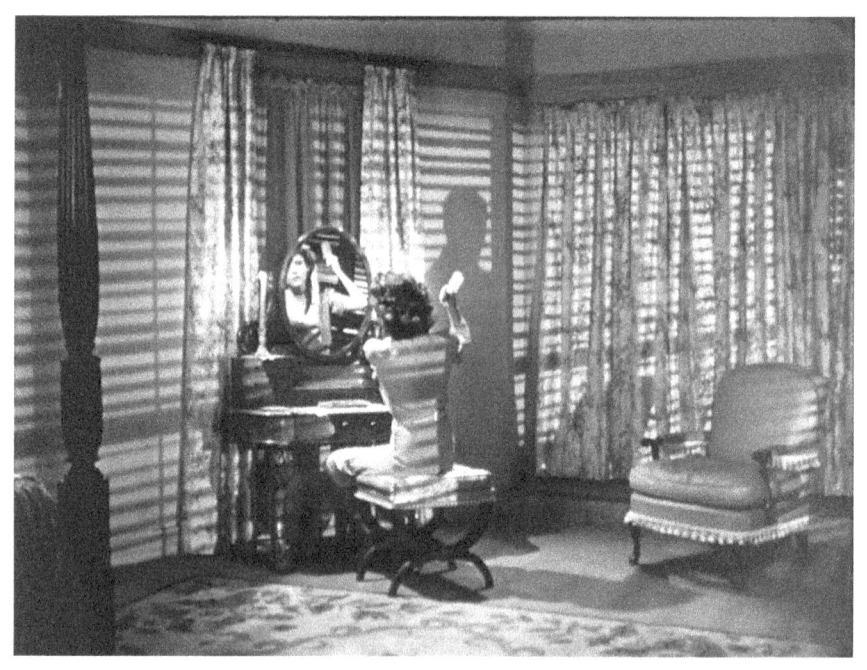

Betsy and the shadow (6b).

7 [6]. The Dining Room

    PRO: dinner (ii): the family

    HER: enigmas surrounding Mrs. Rand (runs dispensary but not a doctor; doesn't live in her own home); Jessica (Wesley's tone of voice)

    SEM: male authority—the two fathers (Holland/capitalism, Rand/religion, both names carrying connotations of South Africa, imperialism, oppression of blacks)

    SYM: the system of oppositions: the half brothers, dominance/subordination ("Masters of the house")

8 [16]. The Dining Room (Later)

    PRO: dinner (iii): completion

    HER: reasons for Wesley's hostility to Paul, and for his heavy drinking; the tower, the obscure door, Jessica's dinner

SEM: Wesley's weakness, bitterness, envy and enmity; deceptiveness of appearances (the work drum and "voodoo")

SYM: the half brothers (British/American, dominant/subordinate); Christianity/voodoo (the drums linked to mention of Mr. Rand as missionary)

9 [7]. Betsy's Bedroom

PRO: preparation for bed, first sight of patient

HER: Jessica, the tower, her illness

SEM: association of Jessica with darkness, nature, mystery, beauty

SYM: light/darkness (the abrupt switch from clear-cut image to crisscross of shadows, in which Betsy herself is included)

10 [39]. The Tower

PRO: Betsy's job, encountering her patient

HER: Jessica's strangeness, her unnatural height, threatening movements; nature of her illness

SEM: deceptiveness of appearances, cultural difference (the crying). The crying also signifies oppression, with several forms linked together: (a) Ti-Misery (the visual image), (b) Jessica (who Betsy thinks is the source), (c) the black slaves and their descendants.

SYM: white/black (race—the two united in Ti-Misery); white/black, Jessica in white; brunette/blonde: reversal of conventions, undermining of expectations

Hence:

SEM: Betsy and Jessica as inverse mirror-images

SEM: the real attitude of black servants to white masters (Alma's sarcastic remarks about Betsy: compare next segment)

The nurse meets her patient (10).

11 [9]. Betsy's Bedroom

PRO: breakfast in bed

HER: Jessica's illness: explanation (i) ("She was very sick, and then she went mindless"): explanation vague and unsatisfying, developing rather than resolving the enigma

SEM: cultural difference (method of awakening; the brioche/puff-up); deceptiveness of appearances (the brioche; Alma's obsequiousness—compare previous segment); class division, Betsy's indeterminate place as Jessica's nurse; the dialogue connects Jessica and Betsy (the past and future Mrs. Holland)

NOTE: Jessica referred to as "doll" ("It's just like dressing a great big doll"): compare the "Jessica-doll" of the voodoo scenes.

12 [3]. Paul's Workroom

    PRO: the Betsy/Paul relationship

    HER: Jessica's illness: explanation (ii) ("a mental case"): partial, misleading

    SEM: Betsy's uniform (whiteness, purity, service); fear of "the dark" (commonest symbol for the unconscious)

NOTE: THE watch-pendant (visual motif) introduced here.

13 [8]. Jessica's Bedroom

    HER: Jessica's illness: explanation (iii) ("tropical fever"): false resolution ("blocking"); introduction of notion that Jessica is a zombie (the truth disguised as a joke)

    SEM/CUL: the harp (white culture; woman as angel)

    SYM: harp/voodoo (talk of the zombies)

    SEM: "Isle of the Dead" (Böcklin's painting, also the title of the last of the series of Lewton-produced horror films): borderline between life and death

14 [6]. The Veranda

    PRO: Paul/Betsy relationship

    HER: Paul's actual feelings for Betsy; reasons for his bitterness

    SEM: deceptiveness of appearances (what is "beautiful"?)

15 [2]. St. Sebastian

    PRO: day off, visit to town (i): meeting Wesley

    SEM: cultural difference, whites as aliens

16 [20]. The Cafe: Day

PRO: visit to town (ii): drinks

HER: the song, hints of family scandal, of the background to Jessica's illness and Paul's bitterness

SEM: tensions and disunity within the family; deceptiveness of appearances, problems of interpreting behavior: (a) singer's subservience barely concealing insolence (compare Alma); (b) Paul and the word "beautiful"; (c) Paul's motivation—using Jessica to see Wesley "squirm"

SYM: white/black (race), calypso and "the British Grenadiers": whites as concealers of truth, blacks as revealers of truth

17 [14]. The Cote: Night

PRO: visit to town (iii): concluded

HER: Jessica's illness: explanation (iv): the conclusion of the song links it to adultery, suggests it may be a punishment for immorality

SEM: woman as bringer of discord—parallel between Jessica and Betsy, past and future trouble, in the song; hence:

HER: Will both brothers fall in love with Betsy, repeating past history? (false enigma)

SEM: family tension (the song); Mrs. Rand introduces herself as "Wesley's mother" (she is also Paul's), suggesting favoritism, a further reason for rivalry/resentment

SEM: singer paralleled to Jessica as threat (approaching Betsy out of the darkness); association of Jessica with the blacks (racial oppression, gender oppression)

SYM: light/darkness (the CU lamp, the night); white/black (singer and darkness)

PRO: Betsy to help Wesley (alcohol); Betsy/Paul relationship (hints of Betsy's influence); hence:

SEM: Mrs. Rand's knowledge, and:

HER: Where does she get her information?

300 - Notes for a Reading of *I Walked with a Zombie*

Betsy, Mrs. Rand, Wesley, calypso singer (17).

18 [5]. Fort Holland

>PRO: helping Wesley: Betsy speaks to Paul
>
>SEM: uncertainty of motivation (Paul's refusal)
>
>SYM: clarity vs. confusion or obscurity: silhouette image followed by faces shadowed with lines

19 [20]. The Dining Room

>PRO: helping Wesley (no decanter); the Betsy/Paul relationship (Betsy's influence)
>
>HER: voodoo (conch, drums); question of Paul's treatment of Jessica, secrets in the past
>
>SYM: white rituals/black rituals (formal dinner, voodoo ceremony); home/houmfort (the "home" is also a "fort")

20 [16]. Paul's Room

> PRO: Paul/Betsy relationship: growth of intimacy, mutual attraction
>
> HER: Jessica's illness: explanation (v): the quarrel (note parallel development of dominant action and dominant enigma). Again, the "false" explanation juxtaposed with hints of the true one (the drums, association of Jessica with voodoo).
>
> SEM: Chopin's E major etude, but more familiar to audiences as "So deep is the night..."
>
> SYM: piano/voodoo drums, white culture/black culture

21 [2]. The Sea

> PRO: Betsy's recognition of her love for Paul and her decision to help him determines the entire chain of subsequent actions to the end of the film: the insulin treatment, the visit to the houmfort, the "voodoo" invasion of the white world. It can therefore be claimed as the turning point of the film.
>
> HER: What exactly will Betsy do? Can she save Jessica? Does she really want to?
>
> SEM/SYM: The sea, already established in segment 3 as image of uncertainty; deceptiveness of appearances, linked here to doubts about Betsy's motivation

NOTE 1: Symmetry of classical narrative: the sea at the beginning (segment 3) and end (segments 44–45) of the film, and also at this near midpoint.

NOTE 2: End of Betsy's narration (because she can no longer control a narrative that calls into question her own motivation?).

22 [3]. Jessica's Room (Day)

> PRO: saving Jessica (i.a): insulin shock treatment
>
> SEM: danger (Jessica may be killed—question of Betsy's true motivation)

23 [4]. Jessica's Room (Night)

>PRO: saving Jessica (i.b): failure

>SEM: uncertainty of motivation (Wesley's speech makes this explicit); darkness and the unconscious

>SYM: light/darkness

NOTE: The threatening figure (here Wesley) approaching out of the darkness, recurrent motif (compare Jessica in segment 10, calypso singer in segment 17).

24 [20]. The Veranda

>PRO: saving Jessica (ii.a, voodoo): suggestion ("better doctors")

>HER: witchcraft. Will Betsy take Alma's advice?

>SEM: uncertain motivation (here, Alma in relation to Jessica: help her, or get her to the houmfort for "test"?)

>SEM/SYM: the drawing together of major components of the system of oppositions: white/black, science/voodoo, rationalism/superstition. The collapse of Betsy's rationalist certitude is linked to her troubled, unclear motivation (loss of self-image).

NOTE: Visual motif: the brooch for Ti-Victor (compare Betsy's watch-pendant).

25 [4]. The Dispensary

>PRO: saving Jessica (ii.b., voodoo): proposal

>HER: the houmfort and possibility of danger

>SYM: Christianity/voodoo ("one foot in the church and one in the houmfort"); science/voodoo; church/houmfort, dispensary/houmfort; rationalism/superstition (psychological explanation for Mamma Rose's cure)

26 [1]. The Garden: Sequence Shot

PRO: visit to the houmfort (i): departure

SEM: continuous camera movement to connect Paul, Wesley, Betsy/Jessica, Alma and Ti-Misery: theme of interconnectedness, breakdown of clear divisions, female transgression.

SYM: movement from light to darkness (the black exit)

27 [2]. Outside the Gate

PRO: visit to the houmfort (ii): directions

HER: Will they get lost? What will happen?

SYM: light/darkness (complex image with Alma, flour, flashlight, Betsy's black cape); the voodoo patches (compare Betsy's watch-pendant, Ti-Victor's brooch); black/white (race and clothing), dark/fair

SEM: "Carrefour" (French for crossroads)—passing from one world to another; female transgression

28 [31½]. The Cane Fields

PRO: visit to houmfort (iii): the walk

HER: Will they get lost? significance of the various sinister objects

SEM: voodoo (conch), death, the "living dead" (Jessica linked to images of death, her dress brushing past the skull, etc.); Carrefour—passing the crossroads (point of no return?)

SYM: white/black (clothing, patches), rationalism/superstition; passage from "white" world to "black," from science to voodoo, from conscious to unconscious (the darkness as the world of the unconscious)

NOTE: I have segmented the film here according to precise locations; Betsy and Jessica pass from the cane fields to the site of the voodoo ceremonies, marking the transgression of another boundary, within a single shot, half of which belongs to this segment, half to the next.

Carrefour (Darby Jones) (28).

29 [16½]. The Houmfort

> PRO: visit to houmfort (iv): the ceremony
>
> HER: significance of dance, danger for intruders
>
> SEM: subjugation of women, phallic power (the dancers); possession; Betsy and Jessica linked in frame, like doubles (female transgression)
>
> SYM: development of interlocking systems of oppression: white/black, master/servant, male/female

30 [8]. Outside the Door

> PRO: visit to houmfort (v): plea to Umbala
>
> HER: The door, what is behind it?
>
> SYM: medicine/voodoo; Betsy as white nurse involving herself in irrational practices associated with blacks

31 [22]. Alternating Sequence: Inside and Outside

>PRO: visit to houmfort (vi): revelation, failure; beginning of attempts to reclaim Jessica as zombie

>HER: resolution of some enigmas (Betsy's danger, what is at houmfort: etc.), development of others (nature of Jessica's illness—she doesn't bleed, partial revelation of "true" explanation)

>SEM: compromise, corruption, ambiguity ("there's no easy way to do good, Betsy"—compare Betsy's own behavior and motivation); female transgression (theme connecting Jessica, Betsy and Mrs. Rand)

>SYM: some of the structural oppositions abruptly drawn together in the ambiguous figure of Mrs. Rand: science/voodoo, Christianity/voodoo; darkness/light

Mrs. Rand, the lamp (31).

32 [2]. The Cane Fields

    PRO: visit to houmfort (vii): the return journey

    HER: Will they be pursued?

33 [4]. Fort Holland: The Garden

    PRO: visit to houmfort (viii): homecoming; Betsy/Paul relationship: deeper understanding

    HER: Paul's real feelings about Jessica (explanation)

    SEM: "the nurse who's afraid of the dark"—fear of darkness, the unconscious

    SYM: white music (Chopin theme on soundtrack) contrasted with voodoo drums of preceding segments; "clean, decent thinking" vs. unconscious motivation

34 [8]. The Garden (Day)

    PRO: visit of commissioner

    HER: Reason for visit? Connection with visit to houmfort? Danger of voodoo?

    SEM: class/race difference—the white lady's knowledge of horses; male/female relations (leading horse without looking at him); horse as representative of (male, white) authority (commissioner, police, Paul); uncertain motivation (Alma's "stupidity" as possible cover for eavesdropping?)

35 [1]. The Houmfort (Anticipation of 37)

    PRO: getting Jessica back (i): ritual

    HER: witchcraft, meaning and effectiveness of ritual

    SEM: male domination of women; Jessica as "doll" (compare no. 11)

    SYM: white/black, rationalism/superstition

36 [3]. Jessica's Room

>PRO: Paul/Betsy relationship: mutual respect
>
>HER: Relationship between Jessica and voodoo? Paul's guilt?
>
>SEM: male/female relations: male authority, female submissiveness (deviousness?)
>
>SYM: harp/drums

37 [5]. The Houmfort

>PRO: getting Jessica back (ii): the agent
>
>HER: Precise meaning of ritual? Carrefour as zombie?
>
>SEM: the "living dead": connection between Jessica and Carrefour
>
>SYM: white/black: blurring of boundary

Carrefour and the Jessica doll (37).

38 [5]. The Garden

> PRO: Paul/Betsy relationship: confession of love, need for separation
>
> HER: Will Betsy return to Canada?
>
> SEM: male authority / female submissiveness (deviousness?); male desire to dominate/destroy women—Paul's fear of his own impulses
>
> SYM: Canada / West Indies

39 [43]. Jessica's Room—Garden

> PRO: getting Jessica back (iii): the agent, failure
>
> HER: Carrefour as zombie: Is he dangerous? Will he succeed? Basis of Mrs. Rand's authority over him?
>
> SEM: Mrs. Rand's authority, her usurpation of power, transgression of male order
>
> SYM: home (Fort) / houmfort—transgression of barriers; harp/shadow of Carrefour
>
> SEM: "Isle of the Dead"

40 [34]. The Living Room

> PRO: investigation, confession
>
> HER: Jessica's illness: explanation (vi): the "true" explanation, immediately blocked by Dr. Maxwell (Jessica never died), followed at once by new enigma (Mrs. Rand's "of course")
>
> SEM: family tensions; repression/punishment of female sexual desire; ambiguity of Mrs. Rand's position (she destroyed Jessica in order to protect the patriarchal system within which women are subordinated, siding with the "firstborn," Paul, for whom she never shows any affection, against Wesley, whom she loves); the oppressed become in turn oppressors
>
> SYM: the "white" system (patriarchy, the family) and the "black" system (voodoo) joined as oppressive systems; the major oppositions undermined in Mrs. Rand

Note: Recurrent visual motif: Mrs. Rand's pocket handkerchief as voodoo-patch.

41 [17]. Houmfort, Garden (Alternating Sequence)

    PRO: getting Jessica back (iv): another ritual

    HER: Jessica's illness: explanation (vi) confirmed (removal of "block" by revelation of coma; Jessica's response to ritual)

    SEM: voodoo as black male power

    SYM: the half brothers, the "righteous" and the "sinner," on opposite sides of gate (Paul's skepticism, Wesley's belief in voodoo); echoed by Betsy/Jessica opposition

Note: Recurrent visual motif: the pocket handkerchief as voodoo patch, here associated most prominently with Paul, the apparently "righteous" brother who doesn't believe in voodoo; hence:

    SEM: undermining of moral certainties

42 [6]. The Garden, the Veranda

    PRO: "freeing" Jessica (i): Betsy's complicity sought

    HER: What will become of Jessica?

    SEM: Betsy's "integrity": she can't do deliberately what she has tried to do unconsciously (eliminate Jessica)

    SYM: Ti-Misery (the white/black opposition undermined)

Note: Recurrent visual motif: watch-pendant as voodoo patch.

43 [12]. The Garden, the Houmfort (Alternating Sequence)

    PRO: "freeing" Jessica (ii): Wesley as agent

    HER: Jessica's fate

    SYM: the oppositions joined in Wesley (acting as another "zombie"); use of arrow from Ti-Misery

44 [27]. The Seashore

PRO: "freeing" Jessica (iii): "death"

HER: resolution of problems

SEM: oppression involving both worlds, white/black, Christian/voodoo, rational/irrational: the problematic of transgressive sexual desire (especially female desire) and its punishment or elimination to maintain the patriarchal order

SYM: white/black: possession of Jessica (Wesley/Carrefour)

Wesley with Jessica's body; Carrefour (44).

45 [7]. The Sea

PRO: recovery of bodies (i): the sea

SEM: the sea, as signifier of uncertainty, deceptiveness, ambiguity (compare segment 3)

SYM: voice of minister (black, Christian) begins on soundtrack; hence:

SEM: undermining of oppositions; continuance of oppression

46 [7]. The Garden

> PRO: recovery of bodies (ii): procession home; resolution of Paul/Betsy relationship.
>
> SEM: a. the "happy end"; b. continuance of themes of oppression, ambiguity, undermining of clear-cut oppositions: the black minister, Mrs. Rand, Ti-Misery (on whom the film ends)

Appendix I: Beyond the Grande Syntagmatique

A NUMBER OF CRITICS (notably Raymond Bellour)[74] have pointed out that, while it makes a useful starting point for segmentation and analysis, Metz's Grande Syntagmatique can have the unfortunate side effect of exaggerating the autonomy of the so-called autonomous segments—that the individual segment is invariably contained within larger patterns of alternation, repetition, and symmetry that structure the entire film. It is scarcely possible here to demonstrate this systematically and exhaustively; I have selected three examples that at once illuminate particular aspects of *I Walked with a Zombie* and illustrate the working of classical Hollywood films in general. The first two concern the film's overall structure, the third exemplifies the patterns of symmetry and asymmetry within a segment larger than Metz's classification allows for.

1. *The sea.* As indicated in the foregoing reading, the image of the sea is used symmetrically to mark the beginning and end of the film and the turning point of its action. But this is not to be seen as a mere formal device, mere patternmaking: at the outset of the film (segment 3) the sea is invested with a specific metaphysical meaning ("deceptiveness of appearances," etc.) which has resonances throughout a film in which nothing is what it seems and in which most of the main characters (Paul, Jessica, Mrs. Rand, Betsy herself) turn out to be ambiguous in various ways.

2. *Night/day.* The most obvious structuring principle operating across the film as a whole is the alternation of day and night. Clearly, this has its significance in relation to the film's complex structure of "symbolic" oppositions indicated in the "reading" above (Canada / West Indies, white/black, science/witchcraft, Christianity/voodoo, conscious/unconscious, etc. . . . .).

The alternation can be set forth as follows (the numbers refer of course to the segments in the reading):

Day: 1, 2   4, 5   11–16   18   22   24, 25   34   40
Night: 3   6–10   17   19–21   23   26–33   35–39   41–46

It will be obvious that the alternation is neither consistent nor symmetrical; the imbalance takes on great resonance in relation to the overall thematic and dramatic movement of the film. In the earlier part, there is a fairly even distribution of day and night scenes; in the later part, night progressively takes over. From segment 26 (the departure for the houmfort, very strongly marked as the film's only true sequence shot), only two of the twenty-one segments are set in daylight.

3. *Symmetry within a larger segment.* The formal principles of symmetry, alternation, repetition operate within classical Hollywood cinema at all levels. The arrangement of shots within an individual sequence will show a frequent tendency to a rough symmetry. An example from *I Walked with a Zombie* chosen at random: segment 3 (the ship), composed of thirteen shots, begins and ends by crosscutting between Paul and Betsy in isolation, separated on the boat; the central shot (no. 7) is both (a) by far the longest take in the sequence and (b) the shot in which Paul moves into Betsy's space, so that they are in frame together.

Here, however, I want briefly to indicate the tendency to symmetry over a larger segment than a single sequence. I have chosen the visit to the houmfort, because it is the core of the film. The segment divides between four (continuous) locations, which we may identify as follows:

    A. The garden of Fort Holland
    B. The cane fields
    C. The site of the ceremony (dance)
    D. The interior of the houmfort

From segment 26 to segment 33 (inclusive), this gives us the progression ABCDCBA. The central movement (in certain aspects, central to the whole film), the revelation of Mrs. Rand's position, is marked further (within a segment predominantly characterized by darkness) by the abrupt switching-on of a lamp. (It will be noticed that the symmetrical use of locations is qualified by the asymmetry of duration: the recurrence of locations C and B after D is much briefer than their initial appearance.)

Appendix II: The Operation of the Codes

WE CAN, FINALLY, DRAW some conclusions from our tracing of the four codes throughout the film (though the reading of a complex work can never really be concluded).

First, the two linear codes (proairetic, hermeneutic): they are dominant (though not always to the same degree) in every classical Hollywood film, whose first aim and duty has always been to tell a story. Every story, and every telling, depends for its success on the logic of its chain of actions and the maintaining of interest and curiosity through its chain of enigmas. It is not quite possible to imagine a narrative film that entirely lacks a semantic/symbolic structure: as soon as you introduce a good character and a bad character you have the beginnings of one, and even the most childish and simple B Western will produce its set of oppositions (good cowboy wears white hat, rides white horse; bad cowboy wears black hat, rides black horse, etc.). But on that rudimentary and banal level, the only interest of the film is likely to be on the level of what happens next (usually quite predictable, also). One might venture the proposition that the richer and more complex the semantic/symbolic structure, the finer the film.

At the same time, the linear codes represent—in the overwhelming majority of cases—the conscious level of Hollywood filmmaking: even the greatest Hollywood directors (for example, Ford and Hawks) tend to discuss their films predominantly in terms of the story, the action, the characters, apparently being (at most) only vaguely aware of the semantic/symbolic dimension of their work. What is also crucially important is that it is on the level of the linear codes that Hollywood films have always been most vulnerable to censorship in various forms (from studio decisions to the strictures of the Motion Picture Production Code, elaborated to guard against subversion of the dominant norms of society in any form), simply because that is the level of which censorship is conscious, the level that must be seen to conform to the demands of "the dominant ideology." In the Hollywood film, then, the level of the linear codes—roughly, the level of the plot—is likely to be (superficially, at least) conservative, the "restoration of order" at the end being the restoration of the status quo, patriarchy, and the conventional morality that serves it.

One can see this clearly (and typically) in *I Walked with a Zombie*. We have specified the "dominant action" as the development of the Paul/Betsy relationship and the "dominant enigma" as the problem of Jessica (her illness, its cause, its nature, what can be done with her?). One can trace, through the reading of the film offered, the interdependence of the two and their perfect correlation at the end: with Jessica at last dead, and her enigma explained, Paul and Betsy can embrace. To put it another way: the film moves, in a way paralleled in countless other narratives, toward the elimination of the "bad couple" (Wesley, Jessica), who have transgressed the patriarchal moral code, in order finally to construct the "good couple" (Paul, Betsy).

What interests me here above all is the ambiguity of the relationship between the operation of the linear codes and that of the semantic/symbolic structure, which supposedly sustains them but in fact undermines them: I want to claim that the whole linear progress of the film toward its apparently conformist, conventional, reactionary resolution effectively collapses under the weight of semantic/symbolic implication. One can suggest how this comes about by listing the dominant themes that are established, reiterated, and developed: deceptiveness of appearances, uncertainty of motivation, oppression (on many levels, in many forms), female transgression, etc., and by tabulating the intricate structure of binary oppositions indicated as forming the film's symbolic structure:

Canada	West Indies
white	black (race)
white	black (clothing)
day	night
science	witchcraft
Christianity	voodoo
home (fort)	houmfort
light	darkness
conscious	unconscious
harp, piano	voodoo drums
rationalism	superstition

etc. . . .

One must then go on to indicate (as I have done in the reading of the film) how the apparently clear-cut nature of the oppositions (in a simple narrative they would be reducible to "good" [left-hand column] and "evil" [right-hand column]) is systematically undermined as the film progresses, so that all moral certitude is lost, and also to indicate how all this affects our reading of the characters and their actions. I suggest here a few points where linear and nonlinear codes intersect.

1. *Jessica's illness*. We are clearly meant to take explanation vi (Mrs. Rand's confession) as the "correct" one, yet it is clear that it complements rather than disqualifies the preceding ones: Jessica was engaged in an adulterous affair with Wesley; she and Paul had a violent argument in which he said terrible things to her; she fell ill, succumbing to a tropical fever; only then was Mrs. Rand able to intervene. In other words, all the family are implicated in Jessica's condition.

2. *Betsy*. Signified heavily as the "pure," "innocent" heroine ("clean, decent thinking," etc.), Betsy is in fact drawn into the web of moral ambiguity (repeatedly suggested visually, by the intricate lighting effects): the insulin shock treatment and visit to the houmfort (both of which she has been assured are extremely dangerous) can be read as (unconscious) attempts to eliminate Jessica, not save her.

3. *Paul*. Interestingly, one enigma is left conspicuously unresolved, what one might call the chicken-and-egg question of Paul's character; certain elements in the film suggest that he became bitter and cynical because of his wife's infidelity, others suggest (more emphatically and more convincingly) that he was always like that (which can be read as the motivation for Jessica's desire to run away with Wesley). The film's nominal "happy ending" in no way guarantees happiness: as Betsy and Jessica are frequently paralleled in the film, we are free to believe that Betsy's fate will be similar to that of her deceased patient.

4. *The voodoo patches*. The cane-field sequences associate the women's protective voodoo patches with the recurrent theme of ambiguity (white on black, black on white). But this is taken up in the visual motif that runs through the film: Betsy's watch-pendant; the brooch she gives to the baby (segment 24); the pocket handkerchiefs, of which Mrs. Rand's (40) and Paul's (41) are especially prominent, all figure as subtle reminders of the transgression of boundaries, the uncertainty of accepted values.

5. *Ti-Misery*. Arguably, the central symbolic image around which the whole film is organized. Introduced in segment 5 (by verbal reference), he is visually prominent in segments 6, 10, 26, 43, and 46. Combining white Christian saint and black slave, he becomes a generalized image of oppression, transgressing the boundaries between the film's oppositions: it is fitting that the film ends with a tracking shot in on him.

THIS ARTICLE IS DEDICATED to the memory of Ed Lowry, a critic of exceptional promise, who died last October. We had hoped to enlist him as a contributor.

(1986)

The Woman's Nightmare

Masculinity in *Day of the Dead*

It is perhaps the lingering intellectual distrust of the horror genre that has prevented George Romero's Living Dead trilogy from receiving recognition for what it undoubtedly is: one of the most remarkable and audacious achievements of modern American cinema. Now that it has been completed by *Day of the Dead* (1985) one can see it clearly for what it always promised to be: the most uncompromising radical critique of contemporary America that is possible within the terms and conditions of a popular "entertainment" cinema.

One particularly unfortunate and misleading critical strategy has been to collapse the three films into each other as if they were not distinguished by crucial differences. For a start, there is the very marked difference of tone, established most obviously by broad differences of format: grainy black and white for *Night of the Living Dead* (1968), bright lighting, garish colors, lavish decor for *Dawn of the Dead* (1978), subdued lighting, drab colors, a totally depleted decor for *Day of the Dead*.

Corresponding to this is the presence or absence of humor. *Night* has a kind of brutal, sardonic humor mainly directed at the posse of zombie destroyers and the figures of authority (including the father of the family); *Dawn* has a pervasive satirical humor directed at consumer capitalism; unless I have missed it (as the film is banned in Ontario one cannot have the experience of seeing it with a large audience), humor, like bright colors, has been eliminated from *Day* altogether (though its military figures are certainly grotesque, one never finds them funny). More important—and again the differences correspond—one must see the films historically, in terms of Romero's changing responses to changes in American society and ideology: *Day* relates as significantly to

Reaganite America (and to the cinema it has typically produced) as *Night* did to the America of the Vietnam period.

In fact, although certain motifs recur and are developed through the three films (most obviously, the presence of a black as the most intelligent and aware of the male characters), Romero never repeats himself. If the films constitute an assault on the structures and assumptions of patriarchal capitalism, the specific target is different in each, and once that target has been hit the attack is not repeated. Thus *Night* deals centrally with the nuclear family, its inner tensions, its oppressiveness, the resentments and frustrations it tries to conceal or repress (relating the film to the general movement of the genre since *Psycho* [1960]); after that, the family is dropped entirely as a concern of the films. *Dawn* is centered on consumerism, the obsession with status and possessions, and on our culture's (and its cinema's) dominant couple relationships: heterosexual marriage and the male-buddy syndrome. Romero ends *Dawn* by permitting the escape (provisional, because there may be nowhere left to escape to) of the two people (male and female, but not romantically involved) who have learned to extricate themselves from the dominant patterns, the ideological norms; the woman is pregnant. In writing on the film I commented that Romero appeared to have set himself a formidable challenge for the sequel, the challenge to define what new, nonoppressive human relations might be. Perhaps he never saw it in those terms: all three films avoid the conventional happy ending (construction of the heterosexual couple) by finally avoiding the issue of sexuality altogether. *Day* sidesteps the hypothetical challenge in favor of a new assault on patriarchy from another direction: *Dawn*'s subordinate concern with structures of masculinity (in its treatment of the "buddy" relationship and its parodic extension to the motorcycle gang) becomes the central concern of *Day*.

The ending of *Dawn* played upon two emblems of masculinist power: the surviving male surrenders his rifle voluntarily to the zombies; the woman (earlier treated by the men as the traditional "helpless female") pilots the helicopter. Weapons and technology, militarism and science: the emblems of rifle and helicopter represent two of the major extensions of socially constructed masculinity into the symbolic realm. The radical feminist analysis of masculinity is plainly relevant here, and it is obvious from *Day* that Romero understands and endorses it. Whether biologically male or female, we are born both "masculine" and "feminine" (active and passive, etc.) and bisexual; patriarchy separates this out, constructing what our culture regards as "real men" and "real women." This clearly has many ramifications (all detrimental to our common humanity and to human relations of every kind). One is the association of masculinity with power and domination: the symbolic extensions of patriarchal dominance include, for example, imperialism, war (never to be confused with revolutionary uprising), fascism, state terrorism (Reagan's support of the Contras), the arms race. If militarism is the most obvious manifestation of the masculinist ideology, science has also been conscripted in its support. The logical ultimate extension of masculinity is the end of the human race, in the interests of domination.

Day of the Dead is absolutely unequivocal on this issue. All Romero's films tend to the schematic (one might see it as either a strength or a limitation). Each of the trilogy's first two parts is built on a triangular structure: the central group of characters, who represent certain forms of human potential, however compromised, threatened by both the living dead and a malevolent, strongly masculinized human group (the redneck posse in *Night*, the motorcycle gang in *Dawn*). The films then suggest parallels between the three groups, developing patterns of similarity and difference. In *Night*, for example, the father of the nuclear family is given characteristics in common with the rednecks outside, and the family's internal tensions become a literal devouring of each other when family members become zombies; in *Dawn*, the pleasure in gratuitous violence to which Roger surrenders (presented as a kind of hysterical showing off for the benefit of his black buddy) is taken up (after his death) in the mindless devastations of the motorcycle gang. In *Day*, this triangular structure is extended: the central group of sympathetic characters (as in *Dawn*, four people, three men and a woman) is set against three variously monstrous antagonists—the zombies, the military, and the scientist Dr. Logan, appropriately nicknamed "Frankenstein." Again, the members of the group are ambiguously related to all three: themselves either scientists (Sarah) or soldiers (Miguel, her lover) or peripherally attached to the authorities (John the West Indian flies the military helicopter, the Irishman Bill McDermott is the electronics expert), they progressively dissociate themselves through their actions and attitudes from their nominal allegiances.

The increasing bleakness and desperation of the trilogy—scarcely an unreasonable response to America's "progress" into the Reagan era, and certainly not a hysterical one (*Day of the Dead* is a perfectly controlled movie)—is marked most obviously by the increasing power of the zombies. In *Night* they could still, apparently, be contained (though the film's attitude to the forces of containment remained resolutely negative and ironic); in *Dawn* they appeared to be getting the upper hand, though the surviving characters could still fly off with the possibility that there might be somewhere safe where resistance was still feasible. In *Day* they have taken over the world, outnumbering the humans (according to Dr. Logan's calculations) by four hundred thousand to one, and the only place to fly to is a desert island that may exist only in fantasy. Crucial to the sense of all the films is the relationship of the zombies to the humans. In *Night* they are evoked by tensions within the nuclear family (the brother and sister arguing, teasing and antagonizing each other in the cemetery where their father is buried, over which flies the stars and stripes), and there is much emphasis on family members devouring each other. In *Dawn* the notion of consumption is extended to consumer capitalism: the zombies gravitate to the shopping mall because it was important to them when they were alive, and the human characters are for a time fascinated by the prospect of endless and unlimited consumption until they realize that, now void of the capitalist allurements of status and competition, it doesn't mean anything. The progress from *Dawn* to *Day* is epitomized in the films' images of money: in *Dawn* it is still worth helping oneself from the mall bank, "just in case"; in *Day*, money blows about the abandoned city streets, so much meaningless paper.

It is in *Dawn* that the zombies are first defined, by the human characters, as "us," and the definition is taken up in *Day*, though there only by the film's monstrous scientist, embodying his "scientific" view of human nature. Its implications need to be carefully pondered, as it is obviously both true and false. The zombies are human beings reduced to their residual "instincts"; they lack the functions that distinguish human beings, reason and emotion, the basis of human communication and human society. (The zombies never communicate, or even notice each other, except in terms of an automatic "herd" instinct, following a leader to the next food supply.) The characters in all three films are valued precisely according to their potential to distinguish

The zombies have taken over the world in *Day of the Dead* (1985).

themselves from the zombies, their ability to demonstrate that the zombies are not "us." Something clearly needs to be said about my use of the term "residual instincts." I am not referring here (and neither is the film, despite Dr. Logan's commitment to such essentialist notions) to some God- or nature-given human essence. Certainly one might claim the need for food as a "natural" instinct, but *Day* is quite explicit on that score: "They don't eat for nourishment." What we popularly call instincts are in fact largely the product of our conditioning, and the residual instincts represented by the zombies are those conditioned by patriarchal capitalism. Above all, of course, they consume for the sake of consuming (a revelation of *Day*—it was not apparent in the earlier films); all good capitalists are conditioned to "live off" other people, and the zombies simply carry this to its logical and literal conclusion. But it is through Bub, Dr. Logan's prize zombie-pupil, that the theme is most fully developed. What Bub learns—through a system of punishments (beatings) and rewards (raw human flesh) that effectively parodies the basis of our educational system—is "the bare beginnings of civilized behavior": in fact, the conditioned reflex. It is Logan's thesis—his hope for the human future—that the zombies can be trained, and to prove it he trains Bub to perform precisely the actions he was trained to perform in life, saluting and firing guns, subservience and violence. The full savagery of the film's irony can be gauged from the fact that he also responds—with the same automatism—to the Beethoven Choral Symphony. Indeed, Schiller's *Alle Menschen werden Brüder* takes on multiple ironic connotations in relation to all the film's major groups, soldiers, scientists, zombies; and his (already thoroughly conditioned) sexism, which verbally excludes women from the universal "brotherhood," receives its implicit answer in the trilogy's progressive emphasis on women, to which I shall return.

First, however, I want to take up a point from the only review of *Day of the Dead* I have read, in the *Village Voice*, in which the reviewer compared the film to Hawks's *The Thing* (1951), finding that Romero reversed Hawks's values: the earlier film favored the military over the scientists, *Day* favors scientists over military.[75] This rests, I think, on a partial misreading of both films, between which there is indeed a close relationship, and one much more complex than that of simple opposition or reversal. Superficially, it is true that Hawks favors his military men (the airmen of the Arctic base) over at least his leading scientist Dr. Carrington (who has major characteristics in common with *Day*'s Dr. Logan); but they are favored for what they embody as human beings, not at all for militarism. Hawks underplays all sense of hierarchy (along with patriotism, which scarcely interests him at all): the men, whatever their rank, become individual and equally valued members of a typical Hawksian male group. What is celebrated in them (as also in the relationship between Captain Hendry and the woman Nikki) is their capacity for spontaneous affection and mutual respect, the pleasure in contact and communication that is fundamental to any valid community: they correspond, in fact, rather closely to Romero's "good" characters and not at all to his military men.

Romero, of course, being far more politically conscious than Hawks and living in the Reagan era, sees precisely what Hawks—perhaps naïvely, perhaps deviously—chooses to ignore: the fact that the military are an institution, and an institution embodying in its extreme form the masculinism that pervades and structures the entire power hierarchy of our culture. If *Day* as a whole must be seen as a response to Reaganite America, its presentation of masculinity in its military characters is specifically a response to Reaganite cinema—to the contemporary mindless celebration of the masculine in the *Rocky* and

Rambo films, in figures like Chuck Norris and Arnold Schwarzenegger. *Day* presents this in sexual terms (the overvaluation of the phallus, the obsession with "size") and in more general terms of aggression and domination. As there is nothing subtle about the phenomenon, so there is nothing subtle about the presentation: masculinity, here, is rendered as caricature, grotesque and gross, the implication being that there is nothing more to be said about it. Is this presentation, in fact, any more gross than the general celebration of masculinity in contemporary cinema? What Romero captures, magnificently, is the *hysteria* of contemporary masculinity, the very excesses of which testify to an anxiety, a terror. In *Day* the grossness of the characters is answered, appropriately, by the grossness of their deaths: dismemberment and evisceration as the ultimate castration, against the threat of which the Stallone/Norris syndrome can be read as the hysterical reaction. The militarist mentality, and what it produces, gets its ironic comment when Bub, having shot Captain Rhodes, dutifully salutes him as he is torn apart by the zombies.

That the film favors the scientists is, however, another partial misconception. It is true that Sarah, the film's most positive figure, is a scientist, just as Nikki in *The Thing* was associated with the scientists' group (though in the subordinate role of secretary). Yet in both films the woman is valued partly for the way in which she dissociates herself from the values science embodies. "Science" in *Day of the Dead* is "Dr. Frankenstein," and it is revealed as yet another symbolic extension of masculinist ideology. If what distinguishes the human beings from the zombies is their potential for reason and emotion, then the science of Dr. Logan represents the overvaluation of a certain kind of rationality at the expense of other distinctively human qualities. The film is not exactly antiscience; neither was *The Thing*. In Hawks's film the monster is finally destroyed by the functional use of scientific knowledge; in *Day*, technology and knowledge provide the means of escape, in the form of the helicopter and John's ability to fly it. Both films make a similar distinction between knowledge placed at the service of human beings and knowledge as a means to power and domination: if "masculinity" as constructed in our culture has led to war, imperialism, aggression, the arms race, it has equally led to the domination—and destruction—of nature. Rationality has traditionally been claimed by men as an essentially male attribute and as the justification for their power; women are fobbed off with "female intuition" as compensation. One can certainly argue that it is men who are the greater losers. The "rational," from this perspective, is what the conscious mind works out for itself without assistance, while the "intuitive" is what the conscious mind comes to understand when it allows itself close contact with the subconscious and with the emotional levels of human psychic activity. Dr. Logan's science is rational in this limited and limiting sense, its results disgusting, dehumanizing, and ultimately useless (the film presents him as increasingly blood soaked as the action progresses). On the other hand, there is nothing irrational about the decisions and actions of the positive characters: like the sympathetic characters in *The Thing*, they simply permit their reason to remain in touch with actual human needs.

Central to the trilogy's progress is the development throughout the three films of the leading female characters. Barbara in *Night* becomes virtually catatonic near the beginning and remains so through most of the action, a parody of female passivity and helplessness; Fran in *Dawn* is at first thoroughly complicit in the established structures of heterosexuality then learns

Day of the Dead (1985): Rhodes (Joseph Pilato) and Dr. Logan (Richard Liberty) represent the patriarchal forces of militarism and science, respectively.

gradually to assert herself and extricate herself from them (her rejection of marriage is crucial to this development). In *Day* the woman has become, quite unambiguously, the positive center around whom the entire film is structured. Strikingly androgynous in character, she combines without strain the best of those qualities our culture has traditionally separated out as "masculine" and "feminine": strong, decisive, and resourceful, she is also tender and caring, and she shows no desire to dominate. As a scientist, she wants to understand what has produced the zombies so that the process might be reversed; Logan wants to control the zombies, turning them into his slaves. Initially antagonistic, she progressively associates herself with the two men who have opted out of the military-vs.-scientist conflict; she effectively learns, in fact, to abandon any attempt to save American civilization, which the film characterizes as a waste of time. Her lover, Miguel, is the least masculine of the soldiers, tormented indeed (partly under the goads of the other men) by the failure of his masculinity and provoking disasters by his attempts to reassert it.

The film begins and ends with Sarah awakening from a nightmare of being assaulted by the zombies: the overtones of rape link the zombies to the military,

Sarah (Lori Cardille) becomes the positive center around whom the entire film is structured (*Day of the Dead*, 1985).

who repeatedly threaten her with just that. This formal device produces complicated narrative ambiguities. We are given no sense of where the final nightmare (the zombies are inside the helicopter and attack Sarah as she climbs in) begins: it is possible to read the entire film as the woman's nightmare, with the exception of the brief coda where Sarah wakes up on the beach of a tropical island, the two men fishing nearby (though, paradoxically, that ending validates the nightmare's "reality"). However, the abruptness and implausibility of this "happy ending" (a striking instance of what Douglas Sirk called the "emergency exit"[76]) encourages an opposite reading: the body of the film is the reality, the epilogue a wish-fulfillment fantasy (perhaps Sarah's fantasy as she dies, perhaps simply the filmmaker's ironic comment): the island image forms part of the decor of John's room in the underground shelter. Romero allows one to read the film optimistically if one wishes: the final image relates back to John's solution, that they fly away to an island and have babies who will be reared without ever even having to know that the whole legacy of American culture existed. ("Teach them never to come here and dig these records out"—the records of "the top five hundred companies, the defense department budget, the negatives of all your favorite movies . . . ," effectively, the records of the economic base and the ideological superstructure of American capitalism: "This is a great big fourteen-mile tombstone with an epitaph on it that nobody's going to bother to read.") Obviously, the optimism is heavily qualified: the zombies have taken over the entire world, and, while they can't reproduce, they appear not to die unless deliberately slaughtered; and the notion of flying away to an island is established, near the beginning of the film, as a form of hedonistic escapism. The ambiguity renders even this limited hope for any human future tentative and uncertain, and we are permitted no hope whatever for American (Western, masculinist) civilization. It is an extraordinary film to come upon in the midst of the *Rocky*s, the *Rambo*s, the *Back to the Future*s, that dominate our present era: scarcely surprising that a film that goes so strongly against the current of its age has not been a commercial success.

Postscript

DAY OF THE DEAD has been banned in its entirety by the Ontario Censor Board (now known euphemistically as the "Film Review Board"—the hypocrisy is as flabbergasting as many of its decisions). Ontario censorship has become almost proverbial not only in Canada but across the world, and its pitiful provincial absurdities and confusions are perhaps not worth lingering on. A typical detail, however: one of the reasons for banning the film is that it contains "racist slurs." It does indeed: Miguel is referred to as a "spick," and John is called a "jungle-bunny." These racist slurs are put into the mouths of the film's militarist rednecks, who are totally discredited and foregrounded as its more despicable characters; the "spick" becomes the movie's Christ figure, the black is its most positive male character. It appears that in Ontario decisions as to what films we are or are not permitted to see are made by people incapable of reading them on even the most elementary level.

What troubles me more is that no one seems to care. The simultaneous banning of Paul Morrissey's *Mixed Blood* (1984) provoked such an uproar from our local journalist-critics that the censor board relented and allowed a series of limited screenings. I have not seen *Mixed Blood*, but I am familiar with much of Morrissey's earlier work, and I have to say that I think there is something deeply wrong with a film culture that shrieks lustily—and to a degree effectively—about the banning of a Morrissey film, while treating the banning of Romero's masterpiece to date, and one of the very few really intelligent American films of the '80s, with utter indifference.

PPS The latest news is that the film—or mangled shreds of it—may after all get a release in Ontario. The censor board has demanded over one hundred cuts.

[PPS Following a number of high-profile cases, some involving films to be screened at the Toronto International Film Festival, in which films were either banned or cuts required, the Ontario Censor Board was restructured as the Ontario Film Review Board in 1985, and in 2005 the province's antiquated Theatres Act was replaced by the Film Classification Act. The Board's primary function is to rate films according to the Act, as well as videos, DVDs, and video games. Since 2015 the Board has been administered by the Ontario Film Authority—Ed.]

(1986)

Larry Cohen Interview

Robin Wood and Richard Lippe

I had written for television for about ten years, starting when I was in college, first for some of the old live television programs like *Kraft Playhouse* and *United States Steel Hour*. Then when I got out of college, I went to work for three years on *The Defenders*, a top-quality television show that had won Emmy awards every year, and did about thirteen scripts. When I came out to Los Angeles, I created a few television series of my own, like *The Invaders* and *Branded* and *Cool Million*. So I was doing well but getting bored, because the writer did not have any particular involvement in the production of the show and, if you went on the set, the director always seemed to be extremely agitated and nervous until you left. On the live television shows and on *The Defenders*, the writer was always on the set, but up in Hollywood the rule was different. So to escape from boredom, I did a play in New York off-Broadway with Tony Lo Bianco called *Nature of the Crime*. I was present at all the rehearsals, but did not actually direct the play. Soon after the play opened, the director took off to California without even saying goodbye to the actors, and we had to decide to run for a few weeks and see if we got business—the reviews were mixed but we thought we might get a run out of it. I took over directing and really enjoyed the experience. This occurred approximately in 1970, at which time I decided that this was what I would do. I had written the script *for Bone*, an off-beat piece which only involved really four principal actors and which I thought I could handle: I could shoot it in my own house and make it on a limited cost. We decided to make a test, got some crew members together, and did a couple of days of shooting in 16 mm with Yaphet Kotto, Pippa Scott, and Andrew Duggan.

After I looked at the footage, I wasn't happy with Pippa Scott, and I wasn't happy with the 16 mm. So I decided we would make the picture in 35 mm, but that meant considerably more money. Because I had a good reputation as a writer, I had no difficulty getting access to people. Of course, when they heard I wanted to make a picture myself, we usually got turned down. I finally found Nick Vanoff, who was a former producer of *The Hollywood Palace* and *The Steve Allen Show*. He had been very successful—he and his partner Bill Harbach had a corner on the variety market on television, but they wanted to do other things. I made him a proposal which was so ridiculously low he figured that he had a minimal risk in giving me some money to make the picture. He and his partner wrote us a check, and we proceeded to start shooting. We would get the principal photography finished, and he had the option to put up more money for the completion of the picture or else we would have our work print of the film to show to studios and to distribution people in the hope of getting the balance of the money from them.

When we finally did show Vanoff the picture, he wasn't that crazy about it, and he decided that he didn't want to put up any more money. As usual in these cases, the lab bill was left unpaid and deferred salaries were left unpaid, and of course the writer/producer/director—me—usually gets nothing unless we make a sale of the picture. But at least we had money to cover the initial expenses and we weren't in any trouble. Some of the major studios did like the picture. We went back two or three times—Universal, in particular, was interested—all the executives liked it and thought it was quite funny, but then Mr. Lew Wasserman ran it at his home over the weekend, and he thought it was a good picture but not within the image of Universal Studios. Joseph E. Levine ran it in New York a couple of times and told me he thought it was terrific but after two showings he finally put his cards on the table and said that he was out of the distribution business and he had no money. We had a number of experiences like that, where people really wasted our time—were very enthusiastic but then turned out not to have the distribution setup or the money, so we were generally disappointed, but I viewed it with a kind of sense of humor, it was a different side of the business—it was interesting. We must have had dozens of showings of the picture, but we still hadn't made a deal. Then we ran it in the screening room at De Lux Laboratories where Jack Harris, who was a distributor, jumped up at the end of the screening and said, "I love this picture, I want this picture—how much money do you need?" Well, this was delightful because someone was actually saying that they wanted the picture without having to go to somebody else for approval. The industry is full of executives who have no power. So you have to be very careful to show your film to someone who has the authority to make a purchase—otherwise all you're going to do is be passed on 'til eventually you'll get to somebody who can make the decision. All these underlings can only kill your project—they can't buy it. Finally we were in a room with somebody who would buy the picture. We made an arrangement with Mr. Harris very rapidly, and he paid a sufficient amount of money to pay all the negative costs and make me a profit. So I did make a profit on the picture—somewhere around $85,000, which I felt was reasonable.

Anyway, subsequent to this, I was called by Arkoff, who said he'd like to make a film with me. So we had to come up with the right project. Concurrently with this, my agent had put me together with the manager of Sammy Davis Jr., who wanted to be a dramatic movie star. I had an idea for something called *Black Caesar*, which would in effect be a black version of *Little Caesar*, showing the rise and fall of a black gangster in Harlem, his dealings with the white underworld, and his success and then his eventual destruction. This seemed to be something tailor-made for Sammy Davis Jr.—his size as well as his abilities—and they promised me $10,000 to write a treatment. I wrote the treatment, submitted it to them and could not get them to pay the money. They would not come up with the $10,000. I had written something and wasn't going to be paid for it—which was, as usual, disappointing. You hate to have to sue people for money when you don't get it, because it takes three years, and to sue for $10,000 the lawyers eat up all the revenues anyway—it isn't even practical.

My agent took that material over to Arkoff. There had just been a big success with a picture called *Shaft*, and people were starting to think in terms of a black audience who would go to the movies and pay to see pictures with black actors. Arkoff said that he would make *Black Caesar* as my production if we could write a satisfactory screenplay.

A few days before the opening in New York City, we had a sneak preview out in Los Angeles at the Pantages Theater. It was playing very well until the end where the main character died. As soon as that happened, the audience got very upset, and in the lobby afterwards some were even screaming and yelling at me because we killed him at the end. Arkoff had told me a number of times not to kill him at the end, but I wanted to give the picture a conclusion which I felt was strong and had a comment. The wounded Black Caesar staggers back to his home in Harlem where he grew up, which is now a decimated tenement, all burned out among a whole string of ghostlike tenement buildings and vacant lots filled with garbage and debris. He staggers back there, in search of his past, only to be set upon by a gang of young punks who don't realize that he is an important kingpin of the underworld—they think he's just a bum. They see he's got a gold wristwatch on, and they kill him for his wristwatch. He is killed by the next generation of young punks who are going to grow up to be the new Black Caesars. The audience did not like that ending—they wanted to see this guy live. I quickly got on a plane and flew to New York. I arrived at the theater—the Cinerama Theater on Broadway—and ran into the projection room. We got a razor blade and cut out the last scene of the picture, spliced on the end titles, got over to the RKO 57th Street Theater and cut the ending off, got up to the 86th Street Twin and cut the ending off, and having made all the three theaters in New York City, we sat back to see what would happen, and the picture was an enormous hit. We did that with all the prints. Lines were forming round the block and we really had a big success. The picture went to the top of the *Variety* list, and people were lining up. They started the shows at nine in the morning, the last show started at 1:00 a.m., and they raised the prices a dollar at the box office—so we knew we had a hit. Such a big hit that I called Arkoff on the telephone and said, "Listen, we'd better make a sequel to this thing," and he said, "Well, when do you want to do it?" I said, "I think we'd better start tomorrow because otherwise all these actors are going to want an enormous amount of money when the word gets around that this is a success. We're never going to be able to reassemble the cast again." He said, "Well, what are you going to use for a script?" I said, "Well, we'll just make one up as we go along." So Arkoff, being the kind of old-fashioned studio executive he is, said, "Go ahead—I'll put up the money." We started shooting the picture about a week or ten days later with only the barest idea of what we were doing. The film, I think, bears some resemblance to one that had been made up as it went along. *Hell up in Harlem* had plenty of action, plenty of exciting chases, and lots of exciting fight scenes, and the picture itself didn't make too much sense—the action scenes had to be strung together afterwards with some kind of story.

Hell up in Harlem starts with the ending of Black Caesar, doesn't it?

Yes, except that we don't kill him. We docked the scene where the kids gang up on him and kill him, so he survives. In foreign, he gets killed and in domestic, he lives, so in domestic we have the sequel, but in the foreign version I think they decided that a foreign audience would accept the ending. Well, let's face it, the foreign audience is only going to be minimally black.

Now, when you take the two *Black Caesars* and cut them together and make one picture out of them, it works out to be a pretty good picture because you just take out the superfluous scenes and there's enough good action in the second one to couple with the first one to make a very good two-hour movie, which we might release again for cable or for television. Nowadays there's so much use to pictures, other markets that you hadn't anticipated when you originally made them—cassettes, new stations, and pay television. *Black Caesar* made a lot of money, *Hell up in Harlem* did go into profits eventually. *Bone* did not make any profit for its distributor, but it made a profit for those of us who made the picture.

There can be few films that have been through so many title changes.

Five title changes, yes. You never know when it will turn up next. You never know when you may go into a movie theater and find that you are looking at *Bone*. It was called *Bone*, then it was called *Housewife*, then it was called—what was it called in England—*Dial Rat for Terror*—terrible title—after I'd gone through an entire afternoon explaining to the British distributor that the picture was a comedy, which he agreed that it was, so it should be sold that way. He then released the picture in this horrendous fashion only to tell me on the transatlantic phone that he did it because the theater owners did not want comedies, they wanted dramas. It's a difficult enough picture anyway—a comedy about a black rapist and a Beverly Hills housewife. If you are going to spend your money misleading the public, you can't ever hope to succeed.

It was also called *Beverly Hills Nightmare*.

A foreign sales rep took it over to the Cannes festival and was going to give it that title, but I don't know that the title ever appeared on the screen.

And *Bad Day at Beverly Hills*?

That was an alternative title for foreign but the picture was never released under that title anywhere. God only knows what would have happened to my career had that picture been successful. I might have gone off in different directions, rather than going into making exploitation pictures for AIP.

How was *It's Alive* set up?

It's Alive was an idea we had had for many years and had been telling to people, before *Rosemary's Baby* was made. After *Black Caesar* was a hit, my agent said, "If you would just write that script I'm sure we could get a deal on it." We took it around to a few places and finally to Dick Shepherd at Warner Brothers who said he thought it was a terrific script—what kind of a deal would we want? They agreed to take it as a negative pickup, which means that you make the picture and when you deliver it they pay you. But before *It's Alive* was a success, we went through three and a half years of it being more or less buried. It played briefly with a campaign that disguised the content of the picture. Somebody in the advertising department decided that a picture about a monster baby would be unattractive and that, in particular, women would not want to see it. So they put out some kind of an ad that said, "Whatever it is, IT'S ALIVE," and a woman's body lying there covered in blood, so it just looked like any cliché horror picture. I was stunned—I tried to explain that if you don't sell the gimmick, you have nothing to sell. This was the studio that had just made *The Exorcist*, where a little girl masturbates with a crucifix, and all of a sudden they were getting squeamish about a picture about a monster baby. But *The Exorcist* cost them $20 million, so it was class product, and our picture didn't cost much, so it was garbage. By that time, Dick Shepherd had left the studio and his successors said that this was an example of the kind of film that Dick Shepherd did at Warner Brothers and are we lucky that *he's* gone. Office politics and the effort to discredit a former executive played a great part in it. Anyway, as long as that administration stayed in power at Warner Brothers, nothing was ever going to happen with the picture, because in the Hollywood studio system, if they decide that your picture is going to be a failure, they make sure that they're correct. They put it into cities against tough competition with no advertising and, obviously, the picture fails. This picture, however, caught on with a small coterie of theater owners, and it kept playing around the Los Angeles area as a second feature, and as a third feature up and down Hollywood Boulevard for years.

Meanwhile, a new administration came into Warner Brothers, and one of the people was Arthur Manson, who had formerly been at Cinerama and had made a success out of a picture called *Ben*, about a boy who had a pet rat. I told Arthur the story of what had happened to me at Warner Brothers, and he agreed to look at the picture—this was about three years after its original release. He called me back and said, "Hey, I thought it was a wonderful picture, terrific film of its type, and I'm going to let the other executives see it." Everybody agreed it had been badly handled and had potential, so they spent the money for a new ad campaign and tested it in the Midwest, where it did very, very well. "We're going to wait 'til spring and go out with the picture again." So approximately four years after the original run, it came out again with about eight hundred prints and a major advertising campaign and was enormously successful. It became the number-one picture on the box office charts and made a fortune. It ended back on Hollywood Boulevard at the Paramount Theater playing first run for five dollars with lines around the block, and I don't think there's ever been a case of a picture that played up and down the street for years as a second and third feature for ninety-nine cents coming back and playing in a first run theater for five dollars and selling tickets like mad.

Warner Brothers decided we should have a sequel to it, so they gave me a commitment for a negative pickup on a sequel. By the time we came back with it, all their attention was on *Superman* number one, and believe it or not, they did the exact same thing to the second It's Alive picture that the other administration had done to the first. They buried the picture. They had no time to work on an ad campaign, and when the picture didn't perform immediately, they just lost interest in it. When a studio is involved with a big success like a

Superman where they're bringing in tons of money, they have no time to pay any attention to a small picture. So the second *It's Alive* remains over at Warner Brothers, waiting for a time when it can be properly released.

We haven't mentioned *God Told Me To*, which came in between the two *It's Alive* films.

God Told Me To was financed by Edgar J. Scherick, a producer who was formerly head of the ABC television network—he made a fortune by creating work as a package. Then he went on to produce such low-budget movies as *Sleuth*, *The Heartbreak Kid*, and *The Taking of Pelham One Two Three*. I knew him from television—he had bought *The Invaders* from me and we had talked for years about doing a project. He and his associate had their finger on a number of financial people—I don't know who they got the money from, but I'm almost certain they didn't put up the money themselves. For serving as the middlemen between me and these anonymous money figures, they got 25 percent of the pie themselves. But at the time, I didn't care what they got, because my main interest is always in getting the picture made.

Of all your films, it's the one where one senses the biggest gap between the enormous ambitions of the film and the budget. It also feels as if it should be about twenty minutes longer. It seems so compressed, as if ideas are not developed to the point at which they are sufficiently clear.

We cut a lot of scenes out because Scherick felt the picture was too slow—he was constantly telling me to shorten it. I didn't have to do it, of course, but he had made a lot of films and I thought perhaps he was right. You can't really tell about your own pictures because you're never seeing them for the first time. He kept saying, "It's too long—make some cuts, shorten it, tighten it up here, tighten it up there." We would have probably had another eight or ten minutes in the picture had I left it alone. We had an awful lot of spectacular stuff around the big St. Patrick's Day Parade sequence. We went to London and did the special effects at Pinewood Studios, and I think we probably would have had more special effects if we'd had more money. It's one of those pictures where you would love it if somebody said, "This is a terrific picture.

Here's $400,000, go back and shoot some more special effects and some more scenes because we think this could be a blockbuster." Because it might very well have been. It's the picture of mine that more people talk about than anything else.

It's a fascinating film—it has so many ideas and they remain partly obscured. For example, the exact relationship between the god and the businessman-disciples and the hippie and other executants who do the actual killings is puzzling. Just how are we to think of the god as working and what is it trying to achieve, and how is it going to achieve it through this business corporation and the mass killings? Do you have any explanations or do you leave that to the imagination of the audience?

There was only one additional scene with the executives, where you saw them all praying, but we didn't have any scene showing him with the people who performed the murders. The god was just getting to know himself when he realized that he had the power to make people do things. He was just doing it, almost as a whim. Imagine Superman as being bad rather than good, and instead of the power to fly, just the power to have people perform whatever he wants them to do, to perform acts that go against their nature. As the guy says

Detective Peter Nicholas (Tony Lo Bianco) talks with the sniper in *God Told Me To* (1976).

in the picture, "God in the Bible never manifests himself doing good as much as he does doing harm." He's always drowning half the world or bringing cities down in a bolt of lightning and smoke and fire—it's a very violent God the Old Testament tells us about. I mean, this is a very vicious god we're talking about. He is mean. If that's the god we expect to meet some day, we may all tremble.

At the same time, he seems to represent an energy which most of the other characters in the film lack. They seem largely drained, unhappy. Particularly, that seems to have something to do with the tangle of male/female relationships which they're so confused about and so unhappy with.

That's true, particularly the Lo Bianco character is torn between two relationships.

What has that got to do with the god being some kind of hermaphrodite, combining the sexes in one figure? I've never been able to put my finger on what you were doing there.

The Lo Bianco character is given another choice, to unite with the supreme being or else turn back to the imperfection of the other relationships—human relationships in themselves are always imperfect. But I doubt that this character is a god—I always thought of him as an alien. He realizes that he isn't a human being and then, after reading religious literature, becomes convinced that if he isn't a human being, then he must be a god. I think that's why he's so upset over the Lo Bianco character, because he is tracking down information that leads you to realize that this is not a god, but an alien, something for which there is a rational explanation in our minds.

You use Catholicism as an almost oppressive force on the characters—the Sandy Dennis and Tony Lo Bianco characters are very troubled in different ways rather than helped by their religious beliefs.

But that's what it has done in most cases—it has imposed a great deal of tension and pressure. Because we don't really know where we came from, what we really are, out of ignorance always come superstition and religion, as a substitute for knowledge. The Lo Bianco character has always grown up with the strange feeling of isolation, of being alien to everything around him, so naturally he likens that to faith. He believes in God, he feels some kind of unity with a higher power. He talks in one scene, which, I think, was cut from the picture, about having wanted to be a priest.

Although the God is both vicious and destructive, I don't think we feel any satisfaction in his being destroyed at the end. It comes across as a further act of repression. Lo Bianco is not only killing the god who represents energy, he's also repressing energies associated with the alien quality in himself.

In their last scene, the god creature says that what is recessive in him is dominant in Lo Bianco, the human side being dominant in Lo Bianco, whereas the alien side is dominant in the god creature, but they are in effect brothers, there's a unity between them. They're two sides of the same person—the doppelgänger. Lo Bianco destroys that side of himself, or tries to, and then takes himself out of life by putting himself in an insane asylum for the rest of his life. He has this power that he has learned how to use in the pool-room scene where he gets the pimp to kill himself, but he elects not to use it anymore. Yet he can't be part of society anymore: he can't go back to Sandy Dennis or to Debbie Raffin—he can't go back to anybody. He has to bottle himself up in a padded cell for the rest of his life—almost like what happens when Keir Dullea arrives in the other world in *2001*—he's in a little room for eternity, and no one quite understands what that's all about either.

As you say, the picture is complicated, but certainly no more complicated than *2001,* which allows you a lot of interpretations. It's just one of those pictures where you can't figure it out. You should just sit there and look at the picture.

You told me once that at some quite early point in your work, you became aware that virtually everything you wrote had the theme of the double in it.

It's also in a lot of the television scripts, even the early ones—two parallel people with usually the reverse of each other's problems, or who are a mirror image of one another.

It becomes very explicit in *It's Alive* when John Ryan talks about Frankenstein—Frankenstein being the monster . . .

Yes, a confusion of identities.

And, of course, in *God Told Me To* where Tony Lo Bianco and the god are two opposite sides. And Hoover and Dillinger. I wondered if you saw it there in *The Winged Serpent*, in which you seemed to be establishing quite complicated parallels between the monster, the policeman, and Michael Moriarty, which at one viewing I didn't understand.

Certainly there are parallels in that there are human sacrifices performed to this bird god and Michael Moriarty does take the hoodlums up there and performs a human sacrifice to the bird god, which gives him his freedom—a parallel, for sure. But there are no back-to-back, mirror-image characters, as there are in some of the others.

There almost always seems to be the question as to which is the more monstrous, the monster itself or contemporary society. That seems particularly strong in *It's Alive*.

A friend of mine said to me when he saw *It's Alive*, "The monster looked good compared to most of the actors." In the second It's Alive picture the monster's face is less frightening than Eddie Constantine and John Marley in close-up. I deliberately cast them to get the most gnarled and wrinkled faces that you could put on the screen—a festival of wrinkles.

In *It's Alive* you seem to go out of your way to attack contemporary America in terms not only of ugly faces, but of corruption, manipulation within the police—

—the pharmaceutical industry, and all that stuff. Sure, yes, there certainly is no good guy and no bad guy. The monster is no worse than anybody else. Actually, he's trying to survive in an alien society that he didn't ask to be brought into. And in the second picture, it's the effort to save the monster, rather than to kill it, which is the main thrust.

Have you been typed as a horror-film specialist? Do you feel that *It's Alive* is a horror film?

Certainly it was sold as a horror film, but I mean, if you look at the picture, it speaks for itself. If the budget is high enough, then it isn't a horror film. For example, *The Omen* isn't a horror film per se, because Gregory Peck is in it—you know what I mean? It's a quality thriller or something like that. Everybody wants to pigeonhole everything. The pictures that I make are just the ones that, I guess, get willed into creation. Why I would end up making a picture like *The Serpent* or *God Told Me To* or *J. Edgar Hoover*? Who knows? In most cases circumstances evolve, the right actor appears, the right time appears, I have the script, but mainly it's an act of willpower. No picture gets made unless you almost will it into existence.

The Private Files of J. Edgar Hoover was another movie about the monster as a product of American society?

I'd always been fascinated with the FBI and its false image, and I'd always been interested in the McCarthy period, and it manifested itself in a lot of things I wrote for television. I particularly wanted to do this project, and I'd gone to Walter Mirisch, who was a big producer at Universal and president of the Motion Picture Academy. He had produced a film I wrote years before called *Return of the Magnificent Seven*. I thought that maybe he would give me the chance to get into high-budget production. It was written on spec, but Walter was going to be the producer and he was going to get it through. But, of course, once we'd finished it, he couldn't get it by the Universal people—they didn't want to be involved in a politically sensitive subject—and that was the end of Walter Mirisch's involvement. At that time Universal was just negotiating to buy Yosemite National Park from the United States government, and Lew Wasserman was very active in Washington, and I don't think they wanted to get involved in something that could be embarrassing politically to the company. Most movie companies felt that this was not a picture that was worth the amount of trouble that they would have to go through. They weren't sure that there'd ever be any repercussions, but there was always the possibility, and so many movie companies are involved in other things—MGM is in the gambling business, and they have to deal with the FBI, Paramount or Gulf and Western was under indictment for various violations of the Securities and Exchange Commission laws—everybody was doing something that had to do with the Federal Government, and they felt they didn't want to make more trouble for themselves by taking on the FBI. People still live under the fear of what happened during the House Un-American Activities Committee days in Hollywood and the McCarthy period: they walk around bravely, but they're scared out of their minds that somebody's going to come and audit their income tax.

Then we decided to try and get Rod Steiger to play the lead. I got the script to Steiger and he was interested. He'd played everybody else in the world from Napoleon to Mussolini, he was everybody, so I figured he might as well play this and add it to his string of biographies. All boring—it was a mistake, but we needed a name, and I was told that if we deliver Rod Steiger, we would get some money. Then I was told that Rod Steiger had decided to play W. C. Fields and wasn't going to do J. Edgar Hoover. I gave the script to a producer who had just left Paramount; he then went to 20th Century Fox as an independent producer and a few weeks later announced in the papers that he was doing the life of J. Edgar Hoover, but I was nowhere mentioned. He had read my script and was basically stealing the idea. Now I got really annoyed and said, "Nobody's making J. Edgar Hoover but me—and I've got the script and am going into production with it right away." Unlike the other times, I hadn't any financing but, like the lunatic that I can be sometimes, I started going out and making commitments to people and lining up a cast. Finally I went back to my old friend Sam Arkoff, who always seems to be there when I need him. He had declined to make *God Told Me To* in the past—when I called him up about that, he told me that God told him not to make the picture—and when the picture was finished, Arkoff wanted to buy it for AIP. We ended up selling it to New World so we had turned him down, which was always a good position to be in. If they turn you down and you make the picture with somebody else, next time you come to them they think twice about turning you down, because maybe you'll go get the money from somewhere else. And Sam, like everybody else, likes to be in action. I'd given him a couple of hits, and I said to him, "Sam, you've made about five or six million dollars off of me." He said, "Yes, but I'd like to hang on to some of it." So anyway I said to him, "Look, I'm going to make that J. Edgar Hoover picture." He said, "Larry, I've told you, I don't want to make that picture." And I said, "I know you don't want to make the picture, but I've got an Academy Award star to play the lead." He said, "Who?" "I'm not going to tell you," I said, "but it's an Oscar winner, winner of the Academy Award for Best Actor—he's playing J. Edgar Hoover. I need a couple of hundred thousand dollars—do you want in or not?" He said, "OK, you've got a couple of hundred thousand dollars, but when do I get to find out who the star is?" "I'll call you next week." Only a few old-time people who own their own companies could do this and now that Sam Arkoff doesn't have American International anymore (it was acquired by Filmways and then reacquired by Orion) he doesn't exist in the same situation anymore, so there's nobody really that you can call up and do this with. The thing about Sam was that although he made what you would call an "inferior" product, he made plenty of pictures, made money on them, and had a company that always came out in the black. He ran the company and sat behind his desk with his big cigar in his hand. If there was anybody who was an embodiment of what the old-time Jack Warner or Harry Cohn or Darryl Zanuck was, it was him. He was a dinosaur—but a good dinosaur. You could ask this man for money and he could say over the telephone, "Yeah! Go make another *Black Caesar* picture—I'll guarantee to pay the bill," and you knew that when it came time to get your money, you'd get your money. So we went to Washington with Broderick Crawford, the Academy Award-winning star. We had Michael Parks and we had Dan Dailey and then we got Rip Torn, who was recommended by Michael Parks, and we got Jo Ferrer, so by the time I called Sam a week later to ask him for more money we had a pretty good cast. We'd already spent his money from the previous week, but I wouldn't tell him who the star was the second week either, but the third week he demanded it and got it. He was very unhappy when he heard it was Broderick Crawford. He said, "Is he still alive?"

What did he win an Academy Award for?

All the King's Men. A very similar part, which was what put me in mind of him for J. Edgar Hoover. He also had a very strong physical resemblance to

J. Edgar Hoover, and I wouldn't have to spend two and a half to three hours every day putting a false face on somebody, which causes a lot of retakes because if you put a false face on somebody and then the light hits him just the wrong way, it looks like a false face and you've got to do the whole day's shooting over again. Sam had figured it out that the Academy Award-winning star was Rod Steiger, and I said to him, "Sam, Rod Steiger hasn't had a hit picture in twenty years—I don't think he's had a success since *In the Heat of the Night*. So what's the difference? Broderick Crawford will not bring anybody into the theater and neither will Rod Steiger, but Broderick Crawford will be better in the part. Rod Steiger has played some of these biography parts—he's boring. Broderick Crawford is fresh in this part and he looks like J. Edgar Hoover." I finally didn't convince him, but he was already in for so much money that he couldn't leave me in the lurch. It's the old trick of getting somebody so far into the swamp that they have to get you out. I said, "If you don't want to put any more money in, then I'm going to have to close down production and that's it. So take over the picture yourself and finish it or let me finish it." He had to go forward and give me some more money. However, we ended up spending more than we got from Sam, so when the picture was all finished we had lost a few hundred thousand dollars. Then Sam didn't think it was the right picture for American International to distribute. He said he would give me a couple of months to make a deal elsewhere. Warner Brothers liked it and previewed it in Westwood. MGM liked it a lot, but we started facing the same problem again: they didn't think they could do more than three or four million dollars' rental on the picture, which might have made them a couple of million dollars profit, but they just felt that to make a couple of million dollars they'd be exposing themselves to a lot of controversy and possible retaliation by the FBI, which was very active, and still is, in policing piracy. Every can of film that goes out now to the theaters has a sticker that says, "This film is protected by the FBI." Now if one of your prints disappears, you call the FBI and the FBI tries to find out what became of it. If your print is pirated, or videotaped, the FBI breaks up that ring and is supposed to preserve your copyright. Now when you've got all these companies relying on the FBI, they are not going to be too anxious to get on the wrong side of the Bureau by releasing a marginal picture which is not going to make them any money anyway and will stir up a lot of bad feeling. NBC and CBS were interested in a purchase for television, and we got into negotiations with both networks. A television sale would have paid off the movie and made us a substantial profit of probably over a million dollars. Unfortunately, after the creative people of the network agreed to buy the picture, the censors more or less said they felt that the picture was too controversial—they felt that we couldn't back up all the allegations and that it crossed over into the area of news and special affairs, and the networks are divided up into their entertainment division and the news and special-affairs divisions and they were afraid that this picture crossed the line. There was a lawsuit pending at that time regarding one of their big docudramas. So we had to go back to Sam, and he had to distribute the picture, even though he didn't want to, because he had so much money in it already. He wasn't hurt on it, though, because American International sold the picture to a tax shelter, which paid sufficient money for the picture that Sam got his money and I got most of my money back, but it is the only picture I've lost money on.

How much did it cost to make the film?

A couple of million dollars, and we lost about $115,000. But at any rate we made the picture that we wanted to make, we had our shot. The picture's still there and has played in all these festivals and on the BBC and it was successful in England—very good reviews foreign and generally negative reviews in America, but always very favorable reviews in foreign. It's always being played someplace, and it's put on HBO and the other cable systems, and I still think that someday this picture will get a theatrical play. I would have liked it if MGM or Warner Brothers had released it, particularly Warner Brothers, which made all those old FBI movies back in the 1940s. I would have liked the old Warner Brothers logo at the beginning of the picture.

Then I did the play *Trick*, which I had written years before. It was performed in England with Honor Blackman and then on the road, on tour, with Carroll Baker. I was in New York. I had taken some of my ill-gotten gains from *It's Alive* and bought a brownstone in Manhattan, one of the things I had always wanted, a New York townhouse. New York being so theater oriented, I decided I wanted to do this play. It didn't run very long, but I had a great time, directing people like Tammy Grimes. I even performed in it one night when one of the actors was ill—it was a three-character play—so I got to make my Broadway acting debut as well as my Broadway directing debut. I had never directed a stage play before, and I had these experienced actors. Naturally I didn't want any of these people to know that I had never directed a stage play before, so I got all these books on directing stage plays, and then I decided, to hell with it, forget it. I'll go in there and just block it, the way I do movies and see how it works out. It was a lot easier than directing movies. You get to do it from beginning to end: you do act one, then you take a break and you do act two, and you rehearse that way for four or five weeks, so you get to see the play on its feet in continuity. You have loads of time and you don't have to worry about where the cameras are and what's going to cut and what isn't. The only tough part about directing a play is the first lighting rehearsal, which takes maybe eight hours to do a two-hour play. Everything is chaos because all the technicians are there resetting lights, and this is going wrong, and that cue is going wrong, and it's exhausting. Having gone through this hell for the whole day, I suddenly remembered what it reminded me of. It reminded me of every day of making a movie, because every day making a movie is just like the lighting rehearsal of a play. It's a nightmare—thirty days of having the lighting rehearsal on the stage play is the equivalent of making a movie. You've never done the scene before, the lights are being hung for the first time, the camera's here for the first time, everything is being done and tried out for the first time and it's stop and go, and stop and go, and let's do it over again, and this didn't work and then you get the great performance you want and the cameraman says, "No, we have to do it over." We lost focus, or the light wasn't right, or she stepped into somebody else's light and she burns up, and you have to go off and redo the scene, and you're always battling for control.

Have you worked consistently with the same cameramen or set designers?

Yes, I worked with a couple of cameramen over and over again and started more or less with a nucleus of a crew. They always complain about the long hours, but they're always calling up asking when the next picture is going to start. My biggest problem is I don't like to stop for lunch because I know how hard it is to get started again. If you're really cooking and the scene is really playing, you hate to stop, because it's not just the hour for lunch, it's a couple of hours to get everybody back into the rhythm. If the crew goes out and has a few drinks at lunchtime, then it takes you a couple of hours before the booze wears off, before everybody's back to optimum performance again. You get a lot of good work done when you reach the period just prior to total exhaustion, when people's inhibitions have broken down and they're just too tired to do anything but just perform, when their subconscious starts to take over. You've got to be able to outlast them, and I can stand up longer than anybody. It's like they say—the person who can stand up longest gets to be the director. The image of a director is always that canvas chair with your name on the back, but in all the years I have made movies I have never sat down. So I don't need a canvas chair with my name on the back. My wife used to come around when we were doing scenes in New York in the rain and put vitamin C pills in my mouth while I was on the set. Everybody thought she was giving me uppers all the time to keep me on my feet.

After the play, we did *Full Moon High*. Everybody had always said, "You're such a humorous fellow, why don't you do a comedy?" So I wrote what was supposed to be a comedy version of *I Was a Teenage Werewolf*. We went back to American International, who owned the rights to *I Was a Teenage Werewolf* and got them to finance the picture. After what I had done to them on *J. Edgar Hoover*, I have to say that it was very nice of them to do any more pictures with me. We got Adam Arkin, and his father Alan Arkin said he wanted to be in it too, so long as we didn't give him any billing in the ads—we would give him an automobile and he would do the part. Adam was alright. Every time he'd get any difficulty, he'd call his father up on the telephone in New York and his father would tell him to shut up and go back to work. It turned out that audiences were not that keen on a resurgence of werewolf pictures. In the meantime, we came out briefly with the picture. The studio that was releasing it had had a success with *Love at First Bite,* which was a comedy vampire picture, and I suggested that they test it in places where they had done well with that. Of course, they went to Texas and tested it there, only to tell me afterwards that that was one of the markets where *Love at First Bite* didn't do well. With the perfect logic that you always find in the movie industry, they did just the opposite of what they should have done. They also opened the picture the same week as the Houston State Fair, which was the biggest event of the year in Houston, and naturally not a very good week for anybody to go to the movies. How come I always get the information that doesn't seem to be available to the studios? When you get into a small operation, where everybody has certain responsibilities and really cares, then something gets accomplished. You wonder why all these people at the studios are getting salaries every week. It's very much like the United States government—about seven times too many people and, because there are so many people, one arm never knows what the other's doing and nobody tells anybody anything. Everybody just wants to get to work, get to lunch, and get home as fast as possible, and as long as they keep their job, they don't really care what happens to the pictures. It's really not dissimilar to the problems of production where a $2 million picture costs $10 million to make simply because there are so many people around being paid money for making no contribution whatsoever. Similarly, distribution of a picture should cost about one-fifth of what it costs: you get better distribution spending less money and having less people involved. What is there to distributing the picture? If the picture is any good, you open it in one or two cities; if it does business, advertise the business in the newspaper and all the other theaters in America are going to call you up on the phone and ask for the picture. That's all that's really involved, because there's no such thing as making money on a marginal picture. Allegedly, the distributor's job is to collect the money from the theaters because the theater owners are supposedly bigger crooks than the distributors.

Is there still a market for low-budget pictures?

Well, look at what's happening today. MGM made pictures like *Pennies from Heaven* for $15 to 20 million and all those films did no business at all. *Diner*, which cost only a couple of million dollars, made a fortune—the biggest-grossing picture they've had, and it cost so little money that the MGM executives had planned to shelve it. By sheer accident, it got played in a couple of markets and now it's their biggest hit. *Animal House* and *American Graffiti* were low-budget pictures, *Rocky* at $2 million was considered a low-budget picture. Every year you get several low-budget pictures that go right through the roof. In fact, just as many low-budget pictures are successful at the box office as high-budget pictures, so it would be more sense to make more low-budget pictures—and just forget about the high-budget pictures—your chances are just as good.

What happened with *I, the Jury*?

I had acquired the rights to the book *I, the Jury* from the people who had made the original picture in 3D in 1952. I was looking around for something that I could option at a reasonable price. Everything that was new would have cost $25,000 to $100,000 but I could maybe go back and find something with a well-known character which could be optioned for $5,000. I remembered that everybody read Mike Hammer back when I was in high school and college, but Hammer was now an almost forgotten character who had not been used in anything for twenty years. *I, the Jury* was the most popular detective novel ever written, having sold over seven million copies. It was a book that I had read in my adolescence and was perhaps what you would call a "dirty book" during the early '50s. This was a time when pornography was not readily available, and *I, the Jury* was about as close to pornography as a person could get—for twenty-five cents on the newsstands. When I realized what an enormous sale the book had had and what a role it had played in the cultural development of millions of young men, I reread it in the idea of freely adapting it into the modern setting. I wanted to make a James Bond type of character out of it—a lot of sex, a lot of action. Bosley Crowther's original review of *Dr. No* in the *New York Times* said this character deserves to give a deep bow of appreciation to Mickey Spillane's Mike Hammer. That's what gave me the idea. I said, "Hey, this could have been made into another James Bond series if it had been made properly, with some sense of humor and some production values."

Once I'd got the rights, I wrote a screenplay and then started submitting it around. There are various kinds of producers in Hollywood. Some are active line producers who know something about making pictures, others used to be agents and know about making deals; then there are producers like Bob Solo, a former studio executive whose real value was his contacts, since studio executives tend to give jobs to former studio executives (it makes them feel secure—some day they will be former studio executives too and maybe someone will give them a job). That's the way it works. Rather than being a creative producer, Solo can help you make a deal because he has contacts with friends who formerly worked with him at Warner Brothers, for example. The head of publicity and the head of foreign sales at American Cinema were all former Warner Brothers employees who had worked with Solo, and that was really the reason why the picture ended up getting made at American Cinema, a relatively new company that had made a lot of money on Chuck Norris karate pictures and then said that it was going to go into big-budget picture making. It was financed by a northern Californian real-estate conglomerate, but no one really understood where the money was coming from. We had a choice of making this deal with Avco Embassy or with American Cinema. If I'd gone for Avco Embassy, I would have been better off because the people over there were professionals who understood picture making, while the people in American Cinema were new to motion picture making. As it turned out, they didn't have enough money to make all the pictures that they had contracted for and soon found themselves in bankruptcy. By the time American Cinema had made *I, the Jury*, they were already going into receivership; the Bankers Trust Company took over the company and took all the negatives and there were a lot of legal problems.

Because of the imminent directors' strike and a writers' strike, the film had been rushed into production without the normal preparation period—two and a half weeks rather than the eight to ten weeks normal for a production of this kind. Therefore, we were slightly over budget, but certainly not enough to warrant my dismissal. American Cinema wanted to control the film: they did not want a filmmaker, they wanted a director who would follow their instructions. The fact that it was my own screenplay and I had cast all the major parts and picked the location gave me too much power. American Cinema preferred to hire a television director who would come in and shoot the picture as they wanted it. In television, a director usually comes in for an individual episode and then leaves, the creative input on the series coming from the producers who stay with the show week after week. A television director is generally a traffic cop, moving the actors around but not dealing in overall concepts. I cannot comment on the work done by the new director since I have not seen the film. I tend to think that the production went ahead in terms of straight narrative and became a fast-paced private-eye movie. When the new director took over, they went back to the smaller screen and a harsher, more grainy, more realistic look, and I think they played the violence for real, so I think what you got is quite a brutal movie. I can only hope that it's a good film and a successful one since I own the rights to two other Mike Hammer books—*Kiss Me Deadly* and *My Gun is Quick*.

Incidentally, had I gotten David Carradine to play Mike Hammer in *I, the Jury*, then I never would have gotten fired off the picture, because if you and the actor are united, there's nothing that the studio can do about replacing you because David Carradine would have left, too. The difficult part about *I, the Jury* was that I didn't have control. I was in there as an employee doing a job, and what Robert Solo wanted to do was maintain his position, get his salary, so even though I had brought him into the project, I really had nobody to rely upon. If you are in a situation where you have control and the actors are with you, you can have some bargaining position with the studio. In fact, I never even knew what the studio executives in California were complaining about, because they never talked directly to me. They would talk to Solo, but Solo wouldn't communicate it to me. You have to have direct lines of communication with all the people, below you and above you, in order to do any kind of a job like this. It's so much like a military operation—making movies is the closest thing to fighting a war. You've got your supply problems, you've got to move a certain number of feet ahead every day, you've got to deal with the people back in Washington who are giving you your orders. You have to have open lines of communication. Once they become clogged up or you cut off communication, you're in a terrible position. Hopefully, the next time we make a picture, a big-budget picture, and we have some kind of a studio involved, I will be more careful. I made some dreadful errors in terms of self-protection—what major directors learn from years of working in the studio system is that they must protect themselves at all times. But I had made nine pictures for myself, which I was controlling all the time—I felt that nothing could hurt me. Most directors won't allow anybody to come to the dailies. When people come to the dailies they don't know how they're going to be cut together—they don't know what the scene's going to look like. If you let your actors come to the dailies, which I did on this film because Solo told the actors they could come, they're always dissatisfied with their performance, or they want to pick which take they like best. Always insecure. Experienced studio directors are wary of the system and understand that you constantly have to be playing politics and trying to protect yourself. I have nothing to worry about in my own films except working with the actors and making a picture. Nobody gets to see the footage until the picture's edited and finished, then I show them my first cut of the picture, but while I'm shooting it nobody sees dailies. If I want to change the schedule around, I do it; if I want to fire somebody, I do it; if I want to hire somebody, I do it. The actors at least feel that somebody is in total control. I'm the only person they have to deal with. If they have a problem, they always come to me with their problem. On *I, the Jury* they had a producer, an associate producer, a production executive, and they had people from Los Angeles who were constantly coming back and forth. All this only served to divide the authority and to confuse everybody and to create a feeling of insecurity. I had no idea all this was going on. I was in my insular world of working on the creative aspects of the picture and little did I think that anybody was going to be telling anybody anything without going through me. It was a very unpleasant experience. It was very disheartening. However, if it wasn't for that, I wouldn't have gone out and made *The Winged Serpent*.

We were surprised just how quickly you set that up. It seemed to be announced almost immediately after you left *I, the Jury*.

I was inactive, and the directors' strike and the Writers Guild strike would have meant no work for maybe five or six months. I thought, am I going to sit around here and feel sorry for myself? I'd been fired off of a picture—who cares who was right and who was wrong, the fact is that they're going to work every day and I'm sitting around doing nothing. I've got some scripts—maybe I should try and put another picture together. But nothing would have happened if I hadn't bumped into Michael Moriarty. I was eating at a little cafe opposite Lincoln Center and he happened to be at the next table with his wife, and I was talking to a young lady at my table, telling her all about Michael Moriarty and what a wonderful actor he was and what awards he'd won. Michael and his wife heard everything I was saying, and then when

I got up to leave I managed to make eye contact with them and we chatted for a few minutes. Later, I thought maybe he'd be interested in *The Winged Serpent* script, so I called him up and asked him if he'd read it, and sure enough, he liked it. He said, "I'd love this part. My agents won't want me to do it but I'd love to do it." So, finally, even though the William Morris Agency advised him not to do it, he decided to go ahead. And once he agreed to do it, it was relatively easy to get Candy Clark, because she'd always wanted to work with him, and once we were really sure we were doing the picture, got in touch with David Carradine who I'd wanted originally to play Mike Hammer in *I the Jury*.

Were you back to complete control on *The Winged Serpent*?

Yes, absolutely. Once we put *The Winged Serpent* together, I had to prove to myself that I could still make pictures. If I had waited six months until the time the directors' and writers' strikes were settled, I think I would have been a nervous wreck. You always figure that everybody's going to think the worst and you'll never get another job. You read biographies of stars and, as big as they are, they're always terrified that they'll never work again. Which is why *The Winged Serpent* was made—because I had to make a picture. I was in

The Aztec god Quetzalcoatl terrorizes New York City in *Q: The Winged Serpent* (1982).

New York, I had the script, I had an actor, I'd told the location people you've got to get me the Chrysler Building. They said, well, you can't—they don't want any movies shot up there. I said we had to have it. We went back three or four times and finally, the fourth time, they agreed to rent it to us for about $8,000 a day. I guess if we hadn't got the Chrysler Building I wouldn't have done it, because we needed that location. Everything came together.

You mention that *The Winged Serpent* was shot in thirty days. Is this an average shooting schedule for you?

It's Alive was shot in about twenty days; the sequel in about twenty-four days. The question is not how many days we shoot, but how many hours per day. Sometimes we shoot sixteen hours, sometimes eighteen hours a day. We usually shoot a six-day week on location. Then there is second-unit photography, preproduction photography, and special effects which are not figured into the basic shooting schedule, which covers only acting sequences of the principal players. In the case of *The Winged Serpent,* the model animation and special effects took almost six months.

Where did the idea come from? Have you any sense now of how it was generated?

First of all, I had an idea about a giant bird inhabiting the dome of a skyscraper and coming out and picking people up and carrying them off. Just a visual idea, a turn-on for kids. There was an attempt to remake *King Kong* by Dino De Laurentiis which didn't quite come off. But other than that, there hadn't really been any quality monster movies made in twenty or twenty-five years. There was *Them!,* with the giant ants, which was a very good picture, and there were a lot of terrible pictures about giant tarantulas and giant spiders and giant bugs and giant lizards, usually taking some animal like a lizard and photographing it and then projecting it up against some real actors and making it look terrible. But there always seemed to have been some kind of audience for those pictures. Always the characters would be a bunch of scientists, a girl scientist who's in love with another guy who's a scientist—totally unrealistic relationships. I said, let's make one of these things but really get it in tune with real people, real street people, real relationships. The difficult thing would be to bridge that reality with the monster so that you're not making two different pictures but the two do mesh, and I think it worked in the picture—and also the humor worked. I think this is the funniest picture I've made, including the comedy, *Full Moon High*, without ruining it by making fun of the genre.

There is the question that has to be asked about all your films. Is Quetzalcoatl a god or is it a monster?

Like the police commissioner in the film says, "I've got to kill this thing and I'd rather think of killing a monster than killing a god, so tear up that report." It's a lot easier to accept killing a monster than it is killing some kind of a god that has been invoked by supernatural means, but nevertheless that's what Quetzalcoatl is, as we see at the end with the other egg waiting to hatch. I think that's the answer to your question.

Quetzalcoatl is absolutely identified with maleness. Yours is a very phallic monster with that enormous snaky neck, and yet it lays an egg.

A snake is a phallic symbol, but there wouldn't be any snakes if they were all male. Certainly it was like a flying penis, no question about it. Various sexual symbols are in there—the egg, opening people up—it's all in there. The thing is, of course, that once we had a bird up there, I had to figure out what it was and how it got there. I thought having it as some super being made it more colorful and exciting, and also the human-sacrifice idea—Moriarty takes these guys up and sacrifices them to the bird, just similar to the way that the high priest is making human sacrifices to the god. Also, the city was interesting to me because New York City, seen from the air by some kind of a creature, could look like a religious city of temples—all these great towers sticking up. The Chrysler Building looks like it could be a religious temple of some kind. It's covered with bird gargoyles. The aluminum, or whatever it's made of up there, is all feather shaped, and the pinnacle looks almost like a beak. The Chrysler Building would be a terrific temple to a bird god, even that pyramid that he falls and dies on at the end exists on Wall Street, and that was picked for a specific reason—that's the Bankers Trust Building and that's the bank that foreclosed *I, the Jury* and put American Cinema out of business and took the negatives and everything else away and put a few of them in jail. So I thought I would take a little bow at the Bankers Trust by putting them in the place that the great beast finally falls on and dies, but it also looks like a Mexican or Egyptian pyramid and if the bird saw that, it was like a homing thing.

Bernard Herrmann was both a collaborator and a personal friend. How did you come to work with him?

I was in great awe of Bernard Herrmann. I had admired the work he did for Hitchcock. When I needed a composer for *It's Alive,* I didn't think there was any real chance of getting Bernard Herrmann. Someone at Warner Brothers told me that he was going to do the score for *The Exorcist*. Since we had made the film through Warner Brothers, we were aware of what was going on within that company. When Bernard Herrmann left *The Exorcist* because of personal differences with the director, I saw an opportunity to offer him a film immediately. I spoke to him, and I sent him a black-and-white work print to view. He called me from London to say how much he liked the picture and that he would do it. The deal was made, and Bernard Herrmann wrote the music without any further meetings with me. I told him by phone to write whatever he felt was correct. He then invited me to London for the scoring session, and I came immediately after Christmas for the final day of the scoring session. The music was recorded at Cripplegate Church in the city of London, which Mr. Herrmann had chosen because of its resonance and its huge organ. An entire mobile recording studio had to be set up for the session and, because of the power shortage in England, no heat was available, so the musicians all played with their overcoats on and Bernard Herrmann conducted with a warm windbreaker to protect him. We then ran the mixed music tracks against the picture and realized how wonderfully everything matched up. At the time I hired him I had no main title design. We agreed that Benny would write the music and I would make up a title design, independently of one another, and we would trust to luck that the two would match. I made a title treatment featuring flashlights moving through the darkness and multiplying in number, going from half a dozen to several hundred. When we tacked the film onto the beginning of the reel and ran it with the music, the synchronization was amazing. So we were immediately very happy with one another and became good friends. My wife and I lived for eight months in London, during which time we saw Benny and his wife, Norma, several times a week. After my return to Los Angeles, we maintained our friendship. When Benny came to New York for the mix of the music for *Obsession*, we met him there and when he arrived in Los Angeles to do *Taxi Driver* we spent much time with him. Bernard Herrmann was about to begin the score for *God Told Me To*. Late in the day that he conducted the final session for *Taxi Driver*, my wife picked him up and brought him and Norma to Goldwyn Studios where I ran him the work print of *God Told Me To*. Benny was delighted with the picture and already was working on ideas for the score. He took us out to dinner at an Italian restaurant, all evening telling me about his ideas for the music for my film. We brought him back to the Universal Sheraton Hotel about twelve o'clock and agreed to speak the following day. The next morning I received a call from Martin Scorsese's fiancée, who informed us that Bernard Herrmann had passed away during the night. My wife and I rushed out to the Universal Hotel to be with Norma. We then brought her back to our house where she stayed during the funeral arrangements. After the service, Norma and friends came to our house to pay respects. Among them were Brian De Palma, Martin Scorsese, and Robert De Niro. When the rabbi requested ten men to say the prayer for the dead, there were not ten Jewish men available, so the Italian contingent, Scorsese, De Palma, and De Niro, joined the circle and said the prayer. I am sure that Benny would have been touched and amused at this little private service.

Bernard Herrmann was known as a difficult man with a vitriolic tongue, a man who spoke directly from the heart and often offended the pompous and the pretentious. When meeting someone, Benny would often attack almost immediately in order to gauge that person's character, to see if they could take it or not. Once you got past that initial barrage, you could be accepted by him. You could become a friend. But very few got past that initial verbal assault and so very few got to know him as the gentle and sensitive guy that he was. I am convinced that Bernard Herrmann was a genius in writing motion picture music. He was certainly a great influence in my life, and I hope that my films that bear his music are worthy of him.

(1986)

Nosferatu

Nosferatu (1922) was the first film version of *Dracula*; more than seventy years later, it remains easily the most intelligent adaptation of Bram Stoker's novel (its nearest, not very close, rival being John Badham's 1978 version with Frank Langella).

Given the way in which Stoker's vampire aristocrat has haunted popular culture since the appearance of the novel in 1890, the figure's social/ideological significance can scarcely be exaggerated. Conceived at the height of Victorian sexual repression, the Count Dracula of the novel embodies, to varying degrees of explicitness, all the sexual dreads that our culture has still not exorcised or come to terms with: nonprocreative sexuality, promiscuity, bisexuality, the so-called perversions, incest, even (indirectly, through the preferences of the vampirized Lucy) the sexuality of children. Much of our sexual social history can be traced through the transformations the count has undergone from Stoker's novel to Badham's movie. With his origins in sexual repression, he transplants very logically and easily into the climate and ethos of German Expressionism.

Between Stoker's novel and Murnau's film came Freud, to whose theories of repression and the unconscious the Expressionist movement, like the Surrealist movement later, was heavily indebted. The essential difference between the two movements lies in their contrasting inflections of Freudian theory: the Surrealists were committed to liberation and the overthrow of repressive bourgeois norms whatever the costs, whereas the Expressionists consistently conceived of the repressed forces as evil, their release cataclysmic. The extraordinary power, and continuing fascination, of Murnau's film are rooted in this vision.

The distinction of *Nosferatu* can be partly suggested by examining the changes Murnau and his scriptwriter Henrik Galeen made from novel to film. What novel and film have in common (and no other film version to the same degree except the Badham) is the perception that it is the woman who is the center of the conflict, that the work is really about her. The uses made of this insight are, however, quite different. In Stoker's novel the battle is fought for the woman; in Murnau's film she becomes the vampire's active antagonist and destroyer. In Stoker the battle is fought between Van Helsing and Dracula (conceived, in the terms of Victorian sexual morality, as "good" and "evil"—in Freudian terms they represent superego and id); Murnau reduces Van Helsing to an ineffectual old fuddy-duddy who lectures on venus flytraps but contributes nothing whatever to the vampire's overthrow. In the novel, the woman (Mina) must be saved from contagion and corruption: the Victorian dread of a released female sexuality is basic to the conception; in the film, the woman (now called Nina) realizes that only she can save civilization from the vampire's contagion, by offering herself to him. Murnau's Nina is a character of quite extraordinary ambivalence: emaciated, as if drained of blood, she suggests both vampire and Christian martyr; the strange abandon with which she gives herself to Dracula (first throwing open a window, then prostrating herself on the bed) suggests the close relationship between religious ecstasy and sensual fulfillment. The ambiguity is set up much earlier in the film, in the protracted and elaborate cross-cutting between Nina (ostensibly awaiting Jonathan's return) and the journeys of Jonathan and Dracula (a sequence that makes nonsense of Bazin's claim that "in neither *Nosferatu* nor *Sunrise* does editing play a decisive part").[77] Jonathan, who traveled by land, is returning by land; the vampire (having taken over a ship) is coming by sea. Nina sits by the shore, gazing out to sea, awaiting her "husband." Her exclamation, as she awakens from sleepwalking ("He is coming! I must go to meet him!") follows a shot, not of Jonathan, but of Dracula's ship.

Jonathan and Dracula also undergo significant alteration from their originals. Stoker's Jonathan is a conventional "noble hero" (although he doesn't actually achieve much of note). Murnau transforms him into the vampire's double, through an intricate series of "mirror" images involving arch structures: at their first meeting, for example, Jonathan enters the castle under one arch, and this is immediately "answered" by Dracula emerging out of darkness under another. Murnau, following Freud, dramatizes the vampire quite explicitly in terms of repression: he is the repressed underside of Jonathan, of civilization. As he falls under Dracula's influence, Jonathan is reduced to total impotence: even when he discovers the vampire asleep in his coffin, during the day, he can do nothing but cower back; when Dracula visits his bedchamber at night, to suck his blood, he can do nothing but prostrate himself. At the film's climax, when Nina reveals to him the vampire's presence at the window of the house directly opposite, across the water (another mirror image), he once again collapses, helpless.

In the novel, Dracula himself is at first quite old, becoming progressively rejuvenated in England by fresh blood; but he is never as grotesque as Max Schreck in Murnau's version and never as romantically attractive as Frank Langella in Badham's—the two films inflect him, significantly, in precisely opposite directions. Murnau's most striking development of the original material is his elaboration of the vampire. In the novel, Dracula disappears quite early from the surface of the narrative (which is told entirely through letters, diaries, etc.), appearing only in brief glimpses; in the film he becomes the dominant figure, a redevelopment especially clear in the long central section of the voyage (for which the novel has no equivalent). Murnau greatly extends Dracula's association with animals, and with a dark, nocturnal underside of nature: he has pointed ears, is visually connected with a jackal, emerges from his castle as out of the blackness of an animal's lair. Above all, the film associates him with rats and plague: wherever he goes, rats swarm, and the precise nature of the spreading pestilence is kept carefully ambiguous.

The rethinking of Dracula in Badham's film offers a fascinating comparison, an attempt at a "progressive" reinterpretation with a far more positive view of the repressed forces the vampire represents: the heroine becomes a "liberated" woman who freely chooses Dracula as her lover, and it is the father figure, Van Helsing, who is finally impaled on a stake. In fact, what Badham's film proves is the intractability of the material for such a purpose: Dracula becomes a kind of sexual superman, the film develops disturbing fascist overtones, and many of the complex connotations of the vampire are eliminated. While Murnau's film—heavily determined by its Expressionist background—can depict repressed sexuality and its release only in the most negative terms, it manages to endow it with far greater force and potency, dramatizing the basic Freudian quandary—the necessity for repression, yet the appalling cost of repression—with a much more suggestive complexity.

(2000)

The Silence of the Lambs

The Silence of the Lambs (1991) is the most authentically terrifying movie since *Psycho* (1960), and it is appropriate that Hannibal Lecter (as incarnated in the superb performance of Anthony Hopkins) should have established a position within our culture's popular mythology comparable to that of Anthony Perkins's Norman Bates three decades earlier. By "authentically" I mean that the terror the film induces is not merely a matter of contrived shock moments (though, as in *Psycho*, those are not lacking). The film brings us into intimate and disturbing contact with the darkest potentialities of the human psyche and, by locating the existence of the serial killer within a context of "normality," connects it to those manifestations of what one might call the "normal psychosis" of the human race that we read about daily in our newspapers: the practice of "ethnic cleansing," the protracted torture and eventual murder of a teenager by "peacemakers" in Somalia, the horrors of child abuse (sexual, physical, psychological) that are the product of our concept of "family" and the guarantee of their own continuance into future generations.

The humanity of Hannibal Lecter is clearly a central issue: if we see Lecter as only a monster, quite distinct from ourselves, then the film fails, becomes "just another horror movie"; as Jodie Foster says of Lecter in the laser-disc commentary, "He just wants to be accepted as a human being." Therefore, the filmmakers' problem lies in persuading us to do just that without ever becoming complicit in his obsessions (killing and eating other human beings): a difficult and dangerous tightrope to walk. It is their degree of success that distinguishes the film from *The Texas Chainsaw Massacre* (1974), in which the fascination exerted by the monstrous cannibal family is not countered by any adequate positive force, the undercharacterized victims mere objects for torment, the film (for all its undeniable power) degenerating into an exercise in sadism.

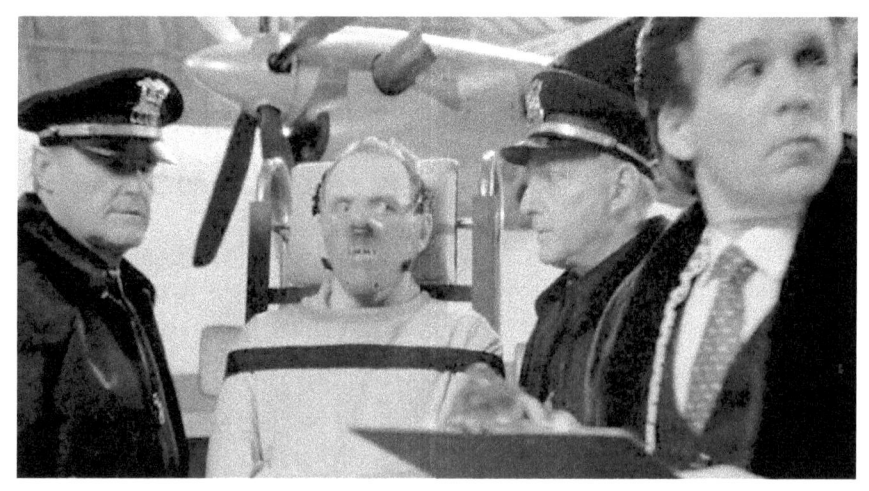

In *The Silence of the Lambs* (1991) Hannibal Lecter (Anthony Hopkins) is both monster and human being.

The success is not complete: it seems to me that Jonathan Demme made two unfortunate errors of judgment. The first is the excision of a crucial sequence that was shot and is included in the supplement to the Criterion laser disc. This sequence includes Lecter's "psychological profile" of the serial killer, accompanied by evocative tracking shots around Jame Gumb's living quarters, in which Lecter explains to Clarice Starling that the serial killer was a severely abused child (a theory for which there is a great deal of factual support) and that Gumb grew up with no sense of identity whatever, so that his attempts to construct one are unreal fabrications. The scene would have partly answered the widespread complaint that Gumb is presented as gay, reinforcing a malicious popular stereotype; it would also have linked the phenomenon of the serial killer to familial practices we now know to be all too common. I find the decision to suppress it inexplicable.

The second error (for which the screenwriter Ted Tally must share responsibility) is the film's famous last line, Lecter's "I'm having an old friend for dinner." Ironically, Tally complains at length (in the commentary on the laser disc's alternative audio track) about the appropriation of Lecter for "camp" purposes, that so many young people find him smart and seductive and even collect Lecter memorabilia: that last line precisely invites such a response, especially in view of the fact that Lecter's imminent victim, Dr. Chilton (Anthony Heald) is presented throughout as irredeemably despicable, enabling the audience to view his fate with equanimity and even satisfaction. The punch line is slick and funny: one can readily understand the temptation, but it is one that should have been resisted.

The film's distinction lies ultimately in its powerful and convincing embodiment of the force for life, in the character of Clarice Starling, Jodie Foster's performance matching that of Hopkins in its strength and vividness. There is another documented fact about serial killers too obvious for the film to have to state explicitly (it is enacted clearly enough): virtually all serial killers are male. Like the issue of child abuse, this reinforces the need to see the phenomenon not in terms of individual and inexplicable "monsters" but as intimately involved in the so-called normal actualities of the culture: the issue of gender as social construction, of the cultural production of "masculinity" in terms of aggression and domination. The achievement of Demme and Foster is to create Starling both as a clearly defined and convincing character and as the embodiment of an ideal: the human being in whom the finest qualities traditionally associated with "masculinity" and "femininity" coexist in perfect balance. The film's title derives from Starling's definitive childhood memory: the young girl's unsuccessful attempt to save one lamb from those waiting to be slaughtered, whose frantic bleating distressed her. The "silence" of the lambs is brought about only by her rescue of Gumb's latest female victim, a feat of heroism requiring a fusion of "masculine" activeness, energy, reasoning, and determination with the capacity for identification with the "feminine" vulnerability, sensitivity, empathy with the oppressed. If we recognize Lecter and Gumb as "human beings" produced by the worst excesses of patriarchal culture, we simultaneously recognize Clarice as the fully human being of a possible future.

(2000)

BRIAN DE PALMA

Robin Wood, updated by Joseph Milicia

THE CONVENTIONAL DISMISSAL OF Brian De Palma—that he is a mere "Hitchcock imitator"—though certainly unjust, provides a useful starting point, the relation being far more complex than such a description suggests. It seems more appropriate to talk of symbiosis than of imitation: if De Palma borrows Hitchcock's plot structures, the impulse is rooted in an authentic identification with the Hitchcock thematic that results in (at De Palma's admittedly infrequent best) valid variations that have their own indisputable originality. *Sisters* (1972) and *Dressed to Kill* (1980) are modeled on *Psycho* (1960); *Obsession* (1976) and *Body Double* (1984) on *Vertigo* (1958); *Body Double* also borrows from *Rear Window* (1954), as does *Blow Out* (1981). The debt is of course enormous, but—at least in the cases of *Sisters*, *Obsession*, and *Blow Out*, De Palma's three most satisfying films to date—the power and coherence of the films testifies to the genuineness of the creativity.

Central to the work of both directors are the tensions and contradictions arising out of the way in which gender has been traditionally constructed in a male-dominated culture. According to Freud, the human infant, while biologically male or female, is not innately "masculine" or "feminine": in order to construct the socially correct man and woman of patriarchy, the little girl's masculinity and the little boy's femininity must be repressed. This repression tends to be particularly rigorous and particularly damaging in the male, where it is compounded by the pervasive association of "femininity" with castration (on both the literal and symbolic levels). The significance of De Palma's best work (and, more powerfully and consistently, that of Hitchcock before him) lies in its eloquent evidence of what happens when the repression is partially unsuccessful. The misogyny of which both directors have been accused, expressing itself in the films' often extreme outbursts of violence against women (both physical and psychological), must be read as the result of their equally extreme identification with the "feminine" and the inevitable dread that such an identification brings with it.

Sisters is concerned single-mindedly with castration: the symbolic castration of the woman within patriarchy, the answering literal castration that is the form of her revenge. The basic concept of female Siamese twins, one active and aggressive, one passive and submissive, is a brilliant inspiration, the action of the entire film arising out of the attempts by men to destroy the active aspect in order to construct the "feminine" woman who will accept her subordination. The aggressive sister Dominique (dead, but still alive as Danielle's unconscious) is paralleled by Grace Collier (Jennifer Salt), the assertive young reporter who usurps the accoutrements of "masculinity" and eventually assumes Dominique's place in the extraordinary climactic hallucination sequence in which the woman's castration is horrifyingly reasserted. *Sisters*, although weakened by De Palma's inability to take Grace seriously enough or give the character the substance the allegory demands, remains his closest to a completely satisfying film: the monstrousness of woman's oppression under patriarchy and its appalling consequences for both sexes have never been rendered more vividly.

Blow Out rivals it in coherence and surpasses it in sensitivity: one would describe it as De Palma's masterpiece were it not for one unpardonable and unfortunately extended lapse—the entirely gratuitous sequence depicting the murder of the prostitute in the railway station, which one can account for only in terms of a fear that the film was not "spicy" enough for the box office (it failed anyway). It can stand as a fitting counterpart to *Sisters*, a rigorous dissection of the egoism fostered in the male by the culture's obsession with "masculinity." It is clear that Travolta's obsession with establishing the reality of his perceptions has little to do with an impersonal concern for truth and everything to do with his need to establish and assert the symbolic phallus at whatever cost—the cost involving, crucially, the manipulation and exploitation of a woman, eventually precipitating her death.

Since *Body Double*—a tawdry ragbag of a film that might be seen as De Palma's gift to his detractors—De Palma seems to have abandoned the Hitchcock connection, and it is not yet clear that he has found a strong thematic with which to replace it. *The Untouchables* (1987) seems a work of empty efficiency; it is perhaps significant that one remains uncertain whether to take the patriarchal idyll of Elliott Ness's domestic life straight or as parody. *Casualties of War* (1989) is more interesting, though severely undermined by the casting of the two leads: one grasps the kind of contrast De Palma had in mind, but it is not successfully realized in between Sean Penn's shameless mugging and Michael J. Fox's intractable blandness. Like most Hollywood movies on Vietnam, the film suffers from the inability to see Asians in terms other than an undifferentiated "otherness": it is symptomatic that the two Vietnamese girls, past and present, are played by the same actress. His return to the film of political protest (and specifically to the Vietnam War) brings De Palma's career to date full circle: his early work in an independent avant-garde (*Greetings* [1968], *Hi, Mom!* [1970]) is too often overlooked. But nothing in *Casualties of War*, for all the strenuousness of its desire to disturb, achieves the genuinely disorienting force of the remarkable "Be Black, Baby" sections of *Hi, Mom!*

Following *Casualties of War*—a film to which he had a deep personal commitment, whatever its success or failure as a comment upon the Vietnam War, violence against women, or the power of traumatic memory—De Palma seemed intent upon remaking his own public image by choosing an unusual property for him, the social satire *The Bonfire of the Vanities* (1990). He did put a personal stamp upon the material, most notably (and paradoxically) by paying tribute to the Orson Welles of *Touch of Evil* (1958), opening the film with an extremely long and intricate tracking shot and using distorting wide-angle lenses almost constantly (though less imaginatively than Welles). Unfortunately, the visual flair did nothing to compensate for some disastrous miscastings and craven attempts to soften the book's scathing cynicism, or for the unfocused script in general and De Palma's own inability to do satiric comedy without obnoxious overemphasis. *Raising Cain* (1992), a return to more comfortable territory—the lurid pop-Freudian thriller, the genre through which De Palma had achieved greatest fame and critical admiration—puzzled those who claimed he was merely repeating himself. But for connoisseurs it was intentionally a delicious self-parody—or at least a virtuoso filmmaker's display of his special talents—most flagrantly in a spectacularly choreographed Steadicam shot in which a psychiatrist spouting endless exposition is always on the verge of walking out of the frame, and in the delirious slow-motion climax.

The delirious slow-motion climax of *Raising Cain* (1992).

Carlito's Way (1983) again harked back to earlier De Palma successes, this time to crime drama, with an emotional intensity somewhere between the hallucinatory *Scarface* (1983) and the more coolly impersonal *The Untouchables*. If the film ultimately could not rise beyond the conventional trajectory of its plot—ex-hood trying to go straight is drawn back into crime by his old buddy, despite the outreach of a saintly woman—it at least boasted a brilliant impersonation of a crooked lawyer by Sean Penn and some splendid De Palma set pieces, like the chase through Grand Central Terminal. The film reminds us that De Palma is unsurpassed among film directors in portraying furies: not the collective surges of violence rendered by a Sam Peckinpah, but the private demons unleashed within or witnessed by (the same thing on dream level) "ordinary" people as well as crime kings and raving lunatics. De Palma's cinematic flourishes have often been called "operatic," but perhaps the better analogy is with the Lisztian keyboard virtuoso, someone who can tap profound emotional depths one moment but skitters over the surface at other times; who frequently improvises upon others' themes but is always unmistakably himself, for better or worse.

(2000)

George Romero

As with Francis Ford Coppola, George Romero's reputation—his position as a major American filmmaker—rests ultimately upon a trilogy. Without the three Living Dead films his work would merit little more than a footnote.

The other films can be dispensed with briefly. The interest of the early ones lies primarily in their relation to the trilogy. *Jack's Wife* (1972) reveals an early interest in feminism that would be fully realized in *Day of the Dead* (1985); *The Crazies* (1973) takes up certain themes of *Night of the Living Dead* (1968) and anticipates the later concern with militarism. The best of these films, *Martin* (1978), stands somewhat to one side, though its insights into alienation and its consequences are consistent with the trilogy's themes. Little need be said of the later films. The liberal attitudes of *Knightriders* (1981) collapse into liberal platitudes—and are the more surprising given the uncompromising radicalism of the trilogy. The five-part anthology film *Creepshow* (1982) is barely distinguishable from the British Amicus horror films of the 1970s: nasty people doing nasty things to other nasty people. *The Dark Half* (1993) is an undistinguished adaptation of one of Stephen King's worst novels. One might rescue *Monkey Shines* (1988), with its intriguing premise, in which Romero seems somewhat more engaged.

The Living Dead trilogy, on the other hand, constitutes, taken in its entirety, one of the major achievements of American cinema, an extraordinary feat of imagination and audacity carried through with exemplary courage and conviction. The intelligence it so convincingly manifests in its sustained significance could scarcely be guessed at from the rest of Romero's work to date. Each of the three films—*Night of the Living Dead*, *Dawn of the Dead* (1978), and *Day of the Dead*—belongs absolutely to its period yet still carries resonance today; together, they constitute an implicit radical sociopolitical critique of the dominant movement of American civilization. *Night of the Living Dead* develops the themes of the modern family horror film inaugurated by *Psycho* (1960):

from its initial brother-sister bickering in the cemetery (which conjures up the first flesh-eating zombie) it proceeds inexorably to the destruction of an entire nuclear family (its members killing and literally feeding on each other, as they had done metaphorically in their lives) and of the young couple (the embryonic future family), characters whose survival has traditionally been generically guaranteed. Unlike its successors, it also kills off its solitary hero figure, mistaken for a zombie and shot down by the sheriff's team. As in the other two films, the hero is black, his color situating him outside the dominant mainstream; the authority figures are treated throughout with bitingly sardonic humor. The whole film is rooted in the disturbance and disillusion of the Vietnam period.

Dawn of the Dead, in the 1970s, focuses its attention on consumer capitalism: the zombies, having taken over a vast shopping mall, proceed to carry on exactly as they did in life, except that they now consume human flesh. As one of the characters remarks, "They are *us*." The film makes clear what was already there but unstated in its predecessor: the zombies do not consume for nourishment, they consume in order to consume. In both the first two films the characters are valued very precisely in relation to their ability to extricate themselves from the socially conditioned patterns of behavior, with the difference that in *Dawn of the Dead* two are permitted to survive. Although male and female, they are not presented as even potential lovers; the woman has earlier rejected marriage to the man (subsequently a zombie) by whom she is pregnant, not because she no longer loves him but as a matter of principle. The implication is that a nonzombie future would necessitate an entire rethinking of the prevailing social-sexual organization.

In *Night of the Living Dead* the main female character is catatonic through most of the film; in *Dawn of the Dead*, Fran is treated by the men as the traditional "helpless female," but at the end, having extricated herself from conformity, she is sufficiently empowered to take over: it is she who pilots the helicopter to a possible though unlikely safety. In *Day of the Dead* the woman, Sarah, becomes central—active, assertive, intelligent throughout. At the same time Romero extends his analysis of contemporary Western culture to a more overtly political level, the critique of "masculinity" now directed at the two main bulwarks of male domination, the scientists and the military. The film is not antiscience: Sarah is herself a scientist. But she detaches herself from the masculinist science of Dr. Logan (a.k.a. "Dr. Frankenstein"). Logan's aim is to prove that zombies can be tamed and trained for use as slaves. The zombies have now taken over the earth, what is left of human life driven underground, and there is nowhere left to fly away to (the tropical island of the close is surely to be understood as fantasy). Logan's solution is represented by his prize pupil, Bub. What Bub learns—through Logan's system of punishments (beatings) and rewards (raw human flesh) that parodies the basis of our educational system—is "the bare beginnings of civilized behavior," in fact, the conditioned reflex. It is understandable that the film has been the least popular of the trilogy: it is unrelievedly dark both in tone and setting, rarely emerging into the light of day, in stark contrast to the brilliant colors and satirical humor of *Dawn of the Dead*, and it systematically demolishes all the central assumptions of our culture. What is inexplicable is its critical neglect and misrepresentation: it seems universally regarded as the weakest of the trilogy, yet it is, besides being the one great American horror film, the only one that is *about* something other than mindless titillation and essentially trivial gory excess since the end of the 1970s, when the genre was invaded and conquered by Michael, Jason, and Freddy. The answer may be that critics see the films only individually, not as panels in a triptych. It seems to be the case that Romero did not conceive them as a trilogy (how could he?—each is a response to a different decade), yet each demands the next, inexorably, and that is how they must be read.

Romero is currently trying to turn the trilogy into a tetralogy, with the addition of *Twilight of the Dead*, but has so far been unable to secure the necessary funding. The apparent finality of *Day of the Dead* makes speculation difficult, but one would certainly want to see what path he can find beyond it.

(2000)

Fresh Meat

Diary of the Dead

I. Retreat and Advance

From the beginning, George Romero's Living Dead movies have been at once mesmerizing, tantalizing, and oddly frustrating. One always has the sense that, beneath the surface shock/horror level, they are making a statement about . . . what, exactly? What do the living dead represent? Our culture, what we used to think of as our civilization, human life itself in all its confusions and unsatisfactoriness? All of the above? When you try to pin it down, something always gets in the way, refuses to fit, resists the meanings we try to impose. Of one thing we may be sure: the films are not about "punishment for sin." Romero's universe is certainly not a Christian one (the occasional religious references are always negative). Rather, we have an accidental universe, an unholy mess, an experiment not even from the familiar mad scientist but from some strange, blind, confused demiurge that didn't know what it was doing but, in its blind fumblings, produced a species that may be responsible for the death of all life on this planet within the next few hundred years. There are signs that the fifth of Romero's Living Dead movies may also be the last (though he has always surprised us, and perhaps himself): it has the feel and appearance of a summation, opening (like the original film) with the first "undead" returning to life, ending on a direct, desperate challenge to the audience, as if demanding our own summation.

Looking back over the five films, one is struck by an inherent contradiction: one cannot believe that they were planned as a sequence, each having its own individual characteristics (there are no carry-overs from one film to the next). Yet the more one reflects upon them the more one is struck by an inherent logic in the overall structure, a logic confirmed by the remarkable new film: the first four in the series cover and demolish, systematically, the central structures of what we still call our civilization, establishing Romero as the most radical of all horror directors.

Night of the Living Dead (1968): The nuclear family (the basis of our culture): the warring brother and sister of the opening, the miserable, squabbling parents and child, the "young couple" (the future nuclear family) of the midsection. All are killed and eaten, the centerpiece being the little girl stabbing her mother to death with a builder's trowel then devouring her father. The zombies—the living dead, dead but still living—are established here as our past; the films are about the impossibility of escaping from it.

Dawn of the Dead (1978): Consumerism, on which our culture's economy depends: free riches in the shopping mall. It will always be the most popular of the series because it's the least disturbing—consumerism is a relatively superficial aspect of our world. It's also the only film in which the couple (but not the romantic couple, not another nuclear family) are permitted to escape, even if the escape is to nowhere. (The tropical island refuge of *Day* is clearly coded as a wish-fulfillment fantasy.)

Day of the Dead (1985): The military—our guardians and defenders—revealed as utterly useless and objectionable, their particularly obnoxious captain literally torn apart by the zombies.

Land of the Dead (2005): Capitalism itself, with the brilliant casting of Dennis Hopper as its supreme embodiment, Easy Rider maturing into its most monstrous tycoon.

Diary of the Dead (2007): Both a return to origins (the first zombies, an entirely new and different starting point, but again with the nuclear family as the origin) and an advance, with young and fresh new actors as the student-film-crew protagonists.

A second substructure uniting the series has proved of equal consistency: the role of black characters.

Night of the Living Dead: The central figure, the "outsider" hero with no apparent family ties, the sole character who survives the zombies (only to be gunned down by the rednecks).

Dawn of the Dead: The most intelligent, responsible, and aware of the three male characters, allowed to escape with the woman.

Day of the Dead: Essentially (of the five) the "woman's picture," but Romero's female protagonist is linked strongly to her black lover.

Land of the Dead: Tantalizingly, the hint Romero gives us of the black zombie who (alone) appears to be developing an embryonic awareness and capacity for thought. Rashly, I had assumed that if there were to be another Living Dead movie he or his counterpart would be the central figure. Was Romero defeated by the obvious problems of spontaneously developing thinking zombies? But instead we have . . .

Diary of the Dead: The group of organized and intelligent blacks who seem closest to controlling and surviving the seemingly uncontrollable situation. If there is, after all, a sixth film, will they be central to it?

The privileged position of the black characters (in all the films) relies on two features, one logical, the other not: as blacks they are outsiders, with a history of oppression, cruelty, and marginalization; they are also, in Romero's movies, unattached, free of the constraints and demands of the nuclear family; they are also always and only male. This gives them a freedom of vision and action from which the white characters are barred, though the total absence of black women makes their future somewhat problematic.

Most seem to agree that *Land* is the weakest of the first four films (Hopper and the black zombie apart, its characters are not very interesting, and too much of the first half merely repeats the now-familiar slaughter). *Diary*, though it lacks the controlled and compressed intensity of *Night* and the bright colors and energy of *Dawn*, may prove to be the series' supreme achievement, Romero's most inclusive statement. Its premise is brilliant. In a gambit of characteristic aplomb, Romero establishes that he has no responsibility for the film we are watching: the opening segment has been downloaded from the internet, and what follows is the work of a group of film students from the University of Pittsburgh, and in particular of an aspiring young filmmaker called Jason Creed (Josh Close), introduced directing his own student horror movie in which a mummy pursues a young woman through the woods at night. When the first news of the zombie attacks comes in, Jason is quite ready to leap at the opportunity to make the abrupt transition to a "reality" movie. We are not permitted to see Jason clearly until well into the film, as he is wielding the handheld camera, blocking his face; his film's title is not *Diary of the Dead* but *The Death of Death*.

Jason (Joshua Close) filming the zombie attack in the hospital (*Diary of the Dead*, 2007).

Romero's decision to attribute his film to a group of students is a masterstroke. The handheld camera continuously underlines the sense of the instability of a world in which nothing is reliable, anyone may turn out to be a zombie. Detached (at least partly) from the nuclear family, looking ahead to a still-undefined future, with a certain freedom of choice, the young people are the ideal protagonists for a Romero movie. Even in the midst of the pervasive horrors, the constant reminders of the handheld camera and the youthful spontaneity and emotional openness of the group also combine to give the film a surprising freshness and exhilaration that's lacking in the previous films (and especially in *Land*), while the group's relative innocence gives the film an unexpected and touching poignancy.

Whatever Romero had in mind when he began, his ambitions, the seriousness of his commitment, have developed and revealed themselves well beyond the expectations we bring to a genre movie. For the record, *Diary* is the first of his films that has made me cry, no doubt partly because the characters, with their youthful energy and thirst for life, remind me of the students in my graduate film-studies courses: they may not be facing zombies but they will also be struggling to survive within a relentlessly disintegrating culture. Romero never idealizes his young people. Jason's motivation, for example, is repeatedly called into question, notably by Debra (Michelle Morgan): is his determination to continue filming through all the horrors callously self-serving, or justified by an authentic desire to establish truth? Both seem present, but Debra's final acceptance of him, and her desire to continue his work after his death, acknowledge a degree of integrity.

II. Structure: A Road Movie with Five Stops

THE FILM'S OPENING SEGMENT—NEWS footage downloaded by Debra from the internet—shows the first case of the dead coming back as zombies: a nuclear family in which the father has committed suicide after killing his wife and son, inverting the central episode of *Night* in which a young girl kills and eats her parents. The ensuing action, beginning haphazardly with a panicky journey of uncertain destination, inevitably takes the form of return to the illusory safety of family homes. Debra sums it up: "You spend so much time resenting your parents . . . but as soon as the shit hits the fan, the only place you want to go is home."

Diary of the Dead is Romero's first "road movie," the last of the five Living Dead films being in strongest possible contrast with the claustrophobic first (in which the continually warring characters are trapped by the zombies in a single house). Its essential progress (a journey with constantly diminishing returns) is from the open road to Debra's final descent into the mansion's panic room, from which we know she will never emerge. Three of the five stops are

The news footage of the first zombie attack (*Diary of the Dead*, 2007).

Fresh Meat - 381

for help, security, and shelter, none of which materialize: the hospital where they take Mary (Tatiana Maslany) after her attempted suicide, and the two homes (Debra's, Ridley's) where they hope to find safety. All prove illusory: Mary, the gentlest and youngest of the group, shoots herself because, as the driver of the group's camper van, she has killed three people who may not all have been zombies. She dies, becomes a zombie, and has to be executed. Debra's parents are already zombies, and Ridley (Philip Riccio), unbeknownst to the group, has already been bitten, and hence may die and become one at any moment. And we must remember that family members, when they die, don't merely become zombies, they *eat* each other: a neat Romeroesque definition of nuclear family relationships.

The other two stops/episodes (the Amish farmer, the militant black group) are stumbled upon accidentally and provide temporary, transient help. The sequence of the confrontation with the black group is especially intriguing as it significantly develops the roles of blacks in the previous films. In contrast to the pervasive hysteria and chaos, they are organized, and the film suggests that what has made this possible is their marginalization within the white world. As their leader tells Debra, "For the first time in our lives, we got the power—because everyone else left." Debra's strength impresses him: he tells her, "I think you're a lot like me." One has the sense that their mutual respect could point ahead to a new development of Romero's pervasive interest in black characters, if we are to have further installments . . .

I wish Romero had ended his film with the withdrawal of Debra, Professor Maxwell (Scott Wentworth), and Tony Ravello (the other surviving student) into the panic room, with Debra's promise that "I'm going to finish his movie. There's got to be more." It expresses the bleak hope that Jason's film may be of value if anyone survives the zombies—an assertion one can take as Romero's hint of a possible sixth film.

I don't understand the brief postscript, introduced by Debra as "the last film Jason shot." Its central image is certainly among the most appalling ever produced within fictional cinema, but the perpetrators of the desecration it depicts are a couple of irrelevant rednecks who played no part in the film. Debra's question ("Are we worth saving? You tell me") has already been answered by the film with a resounding "Yes!" insofar as it applies to the characters—the students—within the narrative, and to Debra's own assertion. I confess to bewilderment . . .

The original *Night of the Living Dead* was welcomed or repudiated as a schlock horror film; *Diary* will probably be welcomed as an art-house movie. But what's in a name? Let us salute a great and audacious filmmaker . . .

(2008)

Revenge Is Sweet

The Bitterness of *Audition*

Audition (1999) stands apart from the rest of Takashi Miike's other films to date: this seems to be the general consensus, and it is confirmed by the three other films by him I have seen. It is the only one of the four that interests—more than interests, fascinates—me.

In general, his reputation (or cult status) appears to rest on his readiness to push further and further the boundaries of portrayable violence, "gross-out" cinema, which doubtless has its sociological interest within a civilization (and I don't mean only Japanese) that seems to be in the process of accepting (and rather enjoying, even celebrating) its headlong race toward extinction: a kind of Japanese Tarantino, perhaps marginally less complacent and self-congratulatory. (I should confess here that I have no right to say this, since I have not seen *Kill Bill: Volume 1* [2003], but after reading the reports, both positive and negative, and with dire memories of *Pulp Fiction* [1994] still lingering like the aftermath of severe food poisoning, I feel I would be wasting my time.)

To put it concisely: The other Miike films are disturbing for what they have to tell us about the state of contemporary civilization; they are not in the least disturbing in themselves, operating on some fantasy level of annihilation, with comic-book violence. *Audition*, on the other hand, is authentically disturbing, and infinitely more horrifying: the first time I watched it—on DVD, at home, after warnings I had received—I was repeatedly tempted, through the last half hour, to turn it off. It is one of those few films, like Pasolini's *Salò, or the 120 Days of Sodom* (*Salò o le 120 giornate di Sodoma*, 1975) that are almost as unwatchable as the newsreels of Auschwitz, of the innocent victims of Hiroshima and Nagasaki and Vietnam, victims of Nazi or American dehumanization, which today, under President Bush, seem not so far apart.

That, however, is a relatively simple issue: the Nazis, the American administration, were dehumanized monsters (who else could knowingly drop an atomic bomb on a city populated predominantly by women, children, and the aged? Surely not a human being). The two central figures of *Audition* are very much human beings—albeit living in our immediately recognizable culture (whether Japanese or American doesn't matter, beyond local cultural difference). They are not "guilty"—in the way in which the Nazis and the American warmongers were guilty. They are simply contaminated by the cultural environment, past and present. They don't deserve their respective fates, except as sacrificial victims of our civilization.

Audition and *Vertigo*

For all their obvious surface differences, *Audition* on close inspection offers striking structural parallels with *Vertigo* (1958). I am not necessarily implying any direct connection, even on a subconscious level (though it would be surprising if Miike has not seen Hitchcock's film—everyone else has). What interests me here is something more fundamental than the tracing of influences: the recurrence of this structure within superficially distinct cultures (both, however, capitalist and male dominated), which suggests that it has a universal relevance today, touching upon deep and sensitive strains of male desire, male anxiety, male guilt, male fears, male masochism...

Both films were made by men, both are about "guilty" women who do some very bad things and are finally punished for them, both male protagonists are presented sympathetically: neither is in any blatant, obvious way "male chauvinist," though neither is exactly untarnished. Male chauvinism remains, despite the feminist movement (which petered out far short of its initial goals), a seemingly universal blight. Juxtaposed, the two male protagonists offer fascinating insights into the current plight of heterosexual relations.

If you look at the characters in the two films, there's no immediately obvious resemblance. But if you reduce each film to a structural skeleton, parallels become clear very quickly. Consider the following:

1. Prelude (separated from the main body of the film by a specified seven years [*Audition*] or an unspecified few months [*Vertigo*]): the male protagonist experiences a profound shock that changes his whole way of life (the death of

his wife, the rooftop accident). In both cases this is experienced as a sense of loss that has to be recuperated, whether swiftly (Scottie) or after a lengthy period of hibernation (Aoyama).

2. The male protagonists. Each is at a loose end, waiting for something to happen: Scottie, after the opening accident, lacks social definition, is ready to "wander" in search of something undefined that will give him a sense of selfhood; Aoyama's aspirations are less romantic, but his placid home life (with a son about to reach manhood and showing an interest in possible romantic attachments) and his apparently more or less "routine" work leave him dissatisfied and uneasy, with the possibility of an empty and lonely future.

3. The female protagonist. Most obviously, she is simply "not what she seems": "Madeleine" is a construct, Asami is not the sweet, helpless, passive, gentle little creature by whom Aoyama is captivated even before he meets her (rather as Scottie is predisposed toward "Madeleine" by Gavin Elster's story). In both cases she presents herself as deeply vulnerable, very much in need of the protection of a strong man: for the male, the ideal temptation/love object, the woman who needs him and whom he can consequently believe himself to be dominating.

4. The alternative partner. In both films the male protagonist is offered a choice, somewhat insistent and aggressive (Midge in *Vertigo*), more passive but always there, waiting, hovering (the secretary in *Audition*). Though the characters again are very different (Midge is sophisticated, attractive, independent, a "career woman," the secretary plain, subservient, a mere employee without apparent ambitions beyond marrying her boss), yet each seems suitable for the position of partner to their respective males, Midge as Scottie's equal, the secretary as humble, home-bound, dutiful, and undemanding wife. With both there is a past history: Midge and Scottie were once engaged until she broke it off (apparently disturbed by his lack of real commitment); Aoyama and the secretary (as revealed in the climactic hallucinatory sequence) once had drunken sex together at an all-night office party; both women have been waiting, never attaching themselves to other partners. Both lack precisely what the man most desires: a certain mystery, fragility, vulnerability, that sense of "needing to be looked after" that brings out the heterosexual male's protective instincts and thereby guarantees his manhood.

5. The tempter. This is far more obvious and explicit in *Vertigo*, where Gavin Elster is clearly one of Hitchcock's "devil" figures who seems to know more about the male protagonist's weaknesses and needs than he does. But it is Elster who sets Scottie up with Madeleine, and it is Yoshikawa, the film producer, who sets Aoyama up for the spurious audition, in which the contestants believe they are applying for a part in a movie but are really there to be inspected and selected as Aoyama's future wife, rather as female slaves were once lined up on display to serve new masters. The producer at least "means well" (as Norman Bates remarks in *Psycho* [1960], "everyone means well"): he is performing a kindness for an old friend. He soothes Aoyama's legitimate worries about the morality of it by telling him, not very convincingly, that he does indeed intend to cast a film as well, but this is obviously an improvised afterthought, and the film hints that Aoyama only believes it because he wants to, to quiet his conscience.

6. The outcome. In *Vertigo* the woman dies, in *Audition* she is severely injured; in both the man survives—just. He is older and (perhaps) wiser—or merely disillusioned. At least Scottie is not subjected to the woman's hideous revenge, though he may be emotionally and psychologically scarred for life. Madeleine/Judy was merely a victim (the most important deviation in the films' correspondences), whereas Asami (with no Gavin Elster behind her, acting as a free agent) is able to enact upon the male the most appalling revenge ever shown on a cinema screen.

Note: Only one significant character in *Audition* has no equivalent in *Vertigo*: Aoyama's son, Shigehiko. He can be read, to a certain extent, as representing a healthier possibility for the future, though Miike subtly undermines even this possibility: he has inherited something of the traditional male attitude to women (see his gesture of male complicity to his father, behind his girlfriend's back, in the scene where he brings her home to dinner, or his later casual remarks about "not understanding girls" when she talks about "a girl thing"). He also lacks his father's depth of feeling and experience of loneliness, but he is still young.

A Thematical Study

AUDITION'S STRUCTURAL RESEMBLANCE TO *Vertigo* (the parallels indicating a basic common concern with male-female relations, with the tragic and devastating outcome of deception, misreadings, incompatible goals and desires) makes it possible to define clearly the specificities of Miike's film, the

Asami (Eihi Shiina) enacts the most appalling revenge upon the male ever shown on a cinema screen (*Audition*, 1999).

uniqueness of its insights, the particular nature of the profound disturbance it engenders, a disturbance left unresolved by the refusal of full closure. I shall examine the film thematically rather than chronologically.

A. The social norms. The two characters who most clearly represent what one might call, for our culture, "normal" behavior are Yoshikawa and Shigehiko. The latter has the excuse of youth, but he already exhibits certain "learned" attitudes to the female sex—casualness, a sense of superiority, condescension about "the girl thing," etc. Yoshikawa, having helped his friend select a possible second wife, immediately has rational qualms about the result, distrusting both the slightly mysterious young woman with the minimal resume and Aoyama's instant and unquestioning obsession with her. His "common sense" attitude, his solicitude for his friend, could have rescued Aoyama from his trap, from hideous physical torture, crippling, and a lifetime of psychological hurt. At the same time its basis in the "everyday," in so-called normal human relations, reveals his ignorance of the possible depths of human feeling, human experience: Aoyama's romanticism, disastrous as it proves, has a grandeur about it that is beyond his grasp. One wants to say, with Hamlet, "There are more things in heaven and earth, Yoshikawa, than are dreamt of in your philosophy"—things deeper, richer, and infinitely more terrifying.

B. Child abuse. It is difficult to think of many films that are centered upon child abuse, its direct effects on both abused and abuser, its potential indirect effects on society beyond. It is a subject most people don't like to think about, perhaps because (if one considers its less extreme manifestations: not only sexual abuse and gratuitous sadism, but the physical abuse that is still regarded in many societies as a parental right and the psychological abuse that seems endemic to the nuclear family itself) it is so widespread. (If I strike a full-grown man in the street he has the right to call the cops; if I strike a small child in my own home, he/she doesn't; I think, if anything, that situation should be reversed.) Asami, of course, is an extreme and special case: the specificity of the abuse has taught her that love and pain must be inseparable. She is at once the "monster" of the traditional horror film and the most touching, vulnerable, and even, in a very real sense, innocent character in the film, although she has performed acts of almost unimaginable horror and been the cause of appalling suffering to men who are at least nominally "innocent" (not, of course, her stepfather, but Aoyama and the man in the sack, who is, I take it, Mr. Shibata, the man from the music industry). I think this is the film's most remarkable achievement. There have been, in the history of the horror film, a number of sympathetic monsters, but none, surely, who moves us as Asami does, none who somehow, to the end, retains that sense of innocence.

C. Guilt. Against Asami's appalling innocence the film sets Aoyama's guilt. It is, of course, totally disproportionate to his punishment, and in fact has only marginally to do with his treatment of her. One might even say that it is his sense of guilt, rather than any guilt most of us might recognize as such. I think the fact that this film has such a powerful effect (it is one I shall never forget, even if I try to) is due less to its physical horrors than to its sense of the injustice of things: Aoyama's transgressions (such as they are) must be read as "standard" within our culture, he is never the "insensitive brute male" who deserves whatever he gets. On one level, his guilt is that, in falling for Asami, he is being unfaithful to his wife—who died seven years ago. But this is compounded by his sense of guilt (unknown to the worldly Yoshikawa) in setting up the audition, which he at least half knows is a fake, bringing in dozens of aspiring young actresses for a film that will never be made. He has other guilts as well, as revealed in the "hallucination" sequence when he has drunk the drugged whisky: he has "used" available women, in the haphazard way men do. In that extraordinary, barely comprehensible sequence (I had to cheat and watch it on my DVD in slow motion to be sure what I was seeing), we learn that his constantly hovering secretary (whom we know would like to marry him, and of whose existence he scarcely seems aware) had sex with him at a drunken office party and that he apparently also had sex (on the staircase?) with Rie, the married woman who comes in to cook and clean for him and his son . . . or did he just want to?—the guilt would perhaps be the same. (She tells him, as she prepares to leave after her work, "Males need female support, otherwise they can't maintain," and the words are repeated verbatim in the hallucination scene as they have sex on the stairs.) But the worst of that guilt is surely that he is, essentially, a scrupulously monogamous man who has occasionally used complicit women as sex objects, and the punishment he receives is greatly in excess of his "crimes."

At the basis of the guilt is Aoyama's wife, Ryoko. She makes five appearances in the film, all very brief: in the precredit sequence, when she dies in the hospital; in two (ambiguous) memory/fantasy shots linked to Aoyama's subjectivity; and twice in the hallucination sequence (the only time she speaks). The opening minutes beautifully and economically establish his dedication to her and to the sense of family, the moments of death shown simply in a slight movement of her lips and the ensuing straightening of the lifeline on the scanner beside the bed, a close-up of their clasped hands, the appearance of the young Shigehiko carrying his elaborate "get well" offering, the father's face almost expressionless as he stares at his son in a silence more eloquent than any demonstration of grief. Then seven years pass before Aoyama decides (after some prompting from his son) that he should remarry. At this stage of the film he shows no guilt at his minor sexual transgressions (of which the spectator knows nothing until much later), but his perusal of the audition applications immediately induces a certain anxiety: as he looks through them he feels compelled to turn Ryoko's photograph (prominent on his desk) away from him. Thus, Miike defines the situation clearly: his guilt is not about minor infidelities, which pose no threat to Ryoko's memory. It is aroused by the sense of replacing his wife.

This reading is confirmed by the two insert shots, which hover between memory and fantasy. As his obsession with Asami develops, he sees Ryoko in a winter landscape, deep snow, moving behind a tree so that she is gradually obliterated, her expression sad, slightly reproachful: perhaps a memory (courtship? honeymoon? holiday?), but it carries clear symbolic meaning. The other insert shot occurs when he reads Asami's application and learns of her irreparably damaged hips after studying ballet for twelve years. Miike cuts to a different angle, Ryoko's photograph now prominent in the foreground: "It's like accepting death." (Earlier we learned that Ryoko danced, though not ballet.) Cut to shot of Ryoko sitting up in her hospital bed at night, distraught, long black hair past her shoulders, looking remarkably like an older Asami . . . and obviously not accepting death. This can hardly be a memory, as she is clearly alone: an imagined memory perhaps, provoked by Aoyama's guilt feelings. The guilt is probably unnecessary, testifying more to his scrupulousness and sensitivity (and his continuing love for Ryoko) than to anything his wife might actually have felt about his remarriage. But the guilt makes him a candidate for punishment, which he subsequently receives out of all proportion.

D. Narrative instability: reality, memory, fantasy, telepathy, hallucination. The opening sequences invite the unwary spectator into what appears to be the stable and consistent world of realist narrative to which mainstream cinema has accustomed us; Miike then proceeds systematically to undermine our sense of security, at first subtly and ambiguously, but gradually increasing our uncertainty until, in the climactic sequence of the hallucinatory drug, all possibility of rational, "realist" explanation dissolves until, like Aoyama, we are floundering in a world in which all logic and coherence dissolve and we no longer know on what level we are to read the images, whether what follows is reality or fantasy. Certitude is restored only by the reentry of common-sense "normality," in the person of Shigehiko. (Here again one can claim a tenuous parallel with *Vertigo*, when Hitchcock teases us with the question of Madeleine's reality: her mysterious, unexplained disappearance from the McKittrick Hotel, the brief moment in the redwoods when she seems to have vanished, to be rediscovered behind a tree.)

From Reality to Psychic Chaos

THE MOVEMENT FROM SOLID reality to some form of unstable, shifting psychic chaos can be traced as follows:

1. Asami in her room. The shot is dimly lit, cut in without explanation; we cannot be certain it is Asami, but for want of a better guess. It proves, however, to be the first of a series that runs through the first half of the film. At this point, no sack is visible.

2. Discrepancies in her story, especially involving Mr. Shibata, her contact in the music industry (during the audition) whom later she confesses to Aoyama (in the restaurant) she has never met, and who (we learn) disappeared a year ago and has never been traced.

3. The memories/fantasies of Ryoko (above).

4. Changing restaurants. The conversation between Aoyama and Asami seems to be continuous (no indication of time change, no hiatus in the dialogue), yet at first the restaurant where they are drinking beer has other customers, then a cut shows it to be empty aside from the couple, then they are abruptly in a different restaurant having dinner.

5. The series of cut-in shots of Asami hunched up against the wall of her room continues; her phone, on the floor, is always in view, and we know she is waiting for Aoyama to contact her. We see, in the background, the sack (just a sack, but obviously containing something). Then, when Aoyama (troubled by Toshikawa's advice not to call her) at last phones, the sack, in the film's first truly unsettling moment, moves and twists about violently, as if something (or someone?) had been awakened or (perhaps?) was desperately trying to make contact, begging to be let out . . .

6. Asami's disappearance from the country hotel, their romantic tryst. Although they are sharing a room and a bed, Aoyama has been the perfect gentleman, never insisting, offering her every delay or alternative. She has responded by removing her clothes, showing him the scars on her thighs (because she wants him to see her imperfections?—because she thinks it will turn him on?), offering herself ("Love me. Only me. Not like the others"), lying back on the bed. We assume they make love, though that seems called into question later, in a brief replay of the scene.

Asami's disappearance is very difficult to interpret, in retrospect from the ending. Has she experienced, for the first time in her life, some kind of authentic tenderness, and leaves because she knows she will harm him? Or is she (as the rest of the film seems to suggest, without quite eradicating the other possibility) just leading him on toward the "satisfaction" she really wants? Does she disappear hoping to spare him the horrors of her desire, or does she already know that he will track her down, into a world of horror and pleasure that the surface world prefers not to know about? (In that she is quite accurate, his obsessive pursuit of her paralleling Scottie's false resightings of Madeleine. Isn't this one of the cinema's most desolate and devastating love stories?)

7. The stepfather, the red-hot sticks. We appear to be in the "real" world of the investigation into a mystery. Yet Aoyama's visit to the one connection he is given is, at the least, very odd: he has to break into an apparently abandoned building (lured on by the sound of a piano) through layers of impediment, to be ignored by the old man seated at the piano. He is, we eventually learn, Asami's stepfather, and the red-hot sticks with which he (lovingly) scarred her thigh are still burning beside the piano, as they burned in the past, though they appear now to serve no purpose . . .

8. The stone fish. Aoyama's quest for truth (and Asami): first he has to break through barriers, now he has to descend two floors into darkness. The bar has been closed for a year (and we should recall that Mr. Shibata disappeared a year ago), since the murder of the female owner, who was involved with a "man from the music industry." May we assume, in terms of narrative logic (for the film has its own complex logic, however unconventional), that she was the aunt who pushed Asami downstairs at the age of seven, when she broke her collarbone? We are not told this, but there seems no other detectable reason for Asami to have murdered a woman and she has not kept any body parts as remembrances. The man, on the other hand, is surely Mr. Shibata, one of Asami's love objects, whom she has not killed but kept for what she perhaps mistakes for their mutual pleasure in torment. The woman's body was dismembered, but its parts were all there; three superfluous fingers and an extra ear baffled the investigators. And there was also a superfluous tongue, which Aoyama then sees, wriggling out from the woodwork. (This, for me, is the film's one lapse: the horror seems superfluous, and I can see no reason why Aoyama would hallucinate such a thing at that moment. It is the only moment in a film I have [reluctantly] come to love that seems gratuitous and slightly silly; it is shown from Aoyama's point of view, so can be taken as his hallucination, an omen he fails to respond to.)

9. Hallucinations. When Aoyama comes home and drinks the doctored whisky, listening to the faintly unnerving message on the machine ("I'm staying away tonight . . . Gang [the dog] is hiding under the house"), the film at last collapses its hesitations and uncertainties as to what is real, what isn't, and what is psychologically real. Aoyama has access to scenes and places and events he couldn't know about in the world of cold logic. The sequence is so complex (on both the technical and emotional levels) that it becomes almost an act of defiance for anyone to attempt to interpret it. I can but try.

Abuse

Aoyama's question about her early life (repeated here verbatim from their earlier restaurant conversation) gets a very different response about her family when she was sent to her uncle's ("That was a terrible place. I only remember being abused. Cold baths in winter, I got pneumonia. She pushed me down the stairs, I broke my collarbone. I was seven years old") and how she was abused by her stepfather (with the disabled legs—the red-hot sticks): "But when I danced it purified the dark side of me. That's the reason I never tried to kill myself." As Aoyama says, "I've been looking for someone like you," he suddenly becomes aware of Ryoko, with friends, at the next table. He offers to introduce her to Asami (Ryoko warns, "No! She isn't good for you!"). Ryoko rises, Asami rises (but in her own room: "I want you. I want you right now"). She is sucking his cock; they are no longer in the restaurant. He closes his eyes and suddenly it's the secretary gazing up at him from the floor ("I expected something from you"). Then Asami ("I'll do anything to give you pleasure")—and suddenly it's his wife, in a sailor suit, and they are in Asami's room (where he has never been, so this is something far beyond any "realist" aesthetic). With Aoyama present (on what level of reality?), the unfortunate member of the music industry, Mr. Shibata, manages, in great agony, to clamber out of the sack in which he has (presumably) survived for the past year. He has (conspicuously) only three fingers on his hand; he can't speak because his tongue is missing. As far as we know, he has done nothing worse than Aoyama has. But, if one is abused to and beyond the point of trauma as a young child, does one make distinctions among adults? Asami feeds him some sort of soup, or slop, and tells him (and Aoyama), "You only love me. Only me."

The stepfather with the red-hot sticks: "Asami, dance for me" (Asami as child). Then Asami as woman lies, opens her legs for the torture. Aoyama appears, watches: Asami, with her metal wires, cuts off her stepfather's head, telling him what he did to her; he appears to enjoy this, though she tells him, "I've never felt unhappy because I've been unhappy all the time." Cut to Rie, sex on the stairs ("Males need female support"), then Yoshikawa in the bar from the early scenes ("Let's have an audition"). Brief shot of Ryoko, then Aoyama in the audition chair, "My son told me that I look old. Why don't I remarry?" The stepfather's head falling off is intercut with Aoyama falling down, as the drug finally takes over.

The End

WHAT CAN ONE SAY about what follows? The first time I saw the film (on DVD) I nearly switched off. It is a love scene—perhaps the most terrible love scene in the history of film. I had, though my endurance level is not the greatest, watched *The Texas Chainsaw Massacre* (1974) and *The Last House on the Left* (1972) without too great a problem and, indeed, with respect (which has survived and surpassed repeated viewings, both seeming to me essential films for our perhaps hopelessly decadent culture). But Miike's film upset me to an extent beyond that: my first reaction was that I was sorry I'd seen it. If one descends to its core, it is a profound film about (among other things) the lingering and spreading effects of child abuse. The climactic scene is above all a consummation—of his misplaced guilt and of her perverted love, which she can express only through the most horrific torture ("You can enjoy the pain and suffer incredibly"). She amputates the lower part of his left leg simply in order to keep him ("You can't go anywhere without feet"), and sticks the needles in his eyelids so that he can't close his eyes—he might miss some of the pain/pleasure. By this point our sense of reality has been so thoroughly undermined that we can ask ourselves whether what we witness is "really" happening or is another fantasy/hallucination. It is only with the reappearance of Shigehiko (the representative of unimaginative sanity) that we are forced to see it as "real."

At the end of the film, after Shigehiko has thrown her down the stairs, she is still alive (though her back may be broken), and it is Asami who is allowed the last words, to Aoyama, continuing her personal love story: "You are the first one to support me. Warmly wrapping me. Trying to understand me. It's hard to forget about." We may recall what Aoyama said to her earlier: "Someday you'll feel that life is wonderful." The final shot shows her as a little girl, tying on her ballet shoes.

Acknowledgment: I feel I must acknowledge the influence on this article of Gustav Mahler—his seventh symphony and especially its central, terrifying Schattenhaft Scherzo—though I can't pin down the exact nature of its contribution. I have been listening to it somewhat obsessively (in recordings by the two greatest Mahler interpreters, Horenstein and Scherchen) throughout the week it has taken to write this, alternating with reviewings of the film, and the two have somehow merged into a single experience. Today the music seems almost like a premonition of what was to come in Germany during the succeeding four decades since the symphony's premiere in 1908: I hear in that central movement the wails of agony, anguish, and despair rising from the concentration camps, ghoulishly juxtaposed with a sort of off-kilter Viennese waltz. What courage it must take to compose such music.

(2004)

What Lies Beneath?

IN 1979, RICHARD LIPPE and I organized and hosted a retrospective of the (primarily) American horror film at the Toronto International Film Festival, then known as the Festival of Festivals. We invited a number of filmmakers to give seminars, and Brian De Palma, George Romero, Wes Craven, and Stephanie Rothman all made public appearances and answered questions, Richard and I interviewing each on stage before turning the questioning over to the audience. As part of this event, we produced a small (one-hundred page) booklet, to which Andrew Britton and Tony Williams also contributed essays, entitled (like the retrospective) *The American Nightmare*. My sections were subsequently included in my book *Hollywood from Vietnam to Reagan*, published by Columbia University Press (1986), with an extension dealing with the genre's development—"degeneration" would be a more appropriate term—in the '80s.

Looking back, it seems to me that our primary motivation was what Howard Hawks always claimed for making his movies: "having fun"—though I would add that, like Hawks, we wanted to make as good a professional job of it as possible and we took our work very seriously. And, of course, we would never have done it had we not believed that we had something to say, at the root of which was our sense that this most despised and ridiculed of genres was worth serious attention. I don't think it occurred to us that what we were doing would come to assume the historic importance that seems to be the case. We never asserted (or believed) that ours was the only way of looking at horror films or that our theories explained every horror film that had ever been made, although much of what has been written since appears to accuse us of exactly that.

At the core of our ideas was the belief (which I don't think anyone is likely to dispute) that the evolution of a genre is strongly influenced by cultural-political evolution, at least as much as by the genre's internal evolution, the fact that later films in a given cycle are nourished by and grow out of what preceded them. How else could one account for the astonishingly abrupt shift in the American horror film from the progressive, exploratory, often radical late '60s and '70s to the reactionary and repressive '80s? The Michael of *Halloween* (1978), the Jason of *Friday the 13th* (1980), the Freddy Krueger of *A Nightmare on Elm Street* (1984), do not develop out of the characteristic monsters of the '70s; they represent a refusal of everything they embodied.

What was crucially determinant of *The American Nightmare* was our political commitment—leftist, radical, with at least an interest in Marxist ideology and especially in the confluence of Marx and Freud in '70s thought. That commitment was vastly more important to us than any desire to tell "the whole truth and nothing but the truth" about the horror film. And I must acknowledge here the key importance of Andrew Britton: his contributions to our booklet were relatively brief, but his influence pervaded the entire enterprise. For myself, Andrew has been for many years the most important film critic writing in the English language; his neglect within academic circles seems to me disgraceful.[78]

If one approaches the American horror film from a radical perspective, one must inevitably find great positive interest in the achievements of the late '60s and the '70s and reject almost everything that has followed. My social-political position has not changed essentially since that time, though in honesty I must admit that two decades of reaction and conservatism have somewhat dulled its edges. In the '70s one felt supported by, at the least, a general disquiet and dissatisfaction, at best a widespread desire for change, which came to a focus in the period's great social movements—radical feminism, the black movement, gay rights, environmentalism. Those movements still exist but have lost much of their momentum, perhaps because of the advances they made: advances that have, to some degree, been recuperated into the establishment at the cost of losing their dangerousness. Perhaps the new American administration will goad people into a new sense of outrage and fury, but it may take the equivalent of the Vietnam war.

Criticism of *The American Nightmare*'s approach has in fact concentrated not on politics but on psychoanalysis, which to us was a valuable weapon that could be used politically. Relatively speaking, our radical political commitment has been generally ignored, despite the fact that it embodies the foundation of our arguments. I would agree today that building an analysis of the horror genre on Freudian theory made it readily vulnerable to attack by those uneasy with our politics. The (supposed) demolition and repudiation of Freud is another '80s phenomenon, again (I would claim) strongly influenced by the social-political climate. Part of the problem lies in that distressingly common tendency either to totally accept or totally reject, as opposed to the principle of *examining critically*. Few today appear to read Freud or Marx with a view to sorting out what is still valid, what can be cast off, what needs to be rethought.

Freudian theory is vulnerable to attack on many points, but not, in my opinion, on the one that formed the psychoanalytic basis of *The American Nightmare*: the theory of repression and the "return of the repressed." We can all trace the workings of this, surely, in our own personal histories and in our daily lives; it continues to have great resonance in relation to the horror film, but only in so far as it is melded with a political awareness. Murnau's *Nosferatu* (1922), made in the very shadow of Freud, strikes me as almost textbook Freud, the monster as "return of the repressed" (and its ultimate re-repression) in almost diagrammatic (yet extremely powerful) form. The Freudian analogy holds good for James Whale's *Frankenstein* (1931), but there, in Karloff's makeup, clothing, gestures, and performance, his threats and pleadings, we can also see the working class, the poor, the homeless, the dispossessed, suggesting a parallel between psychological repression and social oppression. The possibility that the monster (hence "the repressed") might be seen as sympathetic or pitiable (as well as horrifying) was perhaps inherent in the genre from the outset (it is clearly there in Whale's two Frankenstein movies). But it is in the '70s, with the development of radicalism and protest, that the figure of the monster develops a widespread tendency to become (though never unambiguously) the emotional center of many horror films.

That the "return of the repressed" formula does not exhaustively explain all horror movies was demonstrated already in the '70s/'80s by what seems now in retrospect the period's greatest achievement, George Romero's Living Dead trilogy. It has not, I think, been sufficiently recognized that the meaning and function of the zombies change radically from film to film. It is consistent, in fact, in only one way, that the zombies constitute a challenge to the humans, not merely to survive but to change. But the nature of the challenge differs from film to film.

Of the three, *Night of the Living Dead* (1968) corresponds most closely to the psychoanalytic formula, the first zombie emerging not merely from a graveyard but from the precariously repressed familial tensions between brother and sister, tensions derived directly and explicitly from the structures of the nuclear family. Having established this, however, in the first few minutes, Romero relegates the zombies to a subservient and functional position; though powerful because there are so many, they quite lack the dynamic, rebellious energy of other, more characteristic, monsters of the period: the baby of *It's Alive* (1974), Danielle (Margot Kidder) of *Sisters* (1973), Regan (Linda Blair) of *The Exorcist* (1973), or, going further back, the Irena (Simone Simon) of *Cat People* (1942), the Tootie (Margaret O'Brien) of *Meet Me in St. Louis* (1944), or the Erl-king of Goethe and Schubert—whose function is to *demand recognition*. The zombies destroy all the main characters (the existing nuclear family, the "young couple" who represent the future nuclear family) but one simply because they are incapable of change and will merely repeat the repressive patterns of the past. The exception, the film's hero and solitary black, hence an outsider, survives the zombies but, in the film's final irony, is shot down by the sheriff's posse.

The theme is carried over into *Dawn of the Dead* (1978), but with an important difference: the zombies of the shopping mall are the products of consumer capitalism, drawn back to the mall that embodies their utmost desires, the pitiful nonsatisfactions of material possessions by which their culture has taught them to live. The totally passive (literally traumatized) woman of *Night* is transformed into the active and increasingly resourceful heroine of *Dawn*, who learns in the course of the film to free herself from male domination and all the social formations (marriage, traditional family, dependency) that support it, taking over the film's primary symbol of masculine power, the helicopter. Finally, in *Day of the Dead* (1985), the trilogy's lamentably unrecognized crown ("Easily the least of the series," according to Leonard Maltin's lamentably influential *Movie and Video Guide*), at once the darkest, most desperate, and ultimately most exhilarating, of the three films, the woman becomes the central figure, the heart of sanity in a world of masculinity gone mad.

I suspect that the almost total incomprehension (more precisely, refusal of comprehension) with which *Day of the Dead* has been received is simply the result of its late date: by 1985 we had already entered the era of hysterical masculinity that countered the radical feminism of the '70s, Stallone and Schwarzenegger were already major presences, and the reactionary horror movie had already fully established itself. No one wanted to hear about how science and militarism were male-dominated, masculinist institutions threatening to destroy life on the planet (*Day*'s essential theme, even more timely today than it was then, though no one seems willing to pay attention anymore). Though made by a man, it stands (and will probably be recognized as, when it is too late) one of the great feminist movies. It is also, for me, the last great American horror film.

Are significant horror films being made outside America? In the East, in Italy? I am not qualified to answer this question, though it seems necessary to raise it. The Italian horror films of Bava and Argento have their defenders; the few I have seen struck me as obsessively preoccupied with violence against women, dramatized in particularly grotesque images. One European film perhaps qualifies, though it must be seen as marginal to the genre: Michael Haneke's profoundly disturbing and troubling *Funny Games* (1997). Although it barely evokes the supernatural, its relationship to the horror film becomes apparent quite early on.

Two young men enter a bourgeois household on a pretext, then swiftly proceed to make prisoners of the family (father, mother, young son), and subsequently humiliate, torment, and finally kill all three, before going off cheerfully to visit the nearest neighbors for the same purpose. No obvious "explanation" of the young men is offered: they are not noticeably impoverished or underprivileged (rather the contrary); we learn nothing of their background so cannot see them as victims of the conventional nuclear family structure; they appear to humiliate, torment, and kill just for the pleasure of it. One is clearly dominant, and he is credited with the film's only hint of supernatural powers, the ability to rewind the film when things go wrong and replay a scene to his own specifications. Are they "the return of the repressed"? The worst the bourgeois couple can be accused of is complacency, which is what Hitchcock said *The Birds* (1963) is about, and the couple's punishment (if that is how it is to be read) is only a step worse than that meted out to Melanie Daniels (Tippi Hedren).

Funny Games can also be read (and this links it thematically to Haneke's other work) as suggesting that our civilization, by dehumanizing its inhabitants, intrinsically produces psychopaths who therefore require no further explanation. This is one of the most disturbing films I have ever seen (no surprise, really, that it is probably the most widely hated film in modern cinema, critics reacting to it with such an intense resentment of what it does to them that it becomes a tribute to the film's power). Haneke allows his chief "monster" an intimate relationship with the audience, inviting us into the film with his knowing look into the camera, implicating us in the violence (which is for the most part more psychological than physical): do we want to punish this affluent and complacent, yet generally pleasant and harmless, couple? But, simultaneously, we are implicated in an opposed violence, the deliberate tormenting of helpless people reaching a point where we would like to leap into the movie and kill the two young men with our own hands. The film's great danger, it seems to me, is that it might (given that the tormentors appear inexplicable and therefore unreformable) be read as advocating capital punishment.

Aside from *Day of the Dead*, is there any American horror movie made since 1980 that could be championed as any sort of radical statement about our impossible (so-called) civilization? I ask the question seriously, hoping it may get answered in this anthology (for myself, the only possible candidate is Neil Jordan's fascinating and underrated *In Dreams* [1998]).[79] Or is the genre as "living dead" as Romero's zombies, who, while immensely powerful, have nothing to offer but a kind of subhuman nothingness and survive without any real life? The genre's deterioration is easy to chart. Around 1980 it moves crucially from the release of repressed (and therefore terrifying) energies to "teenagers endlessly punished for having sex"—and why has this perversion of the genre been so popular with teenagers? Presumably because, while it is exactly what, at their age, they ought to be doing (besides protesting vigorously about almost everything happening in the dominant culture), their parents make them feel guilty.

From there to the "spoof" is an easy leap (about two inches), stupidity (of the characters, of the films themselves) being already generically inherent. Actually, the "spoof" horror film (unnecessary to give titles, I think) simply carries the "slaughter of sexual teenagers" '80s subdivision of the genre one step further: all those naughty teenagers can now enjoy themselves without taking their punishment seriously. Just one small problem: in all the films I can recall (and they have fused themselves into one horrible confused image of sex and slaughter) the teenagers hardly ever achieve orgasm. The popularity of these films with teenagers is vastly more interesting, and even more depressing, than the films themselves ever are. Given that all these films operate on a very low level of artistic or thematic interest, it is (I suppose) still possible to make certain distinctions. The original *Halloween*, which had the dubious distinction of initiating the entire cycle, and is therefore of historic interest, was a well-made and effective film; the entire Friday the 13th series fully deserves to go, with Jason, to hell; the Nightmare on Elm Street films have a marginally more interesting monster and (especially the first) a certain flair in invention and design. What more can one say?

(2004)

Notes

In Memoriam: Michael Reeves

1. Tom Milne, "*Witchfinder General,*" *Monthly Film Bulletin*, no. 414 (July 1968): 100.

The Shadow Worlds of Jacques Tourneur

2. Michel Mourlet, "Apologie de la violence" [In defense of violence], *Cahiers du cinéma,* no. 107 (May 1960), 24. Reprinted in *Cahiers du Cinéma, the 1960s: New Wave, New Cinema, Reevaluating Hollywood*, ed. Jim Hillier (Cambridge, MA: Harvard University Press, 1986), 133.
3. George A. Huaco, *The Sociology of Film Art* (New York: Basic Books, 1965), 49.
4. "Propos: Jacques Tourneur," *Positif*, no. 132 (November 1971): 10, 14.
5. DeWitt Bodeen, "Val Lewton," *Films in Review* 14, no. 4 (April 1963): 218.
6. "Propos: Jacques Tourneur," 15–16.

Disreputable Genre

7. Film Guide, *Sight and Sound* 42, no. 1 (Winter 1972/73): 62.

Return of the Repressed

8. Juliet Mitchell, *Psychoanalysis and Feminism* (New York: Pantheon, 1974), 6.

Race with the Devil

9. Editors of *Cahiers du cinéma*, "*Young Mr. Lincoln* de John Ford," *Cahiers du cinéma,* no. 223 (August 1970): 29–47. Translated by Helen Lackner and Diana Matias and reprinted in *Screen* 13, no. 3 (1972): 5–44. [Since then it has been reprinted in numerous anthologies of film theory—Ed.]
10. Stephen Heath, "*Jaws*, Ideology and Film Theory," *Framework*, no. 4 (Autumn 1976): 27. Heath's essay is reprinted in *Film Theory and Criticism*, ed. Bill Nichols (Berkeley: University of California Press, 1985), 2: 509–14.

An Introduction to the American Horror Film

11 See Andrew Britton, "The Ideology of *Screen*," *Movie*, no. 26 (Winter 1978–79), 2–28. Reprinted in *Britton on Film: The Complete Film Criticism of Andrew Britton*, ed. Barry Keith Grant (Detroit: Wayne State University Press, 2009), 394–434.

12 Gad Horowitz, *Repression: Basic and Surplus Repression in Psychoanalytic Theory* (Toronto: University of Toronto Press, 1977).

13 Roland Barthes, "Myth Today," in *Mythologies*, trans. Annette Lavers (New York: Hill and Wang, 1977), 151.

14 A. P. Rossiter, *Angel with Horns* (London: Longmans, 1961), 1–23.

15 David Pirie, *A Heritage of Horror: The English Gothic Cinema, 1946–1972* (New York: Avon, 1973).

16 Robin Wood, "Images of Childhood," in *Personal Views*, rev. ed. (Detroit: Wayne State University Press, 2006), 201–5. [See also "The American Family Comedy: From *Meet Me in St. Louis* to *The Texas Chainsaw Massacre*" in this volume—Ed.]

17 Andrew Britton, "*Mandingo*," *Movie*, no. 22 (Spring 1976): 1–22. Reprinted in *Britton on Film*, 241–61.

18 William Shakespeare, *King Lear*, act 4, scene 2.

19 This article owes a considerable debt to the work of Tony Williams. Tony has been writing an MA thesis on the horror film under my supervision, and in the last two years we have exchanged so many ideas that it would no longer be possible to sort out which was whose.

20 Jonathan Rosenbaum, "*Halloween*," *Take One*, January 1979, pp. 8–9.

21 "And my whole philosophy of movies is that movies are not intellectual, they are not ideas, that is done in literature and all sorts of other forms. Movies are *emotional*, an audience should cry or laugh or get scared. I think the audience should project into the film, into a character, into a situation, and react." Williams, "The Mechanics of Repression," in *The American Nightmare*, ed. Robin Wood and Richard Lippe (Toronto: Festival of Festivals, 1979), 67. The comment appeared originally in Todd McCarthy, "Trick and Treat," *Film Comment* 16, no. 1 (January–February 1980): 17–24.

The Dark Mirror

22 [At this point in the earlier version of this essay in *Film Comment* (May–June 1976), the following footnote was included:

The speeded-up film Murnau used for the coach demands some comment. It is certainly one of the aspects of the film that now look most dated—slightly ridiculous, in fact, and an obstacle to our total involvement. Yet it is given added point, I think, by that unearthly moment where the film goes into negative. In negative, the coach is travelling at normal speed. It is as if we were being shown the "underworld" from two viewpoints. From ours it looks unnatural—the speeded-up coach; from its own (taking the use of negative as a simple metaphor for inversion, a "turning inside-out"), everything goes at normal speed, the unnatural becomes natural. The objection to this interpretation is that, for it to stand up logically, either speeded-up motion or negative should have been used consistently (perhaps both in alternation) throughout the vampire scenes. I partly grant this objection but raise the counterobjection that this would have become absurdly cumbersome and awkward. I don't think it is invalid for Murnau, having established his effect by concise poetic metaphor, to move back to normal film and assume the point has been taken.—Ed.]

23 [At this point in the earlier version of this essay in *Film Comment*, the following footnote was included: "Given the admiration of French critics and cineastes for Murnau's film, one can perhaps speak here of direct influence—an impression confirmed by Cocteau's use in *Orpheus* (*Orphée*, 1950) of negative for the car journeys to the underworld."—Ed.]

24 Lotte Eisner, *The Haunted Screen* (Berkeley: University of California Press, 1973), 109–13.

25 André Bazin, "The Evolution of the Language of Cinema," in *The New Wave*, ed. Peter Graham (New York: Doubleday, 1968), 30. The essay also appears in a somewhat different translation in André Bazin, *What Is Cinema?*, ed. and trans. Hugh Gray (Berkeley: University of California Press, 1967), 1: 23–40.

26 D. H. Lawrence, "Snake," in *The Complete Poems of D. H. Lawrence*, ed. Vivian de Sola Pinto and Warren Robert (New York: Viking Press, 1964), 2: 349–51.

27 Raymond Durgnat, *Franju* (Berkeley: University of California Press, 1968), 24–25.

Sisters

28 Roland Barthes, *Mythologies*, trans. Annette Lavers (New York: Hill and Wang, 1977). See esp. "Operation Margarine," 41–42; and "Striptease," 84–87.

World of Gods and Monsters

29 [See "An Introduction to the American Horror Film."—Ed.]
30 Todd McCarthy, "The Exorcism of *The Heretic*," *Film Comment* 13, no. 5 (September–October 1977): 48–49.
31 D. H. Lawrence, "Snake," in *The Complete Poems of D. H. Lawrence*, ed. Vivian de Sola Pinto and Warren Robert (New York: Viking Press, 1964), 2:349–51.
32 Editors of *Cahiers du cinéma*, "Young Mr. Lincoln de John Ford," *Cahiers du cinéma* no. 223 (August 1970): 29–47. Translated by Helen Lackner and Diana Matias and reprinted in *Screen* 13, no. 3 (1972): 5–44.
33 Hege, "*God Told Me To*," *Variety*, December 1, 1972, 38.
34 Tony Williams, "The Mechanics of Repression," in *The American Nightmare*, ed. Robin Wood and Richard Lippe (Toronto: Festival of Festivals, 1979), 67–73.
35 D. H. Lawrence, *Lady Chatterley's Lover* (London: Heinemann, 1961), 148.

The American Family Comedy

36 See Roland Barthes, *Mythologies*, trans. Annette Lavers (New York: Hill and Wang, 1977).
37 Norman O. Brown, *Life Against Death* (Middletown, CT: Wesleyan University Press, 1959).
38 Barthes, *Mythologies*. See esp. "Operation Margarine," 41–42; and "Striptease," 84–87.
39 Robin Wood, "Return of the Repressed," *Film Comment* 14, no. 4 (July–August 1978): 25–32, and included in "An Introduction to the American Horror Film," in *The American Nightmare: Essays on the Horror Film*, ed. Robin Wood and Richard Lippe (Toronto: Festival of Festivals, 1979). See pp. 82–110 here.

Neglected Nightmares

40 Roger Ebert, "Guilty Pleasures," *Film Comment* 14, no. 4 (July–August 1978): 51.
41 John Fraser, *Violence in the Arts* (New York: Cambridge University Press, 1974).

42 Terry Curtis Fox, "Fully Female," *Film Comment* 12, no. 6 (November–December 1976): 46–50.

43 Robin Wood, "Return of the Repressed," *Film Comment* 14, no. 4 (July–August 1978): 25–32; "Gods and Monsters," *Film Comment* 14, no. 5 (September–October 1978): 19–25. [Both are included in this volume.—Ed.]

44 [*There's Always Vanilla* is now available in the DVD box set *George A. Romero: Between Night and Dawn* from Arrow Films (DVD AV108, 2017).—Ed.]

Burying the Undead

45 Only the Browning version tries to "rationalize" Renfield by having him—instead of Jonathan—go to Transylvania, where he is vampirized by the count.

46 The recognition is not shared, at least to the same extent, by the Browning and Fisher versions.

47 Bram Stoker, *Dracula* (New York: Penguin, 1979), 333. Subsequent references to the novel are from this edition and appear parenthetically in the text.

48 Herbert Marcuse, *Eros and Civilization: A Philosophical Inquiry into Freud* (Boston: Beacon Press, 1966), 37.

49 I use the term somewhat loosely, perhaps, since no actual verbal error or substitution of one word for another takes place. Yet the essence of the "Freudian slip" is certainly here: the speaker's words betray a significant slip between conscious and unconscious intention.

50 See my essay "The Dark Mirror: Murnau's *Nosferatu*," in *The American Nightmare: Essays on the Horror Film*, ed. Robin Wood and Richard Lippe (Toronto: Festival of Festivals, 1979), 43–39 [and this volume—Ed.].

51 André Bazin, "The Evolution of the Language of Cinema," in *The New Wave*, ed. Peter Graham (New York: Doubleday, 1968), 30.

52 "Film Guide: *Dracula*," *Sight and Sound* 48, no. 4 (Autumn 1979): 268.

Cronenberg

53 William Beard and Piers Handling, "The Interview," and John Harkness, "The World, the Flesh, and David Cronenberg," both in *The Shape of Rage: The Films of David Cronenberg*, ed. Piers Handling (Toronto: Academy of Canadian Cinema, 1983), 159–98 and 87–97, respectively. Harkness's piece was originally published in *Cinema Canada* 97 (June 1983): 23–25. Page references in the text are to the reprint in *The Shape of Rage*.

54 Robin Wood, "New Cinema at Edinburgh," *Film Comment* 11, no. 6 (November–December 1975): 26.
55 Roland Barthes, "Myth Today," in *Mythologies*, trans. Annette Lavers (New York: Hill and Wang, 1977), 138.
56 Harkness, with what may seem to many callous opportunism, finds my remarks on *Shivers* given "a darkly Cronenbergian irony" by the AIDS epidemic. If this has any point in relation to the film, it is presumably to imply that *Shivers* is somehow validated by its prophecy "coming true." A film (of whatever genre) must be judged according to such features as tone, attitude, imagery; a work of science fiction is no more validated by "coming true" than it is invalidated if it doesn't. To suggest that *Shivers* is some kind of anticipatory film about an actual human tragedy can only make it appear even more distasteful than it already is.

King Meets Cronenberg

57 See previous essay ["Cronenberg: A Dissenting View," in this volume—Ed.].
58 Stephen King, *The Dead Zone* (New York: Viking Press, 1979): 413–14. [The passage is in a letter written by Johnny Smith, the protagonist—Ed.]

Cat and Dog

59 See Stephen King, *Danse Macabre* (New York: Everest House, 1981), chap. 1.
60 Stephen King, *The Mist*, in *Skeleton Crew* (New York: Signet, 1985), 26–27.
61 I develop this in an analysis of Scorsese's film in *Hollywood from Vietnam to Reagan . . . and Beyond* (New York: Columbia University Press, 2003), chap. 12.
62 Stephen King [Richard Bachman], *Thinner* (New York: Simon & Schuster, 1984), 54.
63 Stephen King, introduction to *Skeleton Crew*, 23.
64 Stephen King, *Pet Sematary* (New York: Signet, 1983), 223–24.
65 For a much fuller discussion of this, see Andrew Britton's essay "The Devil, Probably: The Symbolism of Evil," in *The American Nightmare*, ed. Robin Wood and Richard Lippe (Toronto: Festival of Festivals, 1979), 34–42, and reprinted in *Britton on Film: The Complete Film Criticism of Andrew Britton*, ed. Barry Keith Grant (Detroit: Wayne State University Press, 2009), 64–73.
66 The final essay (by Burstyn herself) in Varda Burstyn's anthology *Women Against Censorship* (Vancouver: Douglas and McIntyre, 1985), "Beyond

Despair: Positive Strategies," 152–80, offers magnificent suggestions as to where such roads might lead.

Notes for a Reading of *I Walked with a Zombie*

67 An example ready to hand is an essay on *The Pirate* (1948) by David Rodowick, "Vision, Desire, and the Film-Text," in *camera obscura*, no. 6 (Fall 1980): 55–89. Extreme but not altogether untypical is the author's definition of the fiction film as a "textual mode which privileges the scopic and the auditory." Translation: "Films are seen and heard."

68 See, in particular, Julia Lesage's analysis of *La Regle du Jeu*, "S/Z and Film Criticism," preceded by Judith Mayne's explication of the codes, in *Jump Cut*, no. 12–13 (Winter 1976–77): 45–51. http://ejumpcut.org/archive/jc55.2013/LesageRulesOfGame/index.html.

69 Roland Barthes, *S/Z: An Essay*, trans. Richard Miller (New York: Hill and Wang, 1974), 19.

70 For those unfamiliar with Ophuls's film, the content of the first shot is as follows. A rainy night in a cobbled city street; a horse-drawn carriage is approaching in long shot; the caption "Vienna, about 1900" appears over the image; a clock is striking two. As the carriage draws near and stops outside iron gates, the camera moves in so as to frame the man who gets out (Stefan, played by Louis Jourdan) in the rectangle of the far window. Brief dialogue with the two men who remain inside the carriage: "So you're going through with it?" Stefan (shrugs): "Why not?" "Well, for one thing I hear he's an excellent shot." Stefan: "Oh, it's not so much that I mind getting killed. But you know how hard it is for me to get up in the morning." One of the men tells him that they will return at five o'clock, adding, "And if I were you, no more cognac." The carriage continues on its way, and we see Stefan approaching the gates.

71 See Leavis's series of essays on the novel as dramatic poem in *Scrutiny* in the 1940s and 1950s, and F. R. Leavis, *D. H. Lawrence: Novelist* (London: Chatto and Windus, 1955).

72 The "Grande Syntagmatique" was Metz's attempt to construct a syntax of the narrative film, specifying the possible types of sequence (or syntagma). Its usefulness is very limited (problems arise almost every time one tries to apply it), but it has provided a rough means of breaking a film down into its "autonomous segments." Only a few of Metz's categories are relevant to *I Walked with*

a Zombie: the scene is a sequence in which the action is perfectly continuous in time and space, without ellipses; the ordinary sequence is like the scene but omits stretches of time unnecessary to the narrative (e.g., the walk through the cane fields, segment 28). These two syntagmas account for most of the segments into which I have divided the film. There is also a descriptive syntagma (no. 6), a sequence of shots outside any clear chronological progress establishing a location, etc.; a sequence shot (no. 26) in which an action that might normally require a sequence is filmed in a single take; and an alternate syntagma (I prefer "alternating sequence," no. 31), in which two actions taking place in different locations are intercut.

73 The diegesis is the complete fictional world created within the film, its illusion of reality, including, for example, the action, the characters, the settings, atmosphere, realistic detail . . .

74 Raymond Bellour, "To Segment/To Analyze," in *The Analysis of Film* (Bloomington: Indiana University Press, 2000), esp. 193–97.

The Woman's Nightmare

75 J. Hoberman, "Spielbergism and Its Discontents," *Village Voice*, July 3–9, 1985, 48–49.

76 For Sirk's comments on the endings of his films, see Jon Halliday, *Sirk on Sirk* (London: Martin Secker and Warburg / British Film Institute, 1971), chap. 5.

Nosferatu

77 André Bazin, "The Evolution of the Language of Cinema," in *The New Wave*, ed. Peter Graham (New York: Doubleday, 1968), 30.

What Lies Beneath?

78 [*Britton on Film: The Complete Film Criticism of Andrew Britton*, ed. Barry Keith Grant (Detroit: Wayne State University Press, 2009), was published subsequently. Wood contributed the introduction, "Andrew Britton and the Future of Film Criticism"—Ed.]

79 [This essay was originally published as the preface to the anthology *Horror Film and Psychoanalysis: Freud's Worst Nightmares*, ed. Steven Jay Schneider (New York: Cambridge University Press, 2004), xiii-xviii—Ed.]

Acknowledgments

This book would not have been possible without the cooperation of Richard Lippe, partner and collaborator of Robin Wood for many years, and Annie Martin, senior acquisitions editor for Wayne State University Press, whose support for reprinting Wood's important film criticism has been unwavering. Ian Gordon and the library staff at the James A. Gibson Library at Brock University helped track down and complete some of the more elusive endnotes. Rob Macmorine, media technician in the Department of Communication, Popular Culture and Film at Brock, provided the frame enlargements. At the press, Carrie Downes Teefey, senior production editor, and Rachel Ross, senior designer, provided their usual expertise. Sal Borriello contributed the careful copyediting. Thanks also to John Anderson, Olaf Hedling, Jill Hollis, Daniel Lindvall, Christopher Sharrett, and Heather Szabo, each of whom helped in different ways. Dan Barnowski deserves special mention for selflessly providing his expertise in scanning and digitizing all the files. Dan, too, has learned much from Wood's writings over the years and has been happy to have contributed to this book in return. To all of these people I owe my gratitude, as do the many readers of Robin Wood's work. Finally, I am grateful to all the publishers and editors who have kindly allowed his writings to be reprinted here.

"Psychoanalysis of *Psycho*" was originally published in French as "Psychoanalyse du *Psycho*" in *Cahiers du cinéma*, no. 113 (1960): 1–6, copyright © 1960 *Cahiers du cinéma*. The English text reprinted here is the translation by Deborah Thomas that appeared in *Movie: A Journal of Film Criticism*, no. 2 (May 2011), warwick.ac.uk/fac/arts/film/movie/pastissues/, an online film journal, and it is reprinted with the kind permission of *Cahiers du cinéma*, *Movie*, and the translator.

The following essays originally appeared in *Movie* and are reprinted with the kind permission of Jill Hollis and Cameron and Hollis Publishers:

"In Memoriam: Michael Reeves," *Movie*, no. 17 (1969–70): 2–6.
"*Race with the Devil*," *Movie*, no. 23 (Winter 1976–77): 23–26.
"Larry Cohen Interview," *Movie*, nos. 31–32 (Winter 1986): 118–28.

The following essays appeared originally in *Film Comment* and are reprinted here with the permission of *Film Comment* and the Film Society of Lincoln Center:

"The Shadow Worlds of Jacques Tourneur," *Film Comment* 8, no. 2 (Summer 1972): 64–70.
"The Dark Mirror: Murnau's *Nosferatu*," *Film Comment* 12, no. 3 (May–June 1976): 5–9. This essay was later included in *The American Nightmare: Essays on the Horror Film*, ed. Robin Wood and Richard Lippe (Toronto: Festival of Festivals, 1979).
"Return of the Repressed," *Film Comment* 14, no. 4 (July–August 1978): 25–32. This essay was later included in *The American Nightmare* (1979).
"Gods and Monsters: The Private Films of Larry Cohen," *Film Comment* 14, no. 5 (September–October 1978): 19–25. This essay was later included in *The American Nightmare* and as part of chapter 6 ("Normality and Monsters") in *Hollywood from Vietnam to Reagan* (New York: Columbia University Press, 1986).
"Neglected Nightmares," *Film Comment* 16, no. 2 (March–April 1980): 25–32. This essay was included as part of chapter 8 ("Normality and Monsters") in *Hollywood from Vietnam to Reagan*.
"Fresh Meat," *Film Comment* 44, no. 1 (January–February 2008): 28–31.

The following reviews appeared in *Monthly Film Bulletin* and are reprinted with permission of the British Film Institute:

"*Death Line*," *Monthly Film Bulletin* 40, no. 468 (January 1, 1973): 6.
"*The Creeping Flesh*," *Monthly Film Bulletin* 40, no. 468 (January 1, 1973): 25.
"*Un Hacha para la Luna de Miel* (*Blood Brides*)," *Monthly Film Bulletin* 40, no. 468 (January 1, 1973): 25.

The following pieces appeared originally in *Times Educational Supplement*:

"Disreputable Genre," *Times Educational Supplement*, December 15, 1972, 15.
"Return of the Repressed," *Times Educational Supplement*, December 31, 1976, 12.
"Yet Another Terrible Child," *Times Educational Supplement*, February 11, 1977, 86.

"The Most Horrible Horror Film Ever?" appeared in the *Village Voice*, November 15, 1973. It is reprinted with the kind permission of the *Village Voice*.

The following appeared in *The American Nightmare: Essays on the Horror Film*, ed. Robin Wood and Richard Lippe (Toronto: Festival of Festivals, 1979), copyright © 1979 Festival of Festivals, and they are reprinted courtesy of the Toronto International Film Festival:

"An Introduction to the American Horror Film," in *The American Nightmare: Essays on the Horror Film*, ed. Robin Wood and Richard Lippe (Toronto: Festival of Festivals, 1979), 7–28.
"Der Erlkönig: The Ambiguities of Horror," in *The American Nightmare: Essays on the Horror Film*, 29–33.
"The Dark Mirror: Murnau's *Nosferatu*," in *The American Nightmare: Essays on the Horror Film*, 43–49.
"*Sisters*," in *The American Nightmare: Essays on the Horror Film*, 59–64. Also reprinted in *Movie*, nos. 27–28 (Winter 1980–Spring 1981): 50–54.
"World of Gods and Monsters: The Films of Larry Cohen," in *The American Nightmare: Essays on the Horror Film*, 75–86.
"Apocalypse Now: Notes on the Living Dead," in *The American Nightmare: Essays on the Horror Film*, 91–97.

"The American Family Comedy from *Meet Me in St. Louis* to *The Texas Chainsaw Massacre*" was published originally in *Wide Angle* 3, no. 2 (1979): 5–11, copyright © 1979 Athens International Film Festival (copublished with the Ohio University Department of Film). Reprinted with the permission of the Athens International Film Festival.

The following appeared originally in *Canadian Forum*:

"'Art' and Alligators," *Canadian Forum*, August 1981, 40–41.
"King Meets Cronenberg," *Canadian Forum*, January 1984, 35–36
"Dead End," *Canadian Forum*, January 1985, 41–42.

"Burying the Undead: The Use and Obsolescence of Count Dracula" was first published in *Mosaic* 16, nos. 1–2 (Winter/Spring 1983): 175–87, copyright © 1983 by *Mosaic: An Interdisciplinary Critical Journal*. Reprinted by permission of *Mosaic*.

"Returning the Look: *Eyes of a Stranger*" appeared originally as "Beauty Bests the Beast" in *American Film* 8, no. 10 (September 1983): 63–65, copyright © 1983 American Film Institute and reprinted by permission. This essay was retitled and reprinted in *Canadian Forum*, June–July 1982, 47–48, and in *American Horrors*, ed. Gregory Waller (Urbana: University of Illinois Press, 1987), 79–85, and also was included as the third section of chapter 8 ("Papering the Cracks: Fantasy and Ideology in the Reagan Era") in *Hollywood from Vietnam to Reagan* (New York: Columbia University Press, 1986).

"Cronenberg: A Dissenting View" was first published in the anthology *The Shape of Rage: The Films of David Cronenberg*, ed. Piers Handling (New York: New York Zoetrope, 1983), 115–35, copyright © 1983 Academy of Canadian Cinema & Television. Reprinted by permission of the Academy of Canadian Cinema & Television.

The following essays were first published in *CineAction* and are reprinted with the permission of *CineAction*:

"Cat and Dog: Lewis Teague's Stephen King Movies," *CineAction*, no. 2 (Fall 1985): 39–45.
"Notes for a Reading of *I Walked with a Zombie*," *CineAction*, nos. 3–4 (January 1986): 6–20.

"The Woman's Nightmare: Masculinity in *Day of the Dead*" *CineAction*, no. 6 (Summer/Fall 1986): 45–49. This essay was also included as chapter 14 in *Hollywood from Vietnam to Reagan . . . and Beyond* (New York: Columbia University Press, 2003).

The following were published in the *International Dictionary of Films and Filmmakers*, ed. Sara Pendergast and Tom Pendergast, 4th edition, vol. 1, *Films*, and vol. 2, *Filmmakers* (Detroit: St. James Press, 2000), copyright © 2001 Gale, a part of Cengage Learning, Inc. Reproduced by permission.

"*Nosferatu*"
"George Romero"
"*Silence of the Lambs*"
"Brian De Palma"

"Revenge Is Sweet: The Bitterness of *Audition*" appeared in *Film International* 2, no. 7 (2004): 23–27, and is reprinted with the permission of the editors of *Film International*.

"What Lies Beneath?" was first published as the foreword to *Horror Film and Psychoanalysis: Freud's Worst Nightmares*, ed. Steven Jay Schneider (New York: Cambridge University Press, 2004), xiii–xviii, copyright © Cambridge University Press 2004, and it is reprinted here by permission of Cambridge University Press.

The cover image from George Romero's *Martin* (1978) is copyright © 1977 The MRK Group, Inc., and used with the kind permission of Richard Rubinstein.

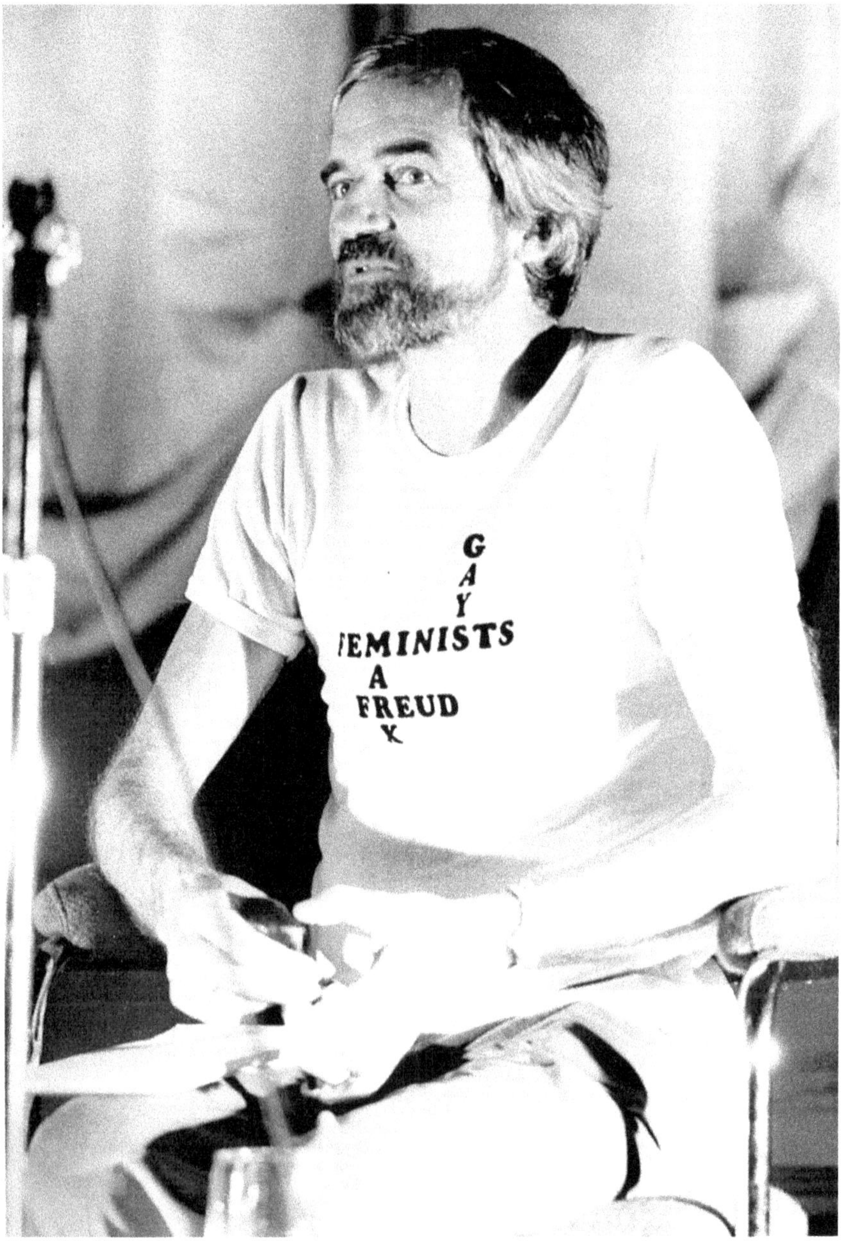

GAY
FEMINISTS
MARX
FREUD

Index

Italicized page numbers indicate photographs.

Age d'Or, L', 219
Alice Adams, 171
Alice Doesn't Live Here Anymore, 139, 172–73
Alien, 80, 107–10
Allen, Sian Barbara, 47
Alligator, 203
All the King's Men, 345
All the President's Men, 155, 157
Altman, Robert, 63
American Graffiti, 350
Andrews, Nigel, 41
Animal House, 350
Antichrist, The, 57
Argento, Dario, 403
Arkin, Adam, 349
Arkin, Alan, 349
Arkoff, Samuel L., 333–34, 344–47
Assault on Precinct 13 (1976), 80, 106, 159, 259
Audition, 386–97, *389*
authorship, 12, 25, 67–68, 255–56

Badham, John, 118, 205–9, 213, 215, 218–20, 361, 363
Baker, Carroll, 347
Balzac, Honoré de, 282–83
Bancroft, Anne, 48
Barrymore, Drew, 277–78
Barthes, Roland, 77, 139, 172, 235, 282–90
Bass, Saul, 4
Bava, Mario, 45–46, 403
Bazin, André, 125, 217, 362
Beast with Five Fingers, The, 83
Beckett, Samuel, 101
Bedlam, 25
Bell, Book and Candle, 278, 279
Bellour, Raymond, 312
Ben, 147
Bergman, Ingmar, 120, 182–84
Berlin Express, 26
Bertolucci, Bernardo, 195
Beyond the Forest, 84
Big Heat, The, 187
Birds, The, 57–58, 89–90, 143, 157, 161–62, 403
Black Caesar, 143, 148–49, 150, 333–34, 335, 336
Black Christmas, 106, *196*
Blackman, Honor, 347
Blade Runner, 241
Blake, William, 62, 95, 248
blaxploitation, 148
Blind Terror, 47
Blood Brides, 45–46

Blood on Satan's Claw, The, 41, 53
Blow Out, 261–62, 369, 370
Boam, Jeffrey, 253
Bodeen, DeWitt, 28
Body Double, 261–64, 369, 370
Body Snatcher, The, 26
Bone, 143,144, 146–48, 150–51, 331, 335
Bonfire of the Vanities, The, 371
Bons Debarras, Les, 201–4
Bosch, Hieronymus, 17
Brand, Neville, 188
Brats, 175
Bride of Frankenstein, 401
Bringing Up Baby, 29, 30, 80, 278
Britton, Andrew, 96, 97, 157, 194, 399–400
Brontë, Emily, 219
Brood, The, 104–5, 234, 244, 246–48, 247
Brown, Norman O., 172, 173
Browning, Tod, 119, 205, 411n45, 411n46
buddy films, 68, 71, 72, 168–69,
Buñuel, Luis, 83,100
Burr, Raymond, 226
Burstyn, Varda, 412–13n66

Cabinet of Dr. Caligari, The, 87, 88, 130, *131*, 223
California Split, 68
Canyon Passage, 26–27
Car, The, 89
Carlito's Way, 372
Carpenter, John, 106–7, 159, 221, 244, 259–60, 277

Carradine, David, 353, 355
Carrie (1976), 63–65, 89, 139, 141, 144, 145, 178, 264, 265
Castle of the Living Dead, 11–15, 17–18, 23
Casualties of War, 371
Cathy's Curse, 89
Cat People (1942), 25, 27–35, *29*, *34*, 37, 38, 80, 92–93, 110, 278, 402
Cat's Eye, 277–79
Chitty Chitty Bang Bang, 120
Chosen, The. See Holocaust 2000.
Christine, 277
Cimino, Michael, 187, 241
Clark, Bob, 181, 195–97
Clark, Candy, 355
Close Encounters of the Third Kind, 177
Cocteau, Jean, 124, 409n23, 194
Cohen, Larry, 81, 134, 141–60, 192, 194–95, 198, 234, 239, 321–59
Cohn, Harry, 345
Coleridge, Samuel Taylor, 120
comedy, 67, 68, 171–79
Conformist, The, 195
Conqueror Worm, The. See Witchfinder General
Conrad, Joseph, 120
Constantine, Eddie, 342
Conway, Tom, 27
Coppola, Francis Ford, 373
Coquillon, John, 12
Craven, Wes, 181–90, 191, 195, 233, 399
Crawford, Broderick, 143, 345–46
Crazies, The (1973), 164–65, 166, 167, 168, 195, 198–99, 373

422 - Index

Creeping Flesh, The, 43–44
Creepshow, 373
Crimes of the Future, 248–50, 251, 252
Cronenberg, David, 104–6, 181, 191, 231–52, 253–57, 265
Crowther, Bosley, 351
Cruising, 235
Cujo, 256, 265–66, *273–77*, 278, 279
Cunningham, Sean S., 222
Curse of the Cat People, The, 111
Curse of the Demon, 26

Dailey, Dan, 143, 345
Damien: Omen II, 141
Dark Half, The, 373
Dark Star, 106, 259
Davis, Sammy Jr., 333
Dawn of the Dead (1968), 102, 161–69, 192, 194, 197, 198–99, 246, 319–22, 326–27, 373–74, 378–79, 401–2
Day of the Animals, 89
Day of the Dead, 161, 319–29, *323*, *326*, *327*, 373–75, 378–79, 401–3, 404
Days of Glory, 26
Dead of Night (1974), 181, 186, 196
Dead Zone, The, 242, 253–57, *256*, 265
Deathdream. See *Dead of Night*
Death Line. See *Raw Meat*
Death Trap. See *Eaten Alive*
De Laurentiis, Dino, 277, 356
De Niro, Robert, 359
De Palma, Brian, 63–65, 80, 134–39, 141, 142–45, 159, 181, 191, 192, 221, 225, 233–34, 261–64, 265, 369–72, 399
De Simone, Tom, 224

Deer Hunter, The, 187–88, 235, 291
Demme, Jonathan, 366–67
Demon. See *God Told Me To*
Diary of the Dead, 377–83, *380*, *381*
Dietrich, Marlene, 139
Diner, 350
disaster films, 61
Donne, John, 32
Don't Go in the House, 201
Dracula (1931), 92, 205, 411n45, 411n46
Dracula (1979), 118, 205–9, *207*, 213, 215, 218–20, *219*
Dracula's Daughter, 92
Dressed to Kill (1980), 221, 224–25, 261–62, *263*, 264, 369
Dreyer, Carl, 121
Dr. No, 351
Drums along the Mohawk, 71, 78
Duel in the Sun, 291
Duggan, Andrew, 331
Duke, Patty, 48
Durgnat, Raymond, 130
Dwyer, Hilary, 22

Easy Living, 26
Easy Rider, 68
Eaten Alive, 101, 188
Ebert, Roger, 181–82
Eisner, Lotte, 124
Ellison, Joseph, 225
Escape from New York, 259
E.T.: The Extra-Terrestrial, 239, 243, 248
Exorcist, The, 57, 59, 61, 68, 69, 81, 89, 103, 106, 111, 150, 154, 178, 336, 402

Exorcist II: The Heretic, 82
Experiment Perilous, 26, 28
Exterminating Angel, The, 83
Eyes of a Stranger, 225–29, *226*

Face to Face, 120
Fast Company, 248–49
Father of the Bride, 91, 171, 174, 175, 177
Fellini, Federico, 12
Ferrer, Jose, 143, 345
Ferris, Paul, 23, 44
film noir, 68, 155
Finley, William, 138
Firestarter, 265
First Blood, 325
Fischer-Dieskau, Dietrich, 112
Fisher, Terence, 53, 119, 205, 411n46
Flaherty, Robert J., 132
Fleischer, Richard, 12
Florey, Robert, 86, 88
Fly, The (1958), 83
Fog, The (1980), 259, 260
Fonda, Peter, 68
Ford, John, 67, 78, 98, 155, 171–72, 272, 314
Foster, Jodie, 365, 367
Fox, Michael J., 371
Fox, Terry Curtis, 191, 192
Franju, Georges, 83, 130, 194
Frankenstein (1931), 42, 80, *81*, 85, 92, 152, 157, 224, 401
Fraser, John, 187
Frenzy, 261
Freud, Sigmund, 8, 35, 59, 73–74, 83, 173, 211–12, 214, 238, 247, 252, 262, 268, 270, 274, 361, 362, 369, 400–401
Freund, Karl, 87
Friday the 13th, 221–23, 241, 400, 405
Friday the 13th Part III, 221–22
Friday the 13th Part 2, 221
Fright, 47
Frightmare, 57, 89, 90
Frogs, 57, 89
Full Moon High, 349–50, 357
Funny Games (1997), 403–4
Fury, The, 89, 143, 144, 159, 264

Galeen, Henrik, 361
gangster films, 82, 143, 148
genre, 41–42, 67–68, 82–83, 84, 164, 174, 193, 201–4, 223, 399
German expressionism, 29, 79, 84, 124, 130–31, 217, 361
Go-Between, The (1971), 53
Godard, Jean-Luc, 111, 146
God Told Me To, 81, 82, 89, 102, 110, 115, 139, 143, 144, 152–54, *153*, 157, 158, 159, 192, 338–42, *339*, 343, 359
Goethe, Johann Wolfgang von, 111–16, 402
Good Sam, 175
Greene, Graham, 30
Greetings, 63, 143, 371
Grimes, Tammy, 348
Group Marriage, 192, 194
Gwenn, Edmund, 94

Hacha para la Luna de Miel, Un. See *Blood Brides*
Haggard, Piers, 41, 53

Halloween (1978), 81, 106–9, *108*, 110, 116, 160, 221, 229, 244, 259, 260, 400, 405
Halloween II, 260
Hammer Films, 53, 89
Hands of the Ripper, 41, 53, 89
Haneke, Michael, 403–4
Harbach, Bill, 332
Harkness, John, 232–33, 235, 236–37, 250, 251, 412 n56
Harris, Jack, 332–33
Haunting, The (1963), 92
Havoc, June, 143
Hawks, Howard, 106, 144, 164, 203, 250, 259, 260, 314, 324–25, 399
Heartbreak Kid, The, 338
Heath, Stephen, 70
Heaven Can Wait (1978), 110
Heaven's Gate, 239, 241, 287
Heilbron, Lorne, 44
He Knows You're Alone, 201, 225, 227
Hell Night, 224
Hell Up in Harlem, 143, 149–50, 334
Herrmann, Bernard, 143–44, 358–59
Herzog, Werner, 205
Heston, Charlton, 27
Hi, Mom!, 63, 142–43, 371
High Noon, 144
High Plains Drifter, 89, 91
Hill, Debra, 253
Hills Have Eyes, The (1979), 89, 90, 99, 100, 190, 195
Hitchcock, Alfred, 3–10, 35, 412, 63, 68, 120, 134, 136, 143, 159, 191, 224, 228, 241–42, 259, 261, 277, 286, 358, 369–70, 386–88, 392, 403

Hoffman, Dustin, 155
Holm, Celeste, 143
Holocaust 2000, 141
Homicidal, 57–58, 89
Hooper, Tobe, 95, 111, 143, 187–88, 221, 233, 260, 269
Hopkins, Anthony, 365, 367
Hopper, Dennis, 26, 378
Horowitz, Gad, 74
Horror of Dracula, 205, 411n46
Huaco, George A., 28
Hungry Wives. See *Jack's Wife*
Hurt, John, 110

I, the Jury (1982), 351–54, 355, 358
Images, 146
In Dreams, 404
In the Heat of the Night, 346
Invasion of the Body Snatchers (1956), 161, 198, 246
Ionesco, Eugene, 101
I Remember Mama, 171
Island of Lost Souls, 80, 88, 92
Isle of the Dead, 299
It Lives Again, 81, 143, 144, 159, 160, 194, 337–38, 342, 356
It's a Wonderful Life, 171, 174
It's Alive (1974), 57, 59, 60, 81, 82, 89, 92, 105, 116, 143, 144, 148, 149, 150–52, 151, 154, 156, 158, 160, 194, 196, 234, 239, 336–38, 342, 356, 402
It's Alive II. See *It Lives Again*
I Walked with a Zombie, 25, 27–28, 31, 35–40, *36*, 58, 93, 134, 281–317, *293*, *294*, *298*, *301*, *305*, *306*, *308*, *311*, 413–14n72
I Was a Teenage Werewolf, 349

Jack's Wife, 181, 198–200, 373
Janáček, Leoš, 248
Januskopf, Der, 84, 124
Jaws, 70, 103–4
Jaws 2, 103–4
John Carpenter's The Thing. See *The Thing*
Jones, Ceri, 54
Jordan, Neil, 404
Jourdan, Louis, 205, 209
Jurgens, Curt, 27

Kael, Pauline, 184
Karloff, Boris, 25, 42, 401
Kiefer, Warren, 11, 14
Kill Bill: Volume I, 385
King Kong (1933), 87, 92, 157, 279
King Kong (1976), 356
King of Comedy, The, 241
King, Stephen, 242, 253–57, 265–79
Knightriders, 373
Kotto, Yaphet, 331
Kubrick, Stanley, 265, 268

Lacan, Jacques, 74
Ladd, David, 54
Laing, R. D., 173
Lamour, Dorothy, 78
Land of the Dead, 378–80
Lang, Fritz, 35, 187
Langella, Frank, 209, 361, 363
Last House on the Left, The, 181–88, 185, 192, 233, 396
Last Tango in Paris, 147
Laurel and Hardy, 175

Lawrence, D. H., 122, 129–30, 160
Leavis, F. R., 288
Leigh, Janet, 6
Leopard Man, The, 26, 93
Letter from an Unknown Woman, 232, 283–90, 413n70
Levene, Sam, 143
Levine, Joseph E., 332
Lewton, Val, 25–27, 31, 58, 92–93
Life with Father, 171
Lippe, Richard, 157, 181, 186, 194, 279, 399
Little Big Man, 189
Little Caesar, 143, 149, 333
Lo Bianco, Tony, 331
Long, Long Trailer, The, 91
Looking for Mr. Goodbar, 110
Loose Ends, 68
Losey, Joseph, 184–85
Love Affair, or the Case of the Missing Switchboard Operator, 17, 147
Love at First Bite, 349
Lucas, George, 241, 243
Lugosi, Bela, 92

Mahler, Gustav, 397
Makavejev, Dusan, 147
Make Way for Tomorrow, 175
Maltin, Leonard, 402
Mandingo, 98, 176
Manitou, The, 80
Mankiewicz, Francis, 202, 204
Mann, Anthony, 84
Man of the West, 84, 98
Manson, Arthur, 337

Marcuse, Herbert, 73, 212
Margie, 171
Marley, John, 342
Marnie, 29, m53, 63, 143, 278
Martin, 118, 162, 196, 197–*200*, 373
Marx, Karl, 73, 75, 79, 400–401
Mastroianni, Armand, 225
McCarey, Leo, 144, 175
Meet Me in St. Louis, 58–59, 91, 106, 171, 175–79, *177*, 259, 402
melodrama, 8, 67, 84, 171–79, 265, 274
Melville, Herman, 84
Metropolis, 84
Metz, Christian, 292, 312, 413–14n72
Mickey One, 146, 148
Middle Age Crazy, 203
Miike, Takeshi, 385–97
Milne, Tom, 11
Miner, Steve, 222
Minnelli, Vincente, 58, 175
Miracle Worker, The, 48
Mirisch, Walter, 343
Mitchell, Juliet, 173
Mitchum, Robert, 27
Mixed Blood, 329
Mizoguchi, Kenji, 37, 187
Mlodzik, Ron, 249–50
Monkey Business (1952), 164
Monkey Shines, 373
Moriarity, Michael, 354–55
Morrissey, Paul, 329
Mourlet, Michel, 27
Mulligan, Robert, 250
Murder by Decree, 196

Murders in the Rue Morgue (1932), 86–89, *87*, 92
Murnau, F. W., 80, 84, 119–31, 158, 205–10, 213, 215, 217–18, 220, 361–63, 401
musicals, 67, 176
My Bloody Valentine, 201–3
My Darling Clementine, 98

Nelligan, Kate, 218
Night Legs. See *Fright*
Nightmare on Elm Street, A, 400, 405
Night of the Demon. See *Curse of the Demon*
Night of the Lepus, 57, 89
Night of the Living Dead (1968), 55, 57, 59, 89, 90, 91, 99, 102, 106, 110, 162–69, *163*, 178, 182, 184, 194, 197, 198–99, 233–34, 246, 259, 319–22, 326, 373–74, 377–79, 383, 401–2
Night Walk. See *Dead of Night*
Night Walker, The. See *Dead of Night*
Norris, Chuck, 325, 352
North by Northwest, 3
Nosferatu (1922), 13, 28, 54–55, 58, 80, 84, 88, 115, 119–31, 123, 126, 127, 158, 205–10, 213, 215, 217–18, 220, 361–63, 401
Nosferatu the Vampyre (1979), 205
Notorious, 277

Obsession (1976), 63–64, 143, 144, 262, 359, 369
Ogilvie, Ian, 20
O Lucky Man!, 53

Omen, The (1976), 57, 60–62, 64, 81, 85, 89–90, 94–97, *96*, 101, 103, 116, 139, 141, 150, 178, 342
O'Neill, Jennifer, 250
Ophüls, Max, 283
Ordinary People, 203
Orphée, 409 n23
Out of the Past, 26–27, 35

Pakula, Alan, 63, 155
Parallax View, The, 155
Parasite Murders, The. See *Shivers*
Parks, Michael, 345
Pasolini, Pier Paolo, 385
Peck, Gregory, 61, 343
Peckinpah, Sam, 63, 372
Penn, Arthur, 48, 63, 148
Penn, Sean, 371, 372
Pennies from Heaven (1981), 350
Perkins, Anthony, 6, 365
Persona, 120
Phantom of the Opera (1925), 143
Phantom of the Opera (1943), 143
Phantom of the Paradise, 138, 143
Pirate, The, 413n67
Pirie, David, 53, 89
Pleasence, Donald, 21, 42, 55
Poe, Edgar Allan, 84, 98, 124, 176
Poltergeist, 248
pornography, 238
Possession of Joel Delaney, The, 80, 89
Price, Vincent, 21
Private Files of J. Edgar Hoover, The, 143, 144, 155–57, 158, 342, 343–47, 349
Prophecy, 80

Psycho (1960), 3–10, 5, 7, 8, 19, 20, 41, 54, 57–58, 63, 82, 89, 90, 91, 92, 94, 98, 106, 120, 134, 143, 174, 176, 177, 221, 223, 259, 274, 320, 365, 369, 373, 388
Pulp Fiction, 385
Puzzle of a Downfall Child, 146

Q, 342, 343, 354–58, *355*
Quinn, Anthony, 27
Rabid, 104, 244, 246, 248, 251, 252
Race with the Devil, 67–72, 80, 89
Raging Bull, 241–42, 269
Raising Cain, 371
Rampage (1963), 278
Raw Meat. See *Death Line*
Ray, Nicholas, 27
Rear Window, 3, 226, 228, 369
Redford, Robert, 155
Reeves, Michael, 10–24, 53
Reglè du jeu, La. See *Rules of the Game*
Repulsion, 89
Return of the Jedi, 239–40
Return of the Magnificent Seven, 343
Revenge of the Blood Beast, 11, 15–18, 20, 22, 23
Rio Bravo, 106, 144, 232, 259
Ritchie, Michael, 63
Robson, Mark, 25
Rocky, 110, 243, 248, 325, 350
Rocky Horror Picture Show, The, 81, 195
Rodowick, David, 413n67
Romero, George A., 59, 106, 111, 118, 162–69, 181, 191, 192, 194–95, 196, 197–200, 233, 246, 259, 319–29, 373–75, 377–83, 399, 401–3

Rose, Louisa, 80, 192
Rosemary's Baby, 57, 59, 60, 68–69, 81, 89, 91, 92, 150, 157, 162, 336
Rosenbaum, Jonathan, 107
Rossellini, Roberto, 12
Rossiter, A. P., 85
Rothman, Stephanie, 181, 191–95, 233, 399
Rozsa, Miklos, 143
Ruggles of Red Gap, 174
Rules of the Game, 232

Sailor Who Fell from Grace with the Sea, The, 57
Salem's Lot, 269
Sallinen, Aulis, 246
Salò, or the 120 Days of Sodom, 385
Sansho the Bailiff, 187
Sarris, Andrew, 26, 27
Sasdy, Peter, 41, 53
Scanners, 250–51
Scarface (1932), 143, 148, 149
Scarface (1983), 262, 372
Scarlet Empress, The, 242
Schatzberg, Jerry, 63
Schatzman, Morton, 173
Scherick, Edgar J., 338
Schizo, 57, 89
Schreck, Max, 209, 363
Schubert, Franz Peter, 111–18, 402
Schwarzenegger, Arnold, 325, 403
Scorsese, Martin, 240–42, 269, 359
Scott, Pippa, 331
Scott, Ridley, 241
Searchers, The, 84
Season of the Witch. See *Jack's Wife*

Secret Beyond the Door,
See No Evil. See *Blind Terror*
Sentinel, The, 103, 137
Seventh Seal, The, 21
Seventh Victim, The, 92–93
Shadow of a Doubt, 68, 92, 143
Shaft (1971), 333
Shakespeare, William, 12, 85, 116, 127, 184, 287, 288
She Beast, The. See *Revenge of the Blood Beast*
Shelley, Mary, 210
Shepherd, Dick, 336
Sherman, Gary, 41, 51, 53–54, 56, 89, 120
Shining, The, 265, 268, 276
Shivers, 104, *105*, 232, 243, 244–46, 412n56
Siegel, Don, 198
Silence of the Lambs, The, 365–67, *366*
Simon, John, 184
Siodmak, Curt, 28
Sirk, Douglas, 328
Sisters (1972), 57–58, 63, 80, 89, 102, 105, 110, 133–39, 141, 142–43, 144, 192, 233, 262, 264, 369–70, 402
slasher films, 229, 260, 404–5
Sleuth, 338
Solo, Bob, 351–53
Son of Frankenstein, 85
Sorcerers, The, 11, 15, 18–21, 22, 23, 53
Spellbound, 35, 158
Spielberg, Steven, 103–4, 239, 241, 243
Spillane, Mickey, 351
Squirm, 57–58, 60, 89–90

Index - 429

Stallone, Sylvester, 325, 403
Starrett, Jack, 68
Stars in My Crown, 35
Star Wars [*Star Wars Episode IV—A New Hope*], 110, 243
Steele, Barbara, 16, 18
Steiger, Rod, 344, 346
Stereo, 248–50, 252
Sternberg, Josef von, 139, 241–42
Stevenson, Robert Louis, 84, 115, 124, 210
Stoker, Bram, 119, 120, 205–20, 361–63
Straw Dogs, 147
structuralism, 281–317, 361
Sunrise, 29, 119, 131, 362
Superman (1979), 337–38
Sure Thing, The, 285
surrealism, 83, 194, 219
Switchboard Operator. See *Love Affair, or the Case of the Missing Switchboard Operator*
Sydney, Sylvia, 143
Szwarc, Jeannot, 104

Tabu: A Story of the South Seas (1931), 119, 127, 131
Taking of Pelham One Two Three, The, 338
Tales from the Crypt, 43
Tally, Ted, 366
Tarantino, Quentin, 385
Taxi Driver, 235, 359
Taylor, Robert, 27
Teague, Lewis, 256, 265, 276, 278
Terminal Island, 191–95, 233

Texas Chainsaw Massacre, The (1974), 57, 60–61, 70, 80, 89, 90, 94–101, *99*, 102, 106, 110, 139, 143, 176, *178–79*, 187, 221, 229, 233, 260, 365, 396
Them!, 93, 152, 356
There's Always Vanilla, 198
Thing, The, 259, 260
Thing from Another World, The, 85, 93, 108–9, 157, 203, 260, 324–26
thrillers, 67
Thunderbolt and Lightfoot, 68
Tokyo Story, 232
Tolstoy, Leo, 285
Tonti, Aldo, 12
Torn, Rip, 345
Touch of Evil, 371
Tourneur, Jacques, 25–41, 58, 110
Tourneur, Maurice, 28
2001: A Space Odyssey, 341

Ugetsu Monogatari, 37
Uninvited, The, 92
Unmarried Woman, An, 173
Untouchables, The, 370–71

Vampyr, 121
Vanoff, Nick, 332
Veidt, Conrad, 124
Velvet Vampire, The, 191–95, *193*
Vertigo, 3, 4, 9, 63, 143, 232, 242, 286, 369, 386–88, 392
Videodrome, 241, *242*, 244, 250, *251*–52
Vidor, King, 84
Virgin Spring, The, 182–84
Visconti, Luchino, 12, 250

Wagonmaster, 98
Walker, Michael, 21
Walker, Pete, 90
Warner, Jack, 345
War of the Worlds, The, 133–34
Wasserman, Lew, 332, 343
Weekend, 146–47
Welles, Orson, 371
West, Mae, 156
westerns, 67, 69, 71, 77, 82, 84, 88, 89, 91
Whale, James, 80, 85, 152, 224, 401
Wiederhorn, Ken, 225–29
Wild Angels, The, 68
Wild Bunch, The, 91

Wilde, Oscar, 124
Willard (1971), 147
Williams, Tony, 107, 159, 399
Williamson, Fred, 148, 149
Winged Serpent, The. See Q
Winner, Michael, 137
Wise, Robert, 25
Witchfinder General, 11, 12, 14, 16, 18, 20–24, *21*, *23*, 44, 53

You Can't Take It with You, 171
You'll Like My Mother, 46–47
Young Mr. Lincoln, 67, 155

Zanuck, Darryl F., 345

Contemporary Approaches to Film and Media Series

A complete listing of the books in this series
can be found online at wsupress.wayne.edu.

General Editor

Barry Keith Grant
Brock University

Advisory Editors

Robert J. Burgoyne
University of St. Andrews

Caren J. Deming
University of Arizona

Patricia B. Erens
School of the Art Institute of Chicago

Peter X. Feng
University of Delaware

Lucy Fischer
University of Pittsburgh

Frances Gateward
California State University, Northridge

Tom Gunning
University of Chicago

Thomas Leitch
University of Delaware

Walter Metz
Southern Illinois University